INTERNATIONAL LAW ISSUES IN THE SOUTH PACIFIC

International Law Issues in the South Pacific

Edited by

GEOFF LEANE and BARBARA VON TIGERSTROM
University of Canterbury, New Zealand

LONDON AND NEW YORK

First published 2005 by Ashgate Publishing

Reissued 2018 by Routledge
2 Park Square, Milton Park, Abingdon, Oxon OX14 4RN
605 Third Avenue, New York, NY 10017

First issued in paperback 2021

Routledge is an imprint of the Taylor & Francis Group, an informa business

© Geoff Leane and Barbara von Tigerstrom 2005

Geoff Leane and Barbara von Tigerstrom have asserted their right under the Copyright, Designs and Patents Act, 1988, to be identified as the editors of this work.

All rights reserved. No part of this book may be reprinted or reproduced or utilised in any form or by any electronic, mechanical, or other means, now known or hereafter invented, including photocopying and recording, or in any information storage or retrieval system, without permission in writing from the publishers.

A Library of Congress record exists under LC control number: 2005013245

Notice:
Product or corporate names may be trademarks or registered trademarks, and are used only for identification and explanation without intent to infringe.

Publisher's Note
The publisher has gone to great lengths to ensure the quality of this reprint but points out that some imperfections in the original copies may be apparent.

Disclaimer
The publisher has made every effort to trace copyright holders and welcomes correspondence from those they have been unable to contact.

ISBN 13: 978-0-815-38979-8 (hbk)
ISBN 13: 978-1-351-15548-9 (ebk)
ISBN 13: 978-1-138-35616-0 (pbk)

DOI: 10.4324/9781351155489

 Printed in the United Kingdom
by Henry Ling Limited

Contents

List of Contributors	*vi*
List of Abbreviations	*vii*
Map of the South Pacific Region	*xi*

	Introduction *Geoff Leane and Barbara von Tigerstrom*	1
1	Mass Refugee Flows and Burden-sharing in the South Pacific *Michael Barutciski*	9
2	Regional Cooperation in the Suppression of Transnational Crime in the South Pacific *Neil Boister*	35
3	International Terrorism and the South Pacific *Alex Conte*	95
4	The Law of the Sea and Freedom of Navigation in Asia Pacific *Scott Davidson*	127
5	Climate Change in Oceania: Responses to the Kyoto Protocol *Geoff Leane*	161
6	What Bioprospecting Means for Antarctica and the Southern Ocean *Michelle Rogan-Finnemore*	199
7	Development and the International Trade Regime: Challenges for South Pacific Island States *Barbara von Tigerstrom*	229

Index	*275*

List of Contributors

Michael Barutciski, BA (McGill), LLB (Montreal), LLM (Osgoode), Doctorate in Law (Paris). Assistant Professor, International Studies Programme, Glendon College, York University.

Neil Boister, BA, LLB, LLM (Natal), PhD (Nottingham). Senior Lecturer, School of Law, University of Canterbury.

Alex Conte, LLB (Canterbury), LLM (Hons) (Victoria University of Wellington). Senior Lecturer, School of Law, University of Canterbury.

Scott Davidson, MA (Cambridge). Pro-Vice-Chancellor and Dean, School of Law, University of Canterbury.

Geoff Leane, BEc (Hons) (Adelaide), LLB, LLM (British Columbia), LLM (Harvard). Senior Lecturer, School of Law, University of Canterbury.

Michelle Rogan-Finnemore, BSc (Hons) (Pittsburgh), LLB (Canterbury). Centre Manager, Gateway Antarctica, University of Canterbury.

Barbara von Tigerstrom, BA (Alberta), MA (Toronto), LLB (Toronto), PhD (Cambridge). Senior Lecturer, School of Law, University of Canterbury.

List of Abbreviations

ACP	African, Caribbean and Pacific
AFP	Australian Federal Police
AG	Attorney General
AGO	Australian Greenhouse Office
AIJ	Activities Implemented Jointly
AOSIS	Alliance of Small Island States
APCs	Asia Pacific Consultations
APEC	Asian Pacific Economic Cooperation
APG-ML	Asia Pacific Group on Money Laundering
ASEAN	Association of South East Asian States
AT	Antarctic Treaty
ATCM	Antarctic Treaty Consultative Meeting
ATS	Antarctic Treaty System
Austrac	Australian Transaction Report and Analysis Centre
CBD	Convention on Biological Diversity
CCAMLR	Convention for the Conservation of Antarctic Marine Living Resources
CDM	Clean Development Mechanism
CER	Closer Economic Relations Australia/New Zealand Trade Agreement
CHM	Common Heritage of Mankind
CLAGS	Combined Law Agency Groups
COMNAP	Council of Managers of National Antarctic Programmes
COMSEC	Commonwealth Secretariat
COPs	Conferences of the Parties
CRAMRA	Convention for the Regulation of Antarctic Mineral Resource Activity
CSCAP	Council for Security Cooperation in the Asia Pacific
CTD	Council on Trade and Development
DDA	Doha Development Agenda
DPOS	Domestic Policy Option Statement
DSU	Dispute Settlement Understanding (Understanding on Rules and Procedures Governing the Settlement of Disputes)
EBA	Everything But Arms
EC	European Communities
EEZ	Exclusive Economic Zone
EITs	Economies in Transition
EPA	Economic Partnership Agreement
EXCOM	Executive Committee (UNHCR)
FADTC	Foreign Affairs, Defence and Trade Committee

FATF	Financial Action Task Force (OECD)
FFA	Forum Fisheries Agency
FIU	Financial Intelligence Unit
FLNKS	Kanak Socialist National Liberation Front
FON	Freedom of Navigation
FORUM	Pacific Islands Forum
Forumsec	Forum Secretariat
FRSC	Forum Regional Security Committee
FICs	Forum Island Countries
GAM	Aceh Liberation Front
GATS	General Agreement on Trade in Services
GATT	General Agreement on Tariffs and Trade
GDP	Gross Domestic Product
GHGs	Greenhouse Gases
GSP	Generalized System of Preferences
GSTP	Generalized System of Trade Preferences
IAEA	International Atomic Energy Agency
ICJ	International Court of Justice
IGY	International Geophysical Year
IMB	International Maritime Bureau
IMDG	International Maritime Dangerous Goods
IMO	International Maritime Organization
INF	Irradiated Nuclear Fuel
IP	Information Paper
IPCC	Intergovernmental Panel on Climate Change
IPR/IP	Intellectual Property Rights/Intellectual Property
ISA	International Seabed Authority
IUU	Illegal, Unreported and Unregulated
IWC	International Whaling Convention
JI	Joint Implementation
JUSCANZ	Japan, US, Canada, Australia and New Zealand
LDC	Least Developed Country
LECP	Law Enforcement Cooperation Program
Lomé IV	Fourth ACP-EEC Convention of Lomé
MFN	Most Favoured Nation
MLAT	Mutual Legal Assistance Treaty
MOU	Memorandum of Understanding
MRET	Mandatory Renewable Energy Targets
MSG	Melanesian Spearhead Group
Mt CO_2	Million tonnes of Carbon Dioxide
NEECS	National Energy Efficiency and Conservation Strategy
NGA	Negotiated Greenhouse Agreement
NGO	Non-governmental Organization
NGRS	National Greenhouse Response Strategy
NGS	National Greenhouse Strategy
NZP	New Zealand Police

List of Abbreviations

OCO	Oceania Customs Organisation
ODA	Official Development Assistance
ODCCP	Office for Drugs Control and Crime Prevention (UN)
OECD	Organisation for Economic Co-operation and Development
OFC	Offshore Financial Centre
PACER	Pacific Agreement on Closer Economic Relations
PACRIM	Pacific Rim Immigration Intelligence Officer's Conference
PACTRA	Agreement on Trade and Commercial Relations between the Government of Australia and the Government of Papua New Guinea
PICs	Pacific Island Countries
PICCAP	Pacific Island Climate Change Assistance Program
PICTA	Pacific Island Countries Trade Agreement
PIDC	Pacific Immigration Directors Conference
PILOM	Pacific Islands Law Officers Meeting
PNG	Papua New Guinea
PSI	Proliferation Security Initiative
PSSA	Particularly Sensitive Sea Areas
RMA	Resource Management Act
RTA	Regional Trade Agreement
SCAR	Scientific Committee for Antarctic Research
SCM	Subsidies and Countervailing Measures
SDT	Special and Differential Treatment
SIDS	Small Island Developing States
SIS	Small Island States
SLOC	Sea Lines of Communication
SNEC	Safety Navigation and Environment Committee
SOLAS	Safety of Life at Sea
SPARTECA	South Pacific Regional Trade and Economic Cooperation Agreement
SPCPC	South Pacific Chief of Police Conference
SPREP	South Pacific Regional Environmental Programme
SUA	Suppression of Unlawful Act (Against the Safety of Navigation)
SUAPROT	Protocol for the Suppression of Unlawful Acts Against the Safety of Fixed Platforms Located on the Continental Shelf
TBT	Technical Barriers to Trade
TRIPS	Trade-Related Aspects of Intellectual Property Rights
UDHR	Universal Declaration of Human Rights
UN	United Nations
UNCLOS	United Nations Convention on the Law of the Sea
UNESCAP	United Nations Economic and Social Commission for Asia and the Pacific
UNFCCC	UN Framework Convention on Climate Change
UNHCR	United Nations High Commissioner for Refugees
UNODC	UN Office on Drugs and Crime
UNSC	United Nations Security Council

WMD	Weapons of Mass Destruction
WP	Working Paper
WTO	World Trade Organization

Map of the South Pacific Region

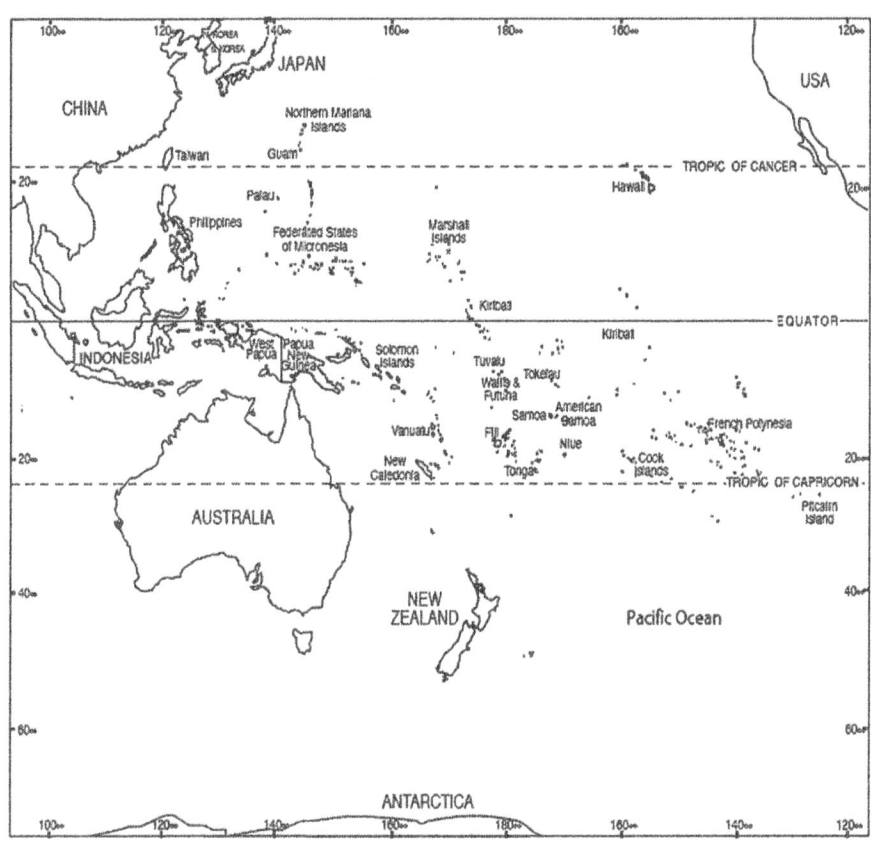

Source: Geography Department, University of Canterbury

Introduction

Geoff Leane and Barbara von Tigerstrom[*]

The South Pacific is a distinctive and fascinating region that too often escapes the attention of the global community. This book seeks to inform on some of the international legal issues and challenges facing the South Pacific and its varying subject matter reflects the diversity of those issues and challenges. The authors collectively constitute the International Law Group at the University of Canterbury School of Law in Christchurch, New Zealand. Their respective interests and expertise converged to produce this first part of an ongoing engagement with a region that represents, in microcosm, many of the contemporary issues and challenges that confront international law and international lawyers everywhere.

One of the first issues facing those with an interest in this region is how the 'region' itself should be defined. A variety of terms – Pacific, South Pacific, Asia Pacific, Oceania – are often used in different contexts. The Pacific Islands Forum provides some structure, and this grouping of sixteen countries[1] is the core focus of many of the chapters in this volume. However, for some purposes, it is useful and even necessary to look beyond its boundaries to the larger Asia-Pacific region (as in Scott Davidson's chapter on freedom of navigation) or to the unique area of Antarctica and the Southern Ocean on its southern edge (as in Michelle Rogan-Finnemore's chapter on bioprospecting). There are also subgroups within the Forum membership, such as the Forum Island Countries (or Pacific Island Countries), referring to the Forum members except Australia and New Zealand; the Small Island States, including the smallest Forum members;[2] and the Melanesian Spearhead Group.[3]

The various groupings reflect differences in size, ethnicity and common or historical ties and hint at the considerable diversity within the region. If we look at matters of culture, ethnicity, geography, demographics or socio-economic indicators in the region, the diversity is such as to render unrealistic any temptation to simplify consideration of these countries as a collective. For example, Australia and New Zealand are developed states whilst the island countries are either developing or least developed countries. Australia has a land mass of some 7.7 million square km and a population of some 19 million of which 90 per cent is of European extraction; the Cook Islands occupies only 240 square km with a

---

[*] The editors would like to acknowledge the assistance of Danie Benkman (LLB student, University of Canterbury) in compiling the index.
[1] Australia, Cook Islands, Federated States of Micronesia, Fiji, Kiribati, Nauru, New Zealand, Niue, Palau, Papua New Guinea, Republic of the Marshall Islands, Samoa, Solomon Islands, Tonga, Tuvalu and Vanuatu.
[2] Cook Islands, Kiribati, Nauru, Niue, Republic of the Marshall Islands and Tuvalu.
[3] Fiji, Papua New Guinea, Solomon Islands and Vanuatu.

population of around 16,000 which is 94 per cent Polynesian; Fiji has a land mass of 18,272 square km with a population of around 800,000 which is a little more than half ethnic Fijian but around 40 per cent Indian.

The region includes diverse ethnic groups whose origins are Polynesian, Melanesian and Micronesian, though ethnicity is not fixed. Some island populations have been denuded by emigration. In the case of Cook Islanders four live in New Zealand for every one remaining in the Cook Islands,[4] whilst in the 1970s Niue began to accept immigrants from other Pacific islands because 80 per cent of its own people had emigrated to New Zealand.[5] Today some 92 per cent of Niueans live in Australia or New Zealand.[6] Of the world's two million Polynesians only 14 per cent live in the independent Polynesian nations (Cook Islands, Niue, Tonga and Tuvalu); the rest live in the United States, Australia and New Zealand.[7] Those emigrant populations have been a critical source of income through remittances. Patterns of migration between the islands have always been a feature of Pacific history and were further complicated by the arrival of metropolitan European powers in the sixteenth century when Spain first settled Guam, later followed by the British, French and Americans. Asian migration also followed later, for example, in Indian migration to Fiji and Chinese migration throughout the region.

The political units of the island countries also demonstrate a fascinating diversity, perhaps more than any equivalent population in the world. They include a kingdom (Tonga), a state in which only chiefs may stand for election (Samoa), a republic with different electorates for different ethnic groups (Fiji) and the world's smallest republic (Nauru). By and large democracy has prospered in the form of regular elections, respect for democratic processes and conformity with constitutions. In only one case (Fiji) has power not devolved to a government elected by majority vote. Generally the Pacific island states have rated highly in respect of political and civil rights, particularly for a region of less developed states.[8] Relations between them are relatively harmonious, perhaps in significant part because they share no land borders. A risk, however, is that in light of the very small populations and (often) a lack of institutional checks and balances, leaders may have irresistible opportunities to run countries as personal fiefdoms and political and bureaucratic elites may wield unhealthy measures of power.[9] All of the island states save Tonga have at some time been colonies, and colonial influence remains strong in many, for example, in the widely adopted Westminster system of government. Independent national governments became the norm in the second half of the twentieth century and most adopted the constitutional arrangements of their former colonizers. However, the region still contains

---

[4] Ron Crocombe, *The South Pacific* (2001) 54.
[5] Ibid 64.
[6] Ibid 66.
[7] Ibid 66-7.
[8] Ibid 482, footnote 7.
[9] See, e.g. Asian Development Bank, *Responding to the Priorities of the Poor: A Pacific Strategy for the Asian Development Bank 2005–2009* (2004) 94 (examples include Nauru, Solomon Islands and Marshall Islands); Crocombe, above n 4, ch. 19.

overseas territories of the United States[10] and France[11] and a non-self-governing territory of New Zealand (Tokelau), as well as countries in free association with New Zealand[12] or the United States.[13] Economic and political ties with former colonial powers in the form of development assistance, trade and other forms of cooperation remain important. The South Pacific receives more international aid per capita than any other region. However, that introduces yet another aspect of vulnerability as aid levels have been declining and average real income per capita is virtually unchanged over the past decade.[14] Australia is the largest aid donor but is being increasingly challenged by East Asian countries and Japan in particular.

The region's resources are diverse and unevenly distributed. Papua New Guinea, for example, is blessed with mineral wealth, forests, agricultural and fish resources and a substantial domestic market of almost five million people, though it is constrained by poor infrastructure and political instability. Fiji enjoys a relatively diversified economy (including tourism, gold mining and sugar) and work force with a population of some 800,000 but is constrained by ethnic and communal tensions and the threat of loss of preferential market access to Europe. Some of the smaller islands are dependent on narrow resource bases which limit their opportunities for diversification. Generally speaking most observers see the region as having under-performed economically given its high level of aid and relatively plentiful natural resources.[15] Economic indicators vary widely; for example, in terms of US$ Gross National Income per capita, Solomon Islands ($580) and Kiribati ($960) lagged well behind Fiji ($2130) and Palau ($6820).[16] Some countries have high levels of poverty despite having relatively plentiful natural resources, some have moderate resources but higher levels of social development, while others have a very small resource base and hence are extremely vulnerable.[17]

Although the smallest islands and those most limited in resources are most at risk in many respects, vulnerability is a quality shared to some degree by all of the island countries in the region. They manifest that vulnerability in a variety of contexts ranging from the physical environment to international markets. They face multiple risks, including volatile markets, resource depletion, crime, political instability and racial tensions, from both internal (for example, very small populations and limited resources) and external (for example, crime and globalization) sources. These vulnerabilities raise the question of whether some of

---

[10] American Samoa, Guam and Commonwealth of the Northern Mariana Islands.
[11] French Polynesia, New Caledonia and Wallis and Futuna. French Polynesia and New Caledonia are now 'overseas countries' of France with greater autonomy.
[12] Cook Islands and Niue. Samoa has a Treaty of Friendship with New Zealand.
[13] Federated States of Micronesia, Palau and Republic of the Marshall Islands.
[14] Crocombe, above n 4, 390.
[15] See, e.g. Asian Development Bank, *Responding to the Priorities of the Poor*, above n 9, ch. 3.
[16] Ibid 41 (Table A3) (2002 data).
[17] Ibid 19. The first group is said to include Papua New Guinea, Solomon Islands and Vanuatu, the second group Cook Islands, Fiji, Federated States of Micronesia, Samoa, Tonga, and the third Kiribati, Republic of the Marshall Islands, Nauru and Tuvalu.

these states are indeed viable, at least in the sense of being functioning and functional states in the modern international order of sovereign, independent states. Whilst all except the Cook Islands and Niue (which are in free association with New Zealand), are members of the United Nations, at least some might be characterized as 'quasi-states, brought into existence by external forces, and shored up by international and bilateral support'.[18] They are cloaked with the mantle of sovereignty but lack the necessary capacities to practise it, and indeed in some cases political independence may not have been either desired or desirable.

One way of dealing with vulnerability and recurring questions about the viability of small island states is to move toward regional integration. Regional institutions in this part of the world are relatively undeveloped compared to most other regions. The Pacific Islands Forum, recently described by its Secretary-General as the 'peak Pacific regional political body',[19] has a Secretariat, holds annual meetings of heads of government and provides a forum for cooperation and dialogue on a range of issues. In the larger Asia Pacific region, Asia Pacific Economic Cooperation (APEC) has an important, though limited, role.[20] Generally regionalist impulses are restricted to institutional linkages, cooperative networks in matters of trade, culture, religion and so forth, but not significant political integration in the sense of compromises of sovereignty to a collective entity such as, say, the European Union. Certainly compared to Europe or even the less developed regional regimes of Africa or the Americas, these regional organizations represent fairly tentative steps toward formalized regional integration. However, as will be seen in a number of the following chapters, pressures for greater integration and cooperation are increasingly felt in the region, for example in trade or security. As this book goes to press, a draft 'Pacific Plan for Strengthening Regional Cooperation and Integration' has been released for public comment.[21]

But regionalist currents are hampered by some commonality of internal problems, for example, endemic corruption, incompetent governance, excessive bureaucracy, racism, political instability, widespread unemployment and, perhaps most importantly, resistance within the island countries themselves to any erosion of a sovereignty only recently attained. More recent crises have included administrative decay and conflict in the Solomon Islands, constitutional crises in Vanuatu and Fiji, ethnic strife in Fiji, class struggle in Tonga, threats of national disintegration in Papua New Guinea, massive emigration from the Cook Islands and Niue, and the tenuous viability of countries like Tuvalu. As much as these

---

[18] A.V. Hughes, *A Different Kind of Voice: Development and Dependence in the Pacific Islands* (Asian Development Bank (Office of Pacific Operations) 1998) 13.

[19] Greg Urwin, 'Preventing Conflict in the Pacific: What Role for the Pacific Islands Forum' (Keynote Address at the Conference on 'Securing a Peaceful Pacific: Preventing and Resolving Conflict', University of Canterbury, 15 October 2004).

[20] Australia, New Zealand and Papua New Guinea are among the 21 'member economies' of APEC.

[21] Pacific Islands Forum Secretariat, 'The Pacific Plan for Strengthening Regional Cooperation and Integration: Working Draft' (2005) New Zealand Ministry of Foreign Affairs and Trade <http://www.mfat.govt.nz/foreign/regions/pacific/pifsec/pacificplan.html> at 22 February 2005.

create challenges for internal governance, they also present obstacles to effective cooperation.

Another impetus to regionalism derives from the desire for greater influence in the international community. In some contexts, the island countries can wield influence disproportionate to their size – although the political units of the South Pacific are the smallest in the world, the fourteen island states of the Pacific Islands Forum, representing seven million people, collectively assert more voting power in some fora than the 3.5 billion people of China, India, Japan and the USA together! However, their economic and political influence are in other important respects severely limited by their small size and remoteness, giving an added incentive for regional integration.

These questions are not directly addressed in the chapters here in, for example, a review of alternative models of regionalism which might redress asymmetries of viability both in the region and globally, or in a comprehensive review of the cooperative arrangements which reflect intra-regional relationships. That would constitute another project which will receive much attention in the coming years.[22] Rather the relationships within and beyond the region are revealed in the context of (mostly) external challenges such as international crime and security issues, the challenges presented by global warming and refugee issues, and difficult resource and geographical challenges to trade. Those regional relationships also reveal the gravitational force and influence asserted by the regional hegemon, Australia, and to a lesser extent New Zealand, both Western liberal democracies geographically located in a diverse region of small island developing states. But as in the wider global order the United States exerts great influence, not just directly in its 'area of influence' but more generally in maritime issues, security issues, trade and the inter-governmental 'management' of external issues such as crime.

The international community is well aware of the region's challenges and also of the fluctuating strategic significance of the region and its component states. The various island countries of the South Pacific are presently in a process of realigning their relations with external powers as the strategic importance of the individual countries is constantly re-evaluated and exploited (by all sides). The region, like much of the global order, appears to be in a period of transition as it moves from a post-colonial, post-Cold War period to a yet-to-be-written future of considerable uncertainty and risk. The island states share serious difficulties in adapting to external forces such as globalization, the need to 'fit' into the global order as functional sovereign states and the need to resist some of the more malevolent forces of that global order, for example, international crime and terrorism.

This collection does not attempt to present a comprehensive overview of the issues facing the Pacific region. Indeed, those with local knowledge will notice the

---

[22] For example, the University of Canterbury School of Law is sponsoring a post-doctoral study of possible models of pooled sovereignty which might serve to empower Pacific Island states in a framework of supra-national regional governance without fatally compromising local aspirations (estimated completion late 2007).

absence of some critically important issues, such as fisheries and regional peace building efforts, from the list of topics covered. Rather these chapters explore a wide variety of issues in international law and seek to relate them to the particular context of the region. In that sense they might be characterized as a range of mostly external global forces to which South Pacific countries are responding, either voluntarily or under pressure from either or both of regional and global powers. Such tensions between authentic local voluntariness and external pressures are clearly at play in most of these chapters.

In the first chapter Michael Barutciski considers the dilemma posed by mass refugee flows, wherein the tension is perhaps best symbolized by Australia's treatment of the Tampa boat people and their subsequent relocation to Nauru. The so-called 'Pacific solution' of offering financial inducements to a third state to accept the refugees can arguably be seen as a pragmatic compromise between advocates of open borders and those who would impose only minimal legal obligations on states in relation to the protection of asylum seekers. It nonetheless poses difficult moral and political issues concerning regional cooperation.

In Chapter 2 Neil Boister considers the issue of transnational crime in the South Pacific and the efforts of Pacific Forum countries to suppress such threats within a framework of international obligations. He argues that the participation of small island states in this global regime is not necessarily benign as local consent is not always authentic and the legitimacy of the regulatory regime is thereby threatened. There is a threat to the sovereignty of reluctant states that may need to be addressed by some kind of empowered regional organization which more effectively represents their interests.

On a parallel topic Alex Conte looks to the implications of international terrorism in the South Pacific in Chapter 3. Whilst the exposure of island states to terrorism, however defined, has been minimal and its immediate relevance therefore questionable it is another example of heightened global concerns manifesting themselves as local issues. As a specific example of transnational crime the risks are as much about island states being used as unwitting conduits for terrorists aiming at third states as they are about the islands themselves representing terrorist targets.

Chapter 4 looks to wider stage as Scott Davidson reviews the law of the sea and freedom of navigation in the Asia Pacific region. The tension between principles of closed seas and of seas being open to all nations appears to be re-emerging and has important implications for island states such as those of the South Pacific, as well as generally. That tension has produced a somewhat unstable relationship between security conscious coastal states and those seeking maximum freedom of navigation for trade, resource exploitation and naval mobility.

Climate change and the Kyoto Protocol, the subject of Geoff Leane's Chapter 5, goes more directly to the vulnerability of small island states in the South Pacific. Their contributions to climate change through greenhouse gas emissions are miniscule yet they are perhaps the most vulnerable of all states to climate change impacts on weather patterns and rising sea levels. As with transnational crime and international terrorism they are forced to react to aspects of globalization which are not of their making and which are largely beyond their control. The policy responses of the regional powers, Australia and New Zealand, reflect the wider international order and give little cause for comfort.

Antarctica typically presents its own peculiar issues in Michelle Rogan-Finnemore's chapter on bioprospecting in Antarctica and the Southern Ocean. As a continent with no permanent population and no widely recognized sovereign it presents unique jurisdictional problems in any attempt at regulating activities there. Bioprospecting is an emerging issue which challenges those states that participate in the Antarctic Treaty System as well as the international community whose interests are less well defined. Australia and New Zealand are claimant states with direct interests but must, like other participating states, seek consensus solutions which will protect the integrity of the continent whilst meeting the legitimate scientific and increasingly commercial interests of the international community.

Finally, in Chapter 7 Barbara von Tigerstrom deals with the challenges of development and international trade in the island states of the South Pacific. Not only is vulnerability an underlying theme but here the question of viability is most directly addressed. In a climate of free trade many of these states simply lack both sizable domestic markets and the necessary efficiencies for an export base to sustain a viable economy. They rely largely on aid, remittances and privileged access to foreign markets, all of which are in some degree uncertain and in some cases presently threatened. The extent to which international trading arrangements adequately respond to the difficulties faced by these countries is questionable, and again questions about the most effective forms of regional cooperation are raised.

It will be apparent to even the casual reader that the outline of a bigger picture emerges from these chapters. As in the wider global order there is a fundamental question that goes to the relevance of international legal rules and principles to less (and least) developed states which lack the resources and infrastructures to fully participate in that order yet are increasingly being pressured to do so. Those pressures are evident here with respect to mass refugee flows, transnational crime, terrorism, law of the sea and trade. The participation of at least the small island states of the South Pacific is sometimes little more than symbolic as they respond to, and sometimes exploit, the pressures from local and global powers. Indeed in many cases the island states have not assented to the various instruments – for example, few have ratified the two main refugee treaties[23] and there has been a mixed degree of consent to the various counter-terrorism instruments.[24]

As a final observation it is probably fair to say that regional issues have been significantly under-researched – models of regional governance, for example, or mitigation options for climate change – but this book represents a contribution toward considering the impacts of international law frameworks as (mostly) external forces requiring local responses. It highlights the growing importance of the interface between these small regional states and the global order which exerts an increasingly powerful gravitational force upon them.

---

[23] See the chapter by Michael Barutciski.
[24] See the chapter by Alex Conte.

Chapter 1

Mass Refugee Flows and Burden-sharing in the South Pacific

Michael Barutciski

Introduction

Commentaries on refugee law are often divided between two polarized views: refugee advocates who tend to present maximalist positions on the entitlements enjoyed by asylum seekers and border control proponents who tend to minimize the protection obligations imposed on States. The problem surfaces when the politics of the situation marginalize the law. For example, in response to recent political troubles in Haiti and concerns about an exodus of migrants toward the coast of Florida, the President of the United States declared that '[US officials] will turn back any [Haitian] refugee that attempts to reach our shore, and that message needs to be very clear as well to the Haitian people'.[1] The fact that US officials were in fact not returning boat people without a screening process indicates the priorities in the public message preoccupying the President's speechwriter: national political leaders have to appear tough on border control and may even be unaware of the actual legal protection accorded to migrants by those implementing official policy.[2] Political leaders are not the only actors using refugee policy to score public opinion points: the response of non-governmental organizations (NGOs) to the President's declaration is equally troubling. Most refugee advocates went on to condemn the supposed policy as a violation of international law,[3] even though they must be aware that the US Supreme Court has already established that their interpretation is not correct in terms of the law as it is applied in the US.[4]

---

[1] Human Rights Watch, 'US: Don't Turn Away Haitian Refugees' (Press Release, 26 February 2004).
[2] See 'Haitians flee to US in boats', CNN, 27 February 2004 <http://www.cnn.com/2004/US/South/02/26/haiti.refugees/index.html> at 8 March 2005 and Rachel L Swarns, 'Advocates for Immigrants Scorn Bush Policy on Haitian Refugees', The New York Times, 27 February 2004, A13.
[3] See, e.g. Human Rights Watch, 'Haiti: US Return of Asylum Seekers Is Illegal' (Press Release, 2 March 2004); US Committee for Refugees and Immigrants, 'President Bush Finally Speaks the Truth about America's Unlawful Treatment of Haitian Refugees' (Press Release, 26 February 2004); Amnesty International, 'Haiti: Refugees and asylum seekers are not part of the conflict' (27 February 2004).
[4] Sale v Haitian Centers Council, 113 S Ct 2549 (1993).

Legal arguments can serve for political purposes even when one knows that they will not stand up in court. The example illustrates how, in different ways, two opposing actors can both position themselves in a manner that marginalizes the law. This kind of politics concerning refugee issues is prevalent throughout the world, including the South Pacific, and it is unfortunately not the basis for a genuine debate on the legal situation of asylum seekers.

The following analysis of refugee policy in the South Pacific emphasizes a positivist approach to certain legal dilemmas created by mass refugee flows. While the public presentation of refugee policy is often used by various actors with wide-ranging political agendas, judicial bodies play a particularly important role in terms of judging the validity of legal arguments. With their decisions that constrain or justify refugee protection policies, courts have developed enough jurisprudence to allow debates on the subject to be framed within certain parameters. This chapter seeks to contribute to the debate surrounding mass refugee flows and burden-sharing in a region of the world that has been forced to confront difficult problems related to boat people.

International law should reflect the actual political conditions found in international society if it is to be relevant to policymakers. While it may be understandable that humanitarian and migration issues tend to attract activist approaches to the role of law, a certain amount of realism is necessary in order to respond to refugee situations in a viable manner. To the extent that it deals with the entry of aliens, refugee law is clearly part of immigration law. The affirmation from advocacy circles that 'refugee law is not immigration law'[5] and that it is actually part of human rights law may be useful in underlining the sensitivity required when dealing with foreigners who claim to flee persecution. In some ways, it may be true that all areas of law can be affected by human rights. However, the suggestion that these fleeing foreigners have special immigration entitlements or that they may trump existing immigration laws[6] does not reflect accurately the current relationship between international law and municipal law. This is a key observation in terms of the problems addressed in this chapter.

By focusing on the dramatic situation of mass refugee flows, the chapter examines the problems of burden-sharing from the perspective of international law. The dynamics mentioned above are illustrated in a particularly effective manner by examples concerning the South Pacific. Indeed, this region is characterized by at least two striking features: it includes a significant number of States not bound by

---

[5] James C Hathaway, 'Refugee Law is Not Immigration Law' (2002) World Refugee Survey 38. See also Amnesty International, 'Refugee Protection is Human Rights Protection' (Amnesty International Statement to the Ministerial Meeting of States Parties to the 1951 Refugee Convention and/or its 1967 Protocol, 1 December 2001).

[6] See, e.g. Refugee Appeal No. 72668/01 (5 April 2002) in which the New Zealand Refugee Status Appeals Authority states that 'refugee status trumps all immigration control and immigration policy' [39].

the 1951 Convention relating to the Status of Refugees,[7] as well as a hegemonic power attempting to coordinate bilateral responses to boat people.

The regional incident that has attracted the most attention in terms of boat people is undoubtedly the Tampa affair. About two weeks before the US was the object of terrorist attacks in 2001, the Australian authorities assisted a Norwegian flagged container ship, the MV Tampa, in rescuing 433 people aboard an Indonesian registered vessel that was sinking in the Indian Ocean. The desperate rescuees were of Iraqi, Afghan and Pakistani origin, and they threatened to commit suicide if they were transported to Indonesia. Contrary to orders from the Australian authorities, the Tampa attempted to enter Australian territorial waters near Christmas Island because the ship's captain was afraid that loss of life was imminent. The ship was boarded by 45 Australian Special Air Service troops who took over control. Federal Court litigation began on 31 August 2001 when a Melbourne-based solicitor filed applications on behalf of the boat people who wanted to seek refugee status in Australia. As the Australian government announced that intergovernmental agreements were reached to transfer the rescuees to Nauru and New Zealand for processing of their refugee claims, the parties to the litigation agreed to allow the courts to resolve certain legal issues. The rescuees were temporarily transferred to an Australian troop ship with medical facilities.

On 11 September 2001, a judge of the Federal Court of Australia ruled that the expulsion of the asylum seekers aboard the Tampa was illegal and that they should be allowed to land on Australian territory in order to apply for protection visas.[8] On 18 September 2001, the full Federal Court of Australia overturned this ruling in a majority decision.[9] The boat people were then sent to Nauru and New Zealand for processing. Over the following weeks, new legislation was enacted in order to validate the government's actions relating to the Tampa affair and to facilitate similar responses in the future. The so-called 'Pacific Solution' adopted by the Australian government was being proposed as a general response to the problem of boat people in the region.

The distinctive features of refugee protection in the South Pacific, and particularly Australia's 'Pacific Solution', have attracted attention from policymakers and criticisms from refugee advocates around the world. In some ways, the region may be at the forefront of some key developments in international refugee law.

Who is a refugee?

As States in the South Pacific have not adopted a regional instrument with a distinct refugee definition, the main international refugee definition applied in the

---

[7] Opened for signature 28 July 1951, 189 UNTS 150 (entered into force 22 April 1954) ('Refugee Convention').
[8] Vadarlis v Ruddock [2001] FCA 1297.
[9] Ruddock v Vadarlis [2001] FCA 1329.

region comes from two complementary treaties approved by the UN General Assembly.

South Pacific States bound by the 1951 Refugee Convention and the 1967 Protocol relating to the Status of Refugees[10] have accepted the following refugee definition:

> For the purposes of the present Convention, the term 'refugee' shall apply to any person who ... owing to a well-founded fear of being persecuted for reasons of race, religion, nationality, membership of a particular social group or political opinion, is outside the country of his nationality and is unable or, owing to such fear, is unwilling to avail himself of the protection of that country; or who, not having a nationality and being outside the country of his former habitual residence as a result of such events, is unable or, owing to such fear, is unwilling to return to it.

According to the Office of the United Nations High Commissioner for Refugees (UNHCR), the above definition is declaratory and not constitutive of refugee status. In other words, a 'refugee' is any person who meets the Convention definition regardless of whether there has been a formal recognition of refugee status by the host State. Indeed, formal recognition of refugee status is not included as one of the conditions of the definition. The logic of UNHCR's argument is the following: when a State grants refugee status, it only 'recognizes' a condition that already existed prior to the State's administrative determination.[11] As a result, a State that mistreats a refugee claimant prior to a decision on the claim runs the risk of violating Convention obligations if the claimant is effectively a refugee.

While the declaratory nature of the Convention definition has generally not posed problems in case law, some doubts have been raised by the MV Tampa affair in 2001 concerning the rescue of 433 boat people near Christmas Island. In its decision on the Australian government's seizure of the Norwegian-owned vessel carrying the asylum seekers, the full Federal Court of Australia refers to a constitutive dimension of the refugee definition:

> The question whether all or any of the rescuees are refugees has not been determined ... nothing done by the Executive on the face of it amounts to a breach of Australia's obligations in respect of non-refoulement under the Refugee Convention.[12]

The reasoning of the majority opinion seems to suggest that asylum seekers do not benefit from the Refugee Convention's guarantees unless they are recognized by the competent Australian authorities. Although this interpretation contributes in making the international refugee protection treaty regime somewhat incoherent, it apparently influences political decision-making and is found occasionally in doctrinal sources.[13]

---

[10] Opened for signature 31 January 1967, 606 UNTS 267 (entered into force 4 October 1967).

[11] UNHCR, Handbook on Procedures and Criteria for Determining Refugee Status (1979) [28].

[12] Ruddock v Vadarlis [2001] FCA 1329, [203] (French J). See also [126] (Beaumont J).

[13] See, e.g. Julius Grey, Immigration Law in Canada (1982) 120.

The bulk of administrative and judicial decisions on refugees in the region concern the interpretation of the various elements of the above definition. Yet the Refugee Convention and its Protocol do not include provisions relating to status determination procedures, thereby leaving this key aspect of refugee protection largely to the discretion of host States. This is supported by article 1(3) of the Declaration on Territorial Asylum: 'It shall rest with the State granting asylum to evaluate the grounds for the grant of asylum'.[14] Given the human rights-related context surrounding refugee protection, it is safe to assume that this discretionary power does not justify arbitrary government decisions.

The above norms apply to States bound by the Convention definition. However, the South Pacific stands out because of the high number of States that are not party to the Convention or its Protocol. The list of non-party States from the region is long: Cook Islands, Kiribati, Micronesia, Nauru, Niue, Palau, Marshall Islands, Tonga and Vanuatu. We could add several significant non-party States if we extend the region to include neighbouring Asia-Pacific countries: Indonesia, Malaysia and Singapore.[15] It appears that the 'Asian values' specificity so prominent in human rights debates[16] also plays an important role in the region's refugee protection policies. The actual role it plays, however, is far from clear: some of the above listed States have an arguably stronger record of refugee reception than many States bound by the Refugee Convention. To a large extent, it is the political and moral constraints found in each society that provide refugees with actual protection.

Another international refugee definition affecting the region that deserves mention is that found in UNHCR's Statute. It is almost identical to the definition found in the Refugee Convention,[17] even though it solely concerns the protection mandate entrusted to UNHCR by the UN General Assembly. The implications of this distinct definition will be explored below.

In a region where a significant number of States are not party to the Refugee Convention and have not implemented domestic legislation on refugees,[18] it is sometimes not easy to answer a simple legal question such as 'who is a refugee?'. This underlines the limited role played by international law in resolving forced migration problems.

---

[14] GA Res 2312 (XXII), 22 GAOR Supp (No 16), 81, UN Doc A/6716 (1967).
[15] Brunei, Thailand and Vietnam are also not bound by the Refugee Convention.
[16] See, e.g. Bilahari Kausikan, 'Asia's Different Standard' (1993) 92 Foreign Policy 24; Aryeh Neier, 'Asia's Unacceptable Standard' (1993) 92 Foreign Policy 42; Joanne R Bauer and Daniel A Bell (eds), The East Asian Challenge for Human Rights (1999).
[17] Statute of the United Nations High Commissioner for Refugees, GA Res 428 (V), 5 UN GAOR Supp (No 20) 46, UN Doc A/1775 (1950) ('Statute') [6].
[18] The following South Pacific States do not have refugee-specific legislation: Cook Islands, Fiji, Kiribati, Micronesia, Nauru, Niue, Palau, Papua New Guinea, Marshall Islands, Samoa, Solomon Islands, Tonga, Tuvalu and Vanuatu.

What protection is guaranteed to a refugee?

Refugee definitions in themselves can be meaningless; it is the corresponding entitlements that give them significance. This section explores the key protection guarantee afforded to refugees by international law.

Refugee advocates often cite article 14(1) of the Universal Declaration of Human Rights (UDHR)[19] to suggest that refugees enjoy a right to asylum: 'Everyone has the right to seek and to enjoy in other countries asylum from persecution'. This provision is well known in advocacy circles and it exerts a considerable amount of influence on protection policies.

However, courts rely generally on binding legal instruments when making decisions and the UDHR was adopted in 1948 as a non-binding instrument. While many rights found in the UDHR were eventually codified in human rights treaties, article 14 was not. In fact, there was an international conference on asylum in the 1970s that was convened in order to adopt a draft Convention on Territorial Asylum.[20] It failed miserably and there have been no further attempts to draft a universal treaty concerning asylum.

The suggestion that the norm found in article 14 is now part of customary international law is also unlikely to be accepted by courts. Practice over the last decades clearly shows that States capable of preventing refugee arrivals generally adopt interdiction policies when they perceive themselves to be threatened by asylum seekers. Regardless of the humanitarian language used by governments to describe their refugee policies in a positive light, this is the harsh reality of the world in which we live. It indicates that evidence is lacking of a general practice accepted as law in relation to an absolute 'right to asylum'.

While courts may use soft law instruments such as the UDHR to interpret existing legal rules, the binding international protection standards granted to a refugee are formulated explicitly in the Refugee Convention. This key instrument is composed largely of socio-economic entitlements that provide a refugee with minimum protection so that he or she can survive in a host State until a durable solution is found. Yet it is the non-refoulement provision found in article 33(1) that constitutes the most basic form of protection afforded to a refugee:

> No Contracting State shall expel or return ('refouler') a refugee in any manner whatsoever to the frontiers of territories where his life or freedom would be threatened on account of his race, religion, nationality, membership of a particular social group or political opinion.

This is as close as the Refugee Convention gets to addressing the issue of territorial asylum. It should be emphasized that the Convention does not oblige States to

---

[19] GA Res 217A (III), UN Doc A/810, 71 (1948).
[20] See Atle Grahl-Madsen, Territorial Asylum (1980) and François Leduc, 'L'asile territorial – Conférence des Nations Unies' (1977) 23 Annuaire français de droit international 221.

provide asylum to a person who satisfies its refugee definition;[21] it simply prohibits refoulement to dangerous territories. In other words, the most basic form of protection found in the Convention, non-refoulement, can be offered in the country of first asylum or in any third country capable of providing refuge. As stated by the full Federal Court of Australia in the Tampa case:

> International law imposes no obligation upon the coastal State to resettle those rescued in the coastal State's territory. This accords with the principles of the Refugee Convention. By Article 33, a person who has established refugee status may not be expelled to a territory where his life and freedom would be threatened for a Convention reason. Again, there is no obligation on the coastal State to resettle in its own territory.[22]

To further complicate the legal situation, the moment at which non-refoulement applies has been the object of considerable debate. For example, one of the grandfathers of international refugee law, Atle Grahl-Madsen, has written that non-refoulement does not apply if the persecuted individual does not actually cross the border of the host State.[23] In some ways, the interpretation in the United States is even stricter: the Supreme Court has established in the Haitian case that the Coast Guard can physically prevent the arrival of boat people on US territorial waters without violating the non-refoulement principle.[24]

As seen from the above quotes, the majority of the full Federal Court of Australia considers that asylum seekers cannot be sent back to a dangerous territory if they are recognized as refugees by the competent authorities. Given that an interdiction operation by Australian forces in international waters can prevent boat people from claiming refugee status in Australia, the court's reasoning arguably makes it possible for the government to return an intercepted boat to a dangerous territory. If such an interpretation is correct, it would represent a considerable step backward in terms of regional protection standards.

In recent years UNHCR's position on this issue appears to be the opposite extreme. In the face of restrictive governmental actions relating to border control and interdiction policies, the UN refugee agency has recently endorsed a paper promoting a rather progressive interpretation of non-refoulement:

---

[21] See, e.g. the declaration by one of the US representatives at the Conference: 'Those who drafted the Convention recognized that governments were not prepared to commit themselves to grant asylum, even to bona fide refugees ... In short, as I understood Article 33, and as I believe all members of the Committee understood Article 33, it amounted to this: a State would not be obliged to admit any refugee. But a State could not seize a refugee in its territory and hand him over to his oppressors.' Affidavit of Louis Henkin, 15 December 1992, reproduced in Harold Hongju Koh, 'Reflections on Refoulement and Haitian Centers Council' (1994) 35 Harvard International Law Journal 45.
[22] Ruddock v Vadarlis [2001] FCA 1329, [126] (Beaumont J).
[23] Atle Grahl-Madsen, The Status of Refugees in International Law (1972) vol 2, 94. See also Neremiah Robinson, Convention relating to the Status of Refugees: A Commentary (1953) 163.
[24] Sale v Haitian Centers Council, 113 S Ct 2549 (1993).

> Non-refoulement is a principle of customary international law ... The principle of non-refoulement embodied in Article 33 encompasses any measure attributable to the State which could have the effect of returning an asylum seeker or refugee to the frontiers of territories where his or her life or freedom would be threatened, or where he or she is at risk of persecution, including interception, rejection at the frontier or indirect refoulement.[25]

While the principle of non-refoulement may indeed be part of customary international law and consequently bind South Pacific States that are not party to the Refugee Convention, its content is far from clear. The debate on this issue will not be resolved in the near future.

In terms of interpreting the content of the non-refoulement principle, the Declaration on Territorial Asylum provides some guidance in its paragraph 3(1): 'No person ... shall be subjected to measures such as rejection at the frontier or, if he has already entered the territory in which he seeks asylum, expulsion or compulsory return to any State where he may be subjected to persecution'. This constitutes a progressive interpretation when considered in light of the consequences of the influential Australian and US court decisions on boat people.

When assessing the practicality and feasibility of burden-sharing mechanisms, it is important to address whether an asylum seeker can choose a country of refuge (or engage in 'forum shopping' as it is called by critics). Indeed, the whole notion of emergency burden-sharing is generally premised on the possibility of transferring refugees to third countries. This implies difficult questions concerning refugee relocations in situations where consent by the affected person may not be forthcoming. At present, there do not appear to be any binding legal rules that suggest a refugee cannot be relocated involuntarily, as long as the principle of non-refoulement is respected. In other words, international law protects refugees from persecution, but it does not allow them necessarily to choose the State where protection will be granted. Furthermore, it appears that the transfer of refugees to other countries without the refugees' consent is not illegal, even if the country of relocation is not party to the Refugee Convention.[26] The issue in terms of international refugee law is whether the refugees will be indirectly refouled (or sent to a dangerous territory).

Yet a practical problem that has contributed in undermining recent burden-sharing proposals is that international human rights organizations are uncomfortable with the idea that a refugee may not always have a choice regarding the territory on which she or he is provided refuge. Until humanitarian actors are willing to accept this limitation on protection options for the asylum seeker, there is limited hope for effective burden-sharing mechanisms in emergency situations. These opposing views reflect the tensions associated with the Tampa affair and similar incidents in the South Pacific.

---

[25] 'Cambridge Roundtable Summary Conclusions – The principle of Non-Refoulement' in Erika Feller, Volker Türk and Frances Nicholson (eds), Refugee Protection in International Law (2003) 179.

[26] Contra Jean-Pierre L Fonteyne, 'All Adrift in a Sea of Illegitimacy: An International Law Perspective on the Tampa Affair' (2001) 12 Public Law Review 249, 251.

Asylum seekers at sea raise specific protection problems that need to be highlighted. Article 98 of the Law of the Sea Convention 'requires the master of a ship flying its flag, in so far as he can do so without serious danger to the ship, the crew or the passengers ... to render assistance to any person found at sea in danger of being lost'.[27] The issue is particularly problematic in the case of asylum seekers because it involves the disembarkation of rescuees who do not want to return to their home State. Yet article 98 does not mention the issue of disembarkation of the rescuees. Neither does the Refugee Convention contain any obligation on this issue. The result is that there is legal controversy over the ultimate responsibility for the fate of people rescued at sea.[28]

As an example of the practical consequences of this legal uncertainty, during the 1970s south-east Asian States denied that they had responsibility to allow disembarkation of Indochinese boat people. The coastal States allowed boat people to disembark only after seeking resettlement commitments from other States. Proposed solutions to this problem will be explored below.

What is a mass flow?

As seen above, the Refugee Convention uses the singular form in its refugee definition and its non-refoulement provision. There is no reference to the specific treatment of groups of refugees in either the Convention or its Protocol. This contrasts with, for example, the Convention Governing the Specific Aspects of Refugee Problems in Africa which refers frequently to 'refugees' in addressing situations that imply group movements.[29]

While the concept of 'mass flow' is not used or defined in any of the above mentioned treaties, it is used in numerous soft law instruments. For example, the Declaration on Territorial Asylum refers to 'a mass influx of persons' in its paragraph 3(2). It does not, however, define the term. Likewise, the concept is found in several conclusions adopted by UNHCR's executive committee (EXCOM) (for example, Conclusion No. 22 on the protection of asylum seekers in situations of large-scale influx[30]) and General Assembly Resolution 58/169 of 22 December 2003 on human rights and mass exoduses. Yet these soft law instruments provide no definition.

The closest example we have of States identifying some of the elements that characterize 'mass flows' is found in EXCOM's Conclusion No. 100 on

---

[27] United Nations Convention on the Law of the Sea, opened for signature 10 December 1982, 1833 UNTS 3 (entered into force 16 November 1994).

[28] See, e.g. Fonteyne, above n 26, 249.

[29] Opened for signature 10 September 1969, 1001 UNTS 45, art 2, 3, 5 (entered into force 20 June 1974).

[30] EXCOM, Protection of Asylum Seekers in Situations of Large-Scale Influx (No. 22 (XXXIII) – 1981) ('Conclusion No. 22').

international cooperation and burden and responsibility sharing in mass influx situations.[31] Its paragraph (a) specifies

> that mass influx is a phenomenon that has not been defined, but that, for the purposes of this conclusion, mass influx situations may, inter alia, have some or all of the following characteristics: (i) considerable numbers of people arriving over an international border; (ii) a rapid rate of arrival; (iii) inadequate absorption or response capacity in host States, particularly during the emergency; (iv) individual asylum procedures, where they exist, which are unable to deal with the assessment of such large numbers.

Governments seem to have a certain amount of discretion in characterizing a group of refugees as constituting a mass flow. As we shall see below, this has crucial consequences in terms of protection obligations.

Does non-refoulement apply to mass flows?

There are a wide variety of opinions concerning the issue of whether the non-refoulement principle applies in mass flow situations. Even though the issue was not as contentious at the time of the drafting of the Refugee Convention, refugee advocates have managed to promote higher protection standards so that this question has actually become one of the more controversial debates in international refugee law today.

The position adopted by UNHCR is summed up in a recent policy paper: 'The principle of non-refoulement applies in situations of mass influx'.[32] Although this paper is based on a relatively lengthy study of non-refoulement,[33] unfortunately the study does not really address thoroughly the various arguments in the debate. Nevertheless, the view that non-refoulement applies in mass flow situations is supported by most non-governmental human rights groups working on refugee issues and it is shared by many academics.[34]

Several soft law instruments adopted by States lend support to this view. EXCOM's first conclusion on the protection of asylum seekers in situations of large-scale influx set a high standard that continues to influence official policy statements by UNHCR. In the section entitled 'Admission and non-refoulement' of Conclusion No. 22, EXCOM expressed support for the concept of first asylum by stating that non-refoulement is to be interpreted as including non-rejection at the border in cases of mass influx:

---

[31] EXCOM, Conclusion on International Cooperation and Burden and Responsibility Sharing in Mass Influx Situations (No. 100 (LV) – 2004) ('Conclusion No. 100').
[32] 'Cambridge Roundtable Summary Conclusions', above n 25.
[33] Sir Elihu Lauterpacht and Daniel Bethlehem, 'The scope and content of the principle of non-refoulement' in Erika Feller, Volker Türk and Frances Nicholson (eds), Refugee Protection in International Law (2003) 89.
[34] See, e.g. Fonteyne, above n 26, 251.

1. In situations of large-scale influx, asylum seekers should be admitted to the State in which they first seek refuge and if that State is unable to admit them on a durable basis, it should always admit them at least on a temporary basis and provide them with protection according to the principles set out below. They should be admitted without any discrimination as to race, religion, political opinion, nationality, country of origin or physical incapacity.
2. In all cases the fundamental principle of non-refoulement including non-rejection at the frontier must be scrupulously observed.[35]

In Conclusion No. 23 on problems related to the rescue of asylum seekers in distress at sea, EXCOM explicitly extended the interpretation to boat people: 'In cases of large-scale influx, asylum seekers rescued at sea should always be admitted, at least on a temporary basis'.[36] It should be noted that both Australia and the United States have been members of EXCOM since its creation in 1958 and that its conclusions are adopted by consensus. Although these instruments are not legally-binding in the sense of immediately enforceable binding commitments, they represent authoritative interpretations that are adopted as political recommendations.

The various EXCOM conclusions on boat people adopted in the 1980s refer to the South China Sea and relate to asylum seekers fleeing from the Indochinese peninsula.[37] Given that the influential western liberal democracies which dominate EXCOM debates were not the coastal States directly impacted by the principle of disembarkation at the next port of call, this begs the question as to whether they intended these high standards to apply to themselves as well as the poorer Asia-Pacific coastal States. We will return to this theme later in the chapter after exploring the actual legal position of the Australian and US governments in court cases.

The preceding comments highlight the importance of distinguishing hard law from soft law, and possibly law from politics. Turning to the text of the Refugee Convention, the answer to the question posed in this section becomes less clear. We have already seen how the refugee definition and the non-refoulement principle found in the Convention are both drafted in the singular form (i.e. 'a refugee').

Recourse to the preparatory work of a treaty is generally accepted as a supplementary means of interpretation.[38] Interestingly, the Convention's *travaux préparatoires* indicate that the issue of mass flows preoccupied many of the State representatives during the Conference of Plenipotentiaries on the Status of Refugees and Stateless Person, convened in Geneva in July 1951.[39] The declarations by government delegations are revealing in terms of the commitments

---

[35] Above n 30, [II(A)].
[36] EXCOM, Conclusion on Problems Related to the Rescue of Asylum Seekers in Distress at Sea (No. 23 (XXXIII) – 1981) [3].
[37] The point is emphasized in Tara Magner, 'A Less than "Pacific" Solution for Asylum Seekers in Australia' (2004) 16 International Journal of Refugee Law 53, 67, 70.
[38] Vienna Convention on the Law of Treaties, opened for signature 23 May 1969, 1155 UNTS 331 (entered into force 27 January 1980).
[39] Conference of Plenipotentiaries on the Status of Refugees and Stateless Persons, Summary Record of the Sixteenth Meeting (held at the Palais des Nations, Geneva, on Wednesday, 11 July 1951, at 3 pm), UN Doc A/CONF.2/SR.16 (1951).

accepted by the States participating in the drafting process. For example, the Swiss representative declared that 'States were not compelled to allow large groups of persons claiming refugee status to cross its frontiers'. The Dutch representative shared this concern and hinted at possible solutions: 'the Netherlands was somewhat diffident about assuming unconditional obligations so far as mass influxes of refugees were concerned, unless international collaboration was sufficiently organized to deal with such a situation'. The link with security concerns was made explicitly by the Italian representative who declared that 'a State could not commit itself not to expel or return large groups of refugees who presented themselves on its territory, and who might endanger public security'.[40]

In fact, during the negotiations on the drafting of the non-refoulement provision (which took place on 11 July 1951, the Convention was signed on the 28th), discussions focused largely on the link between mass flows and destabilization. The *travaux préparatoires* of the Convention show that the signing of this instrument was actually conditional on the understanding that it did not impose any obligations in cases of mass flows.[41] This was noted by the president of the conference on 25 July, allowing the representatives to move on to other issues and eventually sign the Convention three days later. As stated by one of the US representatives at the 1951 Conference: 'Some delegates did express the concern that the right of non-refoulement should not become a vehicle for requiring the admission of massive numbers of migrants ... By expressing a caveat about mass migrations, the delegates were confirming that the right of non-refoulement attached to individual refugees and not to groups'.[42]

A number of doctrinal sources recognize that the non-refoulement principle can be the object of exceptions in mass flow situations.[43] At the very least, we must acknowledge that non-refoulement as expressed in treaty law has been left deliberately imprecise in certain situations. Indeed, the Refugee Convention does

---

[40] Ibid.

[41] Baron van Boetzelaer (Netherlands): '[T]he Netherlands Government attached very great importance to the scope of the provision now contained in article 33. The Netherlands could not accept any legal obligations in respect of large groups of refugees seeking access to its territory. At the first reading the representatives of Belgium, the Federal Republic of Germany, Italy, the Netherlands and Sweden had supported the Swiss interpretation. From conversations he had since had with other representatives, he had gathered that the general consensus of opinion was in favour of the Swiss interpretation. In order to dispel any possible ambiguity and to reassure his Government, he wished to have it placed on record that the Conference was in agreement with the interpretation that the possibility of mass migrations across frontiers or of attempted mass migrations was not covered by article 33.' Conference of Plenipotentiaries on the Status of Refugees and Stateless Persons, Summary Record of the Thirty-fifth Meeting (held at the Palais des Nations, Geneva, on Wednesday, 25 July 1951, at 2.30 pm), UN Doc A/CONF.2/SR.35 (1951).

[42] Affidavit of Louis Henkin, 15 December 1992, reproduced in Koh, above n 21, 45-7.

[43] Grahl-Madsen, Territorial Asylum, above n 20, 42; Patricia Hyndman, 'Asylum and Non-Refoulement – Are these Obligations owed to Refugees under International Law?' (1982) 57 Philippine Law Journal 68; David A Martin, 'Large Scale Migrations of Asylum Seekers' (1982) 76 American Journal of International Law 598.

not contain provisions addressing specifically mass flow situations. This omission suggests that the drafters did not want State reactions to mass inflows to be regulated by international treaty obligations. The lack of precision in the treaty text allows political leaders increased flexibility when dealing with concrete problems related to large refugee movements so that they do not find themselves hampered by unworkable international principles.

Even though refugee advocates will argue that the normative framework has evolved since the drafting of the main refugee protection instrument over a half-century ago, it is far from evident that courts will follow such reasoning to the extent that it is intended to have non-refoulement cover mass flow situations. The restrictive judicial interpretations that have limited the scope of non-refoulement in Australia and the US suggest that a legal strategy based on including mass flows within its sphere of protection is unlikely to win in a court setting. For example, the losing party in the Haitian boat people case never suggested that the government had to admit a large-scale influx on US territory; it simply wanted to prevent the refugees intercepted on the high seas from being sent directly to Haiti.[44] It lost on this minimalist point.

The main example of State practice that confirms the above analysis is found in the treatment of asylum seekers from the former Yugoslavia in Europe during the 1990s. The divergence between the European application of temporary protection measures in relation to these asylum seekers and the Refugee Convention's specific rights regime has been noted by many commentators.[45] As the difference in protection standards was justified largely in exceptional terms resulting from an alleged 'mass inflow', the position of some European States suggests implicitly that they consider the Convention does not apply in situations of mass influx. Although this has not been declared formally by the European Union, it is likely the only way that the various temporary protection policies in the 1990s concerning forced migrants from the former Yugoslavia can be defended on legal grounds.

To the extent that UNHCR approved the ad hoc European temporary protection schemes and accepted that the Convention's rights regime would not apply in this particular case,[46] it is awkward for the UN agency now to insist that the Refugee Convention applies in mass flow situations. Why did it not make this position clear in response to European policies in the 1990s? This problem of different standards applying to different host States is explored below.

The above discussion shows that the drafters of the Refugee Convention did not intend its key protection guarantee, non-refoulement, to apply to mass flows. However, refugee advocates contend that the norms have evolved along with the

---

[44] 'Respondents have never claimed that the Attorney General is obliged to admit a mass Haitian migration across our frontiers or borders, only that Article 33 and § 243(h) [of the 1980 Refugee Act] bar the Attorney General from returning all arriving ships to Haiti.' Koh, above n 21, 55.

[45] See, e.g. Michael Barutciski, 'The Reinforcement of Non-Admission Policies and the Subversion of UNHCR' (1996) 8 International Journal of Refugee Law 49.

[46] UNHCR, Note on International Protection, UN Doc A/AC.96/830 (1994).

development of human rights law over the last few decades. As courts have not dealt directly with this question, there is consequently a certain amount of legal uncertainty over this problem.

How does national security affect State obligations?

It should be noted that in neither the Tampa nor the Haitian case did any party invoke a threat to national security, yet the courts rendered relatively restrictive decisions. It is safe to assume that courts would not be any less restrictive if a threat to national security were actually invoked. Although it involves an individual and not a refugee group, the case of Ahmed Zaoui in New Zealand illustrates the point: he was recognized as a refugee by the country's Refugee Status Appeals Authority,[47] yet the government detained him for two years because it alleges that he has terrorist connections. The country's newly created Supreme Court is still examining the case.

The inclusion in the Refugee Convention of article 9 authorizing provisional measures in cases involving national security is an example of the pragmatic dimension of the principles codified in international law. Article 9 allows the following exceptions:

> Nothing in this Convention shall prevent a Contracting State, in time of war or other grave and exceptional circumstances, from taking provisionally measures which it considers to be essential to the national security in the case of a particular person, pending a determination by the Contracting State that that person is in fact a refugee and that the continuance of such measures is necessary in his case in the interests of national security.

As traditionally conceived, refugee protection principles do not contradict legitimate State interests. It has also become increasingly clear in recent years that courts in liberal democracies are ready to severely restrict rights and liberties when national security is at stake.

The above comments help explain the inclusion of an exception to non-refoulement based on national security reasons in paragraph 2 of the Refugee Convention's article 33:

> The benefit of the present provision may not, however, be claimed by a refugee whom there are reasonable grounds for regarding as a danger to the security of the country in which he is, or who, having been convicted by a final judgment of a particularly serious crime, constitutes a danger to the community of that country.

Although the provision refers to a threat posed by individuals, the destabilization context created by a mass influx suggests that individuals represent a threat due to their membership of a larger group. Any other interpretation would oblige a host

---

[47] Refugee Appeal No 704540/03 (1 August 2003). See also Zaoui v Attorney-General, High Court (Auckland), CIV-2003-404-5872 (19 December 2003).

State to insist that the Refugee Convention's non-refoulement guarantee does not apply to mass flows. The latter interpretation was apparently favoured by the drafters.[48]

The UN General Assembly helps to clarify this issue in its Declaration on Territorial Asylum. Paragraph 3(1) of this non-binding instrument stipulates that a person seeking asylum shall be protected against 'rejection at the frontier or, if he has already entered the territory in which he seeks asylum, expulsion or compulsory return to any State where he may be subjected to persecution'. This provision is followed by an exception in paragraph 3(2) that refers explicitly to security and mass flows: 'Exception may be made to the foregoing principle only for overriding reasons of national security or in order to safeguard the population, as in the case of a mass influx of persons'.

It is interesting to note that UNHCR, as an agency created by the General Assembly, rejects the idea that non-refoulement can be restrained in situations of mass inflows and destabilization. Even after an independent evaluation that was commissioned by the agency and that dealt with the consequences of this problem,[49] the UN refugee agency considers that a State has to admit (at least temporarily) all refugees who present themselves at the border, regardless of whether they are part of a larger group that may destabilize the country. With such absolutist legal opinions, UNHCR exposes itself to harsh criticisms.[50] It also distances itself from its mandate which is to cooperate with UN member States to protect refugees.[51] The agency is not necessarily supposed to be a non-governmental type of watchdog on refugee policy,[52] despite the various suggestions that it assume

---

[48] 'Mr Theodoli (Italy) ... personally felt that a State could not commit itself not to expel or return large groups of refugees who presented themselves on its territory, and who might endanger public security. The Italian delegation would therefore reserve its position on the article, unless some satisfactory explanation was forthcoming.' Conference of Plenipotentiaries on the Status of Refugees and Stateless Persons, Summary Record of the Sixteenth Meeting (held at the Palais des Nations, Geneva, on Wednesday, 11 July 1951, at 3 pm), UN Doc A/CONF.2/SR.16 (1951).
[49] Astri Suhrke et al., The Kosovo Refugee Crisis: An independent evaluation of UNHCR's emergency preparedness and response, UN Doc EPAU/2000/001 (2000).
[50] See, e.g. Guy S Goodwin-Gill, 'The Kosovo Refugee Crisis: An Independent Evaluation of UNHCR's Emergency Preparedness and Response' (2000) 16 Relief and Rehabilitation Network Newsletter 33-4: '[The performance of UNHCR] on first asylum strongly implies that staff initially responsible for protection in the region, and possibly also in Headquarters, are unfamiliar with basic principles. If ... UNHCR seriously considers that first asylum should be considered as an absolute and unconditional legal obligation consistent with the 1951 Refugee Convention, then there is something wrong with its perception of international law ... [F]irst asylum is a fine ideal but it does not reflect general international law or the requirements of the 1951 Convention/1967 Protocol ... [UNHCR] seems to be confused as to its basic legal standing and as to the international law which it is supposed to apply.'
[51] See, e.g. Statute, above n 17, [1], [8], [10].
[52] Adrienne Millbank, 'The Problem with the 1951 Refugee Convention', Parliamentary Library of Australia, Research Paper No 5 (5 September 2000).

something akin to such a role.[53] To the extent that it must follow policy directives from the General Assembly[54] and that it depends on voluntary governmental contributions,[55] the UN refugee agency does not have an appropriate mandate for a watchdog role typically assumed by NGOs.[56]

It is worth emphasizing the uncompromising nature of the position taken by UNHCR and many NGOs on this issue.[57] According to these refugee advocates, States must open their borders to any migrant who claims to be a victim of human rights violations even if there exists a serious fear of destabilization provoked by a massive influx. This proposition does not, however, reflect an interstate consensus. Ironically, it is partly because of this kind of advocacy that western governments seek to contain refugee flows in less affluent regions of the world and to prevent people from poor countries to seek asylum in rich countries.

Indeed, the suggestion that refugees may have an unconditional right to first asylum clashes with some of the most basic premises of legal systems in the South Pacific. As pointed out by Judge French of the Federal Court of Australia:

> The power to determine who may come into Australia is so central to its sovereignty that it is not to be supposed that the Government of the nation would lack under the power conferred upon it directly by the Constitution, the ability to prevent people not part of the Australian community, from entering.[58]

Yet it is rather astonishing that Australia, as a member of UNHCR's executive committee, participated in the adoption of international norms (along with other OECD member States) that actually embrace the unrealistic standard criticized above.

---

[53] See e.g. Saul Takahashi, 'Recourse to Human Rights Treaty Bodies for Monitoring the Refugee Convention' (2002) 20 Netherlands Quarterly of Human Rights 53 and Volker Türk, 'UNHCR's supervisory responsibility', New Issues in Refugee Research, UNHCR Working Paper No 67 (October 2002).

[54] Statute, above n 17, [3].

[55] Statute, above n 17, [20].

[56] For a discussion on UNHCR's mandate, see Michael Barutciski, 'A Critical View of UNHCR's Mandate Dilemmas' (2002) 14 International Journal of Refugee Law 365.

[57] See, e.g. European Council on Refugees and Exiles, 'The Kosovo Refugee Crisis. ECRE's Observations on the independent evaluation of UNHCR's emergency preparedness and response' (Press Release, February 2000); Human Rights Watch, 'Macedonia must keep border open to refugees' (Press Release, 1 April 1999); Amnesty International, 'Former Yugoslav Republic of Macedonia: The Protection of Kosovo Albanian Refugees' (Press Release, 1 May 1999).

[58] Ruddock v Vadarlis [2001] FCA 1329, [193] (French J). See also the remarks by Judge Beaumont ([125]): 'It follows, in my view, that the occupants [of the MV Tampa] had no legal right at common law enforceable in a court to enter Australia. It must follow, in my view, that no foundation existed for the grant of a common law prerogative writ of habeas corpus compelling their entry into Australia ... there is nothing in any of the authorities to contradict the principle that an alien has no common law right to enter Australia. This aspect is beyond argument. For this reason alone, I would allow the appeal.'

As we have seen, EXCOM had already concluded in 1981 that it should call for asylum in the country of first arrival and that this principle applied to mass arrivals as well as individual asylum seekers.[59] It later further concluded that asylum must be unconditional.[60] More recently, EXCOM (including New Zealand as a new member) has confirmed its position on unconditional first asylum in the preamble of Conclusion No. 100.[61]

This leads to the following question: would these EXCOM members insist on having these norms apply to themselves? We know from the Tampa affair and subsequent government policies that Australia does not consider itself bound by such high standards. Likewise, US policy in relation to Haitian and Cuban boat people does not conform to these standards. So why do these States participate in the promulgation of norms that they do not intend to respect if faced with destabilizing mass flows?

While soft law contributes to the evolution of international law, the introduction of a wide range of norms that vary in terms of their legal nature exposes the practice of international law to a type of criticism that is evoked commonly by developing States: a selective use of norms. In other words, it allows powerful States to pick and choose among the norms that are the most convenient for their political goals and their relative ability to impose their political positions on the international scene. After all, if a State does not agree with the particular application of certain norms, it can always resort to a formalist positivist approach generally favoured by courts. We return to power politics in terms of securing international support and legitimacy.

In relation to the particular problem regarding refugees addressed in this chapter, the apparently 'progressive' use of soft norms may actually reinforce the double standards that are implicit in refugee flow containment strategies adopted by affluent States. From a containment perspective, it is entirely consistent to insist on an absolute right of unconditional first asylum, without a complementary commitment to burden sharing. The last point about a lack of commitment is explored in the next section.

It has been noted that the closure of Australian territorial waters on national security grounds may be difficult to justify in the specific case of the Tampa.[62] However, the wider picture might be more complex. At stake are numerous intangible security issues. From a governmental viewpoint, the proliferation of sea-based people smuggling sends a message that Australia is a soft target and an

---

[59] EXCOM, Conclusion No. 22, above n 30.
[60] See, e.g. EXCOM, Conclusion on International Protection (No. 85 (XLIX) 1998).
[61] EXCOM notes 'that persons who arrive as part of a mass influx seeking international refugee protection should always receive it, at least on a temporary basis'. The wording in this important conclusion may suggest a slight shift in tone to a more pragmatic approach to the extent that this provision is now only found in the preamble. Conclusion No. 100, above n 31.
[62] Donald R Rothwell, 'The Law of the Sea and the MV Tampa Incident: Reconciling Maritime Principles with Coastal State Sovereignty' (2002) Public Law Review 118, 122; Cecilia Bailliet, 'The Tampa Case and its Impact on Burden Sharing' (2003) 25 Human Rights Quarterly 741, 750.

attractive destination. Even though the 433 asylum seekers aboard the Tampa may not have directly threatened Australia's security, it was argued by the government that allowing such breaches of the country's maritime boundaries sends a dangerous message and demonstrates Australia's limited capacity to control its borders. After the peak period of 1998–2001 in which the government claims that over 10,000 boat people were smuggled to Australia, there have been only a few boats attempting to reach the Australian mainland.[63] The policies developed in the wake of the Tampa affair are undoubtedly responsible for this development. It is interesting to note that New Zealand also adopted emergency legislation during the early phases of the peak period when public concern was raised about the (far-fetched) possibility that boat people could approach the North Island.[64]

Is there an obligation to share the burden?

The refoulement of refugees to dangerous territories is clearly not an acceptable solution to the problems addressed in this chapter. The arguments presented in the preceding sections are intended to underline the limitations concerning international legal obligations, precisely in order to encourage a genuine debate regarding political solutions and commitments. This section explores one of the key ideas mentioned in the Refugee Convention's preamble: the promotion of international cooperation to alleviate the burden on vulnerable host States. The present analysis suggests that a realist approach offers better chances to implement such a form of international cooperation.

The first point to underline is that there is no binding obligation regarding burden-sharing in the 46 articles found in the Refugee Convention. In fact, international law presently imposes no obligations on States other than the ones that are confronted directly with refugee movements. The unfairness resulting from 'accidents of geography' has inspired detailed proposals from academics and advocates who are interested in introducing authentic burden-sharing mechanisms in international refugee policy.[65] The idea is to conceive an international system in which the State confronted with the refugee flow is not the only one bound by legal obligations. In the current context, it is unlikely that this proposition will be met with a favourable response from States that would have to assume new duties.

Ironically, it may be partly because human rights activists insist that first asylum always be granted unconditionally that it is difficult to impose an

---

[63] Department of Immigration and Multicultural and Indigenous Affairs, Fact sheet no 74: Unauthorised Arrivals by Air and Sea (6 October 2004).
[64] Immigration Amendment Act (No 2) 1999. See also John Armstrong, 'Orion to scan seas for boat people', New Zealand Herald, 17 June 1999, A3; Greg Ansley, 'Trade in people ruthless', New Zealand Herald, 17 June 1999, A15; Editorial, 'Unwelcome by boat', New Zealand Herald, 17 June 1999, A16.
[65] See, e.g. James C Hathaway and R Alexander Neve, 'Making International Refugee Law Relevant Again: A proposal for Collectivized and Solution-Oriented Protection' (1997) 10 Harvard Human Rights Journal 116.

obligation on other States to share the burden of refugee protection. Why should another State commit itself to admit refugees onto its territory if the first State of arrival is obliged to provide unconditional asylum? Numerous intergovernmental negotiations have demonstrated that it is easier for States to shift the burden and avoid any responsibility.

To some extent, this is an example of counterproductive advocacy in the sense that the existence of a (non-binding) standard of unconditional asylum encourages UNHCR not to prepare serious contingency plans for alternative protection measures in case borders are closed.[66] Until recently, its strategy, like that of many NGOs, has been generally to pressure host States into admitting the refugees.

As States and international bodies are increasingly making the link between security and refugee flows in order to restrict admission to asylum seekers, it is necessary to ensure that any reference to the accepted exceptions in the Refugee Convention is done in order to promote burden-sharing and not to defend refoulement. How can this be achieved within the legal framework described above? From a realist perspective, successful burden-sharing initiatives must be based on a combination of principles and diplomacy.

According to article 35 of the Refugee Convention, States have an obligation to cooperate with UNHCR. As the UN agency is mandated to protect refugees regardless of whether a frontline State claims an exception to protection obligations, this suggests a duty to engage in contingency planning for burden-sharing in situations where a host country is too vulnerable to accept a mass influx. The forms of possible sharing relate to the costs of the operational response and provision of territorial asylum in safe countries.

Unfortunately, this has not been the practice of UNHCR to date. If the UN refugee agency were to be persuaded to engage seriously in contingency planning, then this would represent a significant shift in international attempts to implement burden-sharing mechanisms. In this regard, EXCOM Conclusion No. 100 includes several new ideas and provisions that have not been adopted in soft law instruments in the past.

In order to understand the significance of this conclusion, it is important to remember that UNHCR several years ago defended its lack of contingency planning in its response to criticisms:

> [T]he evaluation suggests that UNHCR should have given more and earlier attention to the probability that the refugees would not be admitted to a potential country of asylum, and that alternative protection strategies should have been explored. UNHCR is concerned that contingency planning which assumes that States will not comply with their responsibilities to receive and host new arrivals, particularly in mass influx situations, runs the risk of becoming a self-fulfilling prophecy. At a time when the commitment of States to the institution of asylum appears to be in decline, that risk is real and dangerous.[67]

---

[66] Suhrke et al., above n 49.

[67] Ibid, Appendix D.

The logic to this defence is akin to suggesting that there is no need for a lifeboat aboard a ship because it would undermine the passengers' confidence in the seaworthiness of the ship. Implicitly contradicting UNHCR's views, EXCOM has noted in Conclusion No. 100 the importance of emergency preparedness and response strategies in anticipation of situations likely to lead to a mass influx.[68] EXCOM further notes that UNHCR should convene consultations as early on in a crisis as possible in order to explore refugee protection mechanisms in the spirit of international solidarity involving arrangements among States, regional and international organizations, as well as financial institutions.[69] The fact that EXCOM has requested UNHCR to report regularly on developments regarding burden-sharing in mass flow situations certainly represents a positive step forward.[70]

Given the lack of legally-binding commitments regarding burden-sharing, the political and diplomatic factors that encourage cooperation by regional actors are essential. Here again the South Pacific, along with the Asia-Pacific region more generally, stands out because it includes various States that have managed to cooperate during certain refugee crises over the last few decades. In order to promote burden-sharing, it is necessary to explore the political, moral, institutional and financial factors that made this cooperation possible.

What can we learn from governmental policies?

The above legal analysis helps to understand governmental policies relating to mass refugee flows and burden-sharing in the region. Governments are willing to protect refugees, but only if the measures conform to their immigration concerns and objectives.

Although burden-sharing could theoretically be conceived in different ways, practice shows that it depends generally on the existence of resettlement programmes. Through careful diplomatic initiatives, it is possible to secure a temporary form of initial protection for refugees during mass influxes. However, this initial protection is dependent on assurances that the burden of settling the refugees will be shared with other States. Notwithstanding the language and recommendation in several EXCOM conclusions, practice demonstrates clearly that first asylum is offered only conditionally. The reaction of coastal States to the outflow of Vietnamese boat people during the 1970s and 1980s illustrates this point particularly well. States such as Malaysia, Indonesia, Thailand and the Philippines were willing to grant first asylum, but only after resettlement countries provided quotas for resettlement places.[71] If we want international law to be

---

[68] Above n 31, [(e)].
[69] Ibid, [(g)]-[(h)].
[70] Ibid [(o)].
[71] This 'unwritten arrangement' is described in Sten A Bronee, 'The History of the Comprehensive Plan of Action' (1993) 5 International Journal of Refugee Law 534. See also Astri Suhrke, 'Indochinese Refugees: The Law and Politics of First Asylum' (1983) 467 The Annals of the American Academy of Political and Social Science 102. For a critical

realistic and not simply to indicate aspirations, it may be better to acknowledge this important feature of past burden-sharing schemes, rather than promote standards that do not reflect actual State practice.

To the extent that burden-sharing depends on resettlement, it should be noted that the South Pacific includes two influential States that are recognized by UNHCR as being among the most important refugee resettlement countries in the world: Australia and New Zealand.[72] In recent years, Australia has been resettling between 7,000 and 12,000 people per year for humanitarian reasons, whereas New Zealand has an annual humanitarian resettlement quota of 750 places.[73] During the Tampa crisis, 131 boat people were handed from the Australian authorities to New Zealand for processing and were eventually included in the annual quota.

Despite these significant resettlement programmes, both Australia and New Zealand deal with only a few hundred spontaneous asylum claims per year by individuals who arrive at international airports.[74] This type of uninvited migrant claiming refugee status presents considerably more complicated policy problems than the selection of refugees in overseas camps. While the latter reflects the discretionary powers of an immigration country, the former represents in some ways a failure of border control measures. The picture is relatively clear: States are willing to protect refugees as long as they preserve the impression of controlling their frontiers and the numbers seeking protection are relatively low.

Australia's concerns are worth underlining in order to understand its proposed regional solution to the problems associated with refugee flows. The government believes that the country is facing a serious challenge to its immigration programme due to the increases in the number of illegal migrants entering its territory. The concern relates specifically to people arriving by sea with the help of people-smuggling rackets that have been targeting Australia. Given the country's vast coastline and proximity to south-east Asia, the government is worried that the country's strong economy attracts economic migrants using asylum procedures in order to gain entry. The following comment illustrates the perception motivating governmental policies: 'Australia is the blatant target of

---

assessment, see James C Hathaway, 'Labelling the Boat People: The Failure of the Human Rights Mandate of the Comprehensive Plan of Action for Indochinese Refugees' (1993) 15 Human Rights Quarterly 686.

[72] See, e.g. UNHCR, Resettlement Statistics 2002 (June 2003) which places Australia in 3rd place overall (behind the US and Canada) and New Zealand in 6th place (behind Sweden and Norway).

[73] Department of Immigration and Multicultural and Indigenous Affairs, Fact sheet no 60: Australia's Refugee and Humanitarian Program (20 January 2004). See also the New Zealand Immigration Service (NZIS) website: <www.immigration.govt.nz>.

[74] Department of Immigration and Multicultural and Indigenous Affairs, Fact sheet no 61: Seeking Asylum within Australia (12 November 2003). The figures in Australia have dropped considerably in recent years. Refugee statistics for New Zealand are posted on the NZIS website, ibid.

smugglers who take thousands of dollars to transport human cargoes onto its northern coast'.[75]

In terms of asylum seekers rescued at sea, we have already seen that there is no clear legal obligation to allow boats to enter Australian territorial waters in order to disembark rescuees who intend to seek asylum.[76] A solution needs to explore cooperation between flag States, coastal States and resettlement States. As the port-of-call State is not obliged to accept rescuees for resettlement, practice has been for such States to accept rescuees for disembarkation after obtaining assurances for resettlement from the flag State.[77]

The Australian government's approach to the problems mentioned above is to intercept and detain boat people on offshore territories for processing. To a certain extent, the government's position resembles US initiatives in the Caribbean: the general idea in relation to the interception of Haitian and Cuban boat people is that disembarkation at a transit camp with no specific guarantee of resettlement in the US will discourage asylum seekers from making dangerous sea voyages to the US mainland.

One of the main features of Australia's 'Pacific Solution' is that it involves the use of the Australian Navy to prevent boat people from landing on mainland Australia. The boat people are then transferred to detention centres on offshore Australian territories which have been excised from the country's migration zone where regular immigration rules are in application.[78] Detention centres for such transfers have also been set up on Nauru and Manus Island (Papua New Guinea).[79] As Australia's immigration laws do not apply in these detention centres, the government has assigned Australian officials to apply UNHCR's procedures for determining the legal status of the asylum seekers instead of the domestic procedures.[80] The need for a credible screening process is one of the lessons from the Indochinese boat people crisis of the 1970s and 1980s. The unwritten arrangement involving conditional first asylum was problematic in that resettlement was basically assured for the Indochinese migrants who were rescued and disembarked: this encouraged abuse by some people who were not fleeing persecution.[81]

---

[75] Ryszard Piotrowicz, 'The Case of MV Tampa: State and Refugee Rights Collide at Sea' (2001) 76 Australian Law Journal 12, 13.
[76] Fonteyne, above n 26, 250.
[77] Piotrowicz, above n 75, 16.
[78] The Christmas and Cocos Islands, as well as Ashmore Reef have been excised from the migration zone.
[79] Papua New Guinea was an Australian colony until 1975 and Nauru's foreign relations were handled by Australia until 1975. The territorial application clause found in art 40 of the Refugee Convention was used by Australia to cover Nauru until 1975 (date of receipt of the notification: 22 January 1954).
[80] See, e.g. Graham Thom, 'Human Rights, Refugees and the MV Tampa Crisis' (2002) 13 Public Law Review 110, 110.
[81] For an analysis from a refugee advocate who acknowledges that the arrangement was intended to address the alleged abuse, see Arthur C Helton, 'Refugee Determination under the Comprehensive Plan of Action' (1993) 5 International Journal of Refuge Law 544, 556-7. While the first refugee treaties of the 1920s did not involve screening procedures for the

Unsurprisingly, the controversial 'Pacific Solution' has attracted mixed political reactions: some lawyers morally oppose the government's offloading of asylum claimants on poor and remote territories,[82] while others justify the measures because of the perception that the country has to defend its vast borders in the face of unauthorized boat people arrivals.[83] It is worth emphasizing that courts should generally limit their judgments to the positive law and leave political assessments to the appropriate bodies, even if they may disapprove of the harsh nature of executive actions against boat people. This is one of the basic messages from the full Federal Court of Australia in the Tampa case:

> The steps taken in relation to the MV Tampa which had the purpose and effect of preventing the rescuees from entering the migration zone and arranging for their departure from Australian territorial waters were within the scope of executive power. The finding does not involve a judgment about any policy informing the exercise of that power. That is a matter which has been and continues to be debated in public and indeed international forums. Through that debate and the parliamentary process the Ministers involved can be held accountable for their actions.[84]

The complicated political and moral issues around the 'Pacific Solution' are not explored in this chapter.[85]

In terms of the key international legal obligations, to date there are no reports suggesting that the intercepted boat people have been returned to dangerous countries. Indeed, Australia's assistance with the disembarkation and the determination procedures, along with its financial contributions demonstrate its acceptance of some obligations to facilitate resettlement.

As New Zealand is geographically situated further from refugee-producing areas, it has not been confronted directly with the problems associated with boat people. Government policy is undoubtedly influenced by this favourable context. Yet actions have been taken to protect the country from such eventualities. Indeed, the government has recently conducted interdepartmental exercises to explore various scenarios involving boat people. It is not clear what contingency plans it has prepared in the unlikely case that boat people were to approach New Zealand's

---

designated beneficiaries (eg fleeing Russians and Armenians), by the end of the Second World War it was deemed necessary to have the newly created International Refugee Organization apply what were probably the first individualized determination procedures in public international law. See, e.g. Denis Alland, 'Les organisations internationals et les réfugiés' in René-Jean Dupuy (ed.), Manuel sur les organisations internationals (1998) 496.

[82] For receiving the Tampa asylum seekers, Australia promised Nauru A$10 million worth of fuel, A$3 million for new generators, cancellation of A$1 million worth of hospital bills run by Nauruans in Australia, refurbishment of the small island's sports oval, as well as sporting and educational scholarships for Nauruans to go to Australia.

[83] For an example of a refugee advocate who believes the measures are justified, see Carlos Scott Lopez, 'Australian Immigration Policy at the Centenary: The Quest for Control' (2003) 18 Georgetown Immigration Law Journal 1, 54.

[84] Ruddock v Vadarlis [2001] FCA 1329, [204] (French J).

[85] For a useful and critical discussion on these issues, see OXFAM, Adrift in the Pacific: The implications of Australia's Pacific Refugee Solution (February 2002).

territorial waters,[86] although mass detention in the remote Rangipo desert prison has been discussed in the past.

The above analysis suggests that the regional 'Pacific Solution' to the problem of boat people is politically awkward. However, to the extent that its main promoter, Australia, has seen a dramatic drop in the number of boat people attempting to enter its territorial waters, the approach has been at least partly successful from a border control perspective. This is undoubtedly why several European states have expressed an interest in exploring a similar concept: the establishment of safe areas for refugee processing on the periphery of Europe. As with US attempts to create a similar regional approach in the Caribbean, the combination of interception and offshore processing appears to be limited to an ad hoc response for emergency situations. Australia has taken this approach as far as it has been implemented to date and its experiences indicate that the diplomatic constraints are considerable. The lessons from its experiences will undoubtedly be used by other actors who are interested in pursuing this approach as a generalized policy response to boat people.

Conclusion

States have indicated formally that they intend to protect refugees by adopting the Refugee Convention and its Protocol, along with various soft law instruments. However, the protection commitments are not unconditional. Not only are they placed within the larger context of immigration control, but they are mitigated by discretionary powers concerning security.

Although notions of sovereignty have evolved over recent years, our international system continues to be dominated by the key concept of State sovereignty. This is particularly evident in the area of transnational migration controls. To date States have not even consented to a binding system that grants territorial asylum to individuals who actually meet the legal requirements of the refugee definition in the Refugee Convention. The non-refoulement guarantee that forms the backbone of the international refugee protection system simply prohibits States from sending refugee claimants to dangerous territories where they may fear persecution. In other words, the refugee can be sent to a third country where there is no fear of persecution or risk of being transferred to another dangerous country. From a refugee protection standpoint, this is clearly far from ideal. Yet it is important to underline that this legal situation reflects the actual political commitments that State representatives are willing to assume on the international stage.

Given the context of limited international legal obligations described in this chapter, the struggle for the free movement of people across national borders should not be waged on the back of asylum seekers. This is a particularly vulnerable group of foreigners who risk suffering disproportionately from any xenophobia in host societies. Genuine refugees cannot afford survival strategies based on wishful thinking because they are de facto stateless. Neither should they

---

[86] 'Personnel take part in migrant ship exercise', New Zealand Herald, 8 October 2003.

be encouraged to do so by well-intentioned human rights advocates. The tone of the decision rendered by the US Supreme Court regarding Haitian boat people intercepted by the Coast Guard deserves to be emphasized in order to avoid misguided legal strategies in the future:

> The drafters of the Convention ... may not have contemplated that any nation would gather fleeing refugees and return them to the one country they had desperately sought to escape; such actions may even violate the spirit of Article 33; but a treaty cannot impose uncontemplated extraterritorial obligations on those who ratify it through no more than its general humanitarian intent.[87]

Advocates for open borders should focus their political activism on easing border restrictions between liberal democratic States for this more accurately reflects the positive developments concerning sovereignty and migration in recent years. Indeed, national borders and community membership in some of the affluent parts of the world have been transformed to such an extent that notions of citizenship and nationality are no longer what they used to be in the post-Second World War period. However, it is less evident that this development characterizes exchanges between countries with widely varying cultures and economic performance. Intercontinental migration that involves significant cross-cultural differences continues to be dominated by the key concept of State sovereignty.

The above reflections are crucial to understanding the legal and political dimensions of refugee burden-sharing. Whether it is conceived as an emergency mechanism intended to save refugees from an overburdened host State or as a pre-planned 'insurance' scheme meant to provide a multilateral response to future refugee flows, the issue of burden-sharing has been debated considerably in recent years. Yet despite repeated attempts to establish norms that can be translated into practice, burden-sharing has never been more than an ad hoc and discretionary feature of the current system. Even though thousands of persons displaced by the conflicts in Bougainville and the Solomon Islands have contributed to instability in local host communities, their plight has not attracted the kind of attention that mobilizes third countries to share the burden by providing asylum. Likewise, protection for the thousands of people who have fled Indonesian-ruled West Papua has been limited to refuge in Papua New Guinea and assistance from international organizations.

Acknowledging the circumstances under which refugees can raise regional security concerns helps policymakers respond more effectively in order to manage the problem. Managing refugee movements is, after all, a primary objective of international refugee law. It is not, as suggested by some refugee law scholars, simply to protect refugees. If such were the case, unconditional protection guarantees relating to asylum would have found their way in treaty law. The drafters of the Refugee Convention were clearly preoccupied by other dimensions as well. It is this balancing act that makes refugee law a complicated field.

---

[87] Sale v Haitian Centers Council, 113 S Ct 2549 (1993).

At the beginning of the twenty-first century, refugee protection is an area of international law and policy in which it is often difficult to have a frank debate. This is due largely to the symbolic importance for the key actors to project certain images of themselves when dealing with refugee law. States such as New Zealand and Australia are rightly proud of their contribution to international refugee protection through resettlement programmes, and their governments make good use of this record for public relations purposes. At the same time, domestic political circumstances often dictate the need to appear tough on border control, as was demonstrated by the Tampa affair.[88]

The analysis in this chapter does not encourage potential host States to prevent admission of mass influxes on their territory because that would likely increase tensions in border areas. Temporary admission with assurances of burden-sharing from third States appears to be the only acceptable policy response. It is this form of international solidarity that the chapter seeks to promote. Recognizing the conditionality of admission in such situations simply acknowledges actual State practice, as demonstrated by an examination of the South Pacific, as well as the Asia-Pacific region more generally. This is the realist response to burden-sharing in mass refugee flow situations. It proposes that being upfront about the actual protection obligations assumed by States in terms of binding law is more useful for policymakers than pretending that States will meet vaguely-defined high standards in soft law instruments which may jeopardize national security. The objective is not to avoid any State responsibility in terms of refugee protection, but rather to articulate the commitments in a politically acceptable manner. A genuine debate on this issue must first acknowledge the complicated interplay between law and politics in the field of international refugee protection, as wall as the contrasting interests and agendas that limit what is possible in terms of policy formulation.

---

[88] See, e.g. William Maley, 'Security, people smuggling, and Australia's refugees' (2001) 55 Australian Journal of International Affairs 351 and Mark Beeson, 'Issues in Australian Foreign Policy' (2002) 48 Australian Journal of Politics and History 226, 231-2.

Chapter 2

Regional Cooperation in the Suppression of Transnational Crime in the South Pacific

Neil Boister*

Introduction

The Honiara Declaration on Law Enforcement Cooperation, adopted by the Pacific Islands Forum (hereinafter the Forum) in 1992, initiated a significant regional effort to suppress transnational crime in the South Pacific.[1] This chapter sketches the development of this regional response. It first examines why the Forum has identified certain activities as threats to the region. It then examines how the Forum has attempted to suppress these threats using a regional approach within a framework of international obligations. Finally it examines how effective this process is in getting domestic laws updated and implemented in Forum members. It does so with the further aim of making some general observations about the process of transferring penal norms from the developed to the developing world through regional systems.

The Forum provides a good case study of this process because it consists mainly of poor developing countries (the Pacific Island Countries or PICs) which have been identified as source and transit zones of transnational criminal activity into developed states (Australia, New Zealand and other states outside the region). The transfer of penal policies and associated legal norms from the developed to the developing world is not new; consider, for example, the impact of colonial penal

---

* Versions of this piece were presented at the ANZSIL Conference, Australian National University, 18–20 June 2004, and the SLS Conference, University of Sheffield, 13–16 September 2004. I am grateful to Professor Lawrence Kalinoe, UPNG, for his comments on a draft of this chapter.
[1] The South Pacific may be defined as either region or sub-region. The Forum members are: Australia, Cook Islands, Federated States of Micronesia, Fiji, Kiribati, Nauru, New Zealand, Niue, Palau, Papua New Guinea, Republic of the Marshall Islands, Samoa, Solomon Islands, Tonga, Tuvalu, Vanuatu. The Forum has observer status at the UN. The Forum's 'dialogue partners', states or organizations with significant interests in the region, are: Canada, the PRC, the EU, France, Indonesia, Japan, Republic of Korea, Malaysia, the Philippines, the UK and the US.

codes. In the post-colonial period, however, this process has continued through international law. Transfer usually follows a simple pattern.[2] Developed states initiate formal diplomatic contact with developing states in order to transfer crime control measures. This contact leads to a diplomatic conference and the adoption of a multilateral treaty. Developed states are the active law givers[3] and developing states are largely passive 'law-takers' in this process; they may play a role in the negotiation and adoption of these treaties but the content and enforcement of these treaties is largely in the hands of developed states.

In association with this macro-level process a range of meso- and micro-level contacts occur between law enforcement middle managers and operational officers where the bulk of the actual 'technology transfer' takes place. The technology involves more than laws, it involves policy, practical know-how, administrative arrangements and institutions.[4] Informal contacts set the development of a treaty under way and develop domestic law and practice; the adoption of the treaty provides a formal obligation upon which law enforcement officials from developed states can rely when enthusiasm for cooperation ebbs. The essence of this model is that not only policy is transferred, legal norms are transferred, and not only political pressure is exerted to ensure transfer, international legal obligations are relied upon to ensure transfer. Regional organizations play an intermediate role in developing regional norms and policies to meet global concerns through adapting global models to regional conditions, and serving as conduits for the transfer of these norms and policies. The goal of the process is to harmonize the practice of all states with regard to the definition, punishment and processing of transnational crimes.[5]

The motivation for this transfer is rhetorically the interest of the international community in the internal welfare of its members. This rhetoric conceals concerns about developing states being used as springboards for transnational crimes directed at and harmful or at least potentially harmful to the interests of developed states. Examining the motivation for transfer more closely, if transnational crime is conceptualized as a 'global public bad', and the international and national laws suppressing this crime as a 'global public good',[6] the question is: who benefits from this good? To be a global public good, transnational criminal law must serve the interests of a broad spectrum of states and of a broad socio-economic spectrum

---

[2] These ideas are more fully explored in Neil Boister, 'Transnational Penal Norm Transfer: The Transfer of Civil Forfeiture from the United States to South Africa as a Case in Point' (2003) 16 *South African Journal of Criminal Justice* 271.

[3] See Susan Silbey, '1886 Presidential Address: "Let Them Eat Cake": Globalization, Postmodern Colonialism, and the Possibilities of Justice' (1997) 31 *Law and Society Review* 207, 221.

[4] See David Dolowitz and David Marsh, 'Who Learns From Whom? A Review of the Policy Transfer Literature' (1996) 44 *Political Studies* 343, 344.

[5] See generally Mireille Delmas-Marty, *Global Law: A Triple Challenge* (2003) 81.

[6] See generally Inge Kaul, Isabelle Grunberg and Marc Stern, 'Defining Global Public Goods' in Kaul, Grunberg and Stern (eds), *Global Public Goods: International Cooperation in the 21st Century* (1999) 2ff.

within those states.[7] The development of transnational criminal law is a matter of concern because it is clearly the product of developed states designed to protect their interests. Developing states may not choose to suppress this conduct without pressure from developed states. Having given in to this pressure, they will usually have no alternative but to seek lessons from abroad on how to suppress this conduct because of their impoverishment.[8] In doing so they must ignore the fact that the developed states' policies and practices frequently arise in inefficient, costly, inhumane and discriminatory justice systems.[9]

The danger is that, in general terms, a unidirectional dispersal of norms from certain developed states to the rest of the international community becomes a process of the globalization of laws through their spatial distribution, rather than the universalization of laws through the development of shared meaning.[10] To put this into context, for developed states interested in the South Pacific the key issue is claimed to be effectiveness. But this issue conceals two questions: first, whether there is a genuine consensus to suppress transnational crime in the South Pacific at a national level through the agency of a regional organization, and second, whether these norms will be understood and internalized as obligatory social rules by the inhabitants of the countries to whom they are applied because they recognize these norms as legitimate expressions of authority.[11] Effectiveness cannot be divorced from issues of legitimacy both at a national and personal level.

Transnational crime in the South Pacific

The Forum responds: the Honiara Declaration

There is a plethora of organizations engaged in crime control in the South Pacific. Many cover a broader jurisdiction of which the South Pacific is only a part;[12] others are more specifically focused on the South Pacific.[13] The Forum is the pre-eminent intergovernmental institution working only in the South Pacific. In 1992, responding to an initiative of the Pacific Islands Law Officers' Meeting (PILOM), the Forum identified the need for strengthening regional cooperation in the law

---

[7] Ibid 10-12.
[8] See Tim Newburn, 'Atlantic Crossings: "Policy Transfer" and Crime Control in the USA and Britain' (2002) 4 *Punishment and Society* 165, 170.
[9] Ibid 166.
[10] Delmas-Marty, above n 6, 2.
[11] On the difference see Herbert Hart, *The Concept of Law* (2nd ed, 1994) 56ff.
[12] For example, the Manila Process, Asia Pacific Consultations (APCs), Regional Ministerial Conferences, the Association of South East Asian States (ASEAN), Asian Pacific Economic Cooperation (APEC), Council for Security Cooperation in the Asia Pacific (CSCAP), Pacific Rim Immigration Intelligence Officer's Conference (PACRIM), the Pacific Immigration Directors Conference (PIDC), and the Oceania Customs Organisation (OCO).
[13] For example, the South Pacific Chief of Police Conference (SPCPC) and the Pacific Islands Law Officers Meeting (PILOM).

enforcement field and agreed to a declaration on law enforcement cooperation. Forum leaders set out the rationale for the Honiara Declaration[14] in its opening paragraphs:

1. ... An adverse law enforcement environment could threaten the sovereignty, security and economic integrity of Forum members and jeopardize economic and social development. The threats to the stability of the region were complex and sophisticated, and the potential impact of transnational crime was a matter of increasing concern to regional states and enforcement agencies. The Forum agreed that there was a need for a more comprehensive, integrated and collaborative approach to counter these threats.

2. The Forum considered that law enforcement cooperation should therefore remain an important focus for the region. The scale of criminal activity affecting the region could expand. Forum leaders noted that the balance in economic and social development, the primary goal of all the countries of the region, could not be achieved without the assurance of safety and security. Early action to strengthen the existing framework to tackle potential law enforcement problems should therefore be taken.

The Declaration prioritizes certain law enforcement areas:

3. The Forum noted that certain areas of law enforcement had emerged as particularly important to members. These included necessary legislation on extradition, proceeds of crime (assets forfeiture), mutual criminal assistance, and other aspects of economic crime. In addition, further legislation might be necessary in some areas concerning drug issues.

The Declaration is a regional response to policy makers' perceptions of the growth of transnational economic and drug offences in the South Pacific.[15] Its stated goal is effective law enforcement to suppress these activities through the implementation and use of national legislative measures in the key areas of extradition, mutual legal assistance and money laundering/asset forfeiture.

The justification for this action is the threat presented by transnational crime to the safety and security of Forum members. In 1992, the threat of transnational crime in the South Pacific appeared largely potential; the Declaration states that 'the scale of criminal activity affecting the region could expand'. By 2001,

---

[14] *Declaration by the South Pacific Forum on Law Enforcement Cooperation*, Annex to the *Forum Communiqué*, Twenty-Third Pacific Islands Forum, Honiara, Solomon Islands, 8–9 July 1992 ('Honiara Declaration'); all Forum communiqués were available at The Pacific Islands Forum Secretariat <http://www.forumsec.org.fj/> at 26 January 2005.

[15] A concern repeated over the years by key figures. See, for example, the statement of then Forum Secretary General Noel Levi to the 2001 PILOM Meeting, 22 October 2001, *Press Statement 8101*, The Pacific Islands Forum <http://www.forumsec.org.fj/news/2001/Oct04.htm> at 29 December 2003.

however, the Forum felt able to state that there was 'clear evidence of serious transnational crime moving into the region and posing serious threats to the sovereignty, security and economic integrity of forum members'.[16] These threats included money laundering, terrorist recruitment, identity fraud, West African fraud, people smuggling, issuing passports of convenience, engaging in electronic crimes, small arms trafficking, illegally trading in endangered wildlife, drug trafficking and organized crime.[17] It is worth examining some of these threats more closely.

Money laundering

Prior to the adoption of the Honiara Declaration in 1992, the Forum Secretariat (Forumsec) engaged in a 'Law Enforcement Needs Assessment Study', which identified the South Pacific as a risk area for money laundering activities.[18] Twelve years later, the image of PICs as money laundering centres is pervasive, and it appears to be borne out by the evidence.[19] The opportunity for laundering arose when PICs, relying on foreign legal and commercial skills, began to develop lucrative businesses as Offshore Financial Centres (OFCs) through removing exchange controls, deregulating currency movement, imposing strict bank secrecy legislation and allowing anonymous shareholding.[20] The Cook Islands High Court, for example, confirmed memorably that the purpose of the Cook Islands' haven law was to make it as difficult as possible for creditors to exercise their rights.[21] The incentive to launderers was provided by more restrictive practices elsewhere,[22] the incentive to PICs by the opportunity to acquire alternative sources of revenue.[23] Since the mid-1990s a large number of financial institutions have been registered

---

[16] *Forum Communiqué*, Thirty-Second Pacific Islands Forum, Republic of Nauru, 16–18 August 2001, [38].

[17] *Forum Communiqué*, Thirty-Fourth Pacific Islands Forum, Auckland, New Zealand, 14–16 August 2003, [21]-[25]. See generally, on the criminal threats facing the Pacific, Andreas Schloenhardt, 'Transnational Crime and Island State Security in the South Pacific' in Eric Shibuya and Jim Rolfe (eds), *Security in Oceania in the 21st Century* (2003) 171; UNODC, *Profile on the Pacific Islands* (2003), UNODC Regional Center Thailand <http://www.unodc.un.or.th/material/document/2004/Regional%20Profile%20Pacific%20Island.pdf> at 20 December 2004.

[18] Honiara Declaration, above n 14, [10].

[19] Anthony Van Fossen, 'Money Laundering, Global Financial Instability, and Tax Havens in the Pacific Islands' (2003) 15(2) *Contemporary Pacific* 237, 239-41; Schloenhardt, above n 17, 178-83; UNODC, above n 17, 18.

[20] Van Fossen, above n 19, 362-7; Anselm Herman, 'Money Laundering and the Law in the Republics of Fiji and Vanuatu: A Critical Analysis' (1999) 3 *Journal of South Pacific Law* 17, 18.

[21] High Court of the Cook Islands Civil Division, Plain No 208/94, 6 November 1995, Judgment on Appeal 20 Dec 1995, cited by Ron Crocombe, *The South Pacific* (2001) 364-5.

[22] Herman, above n 20, 21.

[23] Australian Senate Foreign Affairs, Defence and Trade Committee Report, *A Pacific Engaged: Australia's Relations with Papua New Guinea and the Island States of the South West Pacific* (2003) 177, Parliament of Australia, <http://www.aph.gov.au/senate/Committee/fadt_ctte/png/report/C07.pdf> at 7 October 2004.

in OFCs across the Pacific.[24] The discovery in 1995 that the Bank of New York had laundered billions for the Russian Mafia through banks in Nauru resulted in large US banks unilaterally suspending dealing with banks in Nauru, Palau, Vanuatu and Niue.[25] In 1998, the Financial Action Task Force (FATF) claimed that Vanuatu's legislation provided favourable conditions for an increase in money laundering.[26] In 2000, FATF blacklisted as non-cooperative the Cook Islands, Marshall Islands, Niue and Nauru, opening them to counter-measures including heightened security by banks dealing with financial transactions originating from these jurisdictions.[27] The Cook Islands responded by enacting legislation and joining the Asia Pacific Group on Money Laundering (APG-ML), but FATF was unconvinced and the blacklisting is still being maintained.[28] In 2001, FATF recommended sanctions against Nauru[29] and in 2004 complained that Nauru licenced 400 offshore shell banks with no physical presence and maintained excessive bank secrecy provisions.[30] The APG-ML reports a number of cases of money laundering through Vanuatu,[31] but Vanuatu and the Marshall Islands have avoided a similar fate through legislative reform. Ironically, both the pressure to liberalize finance markets and deregulate exchange control regulations and the effort to control money laundering has emanated largely from developed states.[32] Local and global financial stability is said to be at stake,[33] but laundering's potential to cause harm in PICs is difficult to assess. It is said to be able to corrupt weakly regulated local institutions, destabilize legitimate economic activity and discourage development.[34]

Drug trafficking

The location of PICs between Asia and markets in North America, Australia and New Zealand makes them potential way stations for trans-Pacific smuggling. A desire to attract tourists and investors, small police forces, and outdated laws all suggest increased vulnerability. The pattern of drug seizures suggests transit rather than the import or export of drugs. In 1996, nearly a million dollars worth of

---

[24] Australian Bureau of Criminal Intelligence, *Australian Illicit Drug Report 1998–1999* (2000) 115.
[25] Van Fossen, above n 19, 244-8.
[26] Van Fossen, above n 19, 240.
[27] FATF, *Annual Review of Non-Cooperative Countries or Territories* (2004) (*Annual Review 2004*) 1.
[28] In 2004 the Cook Islands still had 1200 companies registered and no relevant information about them, but only 16 offshore banks: see ibid 8.
[29] FATF, *Review to Identify Non-Cooperative Countries or Territories* (2001).
[30] FATF, *Annual Review 2004*, above n 27, 12.
[31] Herman, above n 20, 21.
[32] Herman, above n 20, 22.
[33] Van Fossen, above n 19, 268.
[34] Pierre-Laurant Chatain, 'The World Bank's Role in the Fight Against Money Laundering and Terrorist Financing' (2004) 6 *International Law Forum* 190, 190-91.

cocaine was found in a shipment of Tongan yams bound for Auckland.[35] In 2000, police in Suva seized 350kg of heroin used as a stockpile to supply Australia, New Zealand and Canada.[36] In 2001, 90kg of cocaine was seized transiting New Caledonia, and 100kg of cocaine was seized in Tonga.[37] In 2002, 74kg of methamphetamine was found on a ship in Singapore headed for Fiji and Australia and Hawaiian police broke-up a syndicate that smuggled cocaine and methamphetamine to the US mainland, Tonga, Fiji, Australia and New Zealand, while in 2003, almost 2.5kg of pseudoephedrine, a key ingredient in amphetamines, was found in scuba tanks shipped to Brisbane from Fiji.[38] In 2004, police shut down a large methamphetamine laboratory near Suva apparently intended to supply the market in Thailand, New Zealand and Australia.[39] They found 5kg of methamphetamines and nearly a tonne of precursor chemicals with an estimated street value once refined of $522 million. The Fijian Police Commissioner stated:

> This is a frightening example of transnational organised crime elements using Fiji as a staging ground for their illegal activities. Increasingly we are seeing these elements coming to Fiji and joining up with local organised criminal groups.[40]

A Chinese Malaysian conspiracy allegedly ran the drug factory and bribed a local official to cooperate. In September 2004, 120kg of cocaine was found on a beach in Vanuatu, the largest amount ever discovered in that country.[41] These are not small amounts by any standard.

Summing up the situation, the Australian Federal Police (AFP) warns that the region has been targeted to move drugs and that drug trafficking is a good indicator of the rise in transnational criminal activity.[42] Cooperation is offered as the only solution. Superintendent Larry Reid, acting national manager of the New Zealand Police (NZP), concludes: 'No single country can deal with the problem on its own'.[43] But there are leading players in the cooperative effort. After the raid on the methamphetamine laboratory in Suva in 2004, the Australian Minister for Justice and Customs, Senator Chris Ellison said:

> The success of this operation sends a crystal-clear message to organised drug syndicates that the combined efforts of international law enforcement agencies will ensure that transnational crime will not be allowed to gain a foothold in the region ...

---

[35] Crocombe, *The South Pacific*, above n 21, 370.
[36] Elizabeth Feizkhah, 'Ice: From Gang to Bust', *Time Asia Magazine*, 21 June 2004, Time Online <http://www.time.com/time/asia/magazine/article/0,13673,501040628-655460,00.html> at 28 February 2005.
[37] Australian Senate Foreign Affairs, Defence and Trade Committee Report, above n 23, 194.
[38] Feizkhah, above n 36.
[39] David Fickling, 'Police Bust Fiji Drug Factory', *The Guardian Weekly*, 18–24 June 2004, 5.
[40] Ibid.
[41] 'Record Cocaine Haul in Vanuatu', *Port Villa Presse*, 10 September 2004 <http://www.news.vu/en/news/national/record-cocaine-haul-in-va.shtml> at 28 February 2005.
[42] Australian Senate Foreign Affairs, Defence and Trade Committee Report, above n 23, 195.
[43] Feizkhah, above n 36. See Schloenhardt, n17, 183, for similar sentiments.

Australia has been providing funding and other forms of assistance, such as training, in the Pacific region to ensure that countries in the South Pacific cannot be exploited by drug traffickers and manufacturers, particularly against the backdrop of a world wide growth in amphetamine supply and demand ... The best way to stop drugs harming Australians is for our law enforcement and border protection agencies to work closely with our international partners to attack the illicit drug trade offshore.[44]

Drug trafficking in the region is largely directed at supplying illicit markets elsewhere and has been planned and financed from elsewhere. The authors of a United Nations Office of Drugs and Crime (UNODC) discussion report note that '[t]here is little evidence of a local presence in the Pacific Islands controlling the transhipments; rather most cases reveal criminal syndicates operating from outside the Pacific'.[45] Other than cannabis cultivation for markets within the region, drug production in the region is not significant.[46] The use of drugs in PICs is less easy to quantify. There is extensive use of cannabis in many PICs (Papua New Guinea and Micronesia report the highest prevalence in the world), and in Palau, for example, police ignore public consumption. Consumption of more potent drugs has taken root in Palau and Guam and appears to be increasing in Samoa but it is not a regional epidemic.[47]

Arms smuggling

The proliferation of small arms has had a negative impact on recent regional security threats in the islands, such as the civil wars on Bougainville and in the Solomons, and incidents of violence in Vanuatu, Fiji, the Solomon Islands and Papua New Guinea (PNG).[48] There have been, for example, informal reports of weapons smuggling from Bougainville to the Solomon Islands. The April 2003

---

[44] Quoted in *Massive Drug Bust in Fiji*, 10 June 2004, Findlaw Australia <http://www.findlaw.com.au/news/default.asp?task=read&id=20505&site=CN> at 14 July, 2004.

[45] UNODC, above n 17, 10.

[46] Crocombe, *The South Pacific*, above n 21, 85. This leads Shibuya to suggest that the major supply of drugs originates within the region – Eric Shibuya, 'Oceania's Post 9/11 Security Concerns: Common Causes, Uncommon Approaches' (2003) 2(7) *Asia-Pacific Center for Security Studies* 1, 2, <http//:www.apcss.org/Research/research_publications.html> at 20 December 2004. However, although it records cannabis production in the region, the UNODC reports that none of the islands is considered a major global producer of any kind of drug. See UNODC, above n 17, 8.

[47] Transform Aqorau, *The Pacific: Maintaining the rule of law and regional cooperation* (Unpublished paper presented to the Twenty Second PILOM Meeting, Melbourne, Australia, 20–22 October 2003) 3; Crocombe, *The South Pacific*, above n 21, 86; Mac Marshall, 'Alcohol and Drug Abuse' in Brij V Lal and Kate Fortune (eds), *The Pacific Islands: An Encyclopaedia* (2000) 448. An outbreak of heroin abuse in Palau occurred in 1985–86, but is no longer considered a problem. See UNODC, above n 17, 9-10.

[48] Aqorau above n 47, 5, citing Pacific Islands Forum Secretariat, *Small Arms Control*, PIFS (03) FRSC 11 Session 1, Paper prepared for the Forum Regional Security Committee Meeting, 18–20 June 2003 (2003).

Report Small Arms in the Pacific[49] details the proliferation of arms trading in the Pacific but points to the removal of weapons from police and military armouries as the biggest source of supply. The negative effect has not been felt directly by surrounding developed states. For example, there appears to be little arms trafficking from PNG into Australia.[50]

Terrorism[51]

The Bali Bombings of 12 October 2002 and terrorist activities in the Southern Philippines have raised fears of transnational terrorism in the region.[52] The AFP cites the potential for the South Pacific to serve as an operational base for terrorism because of porous borders, inadequate law enforcement capacity, isolated islands and the presence of 'soft Western targets'.[53] As a concrete example, PNG is concerned about possible terrorist threats to Australian and American interests in PNG through terrorist incursions from Irian Jaya (West Papua), the Indonesian part of New Guinea.[54] The issuing of passports of convenience by Forum members is viewed as a potential risk from the point of view of terrorist activity.[55] At the local level, internal political struggles within PICs have seen the actual perpetration of terrorist acts.[56]

Corruption

Hughes speaks of 'corruption on a relatively wide scale' in PICs[57] and in 2003 Transparency International identified corruption as a major threat to PICs.[58] The evidence suggests that corruption is endemic in the governments of many PICs, official positions are used to attract foreign economic patronage, and official measures to suppress this corruption are ineffective.[59] Crocombe reports corruption

---

[49] Philip Alpers and Conor Twyford, 'Small Arms in The Pacific', *Small Arms Survey Occasional Paper no. 8*, March 2003 <http://www.smallarmssurvey.org/OPs/ OP08Pacifics.pdf> at 27 January 2004.
[50] Australian Senate Foreign Affairs, Defence and Trade Committee Report, above n 23, 182-4.
[51] On terrorism in the Pacific see Alex Conte in this volume.
[52] Aqorau, above n 47, 5.
[53] Australian Senate Foreign Affairs, Defence and Trade Committee Report, above n 23, 194, citing *Committee Hansard*, 27 March 2003, 354, 358 (AFP).
[54] Australian Senate Foreign Affairs, Defence and Trade Committee Report, above n 23, 194.
[55] Aqorau, above n 47, 6.
[56] See the 'Pacific Islands Security: Old Challenges, New Threats', *Report on the Pacific Islands Political Science Association (PIPSA) Conference, University of the Sunshine Coast, 4-6 December 2002*, 3.
[57] Robert Hughes, 'Corruption' in Anita Jowitt and Tess Newton-Cain (eds), *Passage of Change – Law, Society and Governance in the Pacific* (2003) 35, 36.
[58] *The Kooralbyn Declaration*, Transparency International, <http://www.transparency.org.au/ documents/Kooralbyn_Declaration.pdf > at 4 August 2003.
[59] Crocombe, *The South Pacific*, above n 21, 513-15.

in the timber industry, conflicts of business interests, broad small scale corruption, the elimination of government opponents, corruption disguised as tradition and affirmative action, the involvement of whole governments, and the purchase of elections and electors.[60] Some of this activity is transnational in nature, some purely internal. Sometimes the potential is devastating. For example, in 1996 the Vanuatu Ombudsman exposed a financial scam that involved the Prime Minister and Minister of Finance and that had the potential to bankrupt the country.[61] Possible reasons for the proliferation of corruption include the vulnerability of officials and the cultural irrelevance of Western institutions.[62]

Human trafficking and people smuggling

The region is being used as a transit zone for both human trafficking and people smuggling, and identity document fraud compounds the problem.[63] New Zealand is a destination country for trafficking of women from South East Asia for sexual commercial purposes, while Australia is a destination country for women trafficked for commercial sexual exploitation and for people smuggling.[64] However, PICs are themselves the destination for illegal migrants from outside and within the region.[65]

Organized and other crimes

Organized crime appears to be more common in some areas than in others. For example, there is evidence that Asian organized crime has moved into Micronesia.[66] Organized crime groups diversify. Thus identity fraud has been

---

[60] Ibid 520-41.
[61] Herman, above n 20, 21. Ombudsman Marie-Noelle Ferrieux-Patterson denounced the diversion of funds meant for cyclone victim aid, the issuing of false passports and the misappropriation of monies from pension funds – *The World Guide 2001–2002* (2001) 563.
[62] Hughes, above n 57, 46.
[63] Schloenhardt, above n 17, 174. At 175 Schloenhardt notes the use of fraudulent travel documents from Naura, Tonga and the sale by the Marshall Islands of 1000s of passports. See also Shibuya, above n 46, 3.
[64] See *New Zealand*, Human Trafficking.org <http://.www.humantrafficking.org/countries/eap/new_zealand/index.html> at 22 October 2004, and *Australia*, Human Trafficking.org <http://www.humantrafficking.org/countries/eap/australia/index.html> at 22 October 2004. Schloenhardt, above n 17, 176-7, notes reports of transiting migrants through PNG and New Caledonia. These activities have lead Australia to leasing out island state territory for quarantine and processing services – see the statement of the then Secretary General of the Forum Noel Levi to the 2001 PILOM Meeting, 22 October 2001, *Press Statement 8101*, Pacific Islands Forum, <http://www.forumsec.org.fj/news/2001/Oct04.htm> at 29 December 2003.
[65] Schloenhardt, above n 17, 177. The UNODC, above n 17, 24, notes concerns about Fiji becoming a centre for child-sex tourism.
[66] Crocombe, *The South Pacific*, above n 21, 569.

linked to other transnational crimes such as human trafficking, terrorism[67] and the illegal trade in endangered species.[68] The syndicate exposed by Fiji's 2000 heroin seizure was, for further example, also involved in people smuggling and credit card fraud.

Evaluating threats

These threats to external and local interests cannot be individually assessed here. Nevertheless, they have been used to support the process of development of a regional response to transnational crime. The necessity for such a response is, however, buttressed by a number of further motivating factors.

Much reliance is placed on the impact of globalization. At the 2002 Meeting of the Forum in Suva, the Forum endorsed the Nasonini Declaration, which reiterated the commitment made in the Honiara Declaration to act collectively to meet security challenges including the adverse effects of globalization such as transnational crimes.[69] In the rhetoric of the UN criminal justice agencies, transnational crime is a risk run by all.[70] All states are vulnerable because national borders are more porous, there are fewer trade restrictions and finance and telecommunications systems are global.[71] With respect to the South Pacific, Aqorau notes:

> Developments in communications technology suggest that the types of threats and violence facing the region are changing, and could rapidly alter the ability of many Pacific island governments to cope with this shifting dynamic.[72]

However, the hypothesis that criminal activity inevitably follows interconnectedness depends in part on illustrating that the region is interconnected, which is difficult considering its poor infrastructure. A sceptic might argue that what we are witnessing is a global moral panic that constructs transnational crime as a 'folk-devil' deserving of the most serious response, a panic shaped by

---

[67] Aqorau, above n 47, 7, citing Pacific Islands Forum Secretariat, *Identity Fraud: PIFS (03) FRSC.6 Session 1*, Paper prepared for the Forum Regional Security Committee Meeting, 18–20 June 2003 (2003).

[68] Aqorau, above n 47, 7, citing Pacific Islands Forum Secretariat, *Illegal Trade in Endangered Species*, PIFS (03) FRSC.10, Session 1, Paper prepared for the Forum Regional Security Committee Meeting, 18–20 June 2003 (2003).

[69] *Nasonini Declaration on Regional Security*, [1], Annex 1 to the *Forum Communiqué*, Thirty-Third Pacific Islands Forum, Suva, Fiji Islands, 15–17 August, 2002 ('Nasonini Declaration').

[70] See, for example, the *Discussion Guide to the Eleventh United Nations Congress on Crime Prevention and Criminal Justice*, UN Doc. A/Conf.203/PM.1.

[71] Ibid [9].

[72] See Transform Aqorau, *Current Developments on Forum Initiatives to Combat Transnational and Organised Crime: the 2003 Extradition Act* (Unpublished Paper presented to the 2003 Fiji Attorney-General's Conference, Outrigger Hotel, Sigatoka, 14–16 November 2003) 4; Schloenhardt, above n 17, 172.

politicians, the media, the police and the courts rather than entirely by the criminals themselves.[73] Whatever the case, it does seem likely that the global and regional dimensions of crime are not necessarily identical, and that given that PICs are at the global periphery, arguments about the penetration of the region by transnational crime must be buttressed by something other than just 'globalization'.

A more compelling argument for a regional response is the link made between external threats and the manifest internal problems of PICs. Threats to sovereignty and stability, such as land disputes, economic disparities, ethnic tensions, and failures of governance and the rule of law,[74] encourage penetration of the region by transnational crime. The Forum acknowledged this in the 2000 Biketawa Declaration by linking good governance and security.[75] In particular, relative immunity from law enforcement makes developing states attractive bases for criminals to use for provision of illicit goods and services to areas where the risks are higher. Governments may prove unwilling or unable to suppress these activities.[76] In the most severe cases the spectre of a 'failed state' looms.[77] If transnational crime appears to be a contributing factor to potential failure, it justifies pressure from developed states for action against transnational crime. The reverse is also true; failed states may provide safe harbour for transnational crime which will also justify intervention. Crocombe notes that Australia's interest in the 'arc of instability' in the South Pacific grew from the position where it refused to get involved in the Solomons to its wholesale support for intervention, not because of a deep-seated humanitarianism but because of the potential a failed state provided for transnational crime directed at Australia.[78] A problem with this rationalization is that some PICs may not have been established in any meaningful sense as sovereigns in the first instance, which makes demanding that they suppress transnational crime inapt, and portends the likelihood of continued direct suppression by developed states from the colonial into the post-colonial era.

A unique regional factor that compounds the opportunity for transnational crime is the size of the region and the fact that most PICs are completely surrounded by international waters through which private individuals can travel

---

[73] Stanley Cohen, *Folk Devils and Moral Panics: The Creation of Mods and Rockers* (1972) 9.
[74] Aqorau, above n 72, 3. Schloenhardt, above n 17, 172, points out the absence of diversification in island state economies makes them more vulnerable to transnational crime.
[75] *Biketawa Declaration*, Attachment 1 to the *Forum Communiqué*, Thirty-First Pacific Islands Forum, Tarawa, Kiribati, 27–30 October 2000.
[76] Phil Williams and Ernestor Savona, 'Problems and Dangers Posed by Organized Transnational Crime in the Various Regions of the World' in Phil Williams and Ernestor Savona (eds), *The United Nations and Transnational Crime* (1996) 1, 38.
[77] The Australian Strategic Policy Institute Report, *Beyond Bali, ASPI's Strategic Assessment 2002*, November 2002, 28, identified an arc of island states as failing neighbours that could provide potential havens for terrorist groups.
[78] Ron Crocombe, 'The Pacific Plan Among Larger and Smaller Regional Approaches' (Plenary Paper presented at the Conference on Securing a Peaceful Pacific: Preventing and Resolving Conflict in the Pacific, University of Canterbury, Christchurch, New Zealand, 15–17 October 2004).

unimpeded by government regulation until they enter territorial waters.[79] The situation of the region between more developed areas makes this free movement very attractive to smugglers. Kiribati, for example, has an Exclusive Economic Zone (EEZ) the size of the continental US and one Australian sponsored patrol boat to patrol it.[80]

Finally, compulsion for change within the region emanates directly from the vulnerability of developed states outside the region. In early 2004 New Zealand Prime Minister Helen Clark urged PICs to comply with rules aimed at cutting the flow of funds to terrorists and ensuring the security of imports into the US, pointing out: 'All countries face economic risks if they fail to comply with these measures'.[81] These views were echoed by the new Forum Secretary General, Greg Urwin, who noted that Forum members would have to meet new shipping and aviation security requirements or lose markets and tourists and increase the costs of imports.[82] Not surprisingly, the Forum took up this call for compliance at the 2004 Meeting, recognizing the serious risks to the region's trade and tourism of non-compliance.[83] The irony is obvious: developed states tell PICs that they must protect their sovereignty from transnational criminals by enacting new laws when succumbing to such pressure derogates from that sovereignty.

The adoption of the Honiara Declaration by the Forum does not validate the threat of transnational crime; it simply confirms that Forum leaders are receptive to argument that transnational crime is such a threat. Moreover, there is a participation gap in the process of threat-assessment: the leaders of PICs are marginalized when it comes to the establishment of a threat because they receive the threat as a given. What is missing is information. In the light of the difficulties of evaluating risks, it is critical to undertake further research about transnational criminal activities in the region. This will be difficult, given that information about all criminal activities in the region is poor.[84] The appointment of a Law Enforcement Statistics Officer in the Forumsec to input data and produce statistical analyses is a first step.[85] But it is necessary that more is known about the local and external impact of all crime including transnational crime, in order to give regional policymakers rather than law enforcement officials enough information to shape an appropriate response and to expose inappropriate responses. When Europe began to evolve its third pillar of regional cooperation around justice and home affairs, it

---

[79] On freedom of navigation in the Pacific see the chapter by Scott Davidson in this volume.
[80] Shibuya, above n 46, 2.
[81] Tracy Watkins, 'Pacific States Told to Target Security', *The Press* (Christchurch) 15 April 2004, A6.
[82] *Forum Monthly Review*, May 2004, Pacific Islands Forum < http://www.forumsec.org.fj/> at 23 October 2004.
[83] *Forum Communiqué*, Thirty-Fifth Pacific Islands Forum, Apia, Samoa, 3–10 August 2004, [28].
[84] Tess Newton, 'Policing in the South Pacific Region', *University of the South Pacific Occasional Papers Series*, Occasional Paper no. 1, 10.
[85] The LESO as she is known, is responsible for a regional events calendar, a regional illicit drugs database, and the development of other databases: *Pacific Islands Forum Annual Report*, 2001–2002 (2002) 22.

set up independent regional organs to analyse criminal activity in Europe.[86] The establishment of such organs in the South Pacific would be useful to answer a host of questions: how much local participation is there in transnational crime and is it really mainly a foreign intrusion? What are the peculiar features of the different markets for illicit goods? Are there purely South Pacific regional crimes that have no external analogue?

The measures in the Honiara Declaration and subsequent Forum declarations

Introduction

The Honiara Declaration calls for a range of procedural and substantive measures, which have been supplemented by subsequent Forum declarations. These measures are set out below in the order in which the Forum introduced them, and an attempt has been made to sketch the international legal context of the particular measure.

Law enforcement cooperation

Paragraph 3 of the Honiara Declaration makes it clear that rather than duplicate existing regional bodies working in law enforcement, the Forumsec would seek through the Forum Regional Security Committee (FRSC) to serve as a contact point for specialist agencies and to provide advice to Forum leaders on law enforcement issues. Article 9 of the 1988 UN Drug Trafficking Convention[87] provides a multilateral legal basis for such direct contact to exchange information and analysis and also makes provision for cooperation in law enforcement training.

Mutual assistance in criminal matters

Paragraph 7 of the Honiara Declaration states:

> The Forum recognized that the establishment of a framework for mutual assistance in criminal matters between themselves would enhance cooperation between their courts, prosecution authorities and law enforcement agencies.

The purpose of paragraph 7 is to urge Forum members to adopt measures to assist one another in the identification of persons, search and seizure, and the taking of testimony. The most important international legal frameworks for mutual assistance include article 7 of the 1988 UN Drug Trafficking Convention, the 1990

---

[86] In Lisbon, the European Monitoring Centre on Drugs and Drug Addiction (EMCDDA) was established in terms of Council Regulation 1302/93 in order to gather and analyse reliable data on the full range of drug problems and the control strategies being developed in Europe.

[87] *1988 United Nations Convention Against Illicit Traffic in Narcotic Drugs and Psychotropic Substances*, Vienna, 20 December 1988, 185 UNTS 453 (entered into force 11 November 1990).

UN Model Treaty on Mutual Assistance[88] and the 1986 Commonwealth Scheme for Mutual Legal Assistance.[89] These treaties provide part of the framework to enhance cooperation between judicial and law enforcement authorities, while bilateral relations, such as the diplomatic note exchanged by New Zealand and Fiji for mutual assistance in criminal matters allowing video link evidence of witnesses,[90] provides another part. Ultimately, however, new legislation will be required to make legal assistance possible.

Money laundering, asset forfeiture and banking regulation

Paragraph 7 of the Honiara Declaration continues:

> The Forum recognized that large profits from organized crime provide both an incentive to criminal activity together with capital to develop criminal organizations large enough to operate on an international scale. The Forum accepted the need to strengthen national and international legal provisions to enable the proceeds of and instrumentalities of crime to be traced, frozen and seized and acknowledged the need to regulate banking and other financial services to reduce the possible manipulation of these services to 'launder' the proceeds of crime.

The implicit purpose of this part of paragraph 7 is to suppress money laundering, although there is no direct call for its criminalization. Paragraph 7 does call explicitly for provision for the freezing and seizing of criminal proceeds and instrumentalities. This involves locating the proceeds, engaging in forfeiture and enforcing confiscation orders, even if they are made in other states. Paragraph 7 also acknowledges the necessity of regulating the banking and finance industries to prevent their misuse, which involves inter alia the removal of bank secrecy laws. The 1988 Drug Trafficking Convention provides the basic legal framework. Article 3 of the Convention criminalizes drug money laundering.[91] Article 5's anti-money laundering regime obliges states parties to adopt an asset forfeiture regime that inter alia removes bank secrecy and makes it possible to request mutual assistance for asset forfeiture. FATF's Forty Recommendations[92] expand this money laundering regime to an all-crime regime,[93] and provide for stronger regulatory mechanisms. The updated Forty Recommendations add eight Special Recommendations directed at suppressing the funding of terrorism. Paragraph 10 of the Honiara Declaration urges Forum members to adopt and implement these

---

[88] GA Res 45/117, UN GAOR 45th Sess., Supp. No. 49A, 215.
[89] *Scheme Relating to Mutual Assistance in Criminal Matters within the Commonwealth*, Commonwealth Secretariat, London, LMN (86) 13 (as updated).
[90] See Kevueli Tunidau, 'Current Situation and Countermeasures Against Money Laundering' *UNAFEI Resource Material Series* no. 58, December 2001, Tokyo, 399, 400, 409 <http://unafei.or.jp/pdf/58-29.pdf> at 5 October 2004.
[91] Article 3(1)(b) and article 3(1)(c)(i).
[92] FATF, *The Forty Recommendations*, <http://www1.oecd.org/fatf/40Recs_en.htm> at 10 December 2004.
[93] Recommendation 1 refers to 'all serious crimes'.

recommendations as a priority. The direction provided in the Honiara Declaration was supplemented at the 2000 Forum meeting,[94] which endorsed the establishment of domestic Financial Intelligence Units (FIUs). At the 2002 Forum meeting[95] a regional FIU was mooted. The Egmont Group, an informal gathering of the FIU's of 84 different states named after the venue of the first meeting, has adopted a Revised Statement of Purpose that sets out the definitions and functions of FIUs.[96]

Extradition

Paragraph 9 of the Honiara Declaration provides:

> The Forum recognized that while most members have Extradition Acts which reflect the pre-1986 text of the London Scheme for the Rendition of Fugitive Offenders, there was still a need to review extradition arrangements within the region. The Forum agreed that members should review their extradition arrangements and, if required, take steps to introduce and bring into force legislation based on the United Nations Model Treaty on Extradition or on the current London Scheme for the Rendition of Fugitive Offenders within the Commonwealth.

Relaxing the requirements for extradition in new legislation appears to be the aim of paragraph 9 of the Honiara Declaration. This relaxation is driven by the notion that as apolitical transnational crime has increased the risk of the political misuse of extradition has diminished. The 1990 UN Model Treaty on Extradition[97] and the updated London Scheme for Extradition within the Commonwealth[98] provide the international legal framework with regard to extradition. These instruments are designed to smooth the process by reducing the conditions for a valid extradition, such as the prima facie case requirement insisted upon in some common law states, and by restricting the inappropriate use of bars to extradition, such as the political offence and nationality exceptions. Bilateral extradition treaties provide the normal platform for extradition. Bilateral treaties between Forum members[99] and between

---

[94] *Forum Communiqué*, Thirty-First Pacific Islands Forum, Tarawa, Republic of Kiribati, 27–30 October 2000.

[95] *Forum Communiqué*, Thirty-Third Pacific Islands Forum, Suva, Fiji Islands, 15–17 August, 2002.

[96] *Statement of Purpose of the Egmont Group of Financial Intelligence Units*, Guernsey, 23 June 2004, Egmont Group <www.egmontgroup.org./statement_of_purpose.pdf> at 8 December 2004.

[97] GA Res 45/116, 14 December 1990.

[98] *Scheme Relating to Rendition of Fugitive Offenders within the Commonwealth*, London, 1966, as updated at Kingston, Jamaica, 2002, Commonwealth Secretariat, <http://www.thecommonwealth.org/shared_asp_files/uploadedfiles/%7B56F55E5D-1882-4421-9CC1-71634DF17331%7D_London_Scheme.pdf> at 9 December 2004.

[99] For example, the *Agreement on Extradition between the Government of New Zealand and the Government of the Republic of Fiji*, 21 March 1992, annexed to *The Extradition, Republic of Fiji Order, 1992*, New Zealand.

a Forum member and an external state[100] do exist. However, they are rare. Tunidau complains, for example, that there are too many accessible countries with which Fiji has no extradition relations.[101] Domestic legislation that does not depend upon such a treaty or makes it possible to back warrants issued in other states may provide a suitable substitute.

Drugs offences

Paragraph 13 of the Honiara Declaration prioritizes the ratification and implementation of the 1988 Drug Trafficking Convention, which introduces a range of new drug related offences. The 2002 Forum meeting[102] reiterated this call. The 2003 Forum meeting[103] singled out Amphetamine Type abuse as a problem requiring raised awareness and increased cooperation.

Environmental offences

Paragraph 15 of the Honiara Declaration singles out the importance of suppression of breaches of environmental laws such as waste dumping,[104] driftnet fishing,[105] oil spills and other pollution emergencies,[106] and wildlife smuggling to the region.[107]

---

[100] For example, the *Federated States of Micronesia – United States Extradition Treaty of 1986, Compact of Free Association and Agreement on Extradition and Mutual Assistance and Cooperation in Law Enforcement Matters* (entered into force 3 November 1986).

[101] Above n 90, 408.

[102] *Forum Communiqué*, Thirty-Third Pacific Islands Forum, Suva, Fiji Islands, 15–17 August 2002.

[103] *Forum Communiqué*, Thirty-Fourth Pacific Islands Forum, Auckland, New Zealand, 14–16 August 2003.

[104] In contravention of the *Basel Convention on the Control of Transboundary Movement of Hazardous Wastes and other Wastes and their Disposal*, opened for signature 22 March 1989, 1637 UNTS 71 (entered into force 5 May 1992). See also the *Protocol for the Prevention of the Pollution of the South Pacific Region by Dumping*, opened for signature 25 November 1986, 26 ILM 65 (entered into force 18 August 1980).

[105] There are various regional agreements in this regard. For example, the *South Pacific Forum Fisheries Agency Convention*, opened for signature 10 July 1979, 1979 ATS 16 (entered into force 9 August 1979), provides for cooperation in surveillance and enforcement under article 5(2)(c).

[106] See the *International Convention on the Prevention of Pollution from Ships, 1973, as modified by the Protocol of 1978 relating thereto*, opened for signature 2 November 1973, 12 ILM 1319, 17 ILM 546 (entered into force 2 October 1983) ('MARPOL 73/78').

[107] In contravention of the *1973 Washington Convention on International Trade in Endangered Species of Fauna and Flora*, opened for signature 3 March 1973, 12 ILM 1085 (entered into force 1 July 1975) ('CITES').

Terrorism

Paragraph 16 of the Honiara Declaration provides:

> The Forum recognized terrorism as a threat to the political and economic security of the region, and noted the various international conventions in the field. It identified areas of possible cooperation amongst Forum governments, particularly in intelligence gathering, training of personnel and joint exercises in dealing with serious incidents.

The terrorism conventions have multiplied since 1992,[108] adding to many of the areas of possible cooperation tentatively identified by the Declaration and making some of them mandatory. The 2002 Forum meeting noted the threat offered post 9/11 and held the Honiara Declaration up as a 'firm foundation for action'[109] to address new and heightened threats. Forum leaders underlined their commitment to implement anti-terrorist measures such as UN SC Resolution 1373[110] and the FATF Special Recommendations,[111] including associated reporting requirements.

Maritime surveillance

Paragraph 17 of the Honiara Declaration notes the Forum Fisheries Agency's (FFA) increased capacity to engage in maritime surveillance to assist Forum members in managing their fisheries resources and enforcing their sovereignty. The UN Convention on the Law of the Sea and more specifically the 1995 UN Fish Stocks Agreement[112] sets out the coastal state's rights over fisheries. At a regional level article 5 of the 1979 South Pacific Forum Fisheries Agency Convention[113] made possible the agreement of the 1992 Niue Treaty on Cooperation in Fisheries Surveillance and Law Enforcement in the South Pacific Region,[114] which provides under articles 6 and 7 for general cooperation among the parties in enforcement of their fisheries law. It allows for the exchange of information on foreign fisheries licensing, on the location of foreign fishing vessels and on law enforcement and surveillance.[115] It also provides a legal basis for bilateral agreements that allow Parties to use each other's physical enforcement platforms to arrest foreign fishing

---

[108] See the chapter by Alex Conte in this volume.

[109] *Forum Communiqué*, Thirty-Third Pacific Islands Forum, Suva, Fiji Islands, 15–17 August, 2002, [4].

[110] SC Res 1373 (2001), 28 September 2001.

[111] FATF, *The Forty Recommendations*, above n 92.

[112] *Agreement for the Implementation of the Provisions of the United Nations Convention on the Law of the Sea of 10 December 1982 Relating to the Conservation and Management of Straddling Fish Stocks and Highly Migratory Fish Stocks*, opened for signature 4 December 1995, 2167 UNTS 3 (entered into force 11 December 2001).

[113] Above n 101.

[114] Done at Honiara 9 July 1992 (entered into force 20 May 1993), Internet Guide to International Fisheries Law <http://www.oceanlaw.net/texts/niue.htm> at 10 December 2004.

[115] Article 5(1).

vessels in each other's waters and to appear in each other's courts to prosecute for violations that occurred in another state's waters.[116]

Taxation

Paragraph 18 of the Honiara Declaration notes the importance of taxation issues for the development of the economies of the region and suggests further study to identify the specific needs of Forum members. It is unclear whether cooperation in the pursuit of transnational tax evaders is contemplated. Bilateral double taxation conventions provide elements of the international legal framework in this respect.

Prison administration

Paragraph 19 of the Honiara Declaration notes the failure of other bodies promoting cooperation in the region to address adequately the special circumstances of island countries with small prison populations, and endorses a meeting of the heads of regional prison services. The UN Standard Minimum Rules for the Treatment of Prisoners provide elements of the international legal framework here.[117]

Indigenous issues

Paragraph 20 of the Honiara Declaration provides:

> The Forum agreed on the importance of indigenous issues in its member countries. It was stressed that an understanding of indigenous issues, in particular a knowledge of customary laws, was essential to the development and security of the region.

The point being made by the Declaration is that security in the region is impossible without taking indigenous issues into consideration, but what bearing they have on the suppression of transnational crime is left unexplained. The international legal framework in this regard is provided for by the general human rights conventions and those instruments dealing specifically with indigenous people's rights.[118]

Human trafficking

The Honiara Declaration is silent on human trafficking, which was only identified as a threat to the region at the 1999 Forum meeting.[119] The 2000 FRSC Meeting

---

[116] Articles 6-9.
[117] Adopted by the UN Congress on the Prevention of Crime and the Treatment of Offenders, held at Geneva in 1955, and approved by the ECOSOC Res 663 C (XXIV) of 31 July 1957 and 2076 (LXII) of 13 May 1977.
[118] For example, the *UN's Draft Declaration of the Rights of Indigenous Peoples*, 34 ILM 541.
[119] *Forum Communiqué*, Thirtieth Pacific Islands Forum, Koror, Republic of Palau, 3–5 October 1999.

asked the Oceania Customs Organisation (OCO) and the Pacific Immigration Directors Conference (PIDC) to develop a regional perspective on migrant smuggling.[120] The PIDC has also engaged in further discussion on information exchange and regional collaboration in developing migration and passport services. The recent attention to the issue by the Forum parallels the current international emphasis on human trafficking that culminated with the adoption in 2000 of the Protocol to Prevent, Suppress and Punish Trafficking in Persons, Especially Women and Children,[121] which criminalizes this activity in article 5.

Regional security

Paragraph 1 of the 2002 Nasonini Declaration on regional security targets for collective response 'unlawful challenges to nationality and independence' in addition to transnational crime.[122] The link between transnational crime and such challenges is unexplained. The Forum also reiterated the commitment to good governance as a key strategy to address conflict and tension in the region.

Small arms proliferation

The Honiara Declaration does not mention the proliferation of small arms. This is not surprising as it has little external impact, but the 2003 Forum meeting[123] noted poor control of small arms is an integral part of regional insecurity. It is regulated by the Firearms Protocol,[124] and supported by the United Nations Programme of Action to Prevent, Combat and Eradicate the Illicit Trade in Small Arms and Light Weapons in All its Aspects.[125]

Identity fraud

The 2003 Forum[126] also added identity fraud to the list of activities considered by the Forum to be of concern and the Forumsec was directed to explore the

---

[120] See Andreas Schloenhardt, *Migrant Smuggling: Illegal Migration and Organised Crime in Australia and the Asia Pacific Region* (2003) 374.

[121] Supplementing the *UN Convention on Transnational Organised Crime*, opened for signature 14 December 2000, GA Res 55/25, UN GAOR, 55th sess, Supp No 49, 44, UN Doc A/45/49 (Vol I) (2001) (entered into force 29 September 2003).

[122] Above n 69.

[123] *Forum Communiqué*, Thirty-Fourth Pacific Islands Forum, Auckland, New Zealand, 14–16 August 2003.

[124] *Protocol Against the Illicit Manufacturing of and Trafficking in Firearms, Their Parts, Components and Ammunition, Supplementing the United Nations Convention against Transnational Organized Crime*, UN GA Res. 55/25, 15 November 2000, annex to UN Doc A/55/383.

[125] UN Doc. A/Conf. 192/15 (New York: UN Department for Disarmament Affairs, 2001).

[126] *Forum Communiqué*, Thirty-Fourth Pacific Islands Forum, Auckland, New Zealand, 14–16 August 2003.

possibility of Forum members joining the Identity Fraud Register project run by the Australian Crimes Commission.

Corruption

The raising of the issue of good governance in the 2000 Biketawa Declaration, followed by the adoption of the Forum Principles of Good Leadership at the 2003 Forum meeting, led to the 2004 Forum inviting Forum members to consider signing and ratifying the 2003 UN Convention against Corruption[127] in order to strengthen good governance.[128]

Taking appropriate measures

Through the Honiara Declaration and subsequent statements the Forum has adopted a series of measures against transnational crime. The order in which these provisions emerged illustrates that Forum concerns have tracked global concerns. This reactive, incremental process is typical of the development of transnational criminal law. A product of their time, the actions prioritized by the Forum do not specifically include suppression of the full gamut of activities involved in the global criminal economy. Even activities identified as a threat to the region, such as weapons proliferation, smuggling of illegal migrants and corruption, are not specifically subject to control measures. The priority appears to have been to smooth criminal justice processes between different jurisdictions through reducing barriers to all forms of legal assistance including extradition, rather than establish an exhaustive regional criminal law suppressing all possible substantive crimes. This smoothing of interstate criminal procedure has been singled out from the early 1980s as important to the international community as a whole. Only towards the end of the list do the local concerns – fisheries surveillance, prisons, and indigenous issues – begin to emerge, included, it appears, as ineffectual afterthoughts. As a whole, the measures themselves are so broadly worded that it is fairly clear that the Forum's aim is regional harmonization of domestic law through some form of functional equivalence rather than uniformity. They serve as signposts to relevant international treaties and as invitations for detailed legal change though consultation with technical experts.

The legal status of these measures is uncertain. The Forum is the leading intergovernmental organization in the South Pacific in a de facto sense only because it has no treaty basis.[129] Thus participation in a declaration generates no treaty-derived obligation. Indeed, from an international perspective the Forum's

---

[127] *United Nations Convention against Corruption*, opened for signature 9 December 2003, GA Res 58/4, 43 ILM 37 (not in force).
[128] *Forum Communiqué*, Thirty-Fifth Pacific Islands Forum, Apia, Samoa, 3–10 August 2004, [29].
[129] Richard Herr, 'South Pacific Forum' in Brij V Lal and Kate Fortune (eds), *The Pacific Islands: An Encyclopaedia* (2000) 329 notes the lack of a foundation treaty but points out its regional importance and the fact that it operates as an IGO.

objective existence in abstract from its members is debateable. This confusion is mirrored in the Honiara Declaration: sometimes it is the Forum that speaks, sometimes it is the Forum leaders who speak. It is probably most appropriate to consider the Forum as generating state practice of the individual member states. This practice may serve as the basis for emerging regional norms of customary international law given that the statements are couched in normative terms, have been supported by subsequent reiterations of this commitment and have been followed in some instances by formal legislative change and increased cooperation on criminal matters among Forum members. However, the aspirational nature of many of the statements and the poor record of implementation in some cases weakens the case for a customary basis, which has not yet been made out. In result, as a matter of positive law it appears that Forum members are not obliged to adopt the measures recommended. The Declaration depends on multilateral suppression conventions and on bilateral conventions to establish legal obligations that generate implementation.

Legal responses in Forum members

Introduction

This section examines the steps taken by Forum members to respond to the Forum's recommendations. The Honiara Declaration highlights two general issues about implementation: first, the need for Forum members to engage in legislative change; and second, the critical lack of resources to meet the region's emerging needs in law enforcement and the necessity for assistance from the region's international partners to meet these needs.[130] However, before examining legislative modernization, it is apt to examine treaty adherence by Forum members as the Honiara Declaration anticipates that the Forum members should also sign up to the appropriate multilateral suppression conventions and establish the appropriate bilateral relations in order to facilitate such modernization. The function of these multilateral conventions and how they relate to domestic law reform is set out by the UNODC:

> Multilateral conventions form bridges between legal systems and represent a kind of *acquis communitaire* of the international community. They allow the states that are parties to those treaties to deal with challenges posed by transnational organized crime and international terrorism. Modalities of inter-State cooperation in criminal matters that have traditionally been the subject of bilateral agreement are increasingly becoming enshrined in international legal instruments such as the International Convention for the Suppression of Terrorist Bombings (General Assembly resolution 52/164, annex) and the International Convention for the Suppression of the Financing of Terrorism. Matters of extradition, legal assistance, investigative assistance, collection of evidence (hearing of witnesses and the carrying out of searches, for example), transfer of sentenced persons, transfer of documents and penal proceedings,

---

[130] Above n 14, [6] and [5].

seizure and forfeiture of illicit proceeds of crime, as well as the recognition of foreign penal judgements, are issues that can be addressed in such multilateral instruments. In that context, the United Nations Office on Drugs and Crime has, in cooperation with the International Institute of Higher Studies in the Criminal Sciences, been working on model laws to reflect the provisions of international instruments, as well as the revision and updating of manuals on extradition and legal assistance. Furthermore, guidelines on technical assistance are being prepared in order to facilitate international cooperation by strengthening the capacity of national law enforcement agencies to respond promptly to requests for assistance from other states.[131]

The international community is concerned about adherence to these conventions.[132] In this regard, the record of ratification or accession of Forum members to the 1988 Drug Trafficking Convention,[133] perhaps the central treaty in the system of transnational criminal law, is revealing. Although the treaty came into force in 1990 and currently has 169 states parties, of the 16 Forum members only Australia, the Federated States of Micronesia, Fiji, New Zealand and Tonga are currently parties. The participation of PICs in the '*acquis communitaire*' is poor. Initial responses to the much newer 2000 UN Transnational Organized Crime Convention[134] and its protocols on human trafficking,[135] migrants[136] and firearms[137] has been slow,[138] as has the response to the 2003 UN Corruption Convention.[139] The vacuum in international legal obligation with respect to the suppression of transnational crime in the South Pacific contrasts nicely with the general alarm projected by powerful developed states about transnational crime in the region. For example, the US State Department's International Narcotic Control Strategy Report 2003[140] lists as 'countries monitored' Fiji, Marshall Islands, Micronesia,

---

[131] Above n 70, [57].

[132] Above n 70, [14].

[133] Above, n 87.

[134] The *UN Convention on Transnational Organized Crime*, opened for signature 14 December 2000, GA Res 55/25, UN GAOR, 55th sess, Supp No 49, 44, UN Doc A/45/49 (Vol I) (2001) (entered into force 29 September 2003) ('TOC Convention').

[135] Above n 121.

[136] *Protocol Against the Smuggling of Migrants by Land, Sea or Air, Supplementing the United Nations Convention against Transnational Organized Crime*, opened for signature 14 December 2000, GA Res 55/25, UN GAOR, 55th sess, Supp No 49, 65, UN Doc A/45/49 (Vol I) (2001) (entered into force 28 January 2004) ('Migrants Protocol').

[137] *Protocol Against the Illicit Manufacturing and Trafficking in Firearms, their Parts, Components and Ammunition, Supplementing the United Nations Convention against Transnational Organized Crime*, opened for signature 31 May 2001, GA Res 55/255 (not in force).

[138] Australia is a party to the TOC Convention and the Migrants Protocol but has only signed the other instruments; the Cook Islands is a party to the TOC Convention; Fiji is a party to the TOC Convention; the FSM is a party to the TOC Convention; Nauru has signed the TOC Convention and its protocols; New Zealand is party to the TOC Convention and its protocols and has signed the Corruption Convention; and Tonga is party to the TOC Convention.

[139] See n 127.

[140] Bureau for International Narcotics and Law Enforcement Affairs, March 2004.

New Zealand, Niue, PNG, the Solomon Islands and Tonga; as 'countries of concern' the Cook Islands, Palau, Samoa, and Vanuatu; and as a 'major money laundering' countries Australia and Nauru. More serious is the FATF's listing of the Cook Islands and Nauru among the six Non-Cooperative Countries and Territories not meeting international money laundering standards.[141] Yet despite this external pressure to take steps against transnational crime, unlike developing states in other regions, PICs have not even made the formal commitment to suppression conventions. One reason may be disinterest because of the perceived absence of local impact coupled with weak legal and political infrastructures. They may simply not have the money to engage. It is significant that most PICs are unable to attend the negotiations of these treaties. For example, only Australia, New Zealand and PNG attended the 1988 Diplomatic Conference that adopted the Drug Trafficking Convention.[142] There may also be internal reasons for not becoming party, such as jurisdictional conflicts between different law enforcement arms. Nonetheless, pressure for adherence is mounting[143] and appears to be bearing some fruit.[144]

The Honiara Declaration is essentially about promoting legislative reform and the body of this section examines the steps taken by Forum members in response to the Forum's recommendations. Our interest here is not Australia and New Zealand, which claim to have in place the full range of legislation to implement the Honiara Declaration,[145] but the PIC members of the Forum, and the laws that they have enacted in response to regional declarations.[146] In order to provide some sense of what laws have been made, I have provided an Appendix which, using the same subject break-down as is used below, provides a fairly comprehensive list of pertinent legislation together with the year it came into force. Finally, while the upgrade of legislation is the key concern it is not the only concern, and the section also examines changes in law enforcement policy and practice in the various subject areas.

<http://www.state.gov/g/inl/rls/nrcrpt/2003/vol2/html/29919.htm> at 23 October 2004.

[141] FATF, *Annual Review 2004*, above n 27, 1.

[142] *United Nations Conference for the Adoption of a Convention against Illicit Traffic in Narcotic Drugs and Psychotropic Substances, Official Records, Volume I* (New York, 1994) UN Doc E/CONF 82/16, UN Publication Sales No E 94 XI 5, 197.

[143] Australian Senate Foreign Affairs, Defence and Trade Committee Report, above n 23, 192.

[144] For example, since 2003 Palau has ratified almost all of the extant anti-terrorism conventions.

[145] Australian Senate Foreign Affairs, Defence and Trade Committee Report, above n 23, 191.

[146] For a record of legislation enacted in response to the Forum's declarations see *Australian Parliamentary Debates, House of Representatives, Official Hansard* no. 10 of 2004, 30440, Parliament of Australia, <http://parlinfoweb.aph.gov.au/piweb/view_document.aspx?ID=913369&TABLE=HANSARDR> at 14 October 2004. In addition, see the Forumsec Survey on the Implementation of the Legislative Priorities of the Honiara Declaration on Law Enforcement Cooperation, 13 October 2004.

Law enforcement cooperation

Although there appears to be no specific record of legislative change with regard to law enforcement cooperation as a general enterprise, there has been extensive national participation in regional law enforcement activities. At the diplomatic level, the lead organization is the FRSC, an annual meeting of Forum member representatives to review priorities, institutional linkages and resource needs. Significantly, it is preceded by a 'pre-meeting' of law enforcement officials convened by the Forumsec's Law Enforcement Liaison Officer. Other important regional policing and customs meetings addressing current issues and developments in transnational crime and law enforcement include the Pacific Islands Law Officers Meeting (PILOM), the South Pacific Chiefs of Police Conference (SPCPC),[147] OCO and the Australasian and South West Pacific Commissioners Conference. The Forum works closely with these organizations and brings national law enforcement officers together for updates on matters such as border control.[148] In addition to the Law Enforcement Liaison Officer, the Forumsec's Suva-based Political, International and Legal Affairs Division has a Legal Advisor, an Anti-Money Laundering Consultant, Law Enforcement Training Coordinating Advisor and Law Enforcement Statistics Officer. The Forum also cooperates with intergovernmental law enforcement organizations. For example, the Forum cooperated with the UN Office for Drug Control and Crime Prevention (now UNODC) to implement the South Pacific Police – Customs Law Enforcement Project from 1995–1998.[149]

The Forum has also made an effort to establish a training programme for law enforcement personnel to address shortcomings in police training, such as the skills necessary to investigate money laundering.[150] The Forumsec's Law Enforcement Training Coordinator, on secondment from the AFP, is responsible for coordinating all Pacific law enforcement training.[151] Following the 2003 Forum Australia, New Zealand and Fiji announced the establishment of the Pacific Regional Policing Initiative, to be based in Suva, and to be implemented over five years. Australia committed itself to spending A$17 million over three years to strengthen regional police forces and New Zealand added a further NZ$2.5 million. The intention was to support law enforcement efforts in the region through the establishment of a 'virtual police academy' to coordinate and deliver a standardized training to over 900 officers across the Pacific. The PRPI is also intended to strengthen regional policing strategies and foster regional networking

---

[147] It includes all Pacific island states including non-Forum states. The AFP provides travel funds for this meeting.
[148] See the Honiara Declaration, above n 14, [11], [12], and the *Pacific Islands Forum Annual Report*, 2002–2003 (2002) 20.
[149] *ODCCP Statement at the FSC Meeting*, Port Vila, Vanuatu, 12–14 July 2000, see UN Office for Drugs and Crime, <http://www.unodc.un.or.th/factsheet/nontraditional.htm> at 21 October 2004.
[150] Herman, above n 20, 32.
[151] Australian Senate Foreign Affairs, Defence and Trade Committee Report, above n 23, 196.

and the pooling of regional resources. The 2004 Forum called for a focus on forensics analysis and capability, provision of equipment and appropriate training for staff, and maritime and border patrol and surveillance capability.[152]

At an operational level new regional arrangements have been developed. One of the concrete results of the Honiara Declaration has been the formation under the guidance of the AFP and NZP of Combined Law Agency Groups (CLAGS) in Kiribati, Samoa, the Cook Islands, Fiji, the Solomon Islands and Vanuatu. CLAGS draw together officers from the customs, police, coastguard, immigration, and so forth to exchange information and coordinate activities. The principal law enforcement agencies in the region are the police forces and customs organizations of Fiji, PNG, Solomon Islands and Samoa. Joint operations with developed state agencies take place. For example, a 2001 anti-drug operation in Suva involved 20 agents from the Fiji Royal Police Force, the AFP, the Royal Canadian Mounted Police, the US Drug Enforcement Administration and the NZP.[153] The AFP and NZP also played key roles in the 2004 Fijian drug 'bust', backing up Fiji's police. Australian state police also work with island police.[154] The nine-nation mission to restore order to Solomon Islands is considered to be a model of what close cooperation can achieve.[155] However, the most influential operational organization in the region is the AFP. Since the early 1980s, the AFP has posted liaison officers to a number of PICs.[156] The AFP now operates a Law Enforcement Cooperation Program (LECP) in the region to improve cooperation and capacity and to provide for intelligence gathering on transnational organized crime groups threatening Australia's regional interests. From 2002, the AFP through LECP has established Transnational Crime Units in Fiji, Samoa, Tonga, Vanuatu and PNG and plans to establish a unit in the Solomon Islands in 2005.[157] Cooperation from the host PIC is not always forthcoming. In 2004, Vanuatu's new administration decided to expel two AFP members, a move criticized by Australia as breaking pledges by PICs to cooperate in fighting transnational crime.[158] The latest regional development with operational implications is the Pacific Transnational Crime Coordination Centre which opened in Suva on 15 June 2004 as part of an AFP and SPCPC plan to

---

[152] *Forum Communiqué*, Thirty-Fifth Pacific Islands Forum, Apia, Samoa, 3–10 August 2004, [27].
[153] Tunidau, above n 90, 401.
[154] Australian Senate Foreign Affairs, Defence and Trade Committee Report, above n 23, 196.
[155] See also ibid, 205.
[156] In 2003 there were officers in PNG (Port Moresby), the Solomons (Honiara), Vanuatu (Port Vila) and Fiji (Suva). The Fiji office is responsible for all island states to the east of Fiji, while the AFP Region Coordinator Pacific Islands retain responsibility for Micronesia and the French territories: Australian Senate Foreign Affairs, Defence and Trade Committee Report, above n 23, 195.
[157] *AFP Media Release*, 15 June 2004, Australian Federal Police <http://www.afp.gov.au/afp/page/Media/2004/1506suva.htm> at 1 October 2004.
[158] Gratien Tiona, 'AFP – The Doors Remain Open', 16 September 2004, *Port Villa Presse* <http://www.news.vu/en/news/diplomacy/afp-the-doors-remain-open.shtml> at 28 January 2004.

combat transnational crime in the region.[159] The PTCCC is intended to become the hub of a Pacific Transnational Crime Unit Network that will manage and coordinate law enforcement intelligence provided by the network of national law enforcement agencies.[160] Although the Forum did not initiate this development, it welcomed the establishment of the PTCCC.[161] As should by now be apparent, Australia and New Zealand also provide extensive technical support for law enforcement. Australia has trained prosecutors and will provide judicial training in the region.[162] NZAID provides direct police and customs support in some cases and has recently established a Pacific Security Fund to provide training and advice to border control services.

Mutual assistance in criminal matters

Mutual assistance depends on states having legislation that allows the articulation of their criminal procedures with the criminal procedures of other states. Most Forum members have enacted such legislation. The members without new legislation are Nauru, PNG (legislation is before parliament) and Samoa. Drafting assistance, such as that supplied by Forumsec to the Cook Islands to enable adoption of the Mutual Assistance in Criminal Matters Act 2003, has been essential to enable some PICs to meet the recommendations of the Honiara Declaration.

Fiji's Mutual Assistance in Criminal Matters Act, 1997, is a relatively early response to the Honiara Declaration.[163] Requests from foreign states are directed to Fiji's Attorney General (AG) who has the authority to decide whether assistance will be given. If the decision is positive, she forwards the request to the Commissioner of Police or Director of Public Prosecutions depending on whether investigation or judicial action is requested. The Act makes it possible to request assistance from other states. Kiribati's Mutual Assistance in Criminal Matters Act 2003 is among the very latest legislation. It regulates the full gamut of assistance given by or requested by Kiribati to or from other states.[164] The AG determines the conditions under which assistance will be granted, which might include payment of any expenses incurred by Kiribati.[165] An unusual ground of refusal at the AG's discretion is if 'the provision of assistance would impose an excessive burden on the resources of' Kiribati.[166] The Act also makes provision for requests by Kiribati for forfeiture orders, pecuniary penalties and restraining orders to be enforced in a foreign country, and allows for the registration and enforcement of similar foreign

---

[159] See above n 157.
[160] The inaugural team leader is Inspector A Banmatakaui of the Vanuatu Police Force.
[161] *Forum Communiqué*, Thirty-Fifth Pacific Islands Forum, Apia, Samoa, 3–10 August 2004, [27].
[162] Australian Senate Foreign Affairs, Defence and Trade Committee Report, above n 23, 192.
[163] See generally Tunidau, above n 90, 399, 400, 409.
[164] In terms of sections 2 and 4.
[165] Section 9.
[166] Section 11(g).

orders.[167] An interesting feature of the Act is that it allows a defendant to request the court to certify the AG to ask a foreign state for evidence or witnesses to come to Kiribati if it is 'necessary for the proceedings'.[168] This addresses the criticism that legal assistance usually only serves the prosecution.[169] In making this decision the court can take into account inter alia the risk of unfair prejudice to the defendant if the material were not available[170] and whether the foreign state is likely to grant the request.[171] It is unclear what would happen if the foreign state refused the request after the court determined that a risk of injustice exists. Although the Act preserves the right of cross-examination of a witness from whom evidence was taken abroad, it makes it clear that if that person has to be brought to Kiribati, the defendant may have to pay if the cross-examination of the witness was trivial, unnecessary or irrelevant.[172] Resources are an issue, but this legislation is as sophisticated as any.

The extent to which the new mutual assistance legislation has actually been used is unknown. Vanuatu's Financial Services Commissioner is reported as stating that Vanuatu receives many requests for assistance by foreign investigators and that '[w]e provide assistance where we can, but there's a difference between fishing for information and specifics'.[173] A problem is the absence of bi-lateral mutual legal assistance treaties (MLATs) between Forum members. In 2003, Australia did not have an MLAT with any PIC.[174] MLATs are unnecessary when relying on the Commonwealth Scheme Relating to Mutual Assistance because it allows mutual assistance through enabling complementary domestic legislation for those Forum members that are Commonwealth members. Domestic legislation like Kiribati's Mutual Assistance in Criminal Matters Act 2003 assumes that assistance can be requested and provided without a bilateral treaty between the parties, but there would be no obligation to provide it.

Money laundering, asset forfeiture and banking regulation

Preventing money laundering and pursuing the proceeds of crime are the main thrusts of the Honiara Declaration and all Forum members have engaged in some activity in the field. Provision for asset forfeiture seems to have fared better than the criminalization of money laundering, while financial regulation remains a difficult area. PICs are not members of FATF, but Australia, the Cook Islands, Fiji, the Marshall Islands, New Zealand, Niue, Palau, Samoa and Vanuatu are all members of the APG-ML, the purpose of which is to facilitate the adoption and

---

[167] Section 41 and Part 7 generally.
[168] Section 50. This is possible in Fiji but under the *Proceeds of Crime Act 1998*.
[169] See Neil Boister, 'Human Rights Protections in the Suppression Conventions' (2002) 2 *Human Rights Law Review* 199, 200.
[170] Section 51(4)(e).
[171] Section 51(4)(a).
[172] Section 59(2).
[173] See Herman, above n 20, 21.
[174] Australian Senate Foreign Affairs, Defence and Trade Committee Report, above n 23, 193.

implementation of the FATF recommendations, taking into account regional and country factors.[175] Kiribati, Nauru, PNG, the Cook Islands and Tonga have observer status in the APG-ML. Cooperation does not appear, however, to have had as much effect as direct pressure from FATF. For example, blacklisted by FATF in 2000, Niue was de-listed in 2002 after reforming its laws.[176] Technical assistance to facilitate change has been provided by the IMF, the UN, the Commonwealth Secretariat (Comsec), the Forumsec laundering consultant and the NZP. Legislative development, such as the FSM Money Laundering and Proceeds of Crime Act of 2000, has been funded by Forumsec, which also provides for money laundering training needs assessment.[177]

Some Forum members had enacted legislation prior to 1992 but it had limitations. In 1989, Vanuatu enacted the Serious Offences (Confiscation of Proceeds) Act, 1989, but, an established OFC, it lacked the political will to meet the 1988 Drug Trafficking Convention's obligation to remove bank secrecy,[178] the application of this removal to requests by other states for mutual assistance[179] and the duty to cooperate in investigation into the movement of the proceeds of crime.[180] The Basle Committee and FATF's preventative measures such as 'know your customer' rules were equally difficult to accept. Much of the legislation enacted after 1992 was based on Commonwealth models. Fiji's Proceeds of Crime Act, 1997, is a good example.[181] It criminalizes money laundering,[182] but the Fijian offence is harsher than the 1988 Drug Trafficking Convention because it only requires objective fault[183] while the Convention requires subjective fault.[184] In line with the FATF Recommendations the offence is an 'all crimes laundering offence' in that the predicate offence can be of any kind and can occur within or outside of Fiji, the only requirement being that if it had occurred in Fiji it would have been considered 'serious' because it carries a minimum maximum penalty of one year imprisonment.[185] The Act targets the proceeds of serious offences by permitting courts to grant forfeiture and confiscation orders, and together with the Mutual Assistance in Criminal Matters Act, 1997, provides for such orders issued in another state to be given effect in Fiji.[186] The Act's conviction-based value confiscation

---

[175] See Asia Pacific Group on Money Laundering <http://www.apgml.org/content/index.jsp> at 23 October 2004. Forumsec cooperates with the APG-ML through the Coordinating Office for the Participating Countries Anti-Money Laundering Initiative.
[176] FATF, *Annual Review 2004*, above n 27, 15.
[177] See Pacific Islands Forum <http://www.forumsec.org/fj/division/PILAD/Pilad.htm> at 4 October 2004.
[178] Article 5(3).
[179] Article 7(5).
[180] Article 9(1)(b)(ii).
[181] Herman, above n 20, generally.
[182] Section 69(2).
[183] Section 69(3).
[184] Article 3(1)(b)(i).
[185] Section 3.
[186] Tunidau, above n 90, 400.

system[187] may be considered to be of limited value by those who favour civil forfeiture not dependant upon conviction. Although the Act does give authorities extensive powers to lift the corporate veil, to freeze, seize, monitor, disclose and keep records, and obliges banks to report suspicious transactions, it has limitations.[188] For example, the definition of a bank[189] does not cover lawyers who operate in sole partnership, accounting firms, foreign exchange agencies, travel agencies, second hand car dealers and other handlers of finance. The more recent Kiribati Proceeds of Crime Act no. 8 of 2003, includes a range of innovations. It defines 'financial institution' broadly, listing 31 different forms of conduct including acting as a friendly society and money and currency changing and 'any other business prescribed by the minister'.[190] 'Cash dealers' are also subject to the Act and again the definition is broad. Provision is made for the establishment of an FIU within the Kiribati Police.[191] However, the Act protects innocent and perhaps less than innocent third parties by requiring a court making a forfeiture order to take into account 'any right or interest of a third party' and 'any hardship that is reasonably to be expected to be caused to any person by the operation of the order'.[192]

Legislative development with regard to banking regulation has been difficult. FATF pressure resulted in Niue's Financial Transactions Reporting Act 2000, which requires suspicious transaction reporting, the establishment of an FIU and some degree of customer identification. The International Banking Repeal Act 2002 eliminated Niue's offshore banks. The Cook Islands, also blacklisted by FATF, enacted the Financial Supervisory Commission Act 2003, the Banking Act 2003 and the Financial Transactions Reporting Act 2003, to provide for increased regulation of finance and banking regimes, with explicit provisions preventing the establishment of shell banks by requiring 'physical presence'. The latter Act provides for reporting requirements and requires financial institutions to retain information for 6 years in a form that allows the Cook Island's FIU to readily reconstruct a transaction.[193] The Act also empowers the FIU to enter the premises of financial institutions to ensure compliance[194] and specifically overrides the secrecy provisions in other legislation.[195] By 2004, as a result of the 2003 legislation aimed at eliminating shell banks within one year through re-licensing, 9 out of 16 offshore banks had applied for licences.[196] Other PICs have been slower to respond. After Nauru was subject to FATF blacklisting for failing inter alia to provide for customer identification and suspicious transaction reporting,[197] it

---

[187] Section 20(1).
[188] Tunidau, above n 90, 402.
[189] Section 63.
[190] Section 3(1).
[191] Section 16-20.
[192] Section 26(4).
[193] Section 6.
[194] Section 30.
[195] Sections 35 and 36.
[196] FATF, *Annual Review 2004*, above n 27, 8.
[197] Ibid 12.

enacted the Anti-Money Laundering Act of 2001 which provided for such measures, and again under pressure amended the Act to apply to the offshore banking sector. However, FATF was still concerned about the licensing and supervision of the offshore sector. In 2003 Nauru enacted the Corporation (Amendment) Act of 2003 and the Anti-Money Laundering Act of 2003, laws intended to abolish offshore shell banks and prohibit the granting of new licences. Nauru has indicated that it has since revoked the licences of all remaining offshore banks, but FATF has maintained its blacklisting to pressure Nauru to ensure that previously licenced offshore banks are no longer conducting banking activity and are no longer in existence.

Large-scale currency transaction reporting to FIUs in Forum members is a relatively recent development. The Australian Transaction Report and Analysis Centre (Austrac), the Cook Islands Financial Intelligence Unit, the Marshall Islands Domestic Financial Intelligence Unit, New Zealand Police Financial Intelligence Unit, and the Vanuatu Financial Intelligence Unit are all members of the Egmont Group. Aqorau notes that success stories, like the progress made by the Fiji FIU, are invariably the result of individual enthusiasm rather than national design.[198] Austrac is the senior partner here, and the Pacific islands are a priority area for its international work. In terms of the Australian Suppression of the Financing of Terrorism Act 2002, the Director of Austrac has the power to enter into a memorandum of understanding (MOU) with foreign FIUs to facilitate the exchange of financial intelligence but by 2003 it only had an MOU with Vanuatu, although it was working towards signing MOUs with the Cook Islands and the Marshall Islands.[199] The Eminent Persons' Group Review of the Forum suggests the establishment of a regional FIU,[200] and Australia or New Zealand have been mooted as possible locations.[201]

There is evidence of rapid legislative modernization, but the extent to which these new powers have actually been used is uncertain. As we have seen, there have been some concrete results in regulating the banking sector. However, PICs face capacity problems in implementing regional and international directives. Aqorau suggests that Palau, which has had the necessary legislation since 2001, exemplifies these problems. He cites a March 2003 report from an APG-ML Mutual Evaluation which noted that Palau's authorities

> lack [the] resources and financial intelligence to gauge the extent of money laundering resulting from international cross border crimes. It noted Palau's lack of devoted resources and training, the absence of implementing regulations or comprehensive guidance for financial institutions, the absence of an onsite inspection plan, and weaknesses in existing legislation. Although the Bureau of Public Safety and the Office of the Attorney General are currently responsible for enforcing anti-

---

[198] Above n 47, 12.
[199] Australian Senate Foreign Affairs, Defence and Trade Committee Report, above n 23, 198.
[200] The Report is available at New Zealand Ministry of Foreign Affairs and Trade <http://www.mfat.govt.nz/foreign/regions/pacific/pif03/pifreviewdocs/wayforward.html> at 4 October 2004.
[201] Tunidau, above n 90, 402.

money laundering provisions, no funds have been budgeted for this purpose. Thus far there have been no investigations or prosecutions conducted under the anti-money laundering laws.[202]

Moreover, FATF reports indicate the unwillingness of certain PICs to cooperate with law enforcement agencies and international organizations in the suppression of money laundering,[203] and the enactment of new legislation may not change this recalcitrance.

Extradition

Although new extradition laws have been enacted in many Forum members since 1992, some PICs, such as Nauru and PNG, have not updated their laws. After the adoption of the Honiara Declaration, the Forum developed a Model Extradition Law which was tabled at the 1999 PILOM Meeting. The Model Law's purpose is to bring the domestic law of Forum members into line with the Commonwealth's London Scheme for the Rendition of Fugitive Offenders and the UN Model Treaty on Extradition. The Forumsec has also funded new legislation.[204]

Some Forum members engaged in legislative modernization earlier than others. A recent example of legislative reform by a PIC is Fiji's Extradition Act 2003.[205] Although the new Act takes into account the Fiji Bill of Rights and Freedoms,[206] the impact of the UN Model Treaty is patent and illustrates the global tendency towards streamlining extradition. Although the Act still requires offences to carry at least a maximum sentence of one year or more before extradition is allowed (rather than 6 months, which is the recent trend), it allows extradition where the offence carries the death penalty, which may fall foul of Fiji's Bill of Rights and Freedoms.[207] The Act expands the category of extraditable offences to include fiscal and revenue offences,[208] although Aqorau complains that the Act does not make offences against the exploitation of natural resources extraditable despite their serious economic consequences for PICs.[209] He gives the specific example of violation of fisheries laws, where imprisonment is not usually an option thus precluding extradition. The Act removes the political offence exception which raises questions about the vulnerability to extradition of fugitive militants back to

---

[202] Above n 47, 11, citing PACNEWS, 'Money Laundering', *Palau Horizon*, Thursday 24 July 2003.

[203] FATF, *Review to Identify Non-Cooperative Countries or Territories*, above n 29 and FATF, *Annual Review 2004*, above n 27.

[204] For example, the FSM's *Transnational Extradition and Transfer of Convicted Persons Act of 2000 and Interstate Extradition Act of 2000*.

[205] See generally Tunidau, above n 90, 400; Aqorau, above n 72, 3.

[206] *The Fiji Constitution Amendment Act, 1997*, chapter 4.

[207] Section 22.

[208] Section 3(4).

[209] See above n 72, 6.

Pacific hotspots such as the Solomons[210] and PNG. It also abandons the prima facie case requirement for extradition and provides for extradition to requesting Forum members on the backing of warrants issued in those countries.[211] Kiribati's Extradition Act no. 17 of 2003 shows the influence of the Forum's Model Law. Terrorist offences are extraditable and they are expansively defined.[212] Although the prima facie proof requirement has been abandoned, the nationality exception has not.[213] Following a now common approach, the Act permits surrender of fugitives to different states on different bases. Extradition to Commonwealth states other than PICs[214] requires only an authenticated record of the case.[215] The Act provides for extradition to other states on the basis of a treaty or comity, but extradition to Forum members is on a backing of warrants procedure.[216] An unusual reason for refusing surrender that only applies to Forum members is that the 'the prison conditions in the requesting country are not substantially equivalent to the minimum standards for imprisonment in Kiribati',[217] a violation of the rigid rule of non-inquiry into the criminal justice systems of requesting states.[218] Provision is made for Kiribati to establish jurisdiction to prosecute where it refuses to extradite on humanitarian grounds (including poor prison conditions) or because of the nationality exception, as well as provision to surrender for trial only on condition the person is returned to serve their sentence.[219]

The existence of a new cut-down extradition process is only the first step, however; it has to be used properly. Tunidau notes about the Fiji experience:

> Our experience with the extradition cases in the past decade or so has shown that it requires a level of expertise not only in the ability to compare offences in two different countries but also in the ability to work with the Extradition Act and a bi-lateral treaty.[220]

He records a spate of extradition requests by and to Fiji made under the old legislation for offences that included drug and arms smuggling.[221] Yet it is difficult to gauge how many extradition requests have been made by and to Forum members; what little material there is suggests that this legislation is not heavily used. For example, although Australia can conduct extradition under the

---

[210] See Aqorau, above n 72, 8, discussing the presence of Malaita Eagle Force members (Solomon Island militants) in Fiji.
[211] Part 4.
[212] Section 4.
[213] Section 19(2)(a).
[214] Part 3.
[215] Section 24.
[216] Part 4.
[217] Section 36(2).
[218] For a recent example of the rule see *Decision on the extradition of Ricardo Miguel Cavallo* (2003) 47 ILM 888, 902.
[219] Section 59.
[220] Tunidau, above n 90, 408.
[221] Ibid.

Extradition (Commonwealth countries) Regulations with the Cook Islands, Kiribati, Nauru, PNG, Samoa, the Solomon Islands, Tonga, Tuvalu and Vanuatu and under separate non-treaty regulations with Fiji and the Marshall Islands, few actual requests are made. To 2003, Australia had made one request to PNG for four people involved in drug trafficking and PNG had made no successful extradition request to Australia.[222]

Drugs offences

While the impact of more than a century of drug treaty adherence is evident in the legislative record of Forum members, it is remarkable that even post the 1988 Drug Trafficking Convention and the 1992 Honiara Declaration, nine of the fifteen Forum PICs appear to have either outdated or no specialist drug legislation.[223] Experience provided a strong motivation for legal change. For example, the Fiji Dangerous Drugs Act 1938, which reflects its provenance in treaties from 1925[224] and 1931,[225] does not meet the obligations contained in the 1988 Drug Trafficking Convention, which lays out a comprehensive penal regime concerned with suppressing every form of involvement in the illicit traffic. The main offender following the 2000 seizure of 350kg of heroin in Fiji received the existing maximum penalty of eight years' imprisonment for trafficking whereas in Australia he would have received life.[226] Surveillance of the Fijian methamphetamine operation went on for 14 months before it was closed down in 2004 because Fiji's law did not prohibit methamphetamine's precursors. The Illicit Drugs Control Act 2004, which came into force on 9 July 2004, designed to bring Fijian Law up to date with a broader range of offences carrying harsher penalties (it increased the maximum sentence for trafficking to life imprisonment and a million dollar fine), was not ready to put before Parliament until the day of the raid. It appeared that the Chinese conspirators would be prosecuted in Hong Kong rather than in Fiji because of the low maximum sentence available. PNG is also considering new laws, as the maximum penalty under its Dangerous Drugs Act is two years.

The 2000 Forum meeting noted shortcomings in the national drug legislation within the region, and as a result a joint working group of Forum members and the SPCPC and the OCO produced the 'Canberra Framework', the basis for draft

---

[222] Australian Senate Foreign Affairs, Defence and Trade Committee Report, above n 23, 193. In 2001, PNG applied for the extradition of Jimmy Maladina for the infamous National Provident Fund fraud but he returned voluntarily from Brisbane to face charges in 2002.
[223] The Cook Islands, FSM, Fiji, Kiribati, Nauru, PNG, Samoa, Tonga, and Tuvalu.
[224] *International Opium Convention*, signed at Geneva on 19 February 1925, 81 LNTS 317 (entered into force September 1923).
[225] *Convention for Limiting the Manufacture and Regulating the Distribution of Narcotic Drugs*, signed at Geneva on 13 July 1931, 139 LNTS 301 (entered into force 9 July 1933).
[226] Australian Senate Foreign Affairs, Defence and Trade Committee Report, above n 23, 192 (submission by the AFP – see *Committee Hansard*, 27 March 2003, 361). This contrasted starkly with the three month mandatory prison sentence any drug offence including possession, struck down by the courts in 2001 as a breach of the *1997 Bill of Rights*. See the UNODC, above n 17, 33.

model drug legislation.[227] The 2002 Forum meeting endorsed the resulting Illicit Drug Control Bill and encouraged all Forum PICs to examine the possibility of enacting the legislation in its entirety.[228] The working group has also been providing in-country support to law enforcement officers and prosecutors on implementation of the new law. Apart from their input into the Bill, New Zealand and Australian law enforcement agencies have provided technical assistance and training for Pacific island law enforcement agencies.[229] Yet there appears to have been little resulting legislative change.

Effort has also been put into regional drug law enforcement. The 1992–1997 South Pacific Police-Customs Drug Enforcement Project was aimed at improving drug enforcement capabilities of regional law enforcement agencies.[230] In 1999, the UN ODCCP and Forumsec held a Drug Control Master Plan Workshop in Suva, while in 2001, the SPCPC mooted the establishment of a database for drug seizures and requested members to provide details of seizures to the Law Enforcement Liaison officer at the Forumsec.[231] The 2003 Forum encouraged law enforcement agencies to undertake drug awareness campaigns for officers.[232] An area of concern is the general absence of facilities for rehabilitation of drug offenders in the region.[233]

Environmental offences

General regional coordination of the environment is provided by the South Pacific Regional Environment Programme, a stand alone body dating back to 1982, while the South Pacific Applied Geoscience Commission also deals with environmental and resource management issues. The Forum does respond to specific environmental abuses. For example, with regard to wildlife smuggling, the 2003

---

[227] See generally the *Statement by H.E. Mr A. Naidu, Permanent Representative of Fiji to the United Nations on behalf of the Pacific Islands Forum Group at the General Debate of the Third Committee on Item 100 (Crime Prevention and Criminal Justice) and Item 101 (International Drug Control)*, 2 October 2022, United Nations Headquarters, 2, United Nations <http://www.un.int/nauru/pifstatement.o3pdf > at 6 October 2004. UNODC Model laws were used as a template. See the UNODC, above n 17, 33.

[228] *Forum Communiqué*, Thirty-Third Pacific Islands Forum, Suva, Fiji Islands, 15–17 August, 2002, [22].

[229] *NZ Country Report to the UN Commission on Narcotic Drugs, 46th Session, 2003*, National Drug Policy <http://www.ndp.govt.nz/publications/NZCtyRpt03B.pdf> at 8 December 2004.

[230] See Pacific Islands Forum <http://www.forumsec.org/fj/division/PILAD/Pilad.htm> at 4 October 2004.

[231] See UNODC <http://www.unodc.un.or.th/factsheet/nontraditional.htm> at 21 October 2004, and Resolution 7, *Resolutions of the Thirtieth SPCP Conference 2001*, South Pacific Chiefs of Police Conference <http://www.spcpc.org/resolutions_2001.htm> at 4 October 2004.

[232] *Forum Communiqué*, Thirty-Fourth Pacific Islands Forum, Auckland, New Zealand, 14–16 August 2003, [23].

[233] See UNODC, above n 17, 36-7. It recommends preventative rather than rehabilitative responses because of the general shortage of resources.

Forum urged Forum members to provide information on the trade in endangered species and whether or not they are signatories to the CITES convention.[234] Protection of marine resources is the main area of environmental concern involving penal measures and is discussed below under maritime surveillance.

Terrorism

Prior to 9/11, many PICs did not have legislation dealing with terrorism.[235] The 2001 SPCPC meeting highlighted this inadequacy and urged new legislation to ban proscribed terrorist groups, freeze and forfeit terrorist assets and extradite terrorists.[236] After the adoption of the 2002 Nasonini Declaration the Forum agreed that in 2003 an expert working group on terrorism composed of representatives from Forum members and regional law enforcement agencies would develop a regional framework to address terrorism by, in particular, the provision of model legislation.[237] Once the draft legislation was complete in-country visits would take place by legal drafters to adapt the model legislation to local conditions. A framework for compliance with UN SC Resolution 1373 was produced. The unrealistic target date for updating legislation was the end of 2003. However, new laws have been passed in the Marshall Islands and Samoa. In Samoa, for example, the Prevention and Suppression of Terrorism Act 2002 provides for fast track extradition for foreign nationals accused of the commission of a wide range of terrorist and terrorist financing offences. Samoa is also preparing legislation to enable its OFC to comply with a range of post-9/11 international obligations concerning money laundering, terrorism, financing of terrorism and transnational crime. In other PICs there has been debate about the necessity of these draconian laws and who is going to pay for them.[238] Steps have been taken to increase regional law enforcement cooperation on terrorism. In 2003 the Micronesian Presidents agreed to greater information sharing on anti-terrorist measures.[239] A regional security strategy was discussed at a Pacific Round Table on Terrorism held in Wellington from 10–12 May 2004. The 2004 Forum called for enhanced cooperation on counter-terrorism, including the establishment of a network of

---

[234] *Forum Communiqué*, Thirty-Fourth Pacific Islands Forum, Auckland, New Zealand, 14–16 August 2003, [22].
[235] Australian Senate Foreign Affairs, Defence and Trade Committee Report, above n 23, 191.
[236] Resolution 2; see above n 231. The Forumsec also sent a report to the Chair of the UN Committee on Counter Terrorism highlighting ongoing regional counter terrorist activities – *Pacific Islands Forum Annual Report*, 2001–2002 (2002) 20.
[237] Composed of representatives from Australia, Fiji, Kiribati, Marshall Islands, New Zealand, PNG, Samoa, and Vanuatu, as well as two representatives from the OCO, PIDC, SPCPC and PILOM. See *Expert Working Group to Address Pacific Terrorism Issues*, 21 February 2003, Pacific News, <http://www.hellopacificnews.com/news/general/news/2003/02/21/c.hml> at 4 October 2004.
[238] See the chapter by Alex Conte in this volume.
[239] 'Joint Communiqué of the Third Micronesian President's Summit', *Hello Pacific*, 19 August 2003 <http://www.hellopacific.com/news/general/news/2003/08/19/19regmeeting.html> at 4 October 2004.

central contact points and a counter-terrorism working group in advance of the 2005 meeting of the FRSC.[240] It called for further work on extradition and mutual legal assistance, and raised the possibility of a regional counter-terrorism contingency planning exercise.[241]

Maritime surveillance

Maritime surveillance applies to the policing of territorial waters and EEZs for all transnational crimes, but the most effort has been put into fisheries surveillance. The FFA is the key regional agency with an interest in the enforcement of Forum members' national fisheries laws in their EEZs. The legal basis for regulation of fisheries is the Minimum Terms and Conditions for harmonizing foreign fishing vessels' access to fisheries. The FFA has in place a vessel monitoring system, but it was noted at the 2004 Forum meeting that members continue to licence vessels that are not in compliance with this system.[242] National laws, such as Fiji's Fisheries Act 1942 (as amended), makes provision for a range of offences, for extension of jurisdiction to include the EEZ, and for powers to board, search and seize. But penalties are low. The master, owner or charterer of a foreign registered vessel convicted of fishing without a licence in Fiji's waters may be subject to a maximum fine of F$100,000 (US$60,800),[243] which compares unfavourably with the maximum NZ$250,000 (US$181,110) available for the same offence in New Zealand.[244] The actual practice of surveillance appears sporadic. Although patrol boats sponsored by Australia are in operation through the region their under-use has been questioned, and the Australian Senate has recommended maritime surveillance operations using air patrols, satellite surveillance, and coast-watchers.[245] I am not aware of any Forum member that has used the provisions of the Niue Treaty on Regional Fisheries Cooperation and Enforcement to reach agreement with their neighbours to allow their patrol boats to arrest any foreign fishing vessels. At a strategic level, the expansion of a more wide-ranging surveillance policy may be facilitated by the Pacific Islands Regional Ocean Policy and the Pacific Islands Regional Ocean Forum – Integrated Strategic Action framework to be included for consideration in the Pacific Plan.[246]

---

[240] *Forum Communiqué*, Thirty-Fifth Pacific Islands Forum, Apia, Samoa, 3–10 August 2004, [28].
[241] Ibid.
[242] Ibid [14].
[243] Section 10(3).
[244] Section 113(1) read with section 252(3) of the *New Zealand Fisheries Act 1996*.
[245] Australian Senate Foreign Affairs, Defence and Trade Committee Report, above n 23, 205.
[246] *Forum Communiqué*, Thirty-Fifth Pacific Islands Forum, Apia, Samoa, 3–10 August 2004, [14].

Taxation

The Forum takes an interest in taxation through its development of economic cooperation and an open market in the region. The 2002 Forum Economic Action Plan[247] notes the international dialogue on taxation proposed by the IMF, OECD and World Bank, and asked Forumsec to advance Forum members' interests in this regard. However, there appears to have been no attempt to harmonize tax offences other than the harmonization indirectly achieved through adopting money laundering legislation criminalizing the laundering of the proceeds of tax offences, and drugs legislation with excise offence implications. The Australian Customs Service has had regional input through the OCO to provide technical assistance and training to PICs while Japan provides training on tax-collection regimes. Forum members belong to the Pacific Association of Tax Administrators.

Prison administration

Since 1998 an annual Regional Heads of Prisons Meeting has been held, which discusses matters of concern, shares information and ideas, and develops mutual assistance and cooperation on corrections-related matters, among Pacific states generally. Despite the concern expressed in the Honiara Declaration there does not appear to have been any formal study undertaken of the problems prison administrators face on small islands. Given that pursuit of transnational criminals will add a new dimension to the prison population of PICs with the incarceration of individuals who may continue to manage transnational criminality from jail, this seems short-sighted.

Indigenous issues

No effort appears to have been made to integrate a greater understanding of indigenous issues and particularly customary laws into formal legal changes made to address transnational crime. Certainly no new legislation that I have seen acknowledges in any way the importance of indigenous issues or laws; the new laws are analogues of the laws of developed states. Indigenous issues are important in explaining the causes of crime and in the actual practice of law enforcement, but what does a court do when requested to confiscate communally held land under asset forfeiture legislation?

Human trafficking[248]

The legislative development in this area in New Zealand and Australia is advanced, but in the PICs there is a legislative vacuum. To facilitate change, Forumsec has developed model legislation to address people smuggling, human trafficking,

---

[247] See Pacific Islands Forum <http://www.forumsec.org.fj/docs/FEMM/2002/Action%2520Plan.pdf> at 11 November 2004.

[248] See the chapter by Michael Barutciski in this volume.

refugee determination and associated issues. Fiji's Immigration Bill introduced in 2002 imposes serious penalties for failure to provide adequate information,[249] for people smuggling[250] and for harbouring a deportee.[251] Multilateral cooperation on these matters takes place through the Asia-Pacific Consultation (APC) on Refugees, Displaced Persons and Migrants; the Regional Ministerial Conference on People Smuggling, Trafficking in Persons and Related Transnational Crime; and the Pacific Immigration Directors Conference (PIDC). National law enforcement agencies cooperate on human trafficking, people smuggling, and refugee determination, and exchange information and analysis on these matters.[252] But they operate in a sensitive social context, and there have been complaints that PIC police have harassed ethnic minorities during operations aimed at removing illegal immigrants.[253] The most significant national agency operating in the region is the Australian Department of Immigration and Multicultural and Indigenous Affairs. It provides law enforcement training and expert assistance for law reform,[254] and negotiates MOUs to facilitate cooperation in immigration control and border issues.[255] Unsurprisingly, Australia has been a major provider of technical assistance. In 2003, the Australian Government announced an A$20 million package to combat trafficking in persons.

Regional security

Since 2000 the Forum Foreign Affairs Ministers Meeting has been trying to develop proposals for Forum leaders to respond to political instability that has plagued PICs such as the Solomon Islands and Fiji.[256] The Forumsec has commissioned national security studies in individual PICs to help focus attention on the security situation in these countries.[257] The main regional operational initiative has been the Regional Assistance Mission to the Solomon Islands, which required legislation in participating states.[258] The Forumsec has observer status on the

---

[249] F$20,000 or 5 years' imprisonment.
[250] F$75,000 or 20 years' imprisonment.
[251] F$100,000 fine or 7 years.
[252] *Forum Communiqué*, Thirty-Fourth Pacific Islands Forum, Auckland, New Zealand, 14–16 August 2003. Forum states are participants in Customs Asia Pacific Enforcement Reporting System, which has two regional support centres in Australia and New Zealand.
[253] See Newton, above n 84, 12 referring to allegations made by the Fiji Chinese community, reported in the *Fiji Times* 5 April 1999.
[254] Australian Senate Foreign Affairs, Defence and Trade Committee Report, above n 23, 200.
[255] Ibid.
[256] Australian Senate Foreign Affairs, Defence and Trade Committee Report, above n 23, 192.
[257] 2001: Fiji, PNG, Solomon Islands, Kiribati; 2002: Kiribati, Nauru, Samoa, Tonga; 2003: Cook Islands, Niue, Tuvalu; and 2004: FSM, Palau, Marshall Islands. See the *Pacific Islands Forum Annual Report*, 2002–2003 (2003) 21.
[258] See generally, Derek McDougall, 'Intervention in the Solomon Islands' (2004) 93 *The Round Table* 213-223. In a further regional intervention, in terms of the *Joint Agreement on Enhanced Cooperation Between Australia and Papua New Guinea*, Port Moresby, signed 30

Council for Security Cooperation in the Asia Pacific, an NGO of government and private security analysts working on Asia-Pacific security matters.

Small arms proliferation

A specific problem for regional security is the proliferation of small arms. The 2003 Report on Small Arms in the Pacific[259] discusses the lack of adequate legislation covering small arms in the Pacific and the inadequate enforcement of existing laws, and identifies legislative variation as a problem because it creates holes exploited by traffickers.[260] The need for new laws was recognized in 1999 when Forum Leaders agreed to the development of a draft legal framework for weapons control, and in 2000, the SPCPC produced a draft Legal Framework for a Common Approach to Weapons Control. It was taken up by the FRSC and the Forumsec produced a Model Illicit Weapons Control Bill, aimed at providing a proper regulatory framework for controlling small arms,[261] and based on the principle that the possession and use of firearms, ammunition, and other related materials is a privilege conditional on the overriding need to ensure public safety. The model law is designed to improve public safety by imposing strict controls on the importation, possession and use of firearms, ammunition, other related materials and prohibited weapons.[262] No legislative modernization has occurred thus far.

Identity fraud

Legislative change in this area has not been a priority. The 2003 Forum meeting directed the Forumsec to coordinate the formation of a working group to explore the viability for Forum PICs to join and participate in the Identity Fraud Register project.[263]

Corruption

Stocktaking undertaken by the Forum reveals that implementation of the Forum Eight Principles of Accountability is far from complete. However, legislative reform has occurred. For example, the Cook Islands Crimes Amendment Act 2003 creates new offences and widens powers in relation to the corrupt use of official information, conspiring to defeat justice and corrupting juries and witnesses.

June 2004, [2004] ATS 24 (in force 13 August 2004), AFP officers began patrolling the streets of PNG in December 2004.

[259] Alpers and Twyford, above n 49.

[260] Above n 49, xvi-xvii.

[261] See Aqorau, above n 47, 9.

[262] *Forum Communiqué*, Thirty-Fourth Pacific Islands Forum, Auckland, New Zealand, 14–16 August 2003.

[263] Ibid. The first meeting of the group took place at the Australian Crime Commission, Canberra from 5–8 April 2004.

However, the major legislative reform required by the UN Corruption Convention is still to be undertaken.

Ensuring implementation

The implementation of the Honiara Declaration has been a source of concern to the Forum. In 1997, Forum Secretary General Noel Levi stated that '[p]rogress in this area would assist in establishing a regional legislative framework to combat transnational crime'.[264] The 2001 Forum meeting expressed 'serious concerns that, despite the provision of legal drafting assistance, progress in implementing the legislative priorities of the Honiara Declaration had been disappointingly slow'.[265] It ordered the Forumsec to undertake a 'stock-take' of members' progress. At the 2001 PILOM meeting Noel Levi commented: 'If we are failing in our commitments under the Honiara Declaration, what does that say to our commitment to the principles of cooperation, peace and stability that underpin the Declaration?'[266] The 2002 Forum meeting noted that 'while some progress had been made in the implementation of the Honiara Declaration, further urgent action was required of some member states'.[267] A commitment was made to full legislative implementation of the Declaration by 2003.[268] The 2003 Nasonini Declaration called again for a legislative stock-take, in order to explain why implementation has been slow.[269] Noel Levi noted that at this point only five Forum members had enacted most of the legislation, and he termed much of the existing legislation 'archaic'.[270] Yet the 2004 Forum meeting once again 'urged members who had not yet done so to enact and implement existing model legislative provisions'.[271] The new statutes enacted in the last four years provide evidence that the Forum's efforts have borne fruit. However, some members that have had drafts prepared for them by consultants supported by the Forumsec have yet to legislate, and implementation is incomplete.[272] There are a number of possible explanations for the difficulties PICs have had in responding to the Honiara Declaration, all of which bear further investigation.

---

[264] See Herman, above n 20, 31.
[265] *Forum Communiqué*, Thirty-Second Pacific Islands Forum, Republic of Nauru, 16–18 August 2001, [38].
[266] Statement of the then Secretary General of the Forum Noel Levi to the 2001 Pacific Islands Law Officers Meeting, 22 October 2001, *Press Statement 81/01*, Pacific Islands Forum <http://www.forumsec.org.fj/news/2001/Oct04.htm> at 29 December 2003.
[267] *Forum Communiqué*, Thirty-Third Pacific Islands Forum, Suva, Fiji Islands, 15–17 August, 2002, [7].
[268] Ibid [8].
[269] Above n 262.
[270] Radio Australia News, 1 October 2003, Australian Broadcasting Corporation <http://www.abc.net.au/ra/newstories/RANewsStories_957745.htm> at 29 December 2003.
[271] *Forum Communiqué*, Thirty-Fifth Pacific Islands Forum, Apia, Samoa, 3–10 August 2004, [27].
[272] Transform Aqorau, *Implementation of the Honiara Declaration: National Case Study (Draft)*, 2004, 2 (paper on file with the author).

PICs confront a problem of legislative modernization in all areas of law. Newton notes strikingly that 'law reform is not a high priority in most South Pacific jurisdictions, largely due to a lack of available resources'.[273] In criminal justice systems where small numbers of poorly resourced officials[274] still apply colonial era laws, struggle to report cases and update official collections of legislation,[275] enacting and enforcing transnational criminal laws is not going to proceed as smoothly as others might hope. The fact that it has happened at all is because of outside intervention. Only this intervention has overcome the natural response of PICs to prioritize pressing viability issues rather than lawmaking. PICs are almost completely dependant on technical assistance in respect of the legislative response necessary to meet obligations under suppression conventions. The 1998 FRSC Action Plan provided for legal drafting assistance to implement the Declaration. In response, the Forumsec supplies frameworks, model legislation, technical expertise, funds and the necessary impetus to help Forum members to draft and vet the necessary laws. Developed states, heavy funders of the Forumsec,[276] also provide direct assistance. Some PICs may simply have to wait for help. For example, reform of Tuvalu's drug trafficking legislation depends on the finalization of the regional model drug trafficking law and the provision of assistance to implement it. Others may use this as an excuse for inaction. For example, Vanuatu, in turn, has decided to wait to bring the Vanuatu Convention against Illicit Traffic in Narcotic Drugs and Psychotropic Substances Ratification Act No. 27 of 2001 into force until it had 'confirmation that other Pacific countries have enacted the Model law on Illicit Drug Control prepared with the assistance of the Forum Secretariat'. However, the Forumsec is unable to intervene until it is formally requested to do so by the Forum member.[277]

A more formal regional system where members are obliged to bring laws into operation by a specified date and regional organs have greater powers of intervention might overcome such problems. It must be observed, however, that technical assistance is a necessary but not sufficient condition of modernization. Many of these laws struggle through the technical stages of development or are held up in Parliament itself, which suggests that there are other reasons preventing change. Some of these involve the negotiation process and the nature of the organs and individuals involved. Disjuncture between regional declarations negotiated by diplomats and the implementation of these measures by criminal justice officials

---

[273] Tess Newton, 'Sources of Criminal Law in the South Pacific', *University of the South Pacific Occasional Papers Series*, Occasional Paper no. 6, 5.

[274] Australian Senate Foreign Affairs, Defence and Trade Committee Report, above n 23, 192.

[275] Newton, above n 273, 19.

[276] In 2001 PILAD's internal budget (member's contributions) was F$421,000 and it spent F$502,000 while its extra budget (the list of external funders of the Forum for all purposes is Australia, New Zealand, Japan, the EU, France, Portugal, the UNDP, ESCAP, Canada, Taiwan, the UK and US) was F$2,600,000 and it spent F$1,403,000. In 2002 PILAD's internal budget was F$475,000 and it spent F$508,000 while its extra budget was F$4,204,000 and it spent F$2,184000. *Pacific Islands Forum Annual Report*, 2001–2002 (2002) 24 and *Pacific Islands Forum Annual Report*, 2002–2003 (2003) 27.

[277] See Aqorau, above n 272, 4.

can be a problem, which can be compounded by turf wars, poor communication and poor coordination.[278] The use of foreign consultants may be perceived as intrusive and disempowering. Finally, resistance to legal change in PICs may arise through fear or economic benefit to officials and policymakers. Conflicting interests are most obvious around the regulation of OFCs. Formal legal obligations do pose a risk to the 'grey' economies of PICs. Designed to suppress the activities of transnational criminals involved with drugs and small arms, the new laws become equally available against petty traffickers and smugglers of all kinds, tax evaders and participants in the unregulated economy, which brings into prospect a more general resistance to compliance.[279]

These are just some possible explanations for the generally slow pace of legislative modernization under Forumsec tutelage. The further problem is explaining why, when new laws have been enacted, the evidence suggests that implementation of these laws by the law enforcement authorities of PICs is poor. To be fair, these laws may be having an unknowable deterrent effect. Many are new so there may have been little opportunity to use them. Having said that, modelled as they are on the laws of highly developed criminal justice systems and containing a plethora of complex and obscure rules, implementation costs are high and sometimes prohibitive in PICs, so they may not be applied. A significant problem for implementation of these new laws is poor law enforcement capacity. The AFP cites a lack of resources, poor education, inadequate recruitment, poor wages, poor conditions of service, inadequate financial management practices, ineffective leadership, inadequate basic policing skills, stagnant demographics, donor fatigue, inadequate communications and infrastructure, and geographic remoteness as factors compounding this incapacity.[280] Although police to population ratios are significantly lower in the islands than they are in Australia or New Zealand, this may indicate inefficiency and present more of a problem than a solution, particularly when these forces become directly involved in politics.[281] Corruption is a problem for capacity, and although it is low, indications are that it is penetrating police organizations and the potential for direct police involvement in transnational crime should not be ignored.

The solution may be greater provision of resources. However, critics question whether this will help, pointing to the futility of using more resources to shore up developed state policing models that are inappropriate to the social situations in the region.[282] Others suggest that the sharing and enhancing of existing capacity is possible through a cooperative multi-agency approach.[283]

---

[278] Aqorau, above n 272, 3.
[279] Berta Hernandez, 'RIP to IRP – Money laundering and drug trafficking controls score a knockout victory over bank secrecy' (1993) 18 *North Carolina Journal of International Law and Commercial Regulation* 235, 293-5.
[280] Australian Senate Foreign Affairs, Defence and Trade Committee Report, above n 23, 194-5, citing *Committee Hansard*, 27 March 2003, 358 (AFP).
[281] Newton, above n 84, 5-6.
[282] Newton, above n 84, 13-14.
[283] Aqorau, above n 47, 12.

Developed states are obviously cognisant of the problems of capacity. Much of the progress that has been made in modernizing PIC's law enforcement practices can be attributed to technical support from developed states[284] and the Forumsec has become involved in the facilitation of this technical support. But the AFP questions the utility of regional meetings and conferences and of training in Australia and New Zealand when local conditions demand in-country training and 'back to basics' in recruitment and training.[285] A standing regional police to make up for problems of local operational incapacity has been rejected.[286] But it appears unnecessary if that incapacity, at least in respect of transnational crime, is already being met by the AFP and NZP through liaison officers and the PTCCC.

Lastly, we do not know whether, if the new laws are enacted, and problems of implementation are overcome, they will actually work. The South Pacific has only got the examples of developed states to rely upon, and the effectiveness of these laws is highly contentious.[287] Moreover, little provision appears to have been made for actually monitoring the effectiveness of this legislation in suppression of transnational crime. Steps need to be taken at the regional level to ensure that empirical research is done on how the application of individual measures actually impacts on the harm threatened so that these measures can be adjusted appropriately.

Towards a regional transnational criminal law regime in the South Pacific

The South Pacific as a spatial and social entity

It is trite to say that the difficulties of sovereignty, differences in criminal laws and different experiences of crime present enormous obstacles to the development of a regional transnational criminal law regime in the South Pacific. However, borrowing from the literature on globalization,[288] it seems that there are at least two fundamental aspects to any process of regionalizing identification of and response to crime. The first is the objective fact of interconnectedness: the region is in some sense, because of communications, economic and social links, geography and, in certain cases, ethnicity, one place. The International Association of Criminal Law takes this view when it notes that 'regionalisation' equates to 'developing methods of international collaboration linking at least three independent states belonging to

---

[284] For example, Japan has played a significant role in providing technical support, expertise, training and funding to facilitate the combating of crime in the Pacific. See Tunidau, above n 90, 399.
[285] Australian Senate Foreign Affairs, Defence and Trade Committee Report, above n 23, 194-5, citing *Committee Hansard*, 27 March 2003, 358 (AFP).
[286] The Australian Senate Foreign Affairs, Defence and Trade Committee rejected this option – see above n 23, 205.
[287] Consider the war on drugs.
[288] Roland Robertson, *Globalization* (1992) 8.

a clearly specified geographical entity'.[289] This interconnectedness facilitates all human activity including criminal and legal activity. The extent to which the South Pacific is a region in this sense is questionable; it occupies an identifiable geographical space but communications are poor, trade and social contact difficult.[290] It may look more like a region from without than from within. In addition, however, a region exists because the people within it subjectively consider it to be a single place. It is not clear to what extent the peoples of the South Pacific consider themselves as belonging to one place. The region is not socially well integrated;[291] PICs have stronger connections within Micronesia, Melanesia and Polynesia, and individually with New Zealand and Australia, than with states in the South Pacific region as a whole. This makes regional cooperation difficult, and means that responses arise through the agency of the two regional powers. Whether their motivations are selfish, or altruistic, it appears as though the region is partially a construct imposed by these and other developed states in order to police the transnational criminals operating in PICs. Paradoxically, the region is, at least in part, being assembled by foreign criminals and foreign law enforcement agents.

An exercise in hegemony?

Transnational criminal law is a rationalist intrusion based on the suppression of harm into a world of economic globalization driven by desire for goods both licit and illicit.[292] As the Australian Attorney General's Department put it in a report on the criminal environment in the South Pacific, 'there is a need to reconcile two seemingly contradictory aims: trade liberalisation and the effective control of transnational criminal activities'.[293] The 'invisible hand' of the market seeks to supply both licit and illicit demands, but the licit market cannot 'supply' suppression of the illicit market, so the state must. Because PICs are unable to supply this good, developed states do so out of self-interest. Given that, as Hughes puts it, 'much of the agenda of the small island states is written elsewhere',[294] the development of a regional transnational criminal law in the South Pacific is open to the criticism that it is an exercise in hegemony, and not the dispersal of a global public good.

The Honiara Declaration and its antecedents implicitly claim legitimacy because they are a projection of the global rule of law through international law. But international law is not always considered to be the universalist project that it claims to be. Critics condemn it as an instrumental tool for advancing the interests

---

[289] *La Revue Internationale de Droit Pénal* (1994) 21.

[290] See, for example, the travails of Air Pacific and the Pacific Forum Line, set up to link PICs, and despite considerable foreign subsidization, considered failures – Crocombe, *The South Pacific*, above n 21, 606ff.

[291] Crocombe, *The South Pacific*, above n 21, 591ff, is critical of the notion that there is a South Pacific region.

[292] On these two views of globalization see Silbey, above n 3.

[293] Australian Senate Foreign Affairs, Defence and Trade Committee Report, above n 23, 190, citing submission 34, 1 (Attorney-General's Department).

[294] Hughes, above n 57, 47.

of particular peoples, nations and regions at the expense of others.[295] Delmas-Marty warns that:

> ... hegemony is imposed overtly, in the form of what can be called imperial law, or covertly, either through the apparent consent of countries to which dominant legal systems are exported like simple merchandise, or through the appearance of legal no man's lands, where the law of the market reigns.[296]

In her view hegemony encourages a total war without mercy against transnational crime.[297] The specific danger is over-criminalization. She suggests that one response is to assert a criminal justice policy that avoids sole reliance on penalization and uses other sanctions and administrative measures to achieve its goals; another is to impose 'a strict definition of concepts such as terrorism or money laundering, which are too often criminalized for purely political reasons'.[298] Suspicious of a free market in suppression which exports foreign laws to states, she supports a moral trade, and considers that this requires a global criminal law enforceable against everyone, including the most powerful economic or political actors. She believes that the ethical basis of such a law will lead to a supranational conception that aims to protect all humanity.[299]

Given that transnational criminal law is largely instrumental to the needs of developed states concerned about extraterritorial crime, it is difficult to conceive how it can provide a supra-national, universal, ethical criminal law in the sense that Delmas Marty suggests and still remain popular with developed states. To suggest an example, if a PIC that has large scale local usage of cannabis wished to adopt new drug legislation in order to meet its obligations under article 3(2) of the 1988 Drug Trafficking Convention to suppress simple possession by either a) allowing for non-prosecution of possession and diversion, or b) construing possession in a limited way to the same effect, it seems likely that this PIC would be subject to a great deal of international pressure to mend its ways. Silbey is less sanguine about the possibilities of establishing universal human values in this context:

> ... I am concerned about the consequences of marketing specific legal devices as if they were one of those dresses that fit all sizes. I am worried about how local justice can be achieved within a supposedly universal, all purpose, one size fits all law.[300]

She believes that there is no likelihood of pluralism; the globalization of Western laws, including by implication transnational criminal laws, is purely instrumental to Western purposes and will not be appropriated or reconstructed by the locals

---

[295] Makua Wa Matua, 'Critical Race Theory and International Law: The View of an Insider-Outsider' (2001) 45 *Villanova Law Review* 841.
[296] Above n 5, 3.
[297] Mireille Delmas-Marty, 'Criminal Law as Ethics of Globalisation' [2004] *Humanitäres Völkerrecht-Informationsschriften* 4, 4.
[298] Ibid 5.
[299] Ibid.
[300] Above n 3, 222.

themselves.[301] It is unclear precisely how much space for appropriation and adaptation to meet local needs island leaders have when they take these laws. However, it is notable that the regional concerns, such as indigenous issues, added to the end of the Honiara Declaration's catalogue, have since been neglected in the process of legislative modernization.

Why then, do island leaders accept the need for these laws? Ikenberry and Kupchan argue that local elites adopt the hegemon's norms principally because of material incentives, but also because the hegemon changes their substantive beliefs.[302] This socialization is achieved through a combination of technical assistance and advice from policy advisors and pressure groups. The leaders may 'agree' for strategic purposes such as gaining legitimacy in the eyes of international society; however, such 'agreement' is unlikely to result in suppression. Even if the recent legislative reforms mean that island leaders are now convinced that transnational crime does threaten their societies, this may not achieve real change if that acceptance is not shared generally. The populace may be hostile because of over-criminalization and draconian police powers,[303] or they may not consider these laws a priority given their other problems. These views may alter under the impact of media concern and the activities of civil society concerned about, for example, trafficked women and drug-induced harm. Nevertheless, the top-down nature of the modernizing program that is transnational penal norm transfer means that even if elite compliance is achieved, it may not generate the kind of social compliance necessary to effectively suppress these forms of behaviour.

Effectiveness

The absence of such social compliance means that developed states have limited options when it comes to pursuing the effective suppression of extraterritorial crime in the South Pacific. The current option appears to be to use technical assistance to modernize laws and effect surrogate policing through local law enforcement. However, even if these criminal activities also have a negative local impact, this kind of intervention is unlikely to generate popular support for suppression of these offences, and foreign 'supervision' of local policing will generate hostility. An alternative approach would be to wait until these criminal activities begin to have such a negative local impact – through, for example, increased hard drug use – that local populations seek external help. Aside from its ethical problems, this impact may not occur, and even if it does locals may not

---

[301] Above n 3, 223.
[302] John Ikenberry and Charles Kupchan, 'Socialization and Hegemonic Power' (1990) 44 *International Organization* 283, 285ff.
[303] For a case study of such a response see Sappho Xenakis, *The International versus Domestic Pressures on the Development of Organised Crime Policy: The Case of Greece* (Paper presented at the 2nd ECPR Conference, 18–21 September 2003, Marburg), European Consortium for Political Research <http://www.essex.ac.uk/ecpr/events/generalconference/papers/19/10/xenakis> at 15 January 2004.

seek help to suppress activities that do not have a local effect, but do have consequences abroad. A more appropriate option, which does not prioritize the global aspects of transnational crime at the expense of ignoring its local aspects,[304] may be to develop and support laws and law enforcement mechanisms that are versatile enough to be used to suppress both local and transnational criminal activities. Money laundering laws that can be and importantly are used against the laundering of the proceeds of fisheries fraud, or corruption laws that can be and again are used against corrupt local politicians as well as transnational corruption, are likely to engender more local support than laws and enforcement perceived solely to be in the interests of developed states. This approach can be adopted through the negotiation of regional crime control conventions that adequately meet local as well as external concerns, after regional crime control institutions have engaged in adequate empirical research to identify these concerns.

The next steps

The members of the South Pacific Forum are under pressure to regionalize. Some of this pressure comes from outside the region. The European Union, for example, is driving regionalization by linking it to the grant of development aid under the Cotonou Agreement.[305] Some pressure comes from within the region. The Review of the Forum by the Forum Eminent Person's Group in 2003–2004 resulted in the Auckland Declaration, produced by the Forum Leaders Special Retreat in Auckland on 6 April 2004. It proposed a Pacific Plan that 'would create stronger and deeper links between sovereign countries of the region and identify the sectors where the region could gain the most from sharing resources of governance and aligning policies'.[306] The 2004 Forum reiterated that the Pacific Plan was to be the main instrument for the promotion of a new Pacific vision.[307] The desired outcome appears to be efficiency, to discard the more time consuming aspects of the 'Pacific Way'[308] that prevent adaptation to modern conditions. Security from transnational crime is one of a number of forces driving regionalization.[309] Constructed as a

---

[304] See generally Richard Hobbs, 'Going Down the Glocal: The Local Context of Organised Crime' (1998) 37 *The Howard Journal of Criminal Justice* 407-422.

[305] *Partnership agreement between the members of the African, Caribbean and Pacific Group of States of the one part, and the European Community and its Member States, of the other part*, signed 23 June 2000 [2000] OJ L 317/3 (entered into force 1 April 2003). See Malakai Koloamatangi, 'EU, Cotonou and EPAs: the view from the Pacific Islands' (2003) 200 *The Courier ACP-EU* 14.

[306] *Auckland Declaration*, Pacific Island Forum Leaders Special Retreat, Auckland 6 April 2004, [1], Pacific Islands Forum <http://www.forumsec.org.fj/docs/Gen_Docs/Auckland_Declaration.pdf> at 14 December 2004.

[307] *Forum Communiqué*, Thirty-Fifth Pacific Islands Forum, Apia, Samoa, 3–10 August 2004, [3].

[308] See generally Crocombe, 'The Pacific Plan', above n 78, 159.

[309] The Eminent Person's Group Report consider that 'processes for meeting international legal demands' and 'regional law enforcement aimed at transnational crime' are areas that would benefit from greater shared effort. See above n 200.

problem of the integrity of these PICs as sovereign entities,[310] it provides a powerful, if overstated, rationalization for some attenuation of their sovereignty.

However, this shift to greater regionalization is likely to be resisted because it is being imposed on the Pacific by developed states that see it as the best way of managing the region. Moreover, greater regionalization points to tighter legal regulation, which may also be resisted; as Crocombe points out, the Forum has thus far 'successfully kept the lawyers at bay'.[311] On the positive side, a stronger independent regional organization may provide some compensation for loss of sovereignty if it offers PICs a greater opportunity to exercise a new regional sovereignty. In responding to transnational crime, for example, the region may have more control over choosing what to consider criminal, to respond with appropriate legal measures and to adjust this response according to the efficacy of these measures, than an individual state responding to outside pressure. Regionalization may also provide a greater opportunity to counterbalance the negative effects of the suppression of transnational crime by guaranteeing due process in inter-state cooperation on investigation, the gathering of evidence and the transfer of suspects.[312] We can only speculate at this stage about what form greater regional cooperation in the suppression of transnational crime might take, if it occurs at all. While it is likely to go beyond the Honiara Declaration's soft-law, it is unlikely to take the form of supra-national criminal law; even within the EU the regulation of criminal matters is still dealt largely through international treaty.[313] A possible next step for Forum members is to provide either for a regional treaty to suppress a range of transnational crimes or for separate regional treaties focusing on specific crimes.

---

[310] See, e.g. Schloenhardt, above n 17, 191; Shibuya, above n 46, 2, 4.
[311] Crocombe, 'The Pacific Plan', above n 78.
[312] Delmas-Marty, above n 6, vi. This has happened elsewhere: in the European legal space, criminal law cooperation was made palatable by regional human rights cooperation. See Geert Cortsens and Jean Pradel, *European Criminal Law* (2002) generally. It is notable that the Forum has raised human rights as a more recent concern. See the Eminent Person's Group Report, above n 200. The 2000 Biketawa Declaration explicitly links the effective suppression of transnational crime with respect for individual human rights. See generally Steve Peers, *EU Justice and Home Affairs Law* (2000) 15-30, 48-62.
[313] See Peers, above n 312.

Appendix

Mutual assistance in criminal matters

Australia

    Mutual Assistance in Criminal Matters Act 1987 (1987)
    Foreign Evidence Act 1994 (1994)

Cook Islands

    Mutual Assistance in Criminal Matters Act No. 9 of 2003 (2003)

Federated States of Micronesia

    FSM Foreign Evidence Act of 2000 (not yet in force)
    FSM Mutual Assistance in Criminal Matters Act of 2000 (2001)

Fiji

    Mutual Assistance in Criminal Matters Act 1997 (1998)
    Mutual Assistance in Criminal Matters Amendment Bill under discussion

Kiribati

    Mutual Assistance in Criminal Matters Act 2003 (2003)
    Evidence Act 2003 (2003)

New Zealand

    Mutual Assistance in Criminal Matters Act 1992 as amended in 1998 (1992; 1999).

Niue

    Mutual Assistance in Criminal Matters Act 1998 (1998)

Palau

    Mutual Assistance in Criminal Matters Act 2001 (2001)
    Foreign Evidence Act of 2001 (2001)

Republic of the Marshall Islands

    Mutual Assistance in Criminal Matters Act, 2002 (2002)
    Foreign Evidence Act 2002 (2002)

Solomon Islands

    Mutual Assistance in Criminal Matters Act 2002 (2002)

Tonga

    Foreign Evidence Act 2000 (2000)
    Mutual Assistance in Criminal Matters Act 2000 (2000)

Tuvalu

    Mutual Assistance in Criminal Matters Bill drafted but further assistance requested from Forumsec

Vanuatu

    Mutual Assistance in Criminal Matters Act No. 14 of 2002 (2003)

Money laundering, asset forfeiture and banking regulation

Australia

    Proceeds of Crime Act 2002 (2003)
    Division 400 Criminal Code Act 1995 (2003)

Cook Islands

    Financial Transactions Reporting Act No. 10 of 2003 (2003)
    Financial Supervisory Commission Act No. 11 of 2003 (2003)
    International Companies Amendment Act No. 5 of 2003 (2003)
    Banking (substantive Act of 57) No. 7 of 2003 (2003)
    Crimes Amendment Act No. 6 of 2003 (2003)
    Criminal Procedure Amendment Act 2003 (2003)
    Proceeds of Crime Act No. 12 of 2003 (2003)

Federated States of Micronesia

    FSM Money Laundering and Proceeds of Crime Act of 2000 (2001)
    FSM Cooperation in Law Enforcement Act of 2001 (not yet submitted to Congress)

Fiji

    Part V of the Proceeds of Crime Act 1997 (1998)
    Proceeds of Crime Act 1998 (1998)

Kiribati

    Proceeds of Crime Act 2003 (2003)
    Kiribati draft bill on money laundering

Nauru

    Anti-Money Laundering Act, 28 August 2001
    Anti-Money Laundering Act 2003
    Anti-Money Laundering (Amendment) Act 2004
    Draft Proceeds of Crime Act Banking (Amendment) Act 2004

New Zealand

    Proceeds of Crime Act 1991 (1992)
    Crimes Act 1961 (1995)
    Misuse of Drugs Amendment Act 1998 (1999)

Niue

    Proceeds of Crime Act 1998 (1998)
    Financial Transaction Reporting Act 2000

Palau

    Money Laundering and Proceeds of Crime Act of 2001 (2001)
    Financial Institutions Act of 2001 (2001)

Papua New Guinea

    Draft Bill on Proceeds of Crime, 2003

Republic of the Marshall Islands

    Banking (Amendment) Act 2000 (2000)
    Banking (Amendment) Act 2002 (2002)
    Banking (Amendment) Act, 2003
    Proceeds of Crime Act, 2002 (2002)

Samoa

    Money Laundering Prevention Act 2000 (2000)
    Money Laundering Prevention Amendment Act 2000 (2000)

Solomon Islands

    Money Laundering and Proceeds of Crime Act 2002 (2002)

Tonga

    Money Laundering and Proceeds of Crime Act 2000 (2000)

Tuvalu

    Proceeds of Crime Bill drafted but further assistance requested from the Forumsec

Vanuatu

    The Serious Offences (Confiscation of Proceeds) Act 1989
    Proceeds of Crime Act No. 13 of 2002 (2003)
    Financial Transactions Reporting Act No. 33 of 2000 (2000)
    International Banking Act No. 4 of 2002

Extradition

Australia

    Extradition Act 1988 (1988)

Cook Islands

    Extradition Act No. 8 of 2003 (2003)

Federated States of Micronesia

    FSM Trans-national Extradition and Transfer of Convicted Persons Act of 2000 (legislation introduced but not yet passed)
    FSM Interstate Extradition Act of 2000 (legislation introduced but not yet passed)

Fiji

    Extradition Act 2003 (not in force)

Kiribati

    Extradition Act 2003 (2003)

New Zealand

> Extradition Act 1999 (1999)

Niue

> Extradition Act 1998 (1998)

Palau

> Extradition and Transfer Act of 2001 (signed by President but not clear if necessary regulations promulgated)

Republic of the Marshall Islands

> Trans-national Extradition and Transfer of Convicted Persons Act, 2003

Papua New Guinea

> Extradition Act 1975 (1975)

Samoa

> Extradition Act 1974 (1975)
> Extradition Amendment Act 1994
> Prevention and Suppression of Terrorism Act 2002

Solomon Islands

> Extradition Act 1987 (1987)

Tonga

> Extradition Act 1993 (1994)

Tuvalu

> Extradition Bill has passed first reading

Vanuatu

> Extradition Act No. 16 of 2002 (2003)

Drug offences

Australia

> Commonwealth Crimes (Traffic in Narcotic Drugs and Psychotropic Substances) Act 1990 (1990)
> Commonwealth Customs Act 1901 (1901)
> Commonwealth Customs (Prohibited Import) Regulations 1956
> Commonwealth Customs (Prohibited Export) Legislation 1958 (1958)
> Commonwealth Narcotic Drugs Act 1967 (1968)
> Commonwealth Psychotropic Substance Act 1976 (1976)
> National Drug Strategy (for treatment and rehabilitation)
> ACT Poisons and Drugs Act 1978 (1978)
> ACT Drugs of Dependence Act 1989 (1989)
> ACT Drugs of Dependence Regulations 1993 (1993)
> NSW Drug Misuse and Trafficking Act 1985 (1985)
> NSW Poisons and Therapeutic Goods Act 1966 (1966)
> NT Poisons and Dangerous Drugs Act 1983 (1983)
> Misuse of Drugs Act NT 1990 (1990)
> QLD Health Act 1937 (1937)
> QLD Health (Drugs and Poisons) Regulations 1966 (1966)
> QLD Health (Drugs and Poisons Regulations 1996 (1996)
> QLD Drugs Misuse Act 1986 (1986)
> QLD Health Regulation 1966 (1966)
> QLD Health Regulation 1996 (1996)
> SA Controlled Substances Act 1984 (1984)
> Tasmania Poisons Act 1971 (1971)
> Victorian Drugs, Poisons and Controlled Substances Act 1981 (1981)
> Victorian Alcoholics and Drug Dependent Persons Act 1986 (1986)
> WA Poisons Act 1964 (1964)
> WA Poisons Amendment Act 1995 (1995)
> WA Misuse of Drugs Act 1981 (1981)

Cook Islands

> Misuse of Drugs Bill under consideration (not yet in force)

Federated States of Micronesia

> Controlled Substances Act, 11 FSMC section 1101 ff (1982)
> FSM Controlled Substances Act 2000 (pending)

Fiji

> Dangerous Drugs Act 1938, as amended (1938)
> Dangerous Drugs Decree 1990 (1990)

Customs Act 1968 (1968)
Pharmacy and Poisons Act 1938 (1938)
Dangerous Drugs (Amendment) Decree 1991 (not in force)
Illicit Drug Control Act (2004)

Kiribati

Dangerous Drugs Ordinance 1977 (1977)
Pharmacy and Poisons Ordinance
Evidence Act 2003 (2003)

New Zealand

Misuse of Drugs Act 1975 (1977)
Misuse of Drugs Amendment Act 1998 (1999)
Crimes Act 1961 as amended in 1996 (1962; 1996)
Proceeds of Crime Act 1991 (1991)
Financial Transactions Reporting Act 1996 (1996)
Sentencing Act 2002 (2002)
Alcoholism and Drug Addiction Act 1966 (1969)
Mutual Assistance in Criminal Matters Act 1992 as amended in 1998 (1993; 1999)
Evidence Act 1908 (1908)

Niue

Misuse of Drugs Act 1998 (1998)

Palau

Controlled Substances Act, Chapters 30-33 of Title 34 of the Palau National Code

Papua New Guinea

Customs Act 1951 (1951)
Poisons and Dangerous Substances Act 1952 (1952)
Dangerous Drugs Act 1952 (1955)
Drugs Act Ch 229 (1955)
Pharmacy Act Ch. 94 (1955)
Dangerous Drugs (Extension of Definition) Act 1968 (1968)
Dangerous Drugs (Possession) Act 1970 (1970)
Public Health Act 1974 (1974)
Criminal Code Ch. 262 (1975)
Customs (Prohibited Imports) Regulation

National Narcotics Control Board Act 1992 (1992)
Medicines and Cosmetics Act of 1999 (not yet in force)

Republic of the Marshall Islands

Narcotic Drugs (Prohibition and Control Act) 1987 as amended (1987; 1992; 2002)

Samoa

Narcotics Act 1967 (1967)
Food and Drugs Act 1967 (1967)
Pharmacy Act 1976 (1976)
Customs Act 1977 (1977)
Maritime Zones Act 1999 (1999)

Tonga

Regional model legislation currently being vetted by Crown Law Office

Vanuatu

Dangerous Drugs Regulation (Amendment) Act 1984 (original Act 1939)
Convention against Illicit Traffic in Narcotic Drugs and Psychotropic Substances Ratification Act No. 27 of 2001 (?)
The Serious Offences (Confiscation of Proceeds) Act 1989 (1990)

Terrorism

Australia

Crimes (Aviation) Act 1991
Crimes (Ships and Fixed Platforms) Act 1992
Nuclear Non-Proliferation (Safeguards) Act 1987 (in force 1987)
Crimes (Hostages) Act 1989 (in force 1990)
Crimes (Internationally Protected Persons) Act 1976 (in force 1977)
Criminal Code Amendments (Suppression of Terrorists Bombings) Act 2002 (in force 2002)
Suppression of the Financing of Terrorism Act 2002 (in force 2002)

Republic of the Marshall Islands

Counter-Terrorism Act, 2002 (2002)

Fiji

    Penal and Criminal Procedure Codes
    Civil Aviation (Security) Act 1994

Nauru

    Combating Financing Terrorism Bill in process

Palau

    Draft Omnibus Counter-Terrorism Bill introduced in 2003 but still awaiting further legislative action

Samoa

    The Prevention and Suppression of Terrorism Act 2002 (2002)

Maritime surveillance

Australia

    Border Protection Legislation Amendment Act 1999 which implements Article 17 of the 1988 Drug Trafficking Convention (in force 1999)

Federated States of Micronesia

    FSM Controlled Substances Act of 2000 (pending)

New Zealand

    Misuse of Drugs Act 1975 (1977)
    Customs and Excise Act 1996 (1996)
    Mutual Assistance in Criminal Matters Act 1992 as amended in 1998 (1993; 1999)

Samoa

    Maritime Zone Act 1999

Human trafficking

Australia

    Border Protection Legislation Amendment Act 1999 (1999)
    Crimes (Child Sex Tourism) Amendment Act 1994 (1994)

Criminal Code Amendment (Slavery and Sexual Servitude) Act 1999 (1999)
Migration Act 1958, Amendment 1999 (Cth), Division 12 (1999)
Crimes Legislation Amendment Act (Act No. 141 of 2002) (2002)
Human Rights (Sexual Conduct) Act 1994 (1994)

Cook Islands

The Entry, Residence and Departure Act 1971-72

Fiji

Immigration Act 2004 (before Parliament)
Passport Act 2002 (2002)

New Zealand

The Crimes Act 1961, Amendment of 1995 (1995)
The Children, Young Persons and their Families Act 1989 (1989)
Immigration Act 1987 (1987)
Prostitution Reform Act 2003 (2003)

Palau

Draft People Smuggling and People Trafficking Act, 2003, awaiting approval by Congress

Small arms proliferation

Australia

Mutual Assistance in Criminal Matters Act 1987 (in force 1987)
Proceeds of Crime Act 2002 (in force 2003)
Extradition Act 1988 (in force 1988)

Cook Islands

Crimes Act 1969
The CI Arms Ordinance Act 1954

Vanuatu

Penal Code Amendment Bill 2003
United Nations Convention against Transnational Organised Crime Ratification Bill 2003

Chapter 3

International Terrorism and the South Pacific

Alex Conte

Introduction

International terrorism is not a new phenomenon. Indeed, the origin of the word *terrorism* dates back to the French Revolution of 1788 as the label used by the establishment to describe the conduct of revolutionaries.[1] Likewise, terrorism has been a subject of concern with the United Nations since the 1960s, following a series of aircraft hijackings.[2] Notwithstanding the long-held attention of the international community upon terrorism, the subject deserves special attention within this book for several reasons. Terrorism has, some would argue, entered a new phase over recent decades (and as evident in the terrorist attacks of 11 September 2001): an age where trans-national activity has intensified and been made easier, and where technology and the media can be taken advantage of by terrorist entities to further the impact of terrorist conduct and the delivery of messages or fear-inducing images.[3]

Perhaps more importantly, the issue of terrorism is one that has not been responded to in meaningful terms by all Pacific Island countries, many failing to perceive a need for action in the absence of any immediate threat of terrorist conduct within their borders. This brings into play interesting issues concerning the aim of international counter-terrorism and the interface between international, regional and national security. The focus of this chapter, then, is upon the relevance of counter-terrorism to the South Pacific. Against that background, this chapter aims to consider firstly whether counter-terrorism is relevant to the South Pacific. Irrespective of the answer to that question, regard will also be had to the international anti-terrorist obligations of States within the South Pacific. Finally, an examination of the South Pacific response to those obligations will be undertaken.

In undertaking that examination, this chapter will focus its attention upon the South Pacific region, rather than the Pacific at large or the Asia-Pacific region. For

---

[1] French Ambassador to Fiji, His Excellency Berg, 'Terrorism: The New International Challenge' (Paper presented at the public workshop *How Should Fiji Respond to the Threat of Terrorism?*, Suva, Fiji, 17 July 2004, copy on file with author).
[2] Discussed further below.
[3] Berg, above n 1.

the purpose of this chapter, then, the countries upon which it will focus are those that are members of the Pacific Islands Forum, with particular attention paid to New Zealand.[4] It should be noted at this point that one could approach this topic by also addressing the influence of Australia as a 'driving force' behind counter-terrorism in the South Pacific. While it would be fair to do so, this chapter focuses instead on the question of international law and United Nations influences upon counter-terrorism in the region and the relevance of the topic (and responses to it) by the South Pacific in general.

How is counter-terrorism relevant to the South Pacific?

Other than the bombing by French military agents of the *Rainbow Warrior* in New Zealand in 1985, the South Pacific has not been subject to, or had to deal directly with, international terrorism. As such, many public submissions on counter-terrorist legislation within the region have questioned the need for action against international terrorism.[5] Similar views have been expressed by some leaders within the Pacific, seeing the region as an unlikely target of terrorism, such that counter-terrorism should be low on the list of the region's many priorities.[6] The question is valid, although a little simplistic, and the answer partly depends on the definition of terrorism being used. A legal reason for the pursuit of counter-terrorism in the South Pacific is that such action is an obligation at international law for most Pacific Forum members. This is not the same thing as a needs-based explanation for that pursuit. Three particularly important matters do, however, point to the relevance of counter-terrorism to the South Pacific. Before addressing each of those issues, it is important to have regard to the definition of terrorism.

What is terrorism?

In considering international counter-terrorism and its relevance to the South Pacific region, it must be acknowledged that there are problems associated with the definition of the term. The United Nations Terrorism Prevention Branch describes

---

[4] Australia, Cook Islands, Federated States of Micronesia, Fiji, Kiribati, Nauru, New Zealand (incorporating the non-self governing territory of Tokelau), Niue, Palau, Papua New Guinea, Republic of the Marshall Islands, Samoa, Solomon Islands, Tonga, Tuvalu, Vanuatu. This excludes French Polynesian States and American Samoa, being States that are governed by laws of France and the United States respectively.

[5] This was a common theme, for example, in the submissions made to the New Zealand Foreign Affairs, Defence and Trade Committee on the Terrorism Suppression Bill (as redrafted and contained within the Committee's interim report: Foreign Affairs, Defence and Trade Committee, *Interim Report on the Terrorism (Bombings and Financing) Bill*, 8 November 2001).

[6] Greg Urwin, 'The Need for Anti-Terrorism Legislation in Fiji' (Paper presented at the public workshop *How Should Fiji Respond to the Threat of Terrorism?*, Suva, Fiji, 17 July 2004, copy on file with author), [7].

terrorism as a unique form of crime. Terrorist acts, it says, often contain elements of warfare, politics and propaganda. It continues, stating that '[f]or security reasons and due to lack of popular support, terrorist organisations are usually small, making detection and infiltration difficult. Although the goals of terrorists are sometimes shared by wider constituencies, their methods are generally abhorred'.[7]

The inability of the international community to achieve consensus on a global definition of terrorism is one of the major obstacles facing the fight against terrorism. The Executive Director of the International Policy Institute for Counter-Terrorism, Boaz Ganor, has emphasized the point, saying that UN Security Council Resolutions can only have an effective impact once all States agree upon what type of acts constitute terrorism.[8] Despite this, there is still no definition of the term to which all States subscribe.

Generally speaking, the twelve international treaties on counter-terrorism[9] deal with specific forms of terrorist conduct and are therefore precise in nature and not of general application. Furthermore, they are not a solution in themselves, since treaties are only binding upon States parties.[10] Nor does the United Nations Charter contain a definition of the term. The Rome Statute of the International Criminal Court does not include terrorism as one of the international crimes within the Court's jurisdiction.[11] Perhaps most surprising is the fact that Security Council Resolution 1373, which imposes various obligations concerning counter-terrorism, does not define the term.[12]

---

[7] United Nations Office for Drug Control and Crime Prevention, 'UN Action Against Terrorism', <http://www.odccp.org/terrorism.html> at 19 June 2002.
[8] Boaz Ganor, 'Security Council Resolution 1269: What it Leaves Out', 25 October 1999, web site of the International Policy Institute for Counter-Terrorism, <http://www.ict.org.il/articles/articledet.cfm?articleid=93> at 1 June 2002.
[9] To be discussed further in this chapter.
[10] *Pacta tertii nec nocent nec prosunt.*
[11] Statute of the International Criminal Court, opened for signature 17 July 1998, 2187 UNTS 90 (entered into force 1 July 2002). The Court has within its jurisdiction the 'most serious international crimes', according to its preamble. It was proposed, within the draft Statute, to include terrorism within the Court's jurisdiction, but the failure of States to agree upon a definition of the term resulted in the crime being removed from the scope of the Court's jurisdiction and subject matter of the constitutive treaty. There are arguments, however, that terrorist acts fall within the jurisdiction of the Court as constituting crimes against humanity, as crimes under article 7 of the Rome Statute.
[12] Having said this, the lack of definition was most likely due to the fact (as will be seen through subsequent discussions) that there is a lack of consensus on just what amounts to terrorism. In a desire to issue a forceful, and at the same time early, resolution in the wake of September 11 it is likely that the Council saw use of the term, without definition, as the only viable option in the short term. The problem with this approach is that it has left the question of defining the term with individual member States, leading to inconsistent definitions and, arguably, a weak rather than forceful resolution.

Attempts to define terrorism

Attempts to define the term have been made since before the establishment of the United Nations. The Draft League of Nations Convention for the Prevention and Punishment of Terrorism was to provide that terrorism comprised:

> All criminal acts directed against a State and intended or calculated to create a state of terror in the minds of particular persons or a group of persons or the general public.[13]

This provision was never adopted due to dissent over the definition.

There have been suggestions that terrorism be defined as the peacetime equivalent of war crimes. In a report to the UN Crime Branch, Schmidt proposed taking the already agreed upon definition of war crimes (comprising deliberate attacks on civilians, hostage taking and the killing of prisoners) and extending it to peacetime.[14] Terrorism would then be simply defined as the 'peacetime equivalents of war crimes'. Again, however, this did not gain acceptance. Schmidt appears to have been more successful in gaining acceptance of a more complex definition of terrorism, as identified by the UN Office for Drug Control and Crime Prevention (ODCCP):

> An anxiety-inspiring method of repeated violent action, employed by a (semi-) clandestine individual, group or state actors, for idiosyncratic, criminal or political reasons, whereby – in contrast to assassination – the direct targets of violence are not the main targets. The immediate human victims of violence are generally chosen randomly (targets of opportunity) or selectively (representative or symbolic targets) from a target population, and serve as message generators. Threat and violence-based communication processes between terrorist (organisation), (imperilled) victims, and main targets are used to manipulate the main target (audience(s)), turning it into a target of terror, a target of demands, or a target of attention, depending on what intimidation, coercion, or propaganda is primarily sought.[15]

What might be observed is that the common threads throughout this, and various other, definitions are as follows: firstly, that the *physical* targets of a terrorist act are not the *intended* targets (the target against whom a message is being sent, usually a government or international organization); next, that the purpose of the threat or violence is to intimidate and create a situation of fear or terror (hence the term *terror*ism); and, finally, that this is intended to persuade or dissuade the primary target to do or abstain from doing something, in pursuit of some ideological reason(s).

---

[13] Geneva Convention for the Prevention and Punishment of Terrorism (Draft, 1937).
[14] This definition was put to the United Nations Crime Branch by Alexander Schmidt in 1992: see the web site of the United Nations Office for Drug Control and Crime Prevention, 'Definitions of Terrorism', <http://www.odccp.org/terrorism_definitions.html> at 19 June 2002.
[15] Ibid.

Why a lack of consensus?

The sticking point, it seems, is not so much with the technical wording of what physical conduct amounts to a terrorist act (what might be seen as an objective definition). The problem appears to lie with the purpose of the conduct (incorporating subjective elements). For instance, does a bombing carried out by a rebel group, which is directed towards the destabilization of oppressive authorities (the Pol Pot Regime, for example), amount to a terrorist act or an act of 'freedom fighters'? The point to make is that this is not just a cliché. To give two very striking examples, the United States' list of the most wanted terrorists[16] once featured Yasser Arafat and Nelson Mandela (both of whom were subsequently awarded the Nobel Peace Prize); clearly evidence that this is a highly political and controversial issue. An observation made by a journalist on this point encapsulates the issue very nicely, when he noted that 'terrorists are those who use violence against the side that is using the word'.[17]

A number of States argue that a subjective analysis and definition of such conduct (by examining the purpose of the conduct) should therefore be made. The United Nations ODCCP reports that Arab States such as Libya, Syria and Iran have all campaigned for a definition that excludes acts of 'freedom fighters' from the international definition of terrorism by employing the argument that a justified goal may be pursued by any available means.[18]

While it must be acknowledged that these positions are firmly held by a number of States, it should also be pointed out that the majority of States adhere to an objective definition of terrorism (one which does not take into account the motives of the conduct). In 1994, the UN General Assembly adopted the Declaration on Measures to Eliminate International Terrorism.[19] The Declaration was based on the notion of peace and security and the principle of refraining from the threat or use of force in international relations.[20] It pronounced that terrorism constitutes a grave violation of the purpose and principles of the United Nations.[21] While it did not purport to define 'terrorism', it did say that criminal acts intended or calculated to provoke a state of terror in the general public for political purposes are in any circumstances unjustifiable:

---

[16] This is maintained by the United States Federal Bureau of Investigation and may be accessed by internet: <http://www.fbi.gov/mostwant/terrorists/fugitives.htm>.

[17] The Observer, 30 September 2001, quote contained within *Submissions of the Indonesian Human Rights Committee to the Foreign Affairs, Defence and Trade Committee on the Terrorism (Bombings and Finance) Suppression Bill*, TERRO/88, Parliamentary Library, Wellington.

[18] Above n 11.

[19] Declaration on Measures to Eliminate International Terrorism, adopted under GA Res 60, 49 UN GAOR (84th plen mtg), UN Doc A/Res/49/60 (1994).

[20] Ibid, as is evident through its preamble.

[21] Ibid [2].

> The States Members of the United Nations solemnly reaffirm their unequivocal condemnation of *all* acts, methods and practices of terrorism, as criminal and unjustifiable, *wherever and by whomever committed*, including those which jeopardize the friendly relations among States and peoples and threaten the territorial integrity and security of States.[22] [emphasis added]

Of even greater value in this respect, according to the Executive Director of the International Policy Institute for Counter-Terrorism, is the Security Council's Resolution 1269.[23] While the Resolution also fails to define terrorism, it does clearly take an objective approach to the question of terrorist conduct, stating that the Security Council:

> 1. *Unequivocally condemns* all acts, methods and practices of terrorism as criminal and unjustifiable, *regardless of their motivation*, in all their forms and manifestations, wherever and by whomever committed, in particular those which would threaten international peace and security; […] [emphasis added]

The concept of terrorism

One further matter warrants consideration before leaving the issue of definition. The word 'terrorism', particularly in the vocabulary of the media since September 11, has come to be used as a description of a significantly wide range of violent conduct. Little regard is paid in use of the word to the three common threads identified above (differential targets; terror-inducing conduct; to influence a government or organization for ideological ends). It has become all too common, in the observation of the author, for events with some level of 'fear-factor' to be sensationalized as terrorist acts. Care must be taken when considering and assessing situations and how they might impact upon the topic. Civil conflicts where there is no differential targeting should be treated as civil conflicts, not as acts of terrorism. Criminal acts should likewise be dealt with in the context of normal criminal practice and procedure.

This opens the door to an even more fundamental question: *why talk about terrorism at all?* And if one doesn't need to talk about the term, then what need is there for a specific response on the part of Pacific Forum members? An act of 'terrorism', after all, will comprise a series of acts which, in and of themselves, constitute various criminal offences. To take an example, a bombing of an Embassy will likely involve the unlawful possession of explosives, the wilful destruction of property and the wilful injury to or killing of persons. Each element is a criminal offence in most jurisdictions and, as such, is capable of being dealt with by the relevant municipal jurisdiction. In submissions before the New Zealand Foreign Affairs, Defence and Trade Committee on the Counter-Terrorism Bill, for example, Professor Matthew Palmer argued that there are no good policy grounds

---

[22] Ibid [1].
[23] SC Res 1269, 54 UN SCOR (4053rd mtg), UN Doc S/Res/1269 (1999).

to justify a separate, parallel regime of counter-terrorism law.[24] Having regard to the composite nature of terrorist conduct, there is some merit to that argument.

The need to establish a separate regime must also be questioned having regard to the frequency and material effects of terrorist conduct. The annual publication of the United States Department of State, *Patterns of Global Terrorism*, has tracked the following patterns: 208 acts of international terrorism took place in 2003, up slightly from the 198 attacks in 2002, but down from the 355 attacks in 2001; with a corresponding death toll of 625 persons in 2003, 725 in 2002 and 3636 killed and injured in 2001.[25] In the twenty years up to September 11, the incidents of terrorist conduct fluctuated, without any discernable pattern, from the high 200s to the high 600s.[26] While one can never undervalue the loss of human life, it must be acknowledged that there are many more causes of death resulting in higher death tolls than as a result of terrorist conduct. If that is the case, then why add to the extant law?

The answer seems to lie in a combination of factors, not all of which are unique to terrorism, but which cumulatively appear to have been seen by States as calling for a different treatment of the subject matter. The common thread in each factor, or at least in the way each factor can be perceived, is the political interests of States. At least the following factors are relevant to the move by the international community towards treating terrorism as a unique form of crime deserving special attention.[27] The most apparent is the fear-inducing nature of terrorist conduct and the attention this brings to terrorist events through the media and public alike. This in turn adversely affects the credibility of national executive administrations in the eyes of the domestic public, and also the credibility of the United Nations as an institution established to maintain international peace and security in the eyes of the international community. The more severe the terrorist act, the greater the terror induced, to the extent that the public may in fact be paralysed in a real sense, affecting their freedom of movement and association, and enjoyment of life.[28] That again serves to adversely impact upon national and

---

[24] New Zealand, *Counter-Terrorism Bill. Government Bill. Commentary*, as reported from the Foreign Affairs, Defence and Trade Committee (2003) 2. See also Matthew Palmer, 'Counter-Terrorism Law' (2002) *New Zealand Law Journal* 456.

[25] United States Department of State, *Patterns of Global Terrorism 2001*, May 2002, *Patterns of Global Terrorism 2002*, April 2003, *Patterns of Global Terrorism 2003*, April 2004 (Revised 22 June 2004).

[26] The 2001 Report, in reviewing patterns over a twenty-year period from 1981, also identifies that the least number of terrorist attacks, at 274, was recorded in 1998, with the highest number of incidents in 1987 at 666 attacks: ibid.

[27] These are views posited in an attempt to illustrate *some* of the reasons that terrorism has been treated differently by the international community and constituting policy reasons (whether sound or not) for a separate or parallel counter-terrorism regime.

[28] As explicitly recognized within GA Res 164, 54 UN GAOR (83rd plen mtg), UN Doc A/Res/54/164 (2000). The Resolution is very similar to its three predecessors: GA Res 185, 49 UN GAOR (94th plen mtg), UN Doc A/Res/49/185 (1994); GA Res 186, 50 UN GAOR (99th plen mtg), UN Doc A/Res/50/186 (1995); and GA Res 133, 52 UN GAOR (70th plen mtg), UN Doc A/Res/52/133 (1998). Its contents were similarly reaffirmed within

international 'executive' credibility. As will be seen through the discussion of international documents on terrorism that follows, terrorism is therefore viewed as being a crime of 'international concern' (using the wording of the Rome Statute on the International Criminal Court). Terrorism was, as already indicated, proposed to be included within the jurisdiction of the International Criminal Court, to stand beside genocide, war crimes and crimes against humanity.[29]

A further issue of concern to States is the transnational nature of terrorist offending. Whether through Embassy bombings on foreign soil or direct attacks within the territory of a State (such as the September 11 attacks and the Madrid rail bombing), national interest and national security are affected. Through an international framework on counter-terrorism, those interests can arguably be better protected through the ability to secure the extradition of perpetrators of such attacks[30] and cut off the means by which terrorist organizations operate.[31]

A final and individual self-interest of States is that of combating revolutionary or secessionist terrorism, that is, terrorism occurring solely within a State and aimed at destabilizing or overthrowing the established government of the State, or conduct aimed at 'breaking away' from the State. The established government has, in those circumstances, a very real and pressing desire to eradicate terrorism.[32] The international community, in seeking to maintain the integrity of statehood and the stability of regions, also has a vested interest. Examples include the Basque Fatherland and Liberty movement in Spain,[33] the Kurdistan Workers' Party in Turkey[34] and the Liberation Tigers of Tamil Eelam in Sri Lanka.[35] Recent examples within the South Pacific will be discussed below. It should be noted that the classification of some such entities as terrorist organizations is disputed on the basis that these are freedom-fighting or liberation movements, again illustrating the complex nature of defining terrorism and terrorist entities.

---

subsequent resolutions of the General Assembly: GA Res 160, 56 UN GAOR (88th plen mtg), UN Doc A/Res/56/160 (2002); and GA Res 174, 58 UN GAOR (77th plen mtg), UN Doc A/Res/58/174 (2004).
[29] Above n 11.
[30] This being a common feature of the counter-terrorist conventions: see below.
[31] Whether by obliging States to prevent the use of their territories for training facilities or suppressing access to funds, explosives and the like.
[32] By way of example, India's Prevention of Terrorism Act 2002 describes a terrorist act as one including conduct by a person 'with intent to threaten the unity, integrity, security or sovereignty of India' (section 3(1)(a) of the Act).
[33] See Appendix A 'Background Information on Designated Foreign Terrorist Organizations' in Russel Howard and Reid Sawyer (eds), *Terrorism and Counterterrorism. Understanding the New Security Environment (Revised and Updated)* (2003) 507.
[34] Ibid 514.
[35] Ibid 516.

Terrorism and the South Pacific

As intimated, there are three particularly important matters that point to the relevance of counter-terrorism to the South Pacific, beyond the application of international obligations upon particular States. The first is that the region has, depending upon what definition of terrorism is employed, experienced terrorist, or at least secessionist or revolutionary, acts. Secondly, regard should be had to the vulnerability of the region. Finally, and most importantly in the view of the author, the role of the region should be seen as contributing to a wider, international, framework on counter-terrorism.

Terrorist acts in the South Pacific

Having said that the *Rainbow Warrior* bombing was the only incident of international terrorism within the South Pacific, it should be recognized that this statement is dependent (as just mentioned) upon what definition of terrorism is adopted. Certainly, it is the only *international* terrorist act occurring within the Pacific. On 10 July 1985, French military agents Mafart and Prieur bombed and sank the Greenpeace flag-ship the *Rainbow Warrior* in the Auckland harbour port, resulting in the death of a Greenpeace activist on board the vessel. The bombing took place just days before the *Rainbow Warrior* was to undertake a protest voyage to the French nuclear test site at Moruroa Atoll.[36]

Simpson, however, points to various *internal* acts of terrorism within the Pacific.[37] In New Caledonia in the 1980s, the Kanak Socialist National Liberation Front (FLNKS) was denounced as a separatist terrorist movement.[38] It subsequently formed part of the coalition government in 2001 and is now the main opposition party in New Caledonia.[39] The Fiji coups of 1987 and 2000 have likewise been classified as terrorist events,[40] although they might more properly be categorized as internal civil conflicts.[41] The 'civil conflict' in the Solomon Islands during 2000, in contrast, has been said to include terrorist conduct on the part of both main factions, the Malaita Eagles Force and the Isatabu Freedom Movement.[42]

---

[36] Greenpeace, 'The Bombing of the Warrior', <http://archive.greenpeace.org/comms/rw/pkbomb.html> at 16 September 2004.
[37] Stanley Simpson, 'A Brief History of Terrorism in the South Pacific' (Paper presented at the public workshop *How Should Fiji Respond to the Threat of Terrorism?*, Suva, Fiji, 17 July 2004, copy on file with author).
[38] Ibid.
[39] Electionworld.org, 'Elections in New Caledonia', <http://www.electionworld.org/newcaledonia.htm> at 16 September 2004.
[40] Simpson, above n 37.
[41] See the discussion above concerning the misuse of the term 'terrorism' in the absence of differential targeting and fear-inducing conduct.
[42] Simpson, above n 37.

The risk of terrorism in the South Pacific

There is a common view that the likelihood of terrorist acts being perpetrated within the Pacific is remote, such that counter-terrorism should remain at the low end of priorities for the region. While this risk assessment might well be correct, there are various factors that count in favour of a more proactive approach, from even a purely self-serving perspective. As evident from the foregoing discussion, the South Pacific has been subject to terrorist incidents in the past, however defined. Regard should also be had to the possibility and consequences of a direct attack. Of particular relevance to a number of Pacific Island countries, as nations reliant upon the export of commodities such as dairy, meat and fruit,[43] is the biosecurity of those countries. This is a matter dealt with primarily under the domestic legislation of each State including, for example, the Biosecurity Act 1993 in New Zealand. Bioterrorism might, as will be discussed in the examination of the international counter-terrorism framework, fall within the global definition of terrorism under article 2(1)(c) of the Draft Comprehensive Convention on International Terrorism.[44] New Zealand recently took steps towards including bioterrorism as an offence under its domestic law, effected through the Counter-Terrorism Act 2003.[45]

Despite its geographical isolation, the reality of the contemporary world is that globalization has dissolved distances that might have once protected the Pacific Islands. Transport and communications systems, access to the internet, and more efficient means of moving people and money mean that it is easier for the world to interact with the Pacific.[46] Individuals thought to be connected with al-Qaeda have been reported to have been present in New Zealand, Australia and Fiji.[47] Pacific Forum Secretary General, Greg Urwin, adds that while terrorists may not seek to attack citizens and institutions of Pacific countries, the region might prove to be a tempting target, either for an attack like the one in Bali in October 2002, or as a base or staging point from which terrorist cells might undertake

---

[43] By way of example, Statistics New Zealand identifies exports for the years ended June 2001, 2002 and 2003 to be as follows: milk powder, butter and cheese at $5790 million (2001), $5891 million (2002) and $4679 million (2003); meat and edible offal at $4182 million (2001), $4429 million (2002) and $4112 million (2003); logs, wood and wood article at $2192 million (2001), $2378 million (2002) and $2386 million (2003); fish, crustaceans and molluscs at $1374 million (2001), $1402 million (2002) and $1032 million (2003); and fruit at $1045 million (2001), $1159 million (2002) and $1032 million (2003): see Statistics New Zealand online information 'Quick Facts – Economy', <http://www.stats.govt.nz/domino/external/ web/nzstories.nsf/htmldocs/Quick+Facts+Economy> at 17 September 2004.

[44] On that subject, however, see (as a starting point) Richard Hoffman, 'Preparing for a Bioterrorist Attack: Legal and Administrative Strategies', 9(2) (2003) *Emerging Infectious Diseases* 241.

[45] Section 6 of the Act amended the Crimes Act 1961 to include new sections 298A and 298B, making it an offence to contaminate food, crops, water or other products.

[46] Urwin, above n 6, [8].

[47] Ibid [9]. Anecdotal reports are that one of the September 11 hijackers spent a considerable time living in Fiji up until six months prior to the World Trade Centre attacks.

planning for an attack elsewhere.[48] The New Zealand Security Intelligence Service recently reported, for example, that Islamic extremists with links to international terrorist organizations are likely to be operating in New Zealand:

> From the Service's own investigations we assess that there are individuals in or from New Zealand who support Islamic extremist causes. The Service views these developments, most of which have come to attention within 2003/04, with considerable concern. They indicate attempts to use New Zealand as a safe haven from which activities of security concern elsewhere can be facilitated and/or the involvement of people from New Zealand in such activities.[49]

Supporting an international framework on counter-terrorism

The most important point to make is a relatively simple one, although the consequences of it are wide-ranging. The international conventions and protocols, reinforced by customary law and resolutions of the General Assembly, and added to by Security Council resolutions, create an *international* framework for counter-terrorism. A considerable measure of their effectiveness lies in the universal adoption and implementation of the obligations under that framework in order to prevent *any* State being either targeted by terrorists or used by them as a base of operations (whether that be the establishment of physical training camps or the laundering of money to fund activities of terrorist organizations).

Following the train bombing in Madrid on 11 March 2004, in which nearly 200 people were killed, Spain's Ambassador to the United Nations (who also chairs the Security Council Counter-Terrorism Committee) criticized unnamed nations for a 'lack of effort' in countering terrorism.[50] The point was also later made by the US Ambassador to the United Nations, John Danworth:

> [The Counter-Terrorism Committee] must never forget that so long as a few states are not acting quickly enough to raise their capacity to fight terrorism or are not meeting their international counterterrorism obligations, all of us remain vulnerable.[51]

The question is no longer simply one of domestic or regional security in order to prevent attacks from occurring within a State's own borders and, in doing so, assessing the risks of such attacks and the appropriate measures in response. Although those assessments and corresponding national security interests remain, effective counter-terrorism requires (to achieve international security and in light of the manner in which terrorists and terrorist organizations operate) that all States

---

[48] Ibid [10].
[49] New Zealand Security Intelligence Service, *Report to the House of Representatives for the year ended 30 June 2004*, presented to the House of Representatives pursuant to section 4J of the New Zealand Security Intelligence Service Act 1969, 11.
[50] United Nations Foundation, 'Spanish Diplomat Blames Nations for "Lack of Effort" on Terrorism', <http://www.unwire.org/UNWire> at 12 March 2004.
[51] United Nations Foundation, 'Counterterrorism Cooperation Improving, Security Council Told', <http://www.unwire.org/UNWire> at 20 July 2004.

prevent and preclude terrorist conduct and preparations. A high level of threat posed to a State might cause that State to impose measures *above* those required by the international framework, but the reverse does not apply. Even if it is accepted that the South Pacific does not bear any substantial risk of being the subject of a terrorist attack, its role in combating international terrorism through the implementation of anti-terrorism obligations is equal to that of all other States.

All of these various points are reiterated on the website of the New Zealand Security Intelligence Service, equally applicable to other Pacific Island countries:

> The terrorist threat to New Zealand is low, but it cannot be discounted. The country learned at the time of the Rainbow Warrior bombing that relative geographic isolation, in itself, is no guarantee of immunity. The events in the United States on 11 September 2001 confirmed that terrorism is an international phenomenon and terrorists consider the world their stage when they look for a way to advance their cause.
>
> There are individuals and groups in New Zealand with links to overseas organisations that are committed to acts of terrorism, violence and intimidation. Some have developed local structures that are dedicated to the support of their overseas parent bodies. There are also isolated extremists in New Zealand who advocate using violence to impress on others their own political, ethnic or religious viewpoint.
>
> But the threat of terrorism could come equally from beyond New Zealand. Modern transport and communication have effectively made the world a smaller place. Events such as a visit by an overseas dignitary, or a major international gathering may be seen by off-shore terrorists as providing the opportunity to do something spectacular to capture world wide publicity, or to otherwise further their cause.
>
> There is also the risk that individuals or groups may use New Zealand as a safe haven from which to plan or facilitate terrorist acts elsewhere.[52]

Indeed, New Zealand appears to see its role in supporting counter-terrorism within the South Pacific as an important one.[53] It has assessed that, due to an inadequate capacity by some Pacific Island countries for border control and for the control of passports and travel documents, the potential exists for these inadequacies to be exploited by terrorist groups.[54] In its reports to the Security Council Counter-Terrorism Committee, New Zealand has said that it is helping to manage these risks and to provide additional assistance to Pacific Island countries.[55]

The international framework on counter-terrorism

It has been posited that one of the primary reasons for the South Pacific to fully embrace counter-terrorism is the need for it to support and contribute to the

---

[52] New Zealand Security Intelligence Service website, *Protecting New Zealand from Terrorism*, <http://www.nzsis.govt.nz/work/work.html> at 16 November 2004.
[53] See New Zealand's first report to the Security Council Counter-Terrorism Committee, *Report to the Counter-Terrorism Committee pursuant to paragraph 6 of Security Council resolution 1373 (2001) of 28 September 2001, New Zealand*, 2 January 2002, S/2001/1269, 5.
[54] Ibid.
[55] Ibid.

international anti-terrorist framework. Two issues arise from that position. What *is* the international framework on counter-terrorism? How have the Pacific Forum members *responded* to that framework?

The phenomenon of terrorism became an international concern in the 1960s, with a series of aircraft hijackings hitting the headlines. When the 1972 Munich Olympic Games were disrupted by the kidnapping of Israeli athletes by a Palestinian group, the then Secretary-General of the UN, Kurt Waldheim, asked that the issue be placed on the General Assembly's agenda. In the heated debate that followed, the Assembly assigned the issue to its Sixth (Legal) Committee, which subsequently proposed several conventions on terrorism. There are now twelve conventions and protocols on terrorism, all of which have entered into force.[56] In addition to those instruments, a draft Comprehensive Convention on the Elimination of International Terrorism has been under consideration, since 2000.[57] Both the General Assembly and Security Council have also been active in adopting resolutions on the subject.

The international anti-terrorism treaties

Of the twelve international conventions on terrorism, one starts (in chronological order) with the Convention on Offences and Certain Other Acts Committed on Board Aircraft (the Tokyo Convention).[58] The Convention applies to acts affecting in-flight safety. It authorizes the aircraft commander to impose reasonable measures, including restraint, on any person he or she believes has committed or is about to commit an act affecting in-flight safety, when necessary to protect the safety of the aircraft. It also requires contracting States to take custody of offenders and to return control of the aircraft to the lawful commander. The second and third

---

[56] A situation that had not existed at the time of the September 11 terrorist attacks, as discussed below in the context of SC Res 1373, 56 UN SCOR (4385th mtg), UN Doc S/Res/1373 (2001).

[57] Almost one year prior to the September 11 attacks, India had proposed that there be a comprehensive convention against terrorism: the draft Comprehensive Convention on the Elimination of International Terrorism, as contained in the *Report of the Ad Hoc Committee Established under resolution 51/210*, 57 UN GAOR (57th mtg), UN Doc A/57/37 (2002). The draft convention was referred to the Ad Hoc Committee Established by General Assembly Resolution 51/210 (which had been established by the General Assembly in 1996 to work on conventions for the suppression of terrorist bombings and financing of terrorist operations and, thereafter, to address means of developing a comprehensive legal framework dealing with international terrorism): GA Res 210, 51 UN GAOR (88th plen mtg), UN Doc A/Res/51/210 (1996), [9]. As yet, the draft has not been finalized and is likely to be some time away, if it is ever to become a reality. Due to the lack of unanimity on various issues, and the range of issues involved, the Committee has concluded that finalizing a comprehensive international treaty on terrorism will depend primarily on agreement as to whom would be entitled to exclusion from the treaty's scope, and on what grounds. Otherwise, the majority of the 27 articles of the Draft Convention have been preliminarily agreed upon by the Committee.

[58] Opened for signature 14 September 1963, 704 UNTS 219 (entered into force 4 December 1969).

conventions are also concerned with air safety. The Convention for the Suppression of Unlawful Seizure of Aircraft (the Hague Convention),[59] makes it an offence for any person on board an aircraft in flight to 'unlawfully, by force or threat thereof, or any other form of intimidation, seize or exercise control of that aircraft' or to attempt to do so. It requires parties to the Convention to make hijackings punishable by severe penalties. It requires parties that have custody of offenders to either extradite the offender or submit the case for prosecution and also requires parties to assist each other in connection with criminal proceedings brought under the Convention. The Convention for the Suppression of Unlawful Acts Against the Safety of Civil Aviation (the Montreal Convention)[60] makes it an offence for any person unlawfully and intentionally to perform an act of violence against a person on board an aircraft in flight, if that act is likely to endanger the safety of that aircraft; to place an explosive device on an aircraft; and to attempt such acts or be an accomplice of a person who performs or attempts to perform such acts. As for the Hague Convention, it requires parties to make offences punishable by severe penalties and again requires parties that have custody of offenders to either extradite the offender or submit the case for prosecution.

In 1973, the Convention on the Prevention and Punishment of Crimes against International Protected Persons, including Diplomatic Agents (the Protected Persons Convention) was adopted.[61] Internationally protected persons are defined as a Head of State, a Minister for Foreign Affairs, a representative or official of a State or of an international organization who is entitled to special protection from attack under international law (these people being popular terrorist targets). The Convention requires each State party to criminalize and make punishable by appropriate penalties which take into account their grave nature, the intentional murder, kidnapping, or other attack upon the person or liberty of an internationally protected person, a violent attack upon the official premises, the private accommodations, or the means of transport of such person; a threat or attempt to commit such an attack; and an act constituting participation as an accomplice. Also within the theme of protecting persons, the International Convention against the Taking of Hostages (the Hostages Convention)[62] states that 'any person who seizes or detains and threatens to kill, to injure, or to continue to detain another person in order to compel a ... State, an international intergovernmental organization, a natural or juridical person, or a group of persons, to do or abstain from doing any act as an explicit or implicit condition for the release of the hostage' commits the offence of taking of hostages within the meaning of this Convention.

---

[59] Opened for signature 16 December 1970, 860 UNTS 105 (entered into force 14 October 1971).
[60] Opened for signature 23 September 1971, 974 UNTS 177 (entered into force 26 January 1073).
[61] Opened for signature 14 December 1973, 1035 UNTS 167 (entered into force 20 February 1977).
[62] Opened for signature 18 December 1979, 1316 UNTS 205 (entered into force 3 June 1983).

Next in time is the Convention on the Physical Protection of Nuclear Material (the Nuclear Materials Convention).[63] This criminalizes the unlawful possession, use or transfer of nuclear material, the theft of nuclear material, and threats to use nuclear material (to cause death or serious injury to any person or substantial property damage).

The Protocol on the Suppression of Unlawful Acts of Violence at Airports Serving International Civil Aviation 1988 (the Montreal Protocol) was a further addition to air-safety-related counter-terrorist conventions.[64] The Protocol extends the provisions of the Montreal Convention of 1971 to encompass terrorist acts at airports servicing international civil aviation.

The Convention for the Suppression of Unlawful Acts Against the Safety of Maritime Navigation (the Rome Convention) was adopted in 1988.[65] Here, the treaty establishes a legal regime applicable to international maritime navigation that is similar to the regimes established concerning international aviation. More specifically, it makes it an offence for a person unlawfully and intentionally to seize or exercise control over a ship by force, threat, or intimidation; to perform an act of violence against a person on board a ship if that act is likely to endanger the safe navigation of the ship; to place a destructive device or substance aboard a ship; and other acts against the safety of ships. An optional protocol to this Convention, the Protocol for the Suppression of Unlawful Acts Against the Safety of Fixed Platforms Located on the Continental Shelf (the Rome Protocol) was also adopted in 1988,[66] at the same time as its parent Convention. Again by way of extension, the Protocol establishes a legal regime applicable to fixed platforms on the continental shelf (similar to the regimes established with regard to international aviation).

Last in the list of conventions relating to air safety, and within the jurisdiction of the Secretary-General of the International Civil Aviation Organization, is the Convention on the Marking of Plastic Explosives for the Purpose of Identification (the Plastic Explosives Convention).[67] This is designed to control and limit the used of unmarked and undetectable plastic explosives (negotiated in the aftermath of the 1988 Pan Am 103 bombing). Parties are obligated in their respective territories to ensure effective control over 'unmarked' plastic explosive, that is, those that do not contain one of the detection agents described in the Technical Annex to the treaty. Each party must, among other things: take necessary and effective measures to prohibit and prevent the manufacture of unmarked plastic explosives; prevent the movement of unmarked plastic explosives into or out of its territory; ensure that all stocks of such unmarked explosives not held by the military or police are destroyed or consumed,

---

[63] Opened for signature 3 March 1980, 1456 UNTS 124 (entered into force 8 February 1987).
[64] Opened for signature 24 February 1988, ICAO Doc 9518 (entered into force 6 August 1989).
[65] Opened for signature 10 March 1988, 1678 UNTS 221 (entered into force 1 March 1992).
[66] Opened for signature 10 March 1988, 1678 UNTS 304 (entered into force 1 March 1992).
[67] Opened for signature 1 March 1991, ICAO Doc 9571 (entered into force 21 June 1998).

marked, or rendered permanently ineffective within three years; take necessary measures to ensure that unmarked plastic explosives held by the military or police are destroyed or consumed, marked, or rendered permanently ineffective within fifteen years; and ensure the destruction, as soon as possible, of any unmarked explosives manufactured after the date of entry into force of the Convention for that State.

More recent in time is the International Convention for the Suppression of Terrorist Bombing (the Suppression of Bombing Convention).[68] As the name suggests, this creates a regime of universal jurisdiction over the unlawful and intentional use of explosives and other lethal devices in, into, or against various public places with intent to kill or cause serious bodily injury, or with intent to cause extensive destruction in a public place. Finally, there is the International Convention for the Suppression of the Financing of Terrorism (the Suppression of Financing Convention).[69] Of the 12 conventions, this is the most controversial. It requires parties to take steps to prevent and counteract the financing of terrorists, whether direct or indirect, through groups claiming to have charitable, social or cultural goals or which also engage in such illicit activities as drug trafficking or gun running. It commits States to hold those who finance terrorism criminally, civilly or administratively liable for such acts and provides for the identification, freezing and seizure of funds allocated for terrorist activities, as well as for the sharing of the forfeited funds with other States on a case-by-case basis. Bank secrecy will no longer be justification for refusing to cooperate under the treaty.

In summary, then, the twelve anti-terrorism conventions are directed at the protection of potential terrorist targets or at the means through which terrorist organizations operate and do three main things: they criminalize certain conduct, they provide for the prosecution or extradition of perpetrators of such criminal acts, and they impose obligations upon States to suppress the conduct in question. Three potential target groups exist within the twelve conventions: civil aviation (the Tokyo, Hague and Montreal Conventions and the Montreal Protocol); persons (the Protected Persons Convention and the Hostages Convention); and operations at sea (the Rome Convention and Rome Protocol). Four means through which terrorist acts might be executed or facilitated are the subject matter of the remaining four conventions: the Plastic Explosives and Nuclear Materials Conventions and the Suppression of Bombing and Suppression of Financing Conventions.

Utility of the international conventions

The number and scope of these conventions might, at first instance, seem impressive and comprehensive. They have, however, various limitations. To begin with, they only apply to States parties to the conventions. Even then, the conventions themselves are of limited application because of the very precise subject matter of each treaty. The conventions are not of general application but,

---

[68] Opened for signature 12 January 1998, 2149 UNTS 286 (entered into force 23 May 2001).
[69] Opened for signature 10 January 2000, 2179 UNTS 232 (entered into force 10 April 1992).

rather, relate to specific situations in which terrorist acts might have effect, whether on board aircraft, in airports or on maritime platforms.

The only treaty with the potential to impact a wider audience and scope of activity is the International Convention for the Suppression of the Financing of Terrorism. Firstly, the convention mirrors a good number of the suppression of financing obligations contained in Resolution 1373. As a resolution binding upon all members of the United Nations,[70] this has had a significant impact upon the status of the convention. Prior to September 11, 2001, there were just four States parties to the convention and, accordingly, the convention was not in force. Since then, and largely in response to UN Security Council Resolution 1373 and the work of the Counter-Terrorism Committee, almost 120 States have becomes parties to the convention, which has now come into force.[71]

The other reason the Suppression of Financing Convention is of greater relevance is the fact that, in prohibiting the financing of terrorist entities or operations, it defines (for those purposes) what type of acts one may not finance:

> Any other act intended to cause death or serious bodily injury to a civilian, or to any other person not taking an active part in the hostilities in a situation of armed conflict, when the purpose of such act, by its nature or context, is to intimidate a population, or to compel a government or an international organization to do or to abstain from doing any act.

The Convention does therefore have some potentially wider application and is useful for States in determining the type of conduct they are to prohibit.

United Nations action

Beyond the work of the Sixth (Legal) Committee of the General Assembly in working towards the various counter-terrorism conventions discussed, both the General Assembly and Security Council have been working in concert on the issue of counter-terrorism.

In December 1994, the UN General Assembly adopted the Declaration on Measures to Eliminate International Terrorism.[72] The Declaration was based on the notion of peace and security and the principle of refraining from the threat or use of force in international relations.[73] It pronounced that terrorism constitutes a grave

---

[70] By application of article 25 of the Charter of the United Nations.
[71] The convention came into force on 10 April 2002, above n 69. There are now 132 signatories and 117 parties: see <http://untreaty.un.org/ENGLISH/Status/Chapter_xviii/treaty11.asp> at 12 December 2004.
[72] Above n 19. The Declaration has been restated and adopted in subsequent resolutions of the General Assembly, with the contents being much the same: see UNGA Resolutions A/RES/50/53 of 11 December 1995; A/RES/51/210 of 17 December 1996; A/RES/52/165 of 19 January 1998; A/RES/54/110 of 2 February 2000; A/RES/55/158 of 30 January 2001; A/RES/56/88 of 24 January 2002; A/RES/57/27 OF 15 January 2003; and A/RES/58/81 of 8 January 2004.
[73] Ibid, as is evident through its Preamble.

violation of the purpose and principles of the United Nations.[74] While it did not purport to define 'terrorism', it did say that criminal acts intended or calculated to provoke a state of terror in the general public for political purposes are in any circumstances unjustifiable.[75] The Declaration urged all States to consider, as a matter of priority, becoming party to the conventions on terrorism adopted up to that time.[76] It called on States to refrain from organizing, instigating, assisting or participating in terrorist acts, and from acquiescing in or encouraging activities within their territories directed towards the commission of such acts.[77]

In particular, States were directed that, in order to fulfil this obligation, they must refrain from facilitating terrorist activities. Paragraph 5(a) of the 1994 Declaration appears to indicate that a State must be proactive in doing so, obliging States to take appropriate practical measures to ensure that their territory is not used for terrorist installations or training camps, or for the preparation or organization of terrorist acts. Paragraph 5(b) then refers to the obligation to apprehend and prosecute or extradite perpetrators of terrorist acts.

The practical observation to make is that, although compelling and strongly worded, this is a declaration of the General Assembly and therefore does not have the same weight as a convention, nor does it have signatories that are bound by its content. Indeed, article 10 of the UN Charter specifically provides that resolutions and declarations of the United Nations General Assembly are recommendatory only.

More significant, however, are the resolutions of the Security Council, which do place binding obligations upon member States of the United Nations.[78] On the day after the September 11 attacks, the United Nations Security Council (UNSC) adopted Resolution 1368, through which it unequivocally condemned the terrorist attacks and expressed that it regarded them as a threat to international peace and security.[79] It called on all States to urgently work together to bring to justice the perpetrators, organizers and sponsors of the terrorist attacks.[80] Security Council Resolution 1373 was later adopted, through which the UNSC determined that all States were to prevent and suppress the financing of terrorist acts, including the criminalization of such financing and the freezing of funds and financial assets.[81] Described as one of the most strongly worded resolutions in the history of the Security Council,[82] it also

---

[74] Ibid [2].
[75] Ibid [1].
[76] Ibid [6].
[77] Ibid [4].
[78] If made under Chapter VII of the Charter of the United Nations and couched in mandatory language (see later discussion on this point: Charter of the United Nations, art 25.
[79] SC Res 1368, 56 UN SCOR (4370th mtg), UN Doc S/Res/1368 (2001).
[80] Ibid [3].
[81] SC Res 1373, 56 UN SCOR (4385th mtg), UN Doc S/Res/1373 (2001).
[82] Richard Rowe, 'Key Developments: Year of International Law in Review' (Paper presented at the 10th Annual Meeting of the Australian and New Zealand Society of International Law, *New Challenges and New States: What Role for International Law?*, Australian National University, Canberra, Australia, 15 June 2002). Richard Rowe at that time worked in the International Organisations and Legal Division of the Australian Department of Foreign Affairs and Trade. He was the Australian representative and Vice-

requires countries to cooperate on extradition matters and the sharing of information about terrorist networks.[83]

As a decision made under Chapter VII of the United Nations Charter, compliance with Resolution 1373 is mandatory for UN members, imposing certain obligations upon those members.[84] Those obligations can be viewed in two parts. The first is the imposition of specific counter-terrorist obligations, as follows:

Acting under Chapter VII of the Charter of the United Nations,

1. *Decides* that all States shall:
(a) Prevent and suppress the financing of terrorist acts;
(b) Criminalize the wilful provision or collection, by any means, directly or indirectly, of funds by their nationals or in their territories with the intention that the funds should be used, or in the knowledge that they are to be used, in order to carry out terrorist acts;
(c) Freeze without delay funds and other financial assets or economic resources of persons who commit, or attempt to commit, terrorist acts or participate in or facilitate the commission of terrorist acts; of entities owned or controlled directly or indirectly by such persons; and of persons and entities acting on behalf of, or at the direction of such persons and entities, including funds derived or generated from property owned or controlled directly or indirectly by such persons and associated persons and entities;
(d) Prohibit their nationals or any persons and entities within their territories from making any funds, financial assets or economic resources or financial or other related services available, directly or indirectly, for the benefit of persons who commit or attempt to commit or facilitate or participate in the commission of terrorist acts, of entities owned or controlled, directly or indirectly, by such persons and of persons and entities acting on behalf of or at the direction of such persons;

2. *Decides also* that all States shall:
(a) Refrain from providing any form of support, active or passive, to entities or persons involved in terrorist acts, including by suppressing recruitment of members of terrorist groups and eliminating the supply of weapons to terrorists;
(b) Take the necessary steps to prevent the commission of terrorist acts, including by provision of early warning to other States by exchange of information;
(c) Deny safe haven to those who finance, plan, support, or commit terrorist acts, or provide safe havens;
(d) Prevent those who finance, plan, facilitate or commit terrorist acts from using their respective territories for those purposes against other States or their citizens;
(e) Ensure that any person who participates in the financing, planning, preparation or perpetration of terrorist acts or in supporting terrorist acts is brought to justice and ensure that, in addition to any other measures against them, such terrorist acts are established as serious criminal offences in domestic laws and

---

Chairman of the Ad Hoc Committee Established by General Assembly Resolution 51/210 during its Sixth Session, which followed the September 11 attacks.
[83] Above n 81, [3].
[84] Article 25 of the Charter of the United Nations.

regulations and that the punishment duly reflects the seriousness of such terrorist acts;
(f) Afford one another the greatest measure of assistance in connection with criminal investigations or criminal proceedings relating to the financing or support of terrorist acts, including assistance in obtaining evidence in their possession necessary for the proceedings;
(g) Prevent the movement of terrorists or terrorist groups by effective border controls and controls on issuance of identity papers and travel documents, and through measures for preventing counterfeiting, forgery or fraudulent use of identity papers and travel documents;
[...].

This set of obligations expands upon and significantly strengthens the Council's earlier Resolution 1269 of 1999.[85] While Resolution 1269 considered steps to be taken by States to suppress terrorism, deny safe haven to terrorists and cooperate with others in the bringing to justice perpetrators of terrorist conduct, the language of this earlier Resolution is weaker for two principal reasons. First, paragraphs 1 and 2 of Resolution 1373 are considerably more specific in the steps to be taken in countering terrorism. Second, the instructive words of the more recent Resolution provides that 'all States *shall*', whereas the earlier Resolution used a less forceful provision *calling upon* States to take *appropriate steps* to achieve the stated objectives. In short, then, Resolution 1373 takes a considerable step forward in the imposition of counter-terrorism obligations upon members of the United Nations.

The second obligation is a more general requirement to enter into what might be described as a reporting and monitoring dialogue between States and a special committee of the Security Council established under the Resolution, the Counter-Terrorism Committee. Paragraph 6 of the Resolution provides as follows:

6. *Decides* to establish, in accordance with rule 28 of its provisional rules of procedure, a Committee of the Security Council, consisting of all the members of the Council, to monitor implementation of this resolution, with the assistance of appropriate expertise, and *calls upon* all States to report to the Committee, no later than 90 days from the date of adoption of this resolution and thereafter according to a timetable to be proposed by the Committee, on the steps they have taken to implement this resolution;

Since Resolutions 1368 and 1373, there have been further resolutions of the Security Council dealing with the issue of international terrorism.[86] Recognizing

---

[85] Above n 23.
[86] Interestingly, though, the only resolution of the United Nations Security Council prior to September 11 and dealing with terrorism in the international context, rather than relating to and restricted to specific events, is SC Res 1189, 53 UN SCOR (3915th mtg), UN Doc S/Res/1189 (1998). Although the resolution was adopted in response to the 1998 bombings in Nairobi, Kenya and Tanzania, it called upon all States 'to adopt, in accordance with international law and as a matter of priority, effective and practical measures for security cooperation, for the prevention of such acts of terrorism, and for the prosecution and punishment of their perpetrators', [5].

the considerable burden upon States in the domestic implementation process following their party status to the twelve international conventions and in complying with Resolution 1373, the Council tasked the Counter-Terrorism Committee with exploring ways in which States could be assisted.[87] Resolutions 1452 and 1455 concerned themselves specifically with the Taliban and al-Qaida.[88]

Response of the South Pacific to the international framework on counter-terrorism

The response of States within the South Pacific to the international framework just described can be characterized, in the main, as being positive. However, the response of some Pacific Island countries (together with their party status to the UN Charter and the anti-terrorism treaties) creates disparate sets of obligations and legal frameworks within the region. The influence of Asia-Pacific Economic Cooperation Organization and the Organisation for Economic Cooperation and Development (OECD) should also be noted.

Party status to the UN Charter and anti-terrorism treaties

Of the sixteen members of the Pacific Forum, the Cook Islands and Niue are not members of the United Nations and, consequently, are not bound by the provisions of United Nations Security Council Resolution 1373.[89] The binding and substantive obligations contained within paragraphs 1 and 2 of the Resolution (set out earlier) do not therefore apply to those countries, although they have both reported to the Security Council Counter-Terrorism Committee under the procedures established through paragraph 6 of the Resolution.[90]

In terms of the anti-terrorism conventions identified, only Australia, New Zealand and the Marshall Islands are party to all twelve anti-terrorism conventions, and Palau to all but one.[91] At the other end of the scale, Kiribati, Niue and Tuvalu are not party to any of the treaties and the Cook Islands is only party to the

---

[87] SC Res 1377, 56 UN SCOR (4413th mtg), UN Doc S/Res/1377 (2001).

[88] SC Res 1452, 57 UN SCOR (4678th mtg), UN Doc S/Res/1452 (2002), and SC Res 1455, 58 UN SCOR (4686th mtg), UN Doc S/Res/1455 (2003).

[89] Since article 25 of the Charter of the United Nations restricts the need to comply with decisions of the Security Council to members of the organization.

[90] Cook Islands Government, *Report to the United Nations Security Council Counter-Terrorism Committee on counterterrorism activities in the Cook Islands*, 27 December 2001, S/2001/1324 (first report), *Supplementary Report to the United Nations Security Council Counter-Terrorism Committee on counterterrorism activities in the Cook Islands*, 31 May 2002, S/2002/1445 (second report), and *Addendum to Supplementary Report to the United Nations Security Council Counter-Terrorism Committee on counterterrorism activities in the Cook Islands*, 16 September 2003, S/2003/1445/ADD.1 (third report). Niue Government, *Report to the Counter-Terrorism Committee of the United Nations Security Council on resolution 1373 (2001)*, 24 December 2001, S/2001/7 (sole report).

[91] Palau is not a party to the Nuclear Materials Convention.

Suppression of Financing Convention. Fiji, the Solomon Islands and Tuvalu are party to a selection of the treaties relating to civil aviation, most likely reflecting the importance of international tourism to those countries.[92] The final four (Micronesia, Nauru, Papua New Guinea and Samoa) have had a mixed response to the twelve conventions, but are all party to the Suppression of Financing Convention.[93]

Against that background, it is difficult to base international obligations as *the* reason to treat counter-terrorism as relevant to the South Pacific. Indeed, even if all South Pacific States were party to all treaties, there can always be a disparity between party status and the effective implementation of treaty obligations, irrespective of the subject matter. What can be said is that suppression of financing obligations apply to all countries but Niue, since the obligations contained within Resolution 1373 are binding upon all countries but the Cook Islands and Niue, and since the Cook Islands is a party to the Suppression of Financing Convention.

It is also relevant to note that at the thirty-third Pacific Islands Forum in Fiji, Forum Leaders adopted the Nasonini Declaration on Regional Security.[94] The Declaration underlined the commitment of Forum Leaders to the implementation of internationally agreed anti-terrorism measures, with express reference to Resolution 1373, and tasked the Forum Regional Security Committee to review the regional implementation of the Resolution.[95]

Asia-Pacific Economic Cooperation Organization

APEC, made up of 21 'Member Economies',[96] includes three members of the Pacific Forum (Australia, New Zealand and Papua New Guinea) and is predominantly concerned with trade and economic issues. In the wake of the September 11 attacks in 2001 APEC leaders adopted the *Shanghai Counter-*

---

[92] Fiji is party to all four aviation-related conventions (being the Tokyo, Hague and Montreal Conventions and the Montreal Protocol). The Solomon Islands is party to the Tokyo and Montreal Conventions only. Vanuatu is party to all but the Montreal Protocol.

[93] Micronesia is a party to four of the twelve conventions, excluding the Tokyo and Hague Conventions on civil aviation, the two conventions on the protection of persons (the Protected Persons and Hostages Conventions), the Rome Protocol on the safety of maritime platforms, and the Plastics and Nuclear Materials Conventions. Nauru is party to the three civil aviation conventions (but not to the Montreal Protocol), and party to the Suppression of Financing Convention. Papua New Guinea is party to eight conventions, excluding the two maritime conventions and the Plastics and Nuclear Materials Conventions. Samoa is not party to the two protection of persons conventions, nor to the Rome Protocol on maritime platforms, nor the Suppression of Bombings and Nuclear Materials Conventions.

[94] *Forum Communiqué*, Thirty-Third Pacific Islands Forum, Suva, Fiji Islands, 15–17 August 2002, Annex 1, 'Nasonini Declaration on Regional Security'.

[95] Ibid [5] and [9].

[96] Being Australia; Brunei Darussalam; Canada; Chile; People's Republic of China; Hong Kong, China; Indonesia; Japan; Republic of Korea; Malaysia; Mexico; New Zealand; Papua New Guinea; Peru; The Republic of the Philippines; The Russian Federation; Singapore; Chinese Taipei; Thailand; United States of America; Viet Nam.

Terrorism Statement on 21 October 2001.[97] As well as condemning the September 11 attacks, the Leaders characterized terrorism as a direct challenge to APEC's vision of free, open and prosperous economies.[98] Pledging to implement Security Council Resolution 1373, the Statement expressed a commitment to prevent and suppress all forms of terrorism, called for increased cooperation and for the early signing of the anti-terrorism conventions, and identified various practical measures through which Member Economies could cooperate to enhance counter-terrorism.[99] The Shanghai Statement, and the principles within it, were reaffirmed in the APEC Leaders' statements of 2002, 2003, and 2004.[100]

The 2002 Statement on Fighting Terrorism was particularly detailed in setting out ways through which secure trade could be achieved, with focus upon protecting cargo, ships, international aviation, people in transit, and upon cyber security and halting terrorist financing. It established a Counter-Terrorism Task Force, with the mandate to implement and assist with achieving the measures identified (labelled 'STAR', Secure Trade in the APEC Region). By requiring Member Economies to each submit a Counter-Terrorism Action Plan,[101] working with various international organizations,[102] and expanding APEC's extant 'Finance Ministers' Process' to include a focus on the suppression of terrorist financing, the Task Force reports that Member Economies have significantly strengthened counter-terrorist measures.[103]

Of the three countries that are members of both the Pacific Forum and APEC, both Australia and New Zealand have since become party to all conventions,[104]

---

[97] Asia-Pacific Economic Cooperation, 'APEC Leaders' Statement on Counter-Terrorism', Shanghai, People's Republic of China, 21 October 2001, available online at <http://www.apec.org/apec/leaders_declarations/2001/statement_on_counter-terrorism.html>.

[98] Ibid [1 and 2].

[99] Ibid [6].

[100] Asia-Pacific Economic Cooperation, 'APEC Leaders' Statement on Fighting Terrorism and Promoting Growth', Los Cabos, Mexico, 20 October 2002. Asia-Pacific Economic Cooperation, 'APEC Leaders' 2003 Declaration "Bangkok Declaration on Partnership for the Future"', 2. *Enhancing Human Security*, Bangkok, Thailand, 21 October 2003. Asia-Pacific Economic Cooperation, 'APEC Leaders' 2004 Santiago Declaration "One Community, Our Future"', *Enhancing Human Security – Underpinning Economic Growth*, Santiago de Chile, 21 November 2004.

[101] All Member Economies have done so, New Zealand being the most recent to submit a (revised) Action Plan in October 2004. The Action Plans are available on APEC's website at URL <http://www.apec.org/apec/apec_groups/som_special_task_groups/counter_terrorism/counter_terrorism_action_plans.html>.

[102] Including the International Monetary Fund, World Bank, Asia Development Bank, United Nations Counter-Terrorism Committee, Inter-American Committee Against Terrorism and the Association of Southeast Asian Nations (ASEAN).

[103] APEC Counter Terrorism Task Force, 'Counter Terrorism', <http://www.apec.org/apec/apec_groups/som_special_task_groups/counter_terrorism.html> at 7 December 2004.

[104] At 11 September 2001, Australia was party to nine of the twelve conventions (excluding the Plastic Explosives Convention and the Suppression of Bombing and Suppression of Financing Conventions) and New Zealand was party to eight conventions (being those that Australia was not party to, as well as the Nuclear Materials Convention).

while Papua New Guinea has yet to become party to the two maritime conventions and the Plastic Explosives and Nuclear Materials Conventions.

Work of the OECD Financial Action Task Force

The Financial Action Task Force (FATF), a specialist group of the OECD, has been particularly active on the question of money laundering and the suppression of the financing of terrorism. Although only Australia and New Zealand, of the sixteen Pacific Forum members, are members of the OECD, the organization has active relationships with numerous other countries through its Centre for Co-Operation with Non-Members. More importantly, the Nasonini Declaration on Regional Security, as well as committing to implementation of Resolution 1373, saw Pacific Forum Leaders commit to implementation of the FATF Special Recommendations.[105]

Alongside its Forty Recommendations on Combating Money Laundering, the FATF added Eight Special Recommendations on Terrorist Financing.[106] These recommended ratification of the Suppression of Financing Convention and implementation of Resolution 1373, including the criminalizing of financing of terrorist entities, the freezing and confiscating of terrorist assets and the reporting of suspicious transactions related to terrorism.[107] The Special Recommendations also call for international cooperation and for measures to be taken to ensure that alternative remittance, wire transfers and non-profit organizations cannot be used or manipulated by terrorist entities.[108] The Task Force provided guidance on implementing the Special Recommendations,[109] along with a self-assessment questionnaire[110] for States to complete and submit to the agency, as well as guidance for financial institutions.[111]

The international response to this exercise has, according to the FATF, been generally positive, with over 100 non-FATF members undertaking the self-assessment and cooperating with the agency. Regrettably, however, the FATF has identified the Cook Islands, the Marshall Islands and Niue as non-cooperative

---

[105] Above n 108, [5 and 9].
[106] The latter recommendations were adopted 31 October 2001.
[107] Recommendations I to IV inclusive. In the case of New Zealand, these matters are addressed within the Terrorism Suppression Act 2002: sections 8, 9 and 10 prohibiting the financing of terrorism, dealing with terrorist property, and making property or financial or related services available; sections 43 to 47 establish procedures and rules for the reporting of suspicious transactions, lying alongside similar anti-money laundering provisions in the Financial Transactions Reporting Act 1996; and sections 55 to 61 provide mechanisms for the forfeiture of terrorist assets.
[108] Recommendations V to VIII.
[109] Financial Action Task Force, *Annual Report 2002–2003*, 7-8. See also Financial Action Task Force, *Combating the Abuse of Non-Profit Organisations*, 11 October 2002.
[110] Financial Action Task Force, *Self-Assessment Questionnaire: FATF Special Recommendations on Terrorist Financing*, 31 January 2002.
[111] Financial Action Task Force, *Guidance for Financial Institutions in Detecting Terrorist Financing*, 24 April 2002.

countries in its work on money laundering, seen as inherent in the fight against the financing of terrorism (although it has also identified that progress has been made by those States).[112] Countermeasures by OECD members were recommended against Nauru, the FATF considering that inadequate progress had been made by that State.[113]

Reporting to the Counter-Terrorism Committee

As noted, all members of the Pacific Islands Forum, including non-members of the United Nations, have reported to the Security Council Committee under Resolution 1373. By way of example, New Zealand has identified in its reports to the Committee the following features of its domestic legislative framework as measures by which it has implemented the two binding paragraphs, paragraphs 1 and 2, of Resolution 1373:

- *Para 1(a): prevent and suppress the financing of terrorist acts.* Paragraph 1(a), which requires the prevention and suppression of the financing of terrorist acts, is a general provision, expanded upon by the subparagraphs that follow it. In addition to those more specific requirements, New Zealand identified the fact that the Reserve Bank of New Zealand took steps to notify financial institutions of these requirements and prohibitions.[114] Also, funding for security and counter-terrorism has been boosted, with the Minister for Foreign Affairs and Trade identifying the post-September 11 environment as requiring this.[115]
- *Para 1(b): criminalize the provision of funds for terrorist acts.* In compliance with this provision of Resolution 1373, the Terrorism Suppression Act 2002 (the Act) creates offence of the financing of terrorism.[116]
- *Para 1(c): freeze funds and assets of terrorist entities.* The freezing of assets is said to be given effect through various provisions of the Act.[117] New Zealand has described the establishment of various stages in achieving this

---

[112] OECD, 'Financial Action Task Force on Money Laundering, 2000–2001 Report Released',
<http://www.oecd.org/document/57/0,2340,en_2649_201185_1900665_1_1_1_1,00.html> at 9 December 2004 (concerning the Cook Islands). See also Financial Action Task Force, *Annual Review of Non-Cooperative Countries or Territories* (2003) 1 (concerning the Marshall Islands and Niue).

[113] Ibid. See also Financial Action Task Force, *Annual Review of Non-Cooperative Countries or Territories* (2003) 11-12.

[114] See New Zealand's first report to the Counter-Terrorism Committee, above n 145, 6.

[115] The New Zealand Budget for 2003 provided an additional $5.9 million for 2004 and $1.9 million in future years: Hon Phil Goff, 'Funding boost for security, counter-terrorism and emergency responses', Beehive Press Release 12 May 2003, <http://www.behive.govt.nz/PrintDocumentcfm?DocumentID=16723> at 17 Mat 2003.

[116] Section 8 of the Terrorism Suppression Act 2002. See New Zealand's first report to the Counter-Terrorism Committee, ibid 6-7, which also refers to the defining provisions of the Act (sections 4 and 5) and the extraterritorial jurisdiction attached to the offences (sections 14, 15, 17 and 18).

[117] See New Zealand's first report to the Counter-Terrorism Committee, above n 145, 7-9.

obligation.[118] The first stage is to identify the assets to be frozen, through sections 20 to 42 of the Act, which provide a process by which individuals or groups may be designated as terrorist or associated entities. Next, obligations are imposed upon financial institutions to report suspicions of the holding or control of property belonging to or controlled by such entities (sections 43 to 47). Third, section 9 of the Act prohibits dealing with property belonging to terrorist entities. Finally, sections 55 to 61 establish procedures through which terrorist assets can be forfeited.

- *Para 1(d): prohibit the provision of financial or related services to terrorist entities.* Responding to paragraph 1(d) of the Resolution, section 10 makes it unlawful to make property, or financial or related services available to terrorist or associated entities (subject to the express permission of the Prime Minister under section 11).
- *Para 2(a): suppress support to terrorists and eliminate supply of weapons.* In compliance with paragraph 2(a), the Terrorism Suppression Act prohibits the recruitment of persons into terrorist groups, under section 12, and participation in terrorist groups (section 13). New Zealand reported that existing law would see New Zealand comply with the requirement to work towards the elimination of the supply of weapons to terrorists, pointing to the Customs Prohibition Order 1996,[119] the Arms Act 1983,[120] the Crimes Act 1961 (prohibiting the unlawful possession of an offensive weapon),[121] the New Zealand Nuclear Weapons Free Zone, Disarmament and Arms Control Act 1987,[122] and the Chemical Weapons (Prohibition) Act 1966,[123] together with its intended ratification of the Firearms Protocol to the United Nations Convention against Transnational Organized Crime.[124] New Zealand also reported that it would become party to the Plastic Explosives and Nuclear Materials conventions, which would see it create offences under the Terrorism Suppression Act, as required by the treaties and create corresponding offences.[125] This was ultimately done through sections 13B, 13C and 13D of the latter Act.
- *Para 2(b): prevent the commission of terrorist acts.* Additional to the above matters, New Zealand identified measures through which the New Zealand police and intelligence community can investigate groups or organizations of interest.[126] Under the Counter-Terrorism Act, this has seen the creation of authority to obtain interception warrants, warrants to attach tracking devices to

---

[118] As explained within New Zealand's report to the United Nations 1267 Committee, *Response of New Zealand to the Security Council Committee under Security Council resolution 1455 (2003)*, 17 April 2003, 4-7.

[119] Made under the Customs and Excise Act 1996.

[120] See New Zealand's second report to the Counter-Terrorism Committee, *Supplementary report providing additional information on the measures taken by New Zealand to implement the provisions of Security Council resolution 1373 (2001)*, S/2002/795, 19 July 2002, 6.

[121] Ibid.

[122] Ibid.

[123] Ibid.

[124] Not yet in force. See New Zealand's first report, above n 145, 11. See, also, New Zealand's report to the United Nations 1267 Committee, above n 153, 8-9.

[125] See New Zealand's second report, above n 155, 6.

[126] See New Zealand's first report, above n 145, 11.

persons or things, deterrence through more severe penalties, and requiring a computer owner or user to provide information to access data subject to security codes and the like.

- *Para 2(c): deny safe haven.* Sections 7, 73 and 75 of the Immigration Act 1987 (already extant at the time of the adoption of Resolution 1373) were identified by New Zealand as satisfying the requirement to deny safe haven to terrorists.[127]
- *Para 2(d): prevent the use of State territory by terrorists.* The extraterritorial nature of the offences created under the Terrorism Suppression Act, together with extant party liability provisions under the Crimes Act 1961, were identified as further measures to prevent terrorists acting from New Zealand territory against other States or citizens.[128] The further creation of offences of harbouring or concealing terrorists was relied on (offences under 13A of the Terrorism Suppression Act).
- *Para 2(e): ensure prosecution and severe punishment.* As discussed later in this chapter, the various offences created under the Terrorism Suppression Act carry severe penalties.[129]
- *Para 2(f): assist in criminal investigations and prosecutions.* New Zealand again reported that current law permitted New Zealand to comply with this paragraph, referring to the Mutual Assistance in Criminal Matters Act 1992 and the Extradition Act 1999.[130]
- *Para 2(g): effective border controls to prevent the movement of terrorists.* The Passports Act 1992 and Immigration Act 1987 were identified by New Zealand as means through which compliance with paragraph 2(g) of the Resolution could be achieved.[131]

The impact of international counter-terrorism upon executive decision making

One further issue arises from Security Council Resolutions 1373 and 1456, and the impact these resolutions have had upon the decisions of States to enter into treaty relations.[132] Adopted in January 2003, Resolution 1456 calls upon the Counter-Terrorism Committee to intensify its efforts to promote the implementation of Resolution 1373.[133] It also contains the following provisions:

> The Security Council therefore calls for the following steps to be taken:
> 1. All States must take urgent action to prevent and suppress all active and passive support to terrorism, and in particular comply fully with all relevant resolutions of the Security Council, in particular resolutions 1373 (2001), 1390 (2002) and 1455 (2003);

---

[127] See New Zealand's first report, above n 145, 11-12.
[128] Ibid 12.
[129] See New Zealand's first report to the Counter-Terrorism Committee, above n 145, 13-14.
[130] Ibid 14.
[131] Ibid 14-15.
[132] SC Res 1456, 58 UN SCOR (4688th mtg), UN Doc S/Res/1456 (2003).
[133] Ibid [4].

2. The Security Council calls upon States to:
(a) become a party, as a matter of urgency, to all relevant international conventions and protocols relating to terrorism, in particular the 1999 international convention for the suppression of the financing of terrorism and to support all international initiatives taken to that aim, and to make full use of the sources of assistance and guidance which are now becoming available;
(b) assist each other, to the maximum extent possible, in the prevention, investigation, prosecution and punishment of acts of terrorism, wherever they occur;
(c) cooperate closely to implement fully the sanctions against terrorists and their associates, in particular Al-Qaeda and the Taliban and their associates, as reflected in resolutions 1267 (1999), 1390 (2002) and 1455 (2003), to take urgent actions to deny them access to the financial resources they need to carry out their actions, and to cooperate fully with the Monitoring Group established pursuant to resolution 1363 (2001);
[...].

The content of paragraph 1 and paragraphs 2(b) and 2(c), by themselves, do not cause any particular concern. Indeed, they are entirely consistent with earlier resolutions of the Council. It is paragraph 2(a), building upon paragraph 3(d) of Resolution 1373, that raises some issues about the proper role of the Security Council. By calling upon States to become party to all counter-terrorist conventions and protocols, is the Council over-stepping its function and impinging upon State sovereignty?

This is an interesting constitutional question that warrants at least some consideration. On the one hand, member States of the United Nations have to some degree surrendered their sovereignty by becoming a party to the United Nations Charter, to the extent that they have agreed to be bound by decisions of the Security Council.[134] At the same time, however, it could hardly have been intended by those becoming party to the Charter to grant the Security Council the authority to direct members in their treaty-making decision processes. A considerable number of States have complex constitutional rules concerning the executive's treaty-making power which must be complied with before a State can ratify or accede to a treaty. Is the Security Council, by issuing the directions contained in paragraph 3(f) of Resolution 1373 and paragraph 2(a) of Resolution 1456, able to override such domestic constitutional safeguards?

Answering that question appears to lie in one further enquiry: whether any such resolution is indeed binding within the terms of article 25 of the Charter. To avoid an unnecessary examination of this issue (for the purpose of this chapter), it is sufficient to say that it is clear at law that, since paragraph 2 is exhortatory in its nature, it does not impose a legal duty upon States to become signatories to the various international counter-terrorism conventions.[135]

---

[134] Article 25 of the Charter of the United Nations.
[135] For further discussion on this issue, see Alex Conte, *Security in the 21st Century. The United Nations, Afghanistan and Iraq* (Ashgate Publishing Ltd, 2005), 26-8.

Notwithstanding this conclusion at law, it is interesting to note that the resolutions, combined with the interactive dialogue between States and the Counter-Terrorism Committee have resulted in a number of States becoming party to treaties that they might not otherwise have signed or ratified. In the case of South Pacific States, this appears to be a particularly relevant issue. A striking example can be seen in the case of New Zealand's legislative action since 9/11. At the date of adoption of Resolution 1373, New Zealand was not party to the Suppression of Bombing and Suppression of Financing Conventions, nor to the Plastic Explosives or Nuclear Materials Conventions. It became party to the first two conventions once the Terrorism Suppression Act 2002 was enacted.[136] Given the subject matter of those two conventions, there is nothing overly surprising about this. In respect of the Plastic Explosives and Nuclear Materials Conventions, however, the influence of the Security Council's resolutions and Counter-Terrorism Committee are evident.

As treaties that were subject to ratification or accession, New Zealand Parliamentary Standing Order 384 applied,[137] so that the four conventions had to be referred to the Foreign Affairs, Defence and Trade Committee (FADTC)[138] with a National Interest Analysis[139] and then presented to the House.[140] The National Interest Analyses (NIAs), which are contained within the respective international treaty examination reports of the Committee, identify New Zealand's desire to become party to the conventions as being based upon its support of efforts to strengthen the rule of law at the international level[141] and support for an effective and well-supported network of multilateral legal instruments to combat terrorism.[142] In the case of the Plastic Explosives and Nuclear Materials Conventions,

---

[136] As confirmed in New Zealand's third report to the Counter-Terrorism Committee, see *New Zealand Response to the Questions and Comments of the Security Council Counter-Terrorism Committee Contained in the Chairman's Letter of 30 May 2003*, S/2003/860, 5 September 2003, 6-7. New Zealand acceded to the International Convention for the Suppression of Terrorist Bombing on 4 November 2002: as recorded by the United Nations in its record on *Multilateral Treaties Deposited with the Secretary-General*, as at 12 October 2004 at <http://untreaty.un.org/ENGLISH/Status/Chapter_xviii/treaty9.asp>. The International Convention for the Suppression of the Financing of Terrorism was signed by New Zealand on 7 September 2000 but not ratified until 4 November 2002: as recorded by the United Nations, <http://untreaty.un.org/ENGLISH/Status/Chapter_xviii/treaty11.asp>.
[137] See Parliamentary Standing Order 384, [1].
[138] Ibid [3].
[139] Ibid [2].
[140] Ibid [1].
[141] New Zealand Ministry of Foreign Affairs and Trade, *National Interest Analysis, International Convention for the Suppression of Terrorist Bombings*, [2], and *National Interest Analysis, International Convention for the Suppression of the Financing of Terrorism*, [2].
[142] New Zealand Ministry of Foreign Affairs and Trade, *National Interest Analysis, International Convention for the Suppression of Terrorist Bombings*, [2], *National Interest Analysis, International Convention for the Suppression of the Financing of Terrorism*, [2], and *National Interest Analysis, Convention on the Marking of Plastic Explosives for the*

the NIAs noted that New Zealand neither manufactures explosives domestically, nor engages in the transportation of nuclear material.[143] Notwithstanding this, the Analyses pointed to the change in the post-September 11 international context and the call by the Security Council for UN members to become party to all anti-terrorism conventions[144] as sound bases for New Zealand becoming a party to the conventions.[145]

Conclusion

International terrorism has been identified by both the UN General Assembly and Security Council as one of the most serious threats to international peace and security. The terrorist attacks of September 11, 2001, ultimately prompted the intervention in Afghanistan. They also shook the United Nations into concerted action in the fight to eradicate terrorism. Due to a lack of international consensus on the meaning of the term terrorism, however, that action has failed to produce a comprehensive convention on the subject. Despite the considerable work of the Security Council Counter-Terrorism Committee and the Ad Hoc Committee Established under General Assembly Resolution 51/210, the international law on counter-terrorism is mainly based upon twelve very specific conventions that do not have general application and are limited in their binding nature to States parties to those treaties. Given the divergence of party status within Pacific Island countries, this is particularly problematic when considering counter-terrorism in the Pacific. Having said this, the Suppression of Financing Convention does have potentially wider application in its description of conduct that may not be financed. Its effect, either through party status to the Convention or the application of its provisions under Security Council Resolution 1373, is binding on all Pacific Island countries, save Niue.

Both the General Assembly and Security Council have issued numerous resolutions on the topic of counter-terrorism. Although not binding, the General Assembly has built on various guiding principles and expectations in its declarations on measures to eliminate international terrorism. The Security Council established a Counter-Terrorism Committee very soon after the terrorist attacks of September 11, 2001, with the role of liaising with UN members on the implementation of Resolution 1373 and the twelve counter-terrorism conventions,

---

Purpose of Detection, [2], and *National Interest Analysis, Convention on the Physical Protection of Nuclear Materials*, [2].

[143] New Zealand Ministry of Foreign Affairs and Trade, *National Interest Analysis, Convention on the Marking of Plastic Explosives for the Purpose of Detection*, [2], and *National Interest Analysis, Convention on the Physical Protection of Nuclear Materials*, [4].

[144] Resolution 1373, above n 33, [3(d)].

[145] New Zealand Ministry of Foreign Affairs and Trade, *National Interest Analysis, Convention on the Marking of Plastic Explosives for the Purpose of Detection*, [2], and *National Interest Analysis, Convention on the Physical Protection of Nuclear Materials*, [5 and 7].

as well as to provide means by which States could be assisted in doing so. The Committee has seen reports lodged by all Pacific Island countries, even those not members of the United Nations.

The Council has imposed various specific obligations upon States under Resolutions 1373 and 1456. It has been posited, however, that the requirement to become a party to each of the treaties on terrorism remains the sole privilege of State executives and is not a binding provision of Resolution 1456. Notwithstanding that conclusion, it has been observed that the post-September 11 environment, combined with these Resolutions and the work of the Counter-Terrorism Committee, have contributed to States such as New Zealand becoming party to anti-terrorism treaties that might not actually have a great deal of relevance, if any, to those States.

The interface between international, regional and national security is one that is particularly interesting when relating international counter-terrorism to the South Pacific. Although the risk of terrorist attacks within the South Pacific might be assessed as remote, various good reasons exist for Pacific Island countries to act against the threat of international terrorism. Although the region has been fortunate not to be exposed to any considerable history of terrorism, the consequences of a bioterrorist attack could be devastating upon the agricultural and tourist industries. The nature of modern communications and travel, and the lack of infrastructure within some countries, makes the Pacific a potential target for the preparation and planning of terrorist attacks. The OECD Financial Action Task Force has expressed particular concern about the vulnerability of some Pacific countries to being used for the laundering of money and financing of terrorist activities. Both the Task Force and APEC have been active in attempting to redress this vulnerability. Ultimately, if one accepts the position advocated by the current Chair of the Counter-Terrorism Committee, the relevance of counter-terrorism lies not just in national and regional security but also in the establishment and maintenance of an effective international framework.

Chapter 4

The Law of the Sea and Freedom of Navigation in Asia Pacific

Scott Davidson

Introduction

Freedom of navigation is more than a slogan; it represents the essence of a policy which is concerned with the facilitation of maritime trade, the effective disposition of naval forces and the encouragement of hydrographic and marine scientific research. Although it seemed that the seventeenth century debate between Grotius in his *Mare Liberum* (1609) and Selden's *Mare Clausum* (1635) had been resolved in favour of the former, more recent events appear to be displacing Grotius' argument that the seas should be open to all nations and could not be reduced to the sovereignty of any single state. While this principle can be clearly discerned in article 89 of the United Nations Convention on the Law of the Sea 1982,[1] it seems that in recent decades Selden's doctrine of the closed sea has been gaining ascendancy. While a number of states seek to extend their jurisdictional competences ever further seaward, the maritime powers, particularly the United States of America, are concerned to ensure that these developments do not hinder their strategic, commercial and scientific goals in the world's oceans. Given the geography of Asia Pacific, the seaward creep of coastal state jurisdiction has the potential to produce profound consequences for the maintenance and development of seaborne trade and naval mobility. Furthermore, freedom of navigation in Asia Pacific is subject to considerable insecurity through the activities of pirates and maritime robbers who, through their acts of violence and depredation, threaten the often tenuous sea lines of communication in the region.

Before examining the issues affecting freedom of navigation in Asia Pacific, it is perhaps appropriate in a book which is concerned primarily with the South Pacific to say something about the region as a whole. *The Oxford English Dictionary* defines a region as 'an area of land, or division of the earth's surface having definable boundaries or characteristics'. It might be added to this that, in

---

[1] *UN Convention on the Law of the Sea*, opened for signature 10 December 1982, 1833 UNTS 3 (entered into force 16 November 1994) ('UNCLOS'). The full text of the Convention is available at (1982) 21 ILM 1245 and UN Division for Ocean Affairs and Law of the Sea <http://www.un.org/Depts/los/convention_agreements/texts/unclos/closindx.htm>. Art 89 provides: 'No State may validly purport to subject any part of the high seas to its sovereignty'.

geopolitical terms, a region is an area of the earth's surface containing states whose geographical contiguity creates certain political imperatives. In these terms, the Asia Pacific can be more or less defined as an identifiable geographical area with reasonably precise boundaries and shared, if not identical, political imperatives. Certainly, a number of cognate political and economic objectives have been identified by the United Nations Economic and Social Commission for Asia and the Pacific (UNESCAP) and Asia Pacific Economic Cooperation (APEC). At the Track I (governmental) and Track II (mixed governmental and non-governmental) levels the Western Naval Symposium and the Association of Southeast Asian Nations' (ASEAN) Council for Security and Cooperation in Asia Pacific (CSCAP) treat Asia Pacific as a geopolitical whole.

While the narrower geopolitical issues affecting the South Pacific and Southeast Asia differ considerably, in a wider sense, developments in the law of the sea and their impact on freedom of navigation for both commercial and military purposes possess a high level of homogeneity. As we shall see below, the maximization of the right to freedom of navigation which is so important for trade, resource exploitation, scientific developments and naval mobility are in many instances juxtaposed with coastal state security in its widest sense. It is doubtful that an appropriate equilibrium has yet been achieved, but whether a predictable regime which is acceptable to regional and extra-regional states is emerging from the current variety of state practice is also questionable.

Development of maritime zones

Prior to the middle of the twentieth century the limited number of maritime zones meant that the description and content of the right to freedom of navigation was relatively straightforward.[2] Beyond the three mile territorial sea lay the high seas in which the civil or military vessels of all states could navigate and engage in related activities unimpeded.[3] There were certain potential limitations on this right, but these were reserved to the residual public policing function of naval vessels in cases of slave trading and piracy and in the exercise of the right of hot pursuit.[4] From the mid-1970s onward, however, the zonal divisions of the oceans became a much more complex matter, and one which was to have, and still has, a profound impact on the exercise of navigational rights. One of the first major developments

---

[2] This much is evidenced by the fact that only two of the four Geneva Conventions of 1958, the Geneva Convention on the Territorial Sea and the Geneva Convention on the High Seas were primarily concerned with navigational rights. The lacunae in the regulation of navigation in international straits, for example, were regulated by customary international law.

[3] The width of the territorial sea was set at three miles by customary international law. The Geneva Convention on the Territorial Sea 1958 did not contain any reference to the actual width of the territorial sea, since no agreement could be reached on this by the negotiating states at Geneva. See R R Churchill and A V Lowe, *The Law of the Sea* (3rd ed, 1999) 77-81.

[4] The right of hot pursuit permits the public vessels of a coastal state to pursue and arrest on the high seas foreign vessels which have violated the laws of the coastal state. For the conditions under which this might be effected see art 111 UNCLOS.

to occur was the emergence of the 200 nautical mile exclusive economic zone (EEZ).[5] Although the *raison d'etre* of this zone is to allow coastal states to manage and exploit their resources in a sustainable manner, states also enjoy jurisdiction to protect and preserve the marine environment.[6] These jurisdictional capacities raise questions about the extent to which coastal states may interfere with navigational rights to achieve this end. The hybrid nature of the EEZ – a mixture of coastal state jurisdiction and reserved high seas freedoms – has also raised questions about the legitimacy of naval activities in this area.[7]

A further development which occurred during the 1970s and 1980s was the extension in the width of the territorial sea from three to a maximum of twelve miles.[8] This expansion of coastal state sovereignty was not accompanied by any resolution of the question of the limits of the right of innocent passage thus providing further potential for disputes between naval powers and coastal states.[9] In addition, the extension in the width of the territorial sea meant that certain straits became 'zone locked' and thus emerged as 'choke points' potentially restricting the passage of foreign warships.[10] Finally, the emergence of the archipelagic state had the effect of further reducing the area which was formerly high seas by permitting states able to claim this status to enclose large areas of water within straight baselines and subjecting it to their sovereignty.[11]

While most of these developments took place in customary international law and parallel to the United Nations Conference on the Law of the Sea (UNCLOS III, 1973 to 1982), they were incorporated into the architecture of the United Nations Convention on the Law of the Sea (UNCLOS) which was adopted in 1982. Although the Convention had been negotiated as a 'package deal' the administration of US President Ronald Reagan, contrary to the spirit in which UNCLOS had been negotiated, called for its adoption by vote.[12] Although the

---

[5] On the development of the EEZ see David Attard, *The Exclusive Economic Zone in International Law* (1987) 1-42.

[6] See Part V UNCLOS, particularly art 56.

[7] See below.

[8] Art 3 UNCLOS. Churchill and Lowe, above n 3, 80, remark that 'the twelve-mile limit is now firmly established in international law ...'. They also argue that 'the time may soon come ... when customary international law moves beyond the Law of the Sea Convention and regards twelve miles not merely as the maximum, but as the minimum, mandatory limit for the territorial sea'.

[9] See below.

[10] John Noer and David Gregory, *Chokepoints: Maritime Economic Concerns in Southeast Asia* (1996). On the development of the law relating to straits in general see José A de Yturriaga, *Straits Used for International Navigation* (1990) 21-56.

[11] On the development of the archipelagic state concept see Muhammad Munawwar, *Ocean States: Archipelagic Regimes in the Law of the Sea* (1995).

[12] On the negotiating method used at UNCLOS III see Edward Miles, *Global Oceans Politics: The Decision Process at the Third United Nations Conference on the Law of the Sea 1973–1982* (1997); James Sebenius, *Negotiating the Law of the Sea* (1984). See also the series of articles by Bernard Oxman and John Stephenson on UNCLOS III published by the *American Journal of International Law* which appear at (1974) 68 *American Journal of International Law* 1; (1975) 69 *American Journal of International Law* 1; (1977) 71

Convention was adopted, the US, which had profound ideological objections to Part XI UNCLOS on the regime for deep seabed mining, remained aloof and refused to sign; a position which still obtains today despite a subsequent agreement to modify Part XI.[13] The failure of the US to accede to UNCLOS (the Convention has now been in force since 1997) cannot be dismissed lightly since that state is today the world's preeminent naval power with global commercial and strategic interests. Furthermore, it is committed as a matter national policy to maximizing freedom of navigation through its Freedom of Navigation (FON) Program.[14] As Rear Admiral Joseph C Strasser put it in his foreword to the first edition of Roach and Smith's *United States Responses to Excessive Maritime Claims*:

> The national security and international commerce of the United States depend upon the freedoms of navigation and overflight on or over the seas. The Freedom of Navigation Program is designed to further the vital need to protect maritime rights by minimizing efforts of other States to reduce global mobility through the assertion of maritime claims that do not conform to the careful balance of interests reflected in the 1982 United Nations Convention on the Law of the Sea.[15]

While the US FON Program is designed to apply worldwide, there are clear challenges to it in the Asia Pacific region where much of the ocean space has now been incorporated into maritime zones in which coastal states purport to exercise greater or lesser degrees of control over certain navigational activities. This chapter will examine the state practice of a number of Southeast Asian and South Pacific states with a view to assessing the extent to which it impinges upon freedom of navigation, and to reflect on whether there can be any resolution of the 'grey areas' which currently afflict this area of the law of the sea in its current state of development.

American Journal of International Law 247; (1978) 72 *American Journal of International Law* 57; (1979) 73 *American Journal of International Law* 1; (1980) 74 *American Journal of International Law* 1; (1985) 75 *American Journal of International Law* 211 and (1982) 76 *American Journal of International Law* 1.

[13] *Agreement on the Implementation of Part XI of the Law of the Sea Convention of 10 December 1982*, opened for signature 28 July 1994 (1994) 33 ILM 1309 (entered into force provisionally 16 November 1994; definitively 28 July 1996). See Annick de Marffy-Mantuano, 'The Procedural Framework of the Agreement Implementing the 1982 United Nations Convention on the Law of the Sea' (1995) 89 *American Journal of International Law* 814.

[14] The Freedom of Navigation (FON) Program was introduced during the Carter Administration in 1979. The purpose of the FON Program is to maintain navigational freedoms for US naval forces by challenging what the US perceives to be maritime claims in excess of those permitted by extant international law. See 1979 *Digest of US Practice in International Law* 997-8.

[15] J Ashley Roach and Robert W Smith, *United States Responses to Excessive Maritime Claims* (2nd ed, 1996) x.

The Asia Pacific context

The Pacific Ocean is the largest of the world's five oceans. It has a surface area of approximately 156 million square kilometres and occupies about 28 per cent of the world's total surface. The South Pacific Ocean is divided from the North Pacific Ocean by the Equator and is characterized geographically by the presence of a multitude of coral atolls which are either low lying or which fringe mountainous, volcanic islands. The larger coastal states are Australia, New Zealand, Papua New Guinea and the west coast states of Latin America – Chile and Peru. Economically, the South Pacific is of prime importance to its coastal states. It provides the main source of economic sustenance for what are characterized by the United Nations as small island developing states (SIDS), while for regional and extra-regional states it provides access to rich fisheries and a relatively cheap medium for seaborne transport from both North to South and East to West. The main security threats in the South Pacific are not military in character, but relate primarily to issues of human security.[16] These include maritime boundary disputes, fishery disputes between regional and extra-regional states, illegal fishing and pollution, trafficking in drugs, humans and small arms and, more recently, the seaborne transit of ultra-hazardous waste, especially the product of spent nuclear fuel reprocessing.[17]

The maritime configuration of Southeast Asia differs from that of the South Pacific. It is characterized by a high land to sea ratio in which states are densely packed in what is essentially an archipelagic formation with a significant number of enclosed and semi-enclosed seas. The region is connected by a number of straits, some of which are heavily used by civil and military vessels. The Malacca, Lombok, Sunda, Philip and Singapore Straits, for example, are some of the most heavily used straits in the world and form the major sea lines of communication (SLOC) between Southeast Asia and the Pacific.[18] Some of the largest ports on the globe are also located in this region and their security and access has become of even greater significance in the post-September 11 world. Because of the close proximity of the states in this sub-region, there are a number of significant maritime boundary disputes, some of which are a cause of major friction between contesting states.[19] This friction arises not only because of jurisdictional uncertainty in respect of foreign fishing vessels, but because of contested territorial sovereignty, especially in the South China Sea where, despite the adoption of a Code of Conduct to reduce tensions, title to the Spratly Islands is still sharply

---

[16] Sam Bateman, 'The Functions of Navies in the Southwest Pacific and Southeast Asia' in Hugh Smith and Anthony Bergin (eds), *Naval Power in the Pacific: Toward the Year 2000* (1993) 129.

[17] Stanley Weeks, 'Existing Maritime Cooperation Arrangements in the Asia-Pacific Region' in Sam Bateman (ed), *Maritime Cooperation in the Asia-Pacific Region: Current Situation and Prospects* (1999) 1.

[18] Ibid.

[19] For a description of past and current disputes see Jonathan I Charney and Lewis M Alexander (eds), *International Maritime Boundaries* (1993), vol I, 905-1184; vol II, 1195-1474 and vol III, 2295-2368.

contested.[20] There are, however, other activities which hinder freedom of navigation in this region. Southeast Asia is commonly regarded as one of the major 'piracy' hotspots of the world. The word piracy is placed in inverted commas, because what is often colloquially referred to as piracy is nothing of the sort. As will be seen below, piracy *iure gentium* can only occur on the high seas while much of what is referred to as piracy in Southeast Asia is in fact simply criminal activity which takes place in maritime areas under the jurisdiction of coastal states.[21] The possibility of maritime terrorism is also something which needs to be taken into account when considering freedom of navigation in Southeast Asia. While to date there has been minimal interference with shipping by the major terrorist/liberation groups in the region – Abu Sayyef in Malaysia and Jamia Islamia and the Aceh Liberation Front (GAM) in Indonesia – none the less the potential for a major terrorist strike against commercial or military shipping remains a strong possibility, especially in a post-9/11 world.[22]

Freedom of navigation in Asia Pacific: general issues

As noted above, the law of the sea affecting freedom of navigation in the Asia Pacific region has undergone a profound realignment in the last thirty to forty years. The United Nations Convention on the Law of the Sea 1982 (UNCLOS) has increased the potential of coastal states to limit freedom of navigation in areas which were previously characterized as high seas. This potential is further enhanced by the number of so-called 'grey areas' in the law of the sea which can be exploited by states either to minimize or maximize navigational rights.[23] Furthermore, rather than contributing to a stable maritime environment, the differing interpretations of UNCLOS have the capacity to create instability in interstate relations affecting maritime areas. Similarly, progress towards an agreed, common understanding of the relevant provisions of UNCLOS, which has been promoted by certain Track II bodies, is capable of enhancing stability and promoting confidence in maritime relations between regional states.[24]

---

[20] The adoption of a Code of Conduct for the South China Sea might mitigate some of the more extreme aspects of the claims by the contesting states, especially China and Vietnam. See the *Declaration on the Conduct of Parties in the South China Sea*, done in Phnom Penh, Cambodia on 4 November 2002. Text available at <http://www.asean.or.id/13163.htm> at 10 March 2005.

[21] See below.

[22] Scott Davidson, 'International Law and the Suppression of Maritime Violence' in Richard Burchill, Justin Morris and Nigel White (eds), *International Conflict and Security Law* (forthcoming 2005).

[23] Erik Jaap Molenaar, 'Navigational Rights and Freedoms: Grey Areas and Scope for Regional Agreement' in Bateman, above n 17, 97.

[24] The Maritime Cooperation Working Group of the Council for Security and Cooperation in Asia Pacific (CSCAP) has done a significant amount of work in this area. See in particular *CSCAP Memorandum No 6: The Practice of the Law of the Sea in the Asia Pacific* (2002). CSCAP reports to the ASEAN Regional Forum (ARF).

The grey areas in the law of the sea exist largely for one of two reasons: first, since UNCLOS was negotiated as a package deal the Convention embodies a significant amount of compromise.[25] The negotiating states were prepared to trade off their interests in one area of the law of the sea in order to gain advantage elsewhere. In some cases, no agreement could be reached at all and therefore in certain areas UNCLOS represents an agreement to disagree with the relevant provisions designed to have a certain constructive ambiguity. Constructive ambiguity can, of course, turn to destructive ambiguity when confronted with actual circumstances. One area where this issue is particularly acute is the question of the innocent passage of warships in the territorial sea of certain coastal states. The lack of certainty in this area can have the effect of heightening tension if the demands of the coastal state are ignored, as will be demonstrated below. The second reason for the emergence of grey areas is the poor and imprecise drafting of certain provisions of UNCLOS which creates ambiguities. This raises more or less traditional questions of treaty interpretation relating to the ordinary meaning of the words and the intentions of the drafters. Again, given the process which was used to negotiate UNCLOS, the *travaux préparatoires* (preparatory works) are often of little assistance in divining the actual intentions of the parties. An example of this which will be addressed below is the precise content of the right of transit passage in straits used for international navigation, but there are a number of other examples of the use of opaque language and imprecise terminology.

In addition to the so-called grey areas in the law of the sea, there are two further ways in which freedom of navigation in Asia Pacific may be affected by the law of the sea: first, in cases where excessive maritime zones are claimed and, second, by states claiming an excess of jurisdiction within declared zones. Often excessive jurisdictional and zonal claims will be married to create even more objectionable limitations to freedom of navigation. Claims to excessive maritime zones are a world-wide phenomenon with a number of states using methods for delimiting their maritime areas which are not entirely consonant with the applicable law. Sometimes this is because the law lacks clarity, but often it is because the letter of the law is leaned upon rather too heavily or simply ignored. The use of straight baselines is a good – and important – example of this. As will be seen below the wrongful use of straight baselines can have the effect of projecting maritime zones significantly seaward, so that, for example, the outer limit of a state's EEZ might be extended from 200 miles to 250 miles from the coast. Furthermore, the wrongful use of archipelagic baselines can result in the enclosure of thousands of additional square miles of ocean. The second issue is that of coastal states claiming an excess of jurisdiction in certain maritime zones, again most especially the EEZ. As this chapter will show there is a tension between the high seas right of freedom of navigation and the obligation on the coastal state to protect and preserve the marine environment.

---

[25] See the literature cited above at n 12.

The use and abuse of straight baselines

The use of straight baselines in measuring maritime zones (outside closing lines for bays) has been controversial since they first made their appearance in the *Anglo-Norwegian Fisheries* case in 1947.[26] In that case the International Court of Justice (ICJ) declared that Norway was entitled to use a straight baseline system rather than the low water mark for measuring the outer limit of its territorial sea because of the deeply indented nature of the Norwegian coast, because it was fringed by a barrier known as the *skjaergaard* and because of Norway's economic dependence on fisheries. The Court placed limits on the use of baselines but these were restricted to the injunction that they should not depart from the general direction of the coastline and that economic factors should be proven by demonstrable long use. The judgment of the ICJ was adopted by the International Law Commission and codified in article 7 of the Geneva Convention on the Territorial Sea 1958. This provision was subsequently transformed unamended into UNCLOS.

While Article 5 UNCLOS thus adopts the conventional approach that the normal baseline from which the outer limits of a state's maritime zones are measured is the low water mark, Article 7 provides that straight baselines may be used 'in localities where the coastline is deeply indented and cut into, or if there is a fringe of islands along the coast in its immediate vicinity'. Article 7(3) further provides that 'the drawing of straight baselines must not depart to any appreciable extent from the general direction of the coast, and the sea areas lying within the lines must be sufficiently closely linked to the land domain to be subject to the regime of internal waters'. The relevance of a coastal state's economic interests in drawing straight baselines is also retained in Article 7(5). While the constituent elements of Article 7 appear to be self-explanatory, they do, in fact, raise a number of critical questions. It seems that what the drafters of this provision had in mind was a coastline like that of Norway: jagged, precipitous and bounded almost entirely by the outlying *skjaergaard* or a territory in which the land and maritime domain were closely interlinked, if not inseparable. While the words of article 7 are capable of conveying this idea of geographical complexity, they are also capable of other meaning. How, for example, does one gauge what is 'deeply indented'? What does 'a fringe of islands' mean? If straight baselines must 'not depart to any appreciable extent from the general direction of the coast', just how significant must any departure be before it violates the provision? These are unresolved issues which some states have been able to exploit for their own advantage.[27]

---

[26] *Fisheries (United Kingdom v Norway)* [1951] ICJ Rep 116.
[27] The USA, however, has attempted to clarify the position under its FON Program. Roach and Smith, above n 15, 62-3 state that there must be at least three indentations which are in close proximity to each other and that 'the depth of penetration of each deep indentation from the proposed straight baseline enclosing the indentation at its entrance to the sea is, as a rule, greater than half the length of that baseline segment'. In the case of islands, Roach and Smith argue that they must mask at least 50 per cent of the mainland coastline.

Straight baselines are used for the measurement of maritime zones by a number of states in Asia Pacific. These include Australia, Cambodia, China, South Korea and Vietnam. Each of these has been criticized as exceeding the requirements imposed by UNCLOS, but those used by Vietnam and Cambodia have caused particular concern and have elicited protest from the USA.[28] Both these states have drawn their baselines from islands which are minimal in number and, in some cases, more than 50 miles offshore. Since the water enclosed by the baselines became internal waters over which states exercise unrestricted sovereignty, the use of straight baselines by these states had the potential to transform high seas through which there was general freedom of navigation into a maritime zone in which there are limited navigational rights. Furthermore, since the other maritime zones are calculated from the baselines, Vietnam and Cambodia's territorial seas have been projected significantly seaward, with the effect that in some places the outer limits of the territorial sea is 62 miles from the actual coastline.[29] There is certainly no satisfaction of the requirement that the use of straight baselines be predicated on the intimate relationship between the sea and the land domain of the coastal state. Although the water enclosed on the landward side of straight baselines has the characteristics of internal waters over which states are entitled to exercise full sovereignty, article 8 provides that where such waters had not previously been considered as such prior to their enclosure by straight baselines, the right of innocent passage continues to obtain. While this might be regarded as a satisfactory conclusion in the case of merchant vessels, the position is different for warships. The innocent passage of warships is a contentious issue in Asia Pacific with some states claiming that, unlike merchant vessels, warships have no right of innocent passage within the territorial sea.[30] This argument would apply *a fortiori* to internal waters newly enclosed by straight baselines. If one examines the situation in the case of Vietnam which prohibits the passage of warships through its territorial sea without its prior permission, then unnecessarily large areas of the South China Sea are closed to the passage of foreign warships.[31]

Straight baselines can also be used to enclose bays, historic bays and historic waters, as well as atolls and islands having fringing reefs. While the closing line for bays is normally 24 nautical miles, there is no limit on the length of closing lines for historic bays.[32] The effect of this can be that where a state uses straight baselines to enclose large areas of water as internal waters, it once again has the potential to impede navigation. Unlike the use of straight baselines on highly indented coastlines or those fringed with islands, a straight baseline which is used to enclose an historic bay or historic waters is not subject to the proviso in article 8 UNCLOS which retains the right of innocent passage for vessels in the newly enclosed waters. This means that not only might warships be excluded from the zone by the coastal state, but so too might merchant vessels.

---

[28] Roach and Smith, above n 15, 102-103.
[29] Ibid.
[30] See below.
[31] Roach and Smith, above, n 15, 267.
[32] Art 10(6) UNCLOS. See Gayl Westerman, *The Juridical Bay* (1987) 176-8.

UNCLOS does not provide a definition of historic bays, but in the *Tunisia-Libya Continental Shelf Case*[33] the ICJ stated that there was no single legal regime for historic bays and that each case must to be proved on its merits. A 1962 UN study suggested that in order to prove that a bay is 'historic' a state must show that it has claimed the bay as internal waters for a considerable period of time and that it has exercised authority over it during the period in question.[34] It also suggested that such a bay must be so closely linked to the land domain as to be indistinguishable from it. This differs somewhat from the *Digest of US Practice in International Law* which provides that in order to establish a claim to historic waters (a concept which might be wider than that of an historic bay) a state must demonstrate its open, effective, long-term and continuous exercise of authority of the water in question coupled with the acquiescence by other states in the exercise of that authority.[35] Roach and Smith's 'Blue Book' goes on to say that the USA has taken the position 'that an actual showing of acquiescence by foreign states in such a claim is required, as opposed to a mere absence of opposition'.[36]

In the Asia Pacific region there have been few claims of historic bays or waters. Vietnam and Cambodia entered into an agreement in 1982 which claimed part of the Gulf of Thailand as historic waters.[37] The bases of the joint claim were the special geographical conditions of the states and the importance and significance of the waters to each country's national defence and economy. The claim was rejected by the USA on the grounds that these were not valid criteria under international law as that state understands it; that there was no evidence that Vietnam and Cambodia had effectively exercised their authority in the waters in question and that the claim was of too short a duration to be effective.[38] In addition to its claim to part of the Gulf of Thailand, Vietnam also claimed that the Gulf of Tonkin constituted an historic bay. Again, the US suggested that the international legal criteria were not met, but in addition to this, the Gulf was also bordered by China which had not itself claimed the bay as historic and had, in fact, contested Vietnam's boundary with it in the Gulf of Tonkin.[39] Similarly, the claim by Australia that Anxious, Encounter, Lacepede and Rivoli Bays in South Australia are historic bays has been rejected by the USA also on the grounds that they did not fulfil the criteria required by international law.[40]

One area where the use of baselines is provided for in UNCLOS but which seems to have caused few practical problems in Asia Pacific is the case of reefs.[41]

---

[33] *Continental Shelf (Tunisia/Libyan Arab Jamahiriya)* [1982] ICJ Rep 1.
[34] UN Secretariat, 'Juridical regime of historic waters including historic bays', *ILC Yearbook* (1962) vol 2, 1.
[35] *1973 Digest of US Practice in International Law* (1974) 244-5.
[36] Roach and Smith, above n 15, 31.
[37] Ibid 39-40.
[38] Ibid.
[39] Ibid 52-3.
[40] Ibid 35-8.
[41] On reefs generally see P B Beazley, 'Reefs and the 1982 Convention on the Law of the Sea' (1991) 6 *International Journal of Marine and Coastal Law* 281. As Churchill and Lowe, above n 3, 56 observe, the drawing of straight baselines by a number of archipelagic

Article 6 provides that 'in the case of islands situated on atolls or of islands having fringing reefs, the baseline for measuring the breadth of the territorial sea is the seaward low-water line of the reef ...'. The rationale for the adoption of this provision was to protect submerged reefs from environmental damage. As can be seen, however, article 6 only permits reefs which are above water at low tide to form the baseline for other maritime zones. Because of this, there is little to differentiate reefs, whether fringing or otherwise, from drying rocks which have their own regime within UNCLOS. None the less reefs may be designated particularly sensitive sea areas (PSSA) by the International Maritime Organization (IMO) and therefore be subject to special navigational rules.[42] The IMO defines a PSSA as 'an area that needs special protection through action by IMO because of its significance for recognized ecological, socio-economic or scientific reasons, and which may be vulnerable to damage by international shipping activities'.[43] Designation of a maritime area as a PSSA gives coastal states the opportunity to adopt additional protective measures to combat the particular risks associated with international shipping in the area. The only PSSA in the Asia Pacific region to date is Australia's Great Barrier Reef. Here, Australia has introduced a compulsory pilotage system along the Reef's inner shipping route for vessels over 70 metres in length.[44] This would normally be regarded as an impermissible restriction on navigation, but the fact that the Reef is an IMO-approved PSSA remedies this.

Archipelagic states

One of the major potential limitations on freedom of navigation in Asia Pacific has arisen from the emergence of the archipelagic state. Article 46 defines an archipelago as 'a group of islands, including parts of islands, interconnecting waters and other natural features which are so closely interrelated that such islands,

---

states, including Fiji, Kiribati, Nauru, Cook Islands, Tokelau, Tonga and Tuvalu, has obviated the need to apply art 6 UNCLOS.

[42] Guidelines for the designation of special areas under the *International Convention for the Prevention of Pollution from Ships 1973 as Modified by the Protocol of 1978 Relating Thereto*, opened for signature 17 February 1978, 1340 UNTS 61 (entered into force 20 October 1983) and guidelines for the identification and Designation of particularly sensitive sea areas are contained in IMO Resolution A.927(22), 29 November 2001. Roach and Smith comment (at page 459) that 'the concept of [PSSAs] has raised considerable concern because of its potential for upsetting the navigation/environment balance contained in [UNCLOS]'.

[43] Resolution A.927(22), 29 November 2001, Annex II, [1.2].

[44] Australian Maritime Safety Authority, 'Great Barrier Reef Marine Park Authority – Major Issues',
<http://www.amsa.gov.au/About_AMSA/Corporate_information/AMSA_speeches/Shipping_In_The_Asia-Pacific_Conference/Great_Barrier_Reef_Marine_Park_Authority.asp> at 10 March 2005. Peter Ottesen, Stephen Sparkes and Colin Trinder, 'Shipping Threats and Protection of the Great Barrier Reef Marine Park: The Role of the Particularly Sensitive Sea Area Concept (1994) 9 *International Journal of Marine and Coastal Law* 507.

waters and other natural features form an intrinsic geographical, economic and political entity, or which historically have been regarded as such' and an archipelagic state as 'a state which is constituted wholly by one or more archipelagos'. Such a state may draw straight baselines joining the outermost points of the outermost islands and drying rocks of the archipelago, but the main island must be included within the straight baselines and the land (including fringing reefs and atolls[45]) to water ratio must fall within 1:1 to 9:1. The length of straight baselines must not exceed 100 miles, except that up to 3 per cent of the total number of baselines may exceed that length up to a maximum length of 125 miles. The baselines themselves must not depart to any appreciable extent from the general configuration of the archipelago, nor must they be used in such a way as to cut off the high seas, EEZ or the territorial sea of another state. All other maritime zones are drawn from these straight baselines, thus projecting state jurisdiction to maritime areas previously thought of as high seas. Furthermore, the creation by UNCLOS of a new maritime regime – archipelagic waters – has further imposed limitations on navigational rights.

Eight regional states now claim archipelagic state status,[46] and while there appears to be little controversy over these claims, nonetheless the Philippines, rather than claiming the waters enclosed by its straight baselines as archipelagic waters, defines them in its constitution as internal waters with the effect that other states have no navigational rights within the area enclosed by the Philippines' straight baselines.[47] This position is contrary to Article 52 which gives the vessels of third states the right of innocent passage through archipelagic waters. Under article 53 archipelagic states may designate sea lanes and air routes suitable for the continuous and expeditious passage of ships and aircraft through and above archipelagic waters and its adjacent territorial sea. Ships and aircraft using such sea lanes are said to be exercising the right of archipelagic sea lanes passage. In the exercise of this right vessels and aircraft must navigate 'in the normal mode solely for the purpose of continuous, expeditious and unobstructed transit between one part of the high seas or an EEZ and another part of the high seas or an EEZ'. There is some dispute over what constitutes the normal mode of transit for the purposes of these UNCLOS provisions. The naval powers assert that this includes the navigation under water by submarines, formation steaming by surface warships to facilitate their operational security and the launching and recovery of military aircraft from vessels. Roach and Smith argue that 'the provisions regarding the

---

[45] It is not indicated whether the fringing reefs and atolls must be above water at low tide, but to be consistent with arts 6 and 8 UNCLOS it is assumed that this must be so.

[46] These are Fiji, Indonesia, Kiribati, Papua New Guinea, the Philippines, the Solomon Islands, Tuvalu and Vanuatu.

[47] Art 1 of the *Constitution of the Republic of the Philippines* reads, 'The national territory comprises the Philippine archipelago, with all the islands and waters embraced therein, and all other territories over which the Philippines has sovereignty or jurisdiction, consisting of its terrestrial, fluvial and aerial domains, including its territorial sea, the seabed, the subsoil, the insular shelves, and other submarine areas. The waters around, between, and connecting the islands of the archipelago, regardless of their breadth and dimensions, form part of the internal waters of the Philippines.'

width of archipelagic sea lanes were specifically designed to accommodate defensive formations and navigation practices normally used in open waters' thus suggesting that function gives rise to form.[48] It is, however, difficult to square this with the right of innocent passage which exists in other parts of archipelagic waters. Even allowing for the fact that the Philippines requires prior permission for the passage of warships through its territorial sea and archipelagic waters,[49] it would seem that formation steaming could be regarded as a hostile rather than a defensive act and thus inconsistent with the requirements of innocent passage both under customary international law and article 19 UNCLOS.

There is continuing disagreement between the maritime powers and the archipelagic states over the appropriate locations and regimes for archipelagic sea lanes passage. Indonesia and the Philippines restrict the passage of foreign warships and aircraft as well as potentially polluting vessels through designated sea lanes. Indonesia has declared three sea lanes through the Sunda, Lombok and Ombai-Wetar Straits running north-south, but the United States insists that an east-west sea lane through the Java and Banda Seas is a more appropriate route for navigation.[50] As noted above, this causes difficulties where navigation in archipelagic waters outside of an archipelagic sea lane is under the regime of innocent passage. In order to comply with article 19 UNCLOS there must be no overt threat to the coastal state, so according to the Philippines, weapons and radar systems must be deactivated, submarines must navigate on the surface and show their flag, and vessels carrying aircraft can neither launch nor receive them. Indonesia has provided a short east-west sealane in its waters adjacent to Singapore but that is considered insufficient by the United States.[51]

Straits

There are about forty-five international straits in Southeast Asia, over twenty of which are of major strategic importance.[52] The most significant are the Straits of Malacca and Singapore, Luzon, Formosa, Torres, Sunda, Lombok, and Obai-Wetar in Indonesia, and San Bernardino, Surigao and Balut in the Philippines. If the Malacca/Singapore Straits were to be closed the principal link between the Indian and the South Pacific Oceans would be either the Sunda Strait to the South China Sea or the Lombok Strait to the Sulawesi Sea. The alternative route for shipping with tonnage greater than 200,000 gross registered tonnes and drafts too deep for the Malacca-Singapore Straits, would be through the Lombok-Makassar Straits and

---

[48] Roach and Smith, above n 15, 378.
[49] Ibid 267.
[50] The Nippon Foundation Library, 'Threats to Sealane Safety and Security', <http://nippon.zaidan.info/seikabutsu/2001/00800/contents/00007.htm> at 10 March 2005.
[51] Ibid.
[52] The Nippon Foundation Library, 'Asian Sealane Security', <http://nippon.zaidan.info/seikabutsu/2001/00800/contents/00006.htm> at 10 March 2005.

the Sulawesi Sea south of Mindanao, through the Surigao Strait and on through eastern Philippine waters.[53]

The question of straits and their associated navigational rights were a matter of some controversy during the UNCLOS III negotiations. The main complicating issue was that with the extension of the territorial sea regime from three to a maximum of twelve nautical miles a number of straits would have become zone locked by the bordering states' territorial seas. In order to avoid this, a new navigational regime of transit passage was negotiated. Transit passage applies when the straits in question connect one part of the high seas or an EEZ to another part of the high seas or EEZ.[54] In such straits the ships and aircraft of all nations (including military ships and aircraft) enjoy the right of unimpeded passage solely for the purpose of continuous and expeditious transit. Such transit must be in the 'normal mode'.[55]

There is some disagreement over the precise legal status of transit passage with the USA claiming that it has become a right under customary international law and other states asserting that the right is only available to those states which are party to UNCLOS.[56] Given that the USA is not party to UNCLOS the clear implication here is that it should not be entitled to the more liberal regime of transit passage, but should be restricted to the customary law right of non-suspensable innocent passage in straits used for international navigation.[57] As noted above, transit passage, like archipelagic sea lanes passage, exists solely for the expeditious passage of vessels in their normal modes from one part of the EEZ or high seas to another. Like archipelagic sea lane passage, there is no general agreement on what constitutes the normal mode of passage. Again, the USA, the UK and Australia take a consistent position on this and maintain that it permits submarines to navigate underwater; for surface vessels to steam in formation for security purposes and the launching and recovery of aircraft where this is consistent with sound navigational practices.[58] It is reasonably plain that these requirements are designed to maximize the efficacy of naval operations, but coastal states might well perceive them as threats to their national security. The USA would respond that in exercising transit passage rights it is meticulous in observing the requirements that its vessels and aircraft proceed without delay; that it must refrain from the threat or the use of force against the sovereignty, territorial integrity or political independence of nations bordering the strait; and must otherwise refrain from any activities other than those incidental to their normal modes of continuous and expeditious passage.[59] This issue, however, remains unresolved and the possibilities of inter-state tension which might result from this are apparent.

---

[53] Ibid.
[54] Art 37 UNCLOS.
[55] Art 39(1)(c) UNCLOS.
[56] Roach and Smith, above n 15, 24-6.
[57] *Corfu Channel Case (Albania v United Kingdom)* [1949] ICJ Rep 4.
[58] Roach and Smith, above n 15, 282-4.
[59] Ibid.

Innocent passage in the territorial sea

If the extent of the newly created rights of archipelagic sea lane passage and transit passage in international straits is controversial, the same remains true of the question of whether warships have the right of innocent passage in the territorial sea of coastal states.[60] Section 3 UNCLOS is entitled 'Innocent Passage in the Territorial Sea' and Subsection A is headed 'Rules Applicable to All Ships'. Article 17 UNCLOS further provides that 'the ships of all states ... enjoy the right of innocent passage through the territorial sea'. From this and from the alleged existence of a prior rule of customary international law which allowed warships the right of innocent passage, the naval powers argue that it is self-evident that warships have a right of innocent passage in the territorial seas of other states which they are allowed to exercise without interference. In particular the naval powers assert that they are not required to give prior notification or request prior permission for their warships to exercise the right. This, however, is not the view of a number of regional states who argue that warships have no right of innocent passage because such passage represents a threat to their national security.[61] Cambodia, China, Indonesia, South Korea, the Philippines and Vietnam all require prior permission before a foreign warship can enter their territorial waters.[62]

The effect of this disagreement over the true meaning, extent and application of the rights of archipelagic sea lane passage, transit passage and innocent passage contributes to maritime insecurity in the Asia Pacific region.[63] While there has been no incident similar to the Black Sea bumping incident between American and Soviet naval vessels during the Cold War,[64] this does not mean that the situation is free from all risk. In 2001 a squadron of three Australian warships entered Chinese territorial waters without prior permission. Beijing protested to Canberra over this incursion, but the matter remained unresolved with Australia stating that the protest was 'a fairly standard diplomatic procedure'.[65] Given that this incident occurred during a period of heightened international tension between the USA and China over the downing of an American aircraft by Chinese warplanes, it seems clear that the Australian naval incursion was designed to test China's response. While it would seem desirable for regional states to come to some agreement over the nature of the precise content of the various rights of passage, it is apparent that this is unlikely to happen. Attempts to secure agreement on the content of these indeterminate rights have generally served to illustrate the distance by which states

---

[60] F David Froman, 'Uncharted Waters: Non-innocent Passage of Warships in the Territorial Sea' (1984) 21 *San Diego Law Review* 625.
[61] Roach and Smith, above n 15, 251-70.
[62] Ibid, Table 10, 266-7.
[63] *CSCAP Memorandum No 6: The Practice of the Law of the Sea in the Asia Pacific* (December 2002) 1.
[64] John W Rolph, 'Freedom of Navigation and the Black Sea Bumping Incident: How "Innocent" Must Innocent Passage Be?' (1992) 135 *Military Law Review* 137.
[65] Sam Blay, 'Australia's Warships and Innocent Passage' (2001) 75 *Australian Law Journal* 660.

are separated on this matter.[66] In the absence of any agreement therefore, it is clear that there must be some form of confidence building measures which contribute towards regional maritime stability.

The EEZ

The effects of the EEZ regime in Asia Pacific

As noted above, one of the major developments in the law of the sea during the 1970s was the emergence of the EEZ. In the Asia Pacific region this development alone has led to the enclosure of massive areas of maritime territory. With the use of straight baselines and the declaration of archipelagic state status by Indonesia, the Philippines and a significant majority of the South Pacific island states, there has been a considerable projection seaward of coastal state jurisdiction. In the region some states, such as Singapore, have effectively been zone-locked, that is, fully enclosed by the EEZs of neighbouring states, and in the South Pacific, the ocean is now almost fully enclosed by interlocking EEZs leaving very few areas which can truly be described as high seas. One of the salient features of the South Pacific is that the EEZs of the archipelagic small island states are exponentially larger than the land territories on which they are based. As Anthony Bergin points out, 'virtually all the resources and economic uses in this vast area of more than 30 million square kilometres ... (11.5 million square miles ...) are under the control of island states'.[67] Bergin goes on to give some examples of this phenomenon. Kiribati, for example, has a land area of 690 km^2 (266 ml^2) but controls a sea area of 3.5 million km^2 (1.4 million ml^2).[68] While this clearly has significant consequences for marine resource management and protection of the marine environment, it also has the potential to affect navigational rights since there is some disagreement between states as to the extent to which coastal states are able to place limits on freedom of navigation within the EEZ. As Rose has pointed out, 'the EEZ is a modern arena in which the ancient clash between *mare clausum* and *mare liberum* continues to play itself out'.[69] This much is evident in current state practice with states such as China placing clear restrictions on the ability of other states to engage in military or intelligence gathering activities within its EEZ.[70] While

---

[66] An attempt to secure agreement on a uniform interpretation of the right of innocent passage as it relates to warships as the Maritime Cooperation Working Group of CSCAP in Vancouver in December 2001 foundered because of significant differences of opinion. The best that could be achieved was an agreement to disagree which was not ultimately recorded in *CSCAP Memorandum No 6*, above n 63.

[67] Anthony Bergin, 'New Developments in the Law of the Sea' in H Smith and A Bergin (eds), *Naval Power in the Pacific* (1993) 67.

[68] Ibid.

[69] Stephen A Rose, 'Naval Activity in the EEZ – Troubled Waters Ahead?' (1990) 39 *Naval Law Review* 67.

[70] See the dispute between the US and China over the voyage of US vessel *Dowdich* within China's EEZ in September 2002. China claimed that the *Dowdich* was a naval intelligence

South Pacific states have so far not placed restrictions on navigational rights within their EEZs, this does not mean that at some future stage this might not happen. A situation could easily be envisaged where these states, who have already expressed concerns over the transport of reprocessed nuclear waste through their region, might legislate to curb transit of vessels carrying such materials through their individual EEZs.[71] As will be seen below, the New Zealand Green Party has already sponsored a bill which would curtail the navigational rights of vessels carrying nuclear waste through New Zealands's EEZ and while this initiative has not been successful, it gives a lead to regional states who might wish to limit such activities. For the major naval states therefore, the nightmare scenario is an Asia Pacific region in which naval manoeuvres, weapons practice and the transport of certain sensitive cargos are essentially prohibited. The question, of course, is whether UNCLOS is capable of leading to such a result.

The EEZ regime in UNCLOS

Part V UNCLOS contains the major part of the legal regime governing the EEZ. Like other parts of UNCLOS it was negotiated as part of the package deal and therefore represents a compromise in terms of the competing interests of coastal and other states. While this approach might have had the virtue of allowing textual agreement at UNCLOS, it has undoubtedly stored up future conflict in terms of the true extent of navigational rights in this particular maritime area. Attard has argued that the 'delicate, intricate and sometimes ambiguous mechanism' that is the legal regime governing the EEZ will have to be clarified by actual state practice over the years.[72] In essence, the issue is which of the prevailing views will succeed: that which sees the EEZ as a modified form of high seas regime or that which sees it as primarily subject to coastal state jurisdiction: the age old tension between *mare liberum* and *mare clausum*.

While article 55 makes clear that the EEZ is a specific regime in which the competing rights of states are balanced, the content of article 56 gives an indication that the primary *raison d'etre* of the EEZ is resource related. Article 56 provides:

1. In the [EEZ], the coastal State has:
(a) sovereign rights for the purpose of exploring and exploiting, conserving and managing the natural resources, whether living or non-living, of the waters superjacent to the sea-bed and of the sea-bed and its subsoil, and with regard to other activities for the exonomic exploitation and exploration of the zone, such as the production of energy from the water, currents and winds;

---

vessel which required prior permission to enter China's EEZ. See Li Heng, 'What's US Vessel up to in Chinese Waters?', *People's Daily Online*, 30 September 2002, <http://english.people.com.cn/200209/29/eng20020929_104144.shtml> at 10 March 2005.
[71] The South Pacific Forum has already expressed concern over nuclear fuel shipments though its participating states' waters. See Pacific Islands Forum, 'Forum Concerned about Nuclear Waste Shipment' (Press Statement 1499, 2 March 1999).
[72] Attard, above n 5, 66.

(b) jurisdiction as provided for in the relevant provision of this Conventon with regard to:
- (i) the establishment and use of artificial islands, installations and structures;
- (ii) marine scientific research;
- (iii) the protection and preservation of the marine environment;

(c) other rights and duties provided for in this Convention.

From this it is apparent that coastal states have two types of right in the EEZ: sovereign rights which are directly resource related, and jurisdictional rights which are intimately concerned with the exploration, exploitation and protection of resources. The name EEZ is thus derived from its function which is to allow coastal states to explore, exploit and protect resources having *economic* value. It would not therefore seem legitimate for a coastal state to restrict navigational rights unless such rights interfered with its ability to explore, exploit or protect its resources. This delicate balance of rights and duties is alluded to in article 56(2) which provides that:

> In exercising its rights and performing its duties under this Convention in the [EEZ], the coastal State shall have due regard to the rights and duties of other States and shall act in a manner compatible with the provisions of this Convention.

In order to make explicit and further reinforce the balancing of rights and duties between coastal and other states in the EEZ, article 58 provides:

> 1. In the [EEZ] all States ... enjoy, subject to the relevant provisions of this Convention, the freedoms referred to in article 87 of navigation and overflight and of the laying of submarine cables and pipelines, and other internationally lawful uses of the sea related to these freedoms, such as those associated with the operation of ships, aircraft and submarine cables and pipelines, and compatible with the other provisions of the Convention.

The reference to article 87 is particularly crucial to the naval powers who regard it as guaranteeing their ability to conduct military manoeuvres in the EEZs of other states. It will be recalled that article 87, which is regarded as a codification of customary international law, provides that 'the high seas are open to all States' and further that it comprises, *inter alia*, 'freedom of navigation'. The arguable pre-eminence of freedom of navigation is also further underpinned by article 86 which provides that while the provision, which describes the extent of the high seas, does not apply to the EEZ, none the less, 'this article does not entail any abridgement of the freedoms enjoyed by all states in the [EEZ] in accordance with article 87'. As in article 56, however, the freedom of navigation on the high seas must be exercised 'with due regard for the interests of other states in their exercise of the freedom of the high seas'.[73]

---

[73] Art 87(2) UNCLOS.

Balancing rights in the EEZ

The balancing of coastal and non-coastal states' rights in the EEZ is a fertile area for potential dispute. As Song points out, the right of states to conduct military activities in the EEZ of other states was not greatly discussed at UNCLOS III.[74] Upon the signing of UNCLOS, however, Brazil, Cape Verde and Uruguay made declarations to the effect that the Convention did not permit other states to carry out naval manoeuvres or weapons tests in another state's EEZ without that state's prior permission.[75] These declarations elicited strong protest from both Italy[76] and, most pertinently, the USA which consistently maintains that all aspects of military operations on the high seas are preserved by the provisions of UNCLOS.[77] Thus the conduct of naval manoeuvres, weapons testing, the launching and landing of aircraft and other military devices, military surveys and the collecting of intelligence are all regarded as traditional uses of the high sea.

On the other hand, some coastal states such as China argue that the conduct of military activities in the EEZ has the potential to hamper resource exploitation. Say, for example, that the Royal Australian Navy wished to conduct military exercises in China's EEZ which conflicted with the activities of a Chinese fishing vessel. Which state would have the better right to engage in its chosen activity? The coastal state would doubtless assert the 'due regard' provision, especially since it has 'sovereign rights' over the exploitation of resources, while the naval power would most likely assert its high seas freedoms. There is probably no absolute solution to this conundrum since much will depend on the policy adopted by the states in question. The position of the maritime powers on this matter is well known as, equally, is the position of other states in the region, such as China. In general terms, however, the state practice of the South Pacific states on such matters is not clear. The experience of a number of these states in the era of nuclear testing might suggest that they would favour stronger controls over the naval activities of the maritime powers in their region. If this were to occur, then the maritime powers would find their room for manoeuvre much reduced.

Regulating military activities in the EEZ

It can hardly be said that the EEZ regime regarding military activities is satisfactory. In their efforts to secure agreement at UNCLOS III the negotiators have created considerable uncertainty and this uncertainty could easily lead to insecurity if this is not reduced by confidence and security building measures

---

[74] Yann-huei Song, 'The PRC's Peacetime Military Activities in Taiwan's EEZ: A Question of Legality' (2001) 16 *International Journal of Marine and Coastal Law* 625, 635.
[75] UN Division for Ocean Affairs and the Law of the Sea, *United Nations Convention on the Law of the Sea: Declarations Made upon Signature, Ratification, Accession or Succession or Anytime Thereafter*, <http://www.un.org/Depts/los/convention_agreements/convention_declarations.htm> at 10 March 2005.
[76] Ibid.
[77] Roach and Smith, above n 15, 409-14.

among regional states. This much has been foreseen by commentators such as Rose[78] and Boczek[79] who have both recognized the potential of the current regime to lead to international conflict. Where such conflict does arise, as in the *USS Dowdich* case referred to above, article 59 provides for a means of resolution between contesting states. This provides:

> In cases where this Convention does not attribute rights or jurisdiction to the coastal State or to other States within the [EEZ], and a conflict arises between the interests of the coastal State and any other State or States, the conflict should be resolved on the basis of equity and in the light of all the relevant circumstances, taking into account the respective importance of the interests involved to the parties as well as to the international community as a whole.

While article 59 might be regarded as supplementary to the obligation found in article 33 of the UN Charter which requires states to resolve their disputes in a peaceful manner, it is a clear obligation underpinned by the requirement of *pacta sunt servanda*.[80] Thus any action taken by regional states which would lead to a potential military conflict would have to be resolved by way of article 59. As Song indicated, the difficulty with the provision is that 'in the absence of compulsory judicial settlement of disputes concerning military activities in the EEZ, it is very difficult to render an authoritative legal interpretation whenever a dispute arises' and that these matters will only be resolved authoritatively when they are adjudicated by the International Court of Justice or the International Tribunal for the Law of the Sea.[81]

Transportation of hazardous materials through the EEZ

In addition to the disagreement over the extent of the navigational rights of military vessels in the EEZ, there is also potential disagreement over the transportation of hazardous materials through this zone. In the Asia Pacific this has been highlighted most recently by the protests elicited by the transportation of reprocessed nuclear waste from the United Kingdom and France to Japan. The voyages of the armed merchant vessels *Pacific Pintail* and *Pacific Teal* have caused concern on a number of levels.[82] There is some anxiety that in a post 9/11 world such vessels might become targets for terrorists, while for those with environmental concerns the possibility of catastrophic damage to the sea, its ecosystems and human kind which might be brought about by their sinking is a serious concern. Although the voyage details of the nuclear waste vessels is generally kept secret to frustrate those who

---

[78] Rose, above n 69.
[79] Boleslaw Adam Boczek, 'Peacetime Military Activities in the Exclusive Economic Zones of Third Countries' (1989) 19 *Ocean Development and International Law* 452.
[80] *Vienna Convention on the Law of Treaties*, opened for signature 23 May 1969, 1155 UNTS 331 (entered into force 27 January 1980) art 26.
[81] Song, above n 74, 637.
[82] Grant Hewison, 'Return Shipments of Nuclear Material from Europe to Japan' in Bateman, above n 17, 145.

might have designs on hijacking or seriously damaging them, the New Zealand government has requested that they not pass through New Zealand's EEZ.[83] Furthermore, in 2001 the New Zealand Green Party introduced a bill which would have extended the application of New Zealand's anti-nuclear legislation to its EEZ.[84] This would have had the effect of prohibiting vessels carrying nuclear waste from entering New Zealand's EEZ. The justification for this legislation advanced by the Green Party was that it would be consistent with New Zealand's jurisdictional rights to protect the maritime environment and ecosystems of the EEZ. The advice given to the New Zealand Government on this Bill was that it would be contrary to international law as an unjustifiable interference with freedom of navigation.[85] There is little doubt that if New Zealand had proceeded with this legislation it would have elicited protests from a number of maritime states including the UK, France, Japan and the USA contrary to international law.

The issue of whether or not restrictions can be placed on the transit through the EEZ of vessels carrying nuclear waste cannot be resolved simply by examining the current legal regime pertinent to that maritime area, but must be analysed in the light of the various international institutional arrangements which are in existence and which govern the transportation of irradiated materials. These include regulatory arrangements put in place by both the International Atomic Energy Agency (IAEA) and the International Maritime Organization (IMO).[86] Before examining these arrangements, however, it is necessary to consider the relevant provisions of UNCLOS which might have an effect upon the regional transportation of highly active reprocessed nuclear materials.

As noted in the discussion above, while article 56(1)(b)(iii) gives coastal states jurisdiction to protect and preserve the marine environment, this is balanced by article 58 which preserves the high seas right of freedom of navigation which is provided for in article 87. In both cases the rights of the coastal states and states seeking to exercise the right of freedom of navigation in the EEZ is balanced by the need for each to have due regard for the rights of the other. Again, the lack of clarity inherent in this arrangement allows both groups of states to argue on a continuum from absolute freedom of navigation to complete exclusion of vessels carrying certain cargos from the EEZ. Furthermore, in the event of a dispute over such matters, article 59 requires states to resolve their conflict 'on the basis of equity and in the light of all other circumstances, taking into account the respective

---

[83] Ibid 150-51.
[84] The relevant legislation is the *New Zealand Nuclear Free Zone, Disarmament, and Arms Control Act 1987*. The *New Zealand Nuclear Free Zone Extension Bill*, which received a second reading, was sent to the Select Committee on Foreign Affairs, Disarmament and Trade for consideration in 2001. It was returned to Parliament in 2002 and was rejected on 29 June 2002.
[85] For the Green Party's arguments that the Bill was consistent with international law see *New Zealand Nuclear Free Zone Extension Bill*, Parliamentary Network for Nuclear Disarmament, <http://wildrooster.com/~pnndorg/nz_nfz_ext_debate.htm> at 10 March 2005.
[86] See A Suzette V Suarez, 'Post-September 11 Security Challenges to the Legal Regime of the Maritime Carriage of Nuclear and Radioactive Materials' (2003) 18 *International Journal of Marine and Coastal Law* 423.

importance of the interests involved to the parties as well as to the international community as a whole'. Bearing in mind this imprecise legal framework, what arguments can be adduced that could justify limitations on the freedom of navigation of vessels carrying nuclear waste? It is suggested that the primary argument would be based on article 56(1)(b)(i) giving coastal states jurisdiction to protect and preserve the marine environment. Given both the predictable and unpredictable consequences of the introduction of toxic radioactive waste into the marine environment and hence the food chain, it might be argued that prudence dictates action which would prevent such occurrences. The counter-argument would be that the generation of nuclear power is a legitimate activity, as is the reprocessing and storing of spent irradiated fuel. Furthermore, the transportation of nuclear or other inherently dangerous or noxious substances is explicitly recognized by article 23 UNCLOS. Article 23 provides:

> Foreign nuclear-powered ships and ships carrying nuclear or other inherently dangerous or noxious substances shall, when exercising the right of innocent passage through the territorial sea, carry documents and observe special precautionary measures established for such ships by international agreements.

If therefore UNCLOS sanctions the transport of nuclear waste through the territorial sea subject only to certain formalities, then, *a fortiori*, the carrying of such materials through the EEZ where states have only jurisdictional rights and not sovereignty is clearly permissible, subject to similar special precautionary measures established by international agreements where these are in force. Indeed, the very existence of such international agreements governing these activities would tend to suggest that the transport of nuclear waste around the world is clearly envisaged as a lawful, and hence permissible, activity.

Both the IAEA and IMO working individually and in tandem have produced a series of arrangements designed to ensure the safe transportation of nuclear materials.[87] In 1961 the IAEA adopted a recommendatory instrument entitled the Regulations for the Safe Transport of Radioactive Materials. These Regulations were subsequently incorporated into the IMO's International Maritime Dangerous Goods (IMDG) Code which was finally made legally binding by its incorporation into the International Convention for the Safety of Life at Sea (SOLAS) in 2002. The IMDG Code is subject to biannual revision and lays down standards for, among other things, documentation, containment standards, stowage and dealing with contamination. Under SOLAS the IMO also determines the appropriate seaworthiness standards for vessels. In the case of vessels carrying radioactive materials Chapter VII of SOLAS incorporates the Irradiated Nuclear Fuel (INF) Code devised by the IAEA. This code determines the protection standards, including the specifications of containment, for all vessels carrying irradiated material, including highly active waste. While there has been some criticism of the

---

[87] The IAEA and IMO have worked together on these issues since 10 April 1962 when they signed a Cooperation Agreement. See *Cooperation Agreement between IAEA and IMO*, 10 April 1962, IAEA/INFCIRC/20/Add.1.

IAEA/IMO standards,[88] it is none the less apparent that the regulatory framework for the carriage of irradiated materials is an accepted aspect of international maritime commerce. While it might be desirable in the interests of prudence to prohibit the worldwide transport of highly active nuclear waste, it would seem that international law has not yet reached this stage and that in the absence of such a prohibition it is not possible to argue that states have jurisdiction to exclude vessels carrying such waste from their EEZs.

Piracy, armed robbery at sea, maritime terrorism and maritime interdiction of weapons of mass destruction

As noted above, various forms of maritime violence also have the capacity to interfere with freedom of navigation by affecting the security of SLOC. While piracy, and more particularly armed robbery at sea, have been the bane of seafarers and ship and cargo owners in the region for many years, particularly in the waters around Indonesia and the Philippines, in more recent years terrorist activities have become a real threat to navigational security. Furthermore, in the post-9/11 world in which the transport by sea of weapons of mass destruction (WMD), their precursors and delivery systems by non-state actors has become a matter of concern, the US sponsored Proliferation Security Initiative (PSI) has introduced a further mechanism for interfering with navigational freedom.

The nature of the maritime environment in Asia Pacific creates particular challenges for coastal states in the prevention and control of violence at sea. Among the particular factors which make it difficult for regional navies and maritime law enforcement agencies to combat the various species of maritime violence are the archipelagic nature of many of the region's states; the close geographical proximity of many states in Southeast Asia; the large ocean spaces of the South Pacific; territorial and boundary disputes leading to a lack of certainty in jurisdiction; the lack of confidence in political relations between a number of regional states; the absolute or relative poverty of maritime policing resources in certain states, particularly in the South Pacific; and the lack of political will or capacity in some regional states. Taken as a whole, these factors contribute to an exceedingly complex matrix which has to be managed through a combination of unilateral, bilateral and multilateral measures.

Piracy

There is very little true piracy in the modern world since most acts which are described as piracy are, in fact, simply criminal acts within the ports, harbours, internal waters or territorial seas of states.[89] As such, these acts fall squarely within the jurisdiction of the coastal state. The main problems here tend not to be those of

---

[88] See Hewison, above n 82, 156-61.
[89] Scott Davidson, 'Dangerous Waters: Combating Maritime Piracy in Asia' (2000) 9 *Asian Yearbook of International Law* 3.

legal uncertainty, but of detection and apprehension. Very often, those who commit crimes in the coastal waters of regional states are able to flee and hide among the many islands or flee to the coastal waters of neighbouring states, raising the same sorts of problems created by fugitive offenders on land.

Traditional piracy or piracy *jure gentium* is defined by article 101 of UNCLOS as:

(a) Any illegal acts of violence or detention, or any act of depredation, committed for private ends by the crew or the passengers of a private ship or a private aircraft, and directed:
  (i) on the high seas, against another ship or aircraft, or against persons or property on board such ship or aircraft;
  (ii) against a ship, aircraft, person or property in a place outside the jurisdiction of any State;
(b) any act of voluntary participation in the operation of a ship or of an aircraft with knowledge of facts making it a pirate ship or aircraft;
(c) any act of inciting or of intentionally facilitating an act described in subparagraph (a) or (b).

It is noticeable that the definition of piracy in UNCLOS is restrictive as to both the types of act and the *locus* in which those acts take place. The essential requirements of piracy under international law, as opposed to any behaviour which might be classified as such under the domestic law of various states,[90] are that there must be acts of violence, detention or depredation; those acts must be illegal; they must be undertaken for private ends; they must be done by the crew or passengers of a private ship or aircraft; they must be committed on the high seas or in a place outside the jurisdiction of any State; and they must be directed against another ship or aircraft, or persons or property on board a ship or aircraft.

Without analysing each of these requirements in detail, it is apparent that piracy must take place beyond the jurisdiction of states on the high seas, including the EEZ,[91] or on *terra nullius* that is, territory which is not subject to the sovereignty of any state.[92] Furthermore, the relevant illegal acts must be committed by private individuals for private ends.[93] The 'two vessel' requirement also means that a ship upon which a mutiny takes place or which is hijacked by members of the crew or passengers will not be piracy under article 101 of UNCLOS. These two factors appear to have been relevant in the case of the *Santa Maria* where a Portuguese cruise ship was reported to have been captured by pirates in the

---

[90] The laws of a number of states have definitions of piracy which include activities taking place within their coastal waters. These definitions are for the purposes of domestic law alone and do not affect the definition of piracy at international law. See Barry H Dubner, *The Law of International Sea Piracy* (1980).

[91] By virtue of art 58(2) UNCLOS.

[92] Whether this refers to a question of contested and unresolved sovereignty such as the case of the Spratly Islands is a moot point. See Davidson, 'Dangerous Waters', above n 89, 15-17.

[93] On the problems associated with this see Samuel Pyeatt Menefee, 'The Case of the Castle John, or Greenbeard the Pirate?: Environmentalism, Piracy and the Development of International Law' (1993) 24 *California Western International Law Journal* 2.

Caribbean.[94] The Portuguese government issued a request for assistance from the British, Dutch and US navies which began searching for the vessel. Upon further investigation by the State Department, however, it was found that the *Santa Maria* had been boarded by a Captain Henrique Galvao while the ship was in port and had been hijacked on the high seas by Galvao and his men to make a political point prior to elections which were to be held in Portugal. In consequence of this, it was clear that the action was not piracy since it had not been undertaken for private ends, and the US refused to intervene further.[95] In the *Castle John* case,[96] however, certain action by Greenpeace to prevent alleged environmental damage by the dumping of titanium dioxide in the North Sea was held by the Belgian *Cour de Cassation* to be piracy within the meaning of article 15 of the Geneva Convention on the High Seas, since, despite the political colour of the acts in question, they were done for 'personal ends'.

It was also the absence of the two vessel requirement and possibly the existence of a political motivation which prevented the hijacking of the Italian-registered cruise ship *Achille Lauro* in the Mediterranean and the killing of the American hostage, Leon Klinghoffer, by Palestininan terrorists from being classified as piracy *jure gentium*.[97] The four hijackers were eventually apprehended, tried by the Italian courts and convicted of murder. Although the US issued warrants for their arrest on the grounds, *inter alia*, of piracy under 18 USC subsection 1651, it is clear that their actions did not constitute piracy under international law. The hijackers' actions were politically motivated and there was no satisfaction of the two vessel/aircraft requirement. The response of the international community to the lacuna in international law exposed by the *Achille Lauro* affair was to negotiate and adopt the Convention for the Suppression of Unlawful Acts Against the Safety of Navigation 1988 (SUA).[98]

---

[94] Whiteman, *Digest of United States Practice in International Law* (1983), vol 4, 665-7; Dubner, above n 90, 146-9 and Leslie C Green, 'The Santa Maria: Rebels or Pirates?' (1961) 37 *British Yearbook of International Law* 496.
[95] It can also be observed that this incident did not satisfy the 'two vessel' requirement of art 15 of the *Geneva Convention on the High Seas 1958*, opened for signature 29 April 1958, 450 UNTS 11 (entered into force 30 September 1962), whose terms were incorporated without amendment as art 100 UNCLOS. Galvao and his insurgents eventually put into the Brazilian port of Recife and were granted political asylum.
[96] *Castle John and Nederlandse Stichting Sirius v NV Marjlo and NV Parfin* (1986) 77 *International Law Reports* 537.
[97] David Freestone, 'The Convention for the Suppression of Unlawful Acts Against the Safety of Navigation' (1988) 3 *International Journal of Estuarine and Coastal Law* 305; Malvina Halberstam, 'Terrorism on the High Sea: The Achille Lauro, Piracy and the IMO Convention on Maritime Safety' (1988) 82 *American Journal of International Law* 269.
[98] Opened for signature 10 March 1988, 1678 UNTS 222 (entered into force 1 March 1992) ('SUA'); also known as the 'Rome Convention'. On SUA see below.

Armed robbery against ships

As noted above, most acts which are referred to colloquially as piracy are simply crimes under the domestic law of the states in whose coastal waters they take place. A review of most acts of 'piracy' reported to the Piracy Reporting Centre of the International Maritime Bureau (IMB) or to the IMO fall within this category.[99] The IMO makes clear the distinction between piracy proper and armed robbery against ships in its *Draft Code of Practice for the Investigation of Crimes of Piracy and Armed Robbery against Ships*.[100] Under the Code of Practice, 'piracy means unlawful acts as defined by article 101 (UNCLOS)'[101] while 'armed robbery against ships' means:[102]

> Any unlawful act of violence or detention or any act of depredation, or threat thereof, other than an act of 'piracy', directed against a ship or against persons or property on board such ship, within a State's jurisdiction over such offences.

It will be noted that while this definition bears similarity to the definition of piracy in article 101, it omits the two vessel requirement and says nothing about the private motive of such unlawful acts. The main requirement is that the acts be unlawful, presumably under the law of the coastal state. The IMB definition does not make a distinction between piracy and armed robbery, but since it is for statistical purposes alone, this has little significance from a legal point of view.[103] It is interesting, however, that the IMB definition of piracy and armed robbery includes inchoate crimes, as well as those crimes which have been consummated. The definition provides that piracy and armed robbery is:[104]

> An act of boarding or attempting to board any ship with the intent to commit theft or any other crime and with the intent or capability to use force in furtherance of that act.

It will be noted that the *locus* of the offence appears to be irrelevant under the IMB definition, and this is confirmed by a perusal of the many incidents contained in that organization's annual reports.

Both the IMO and IMB definitions are also capable of comprehending crimes which extend beyond the notions of theft or armed robbery. In its 2001 report the IMB noted that a new trend in 'piracy' had emerged in the northern parts of the Malacca Straits in the waters off the Indonesian province of Aceh, where pirates had started to kidnap the crew members of ships for the purposes of holding

---

[99] The IMB is a branch of the International Chamber of Commerce which established its Piracy Reporting Centre in Kuala Lumpur in 1992 in response to the increasing number of armed attacks against ships and their crews. International Chamber of Commerce Commercial Crime Services, *IMB Piracy Reporting Centre* <www.icc-ccs.org/prc/overview.php> at 18 March 2005.
[100] MSC/Circ.984, 20 December 2000.
[101] Ibid [2.1].
[102] Ibid [2.2].
[103] *IMB Report 2001* (2001) 3.
[104] Ibid.

them for ransom.[105] As the IMB report observed, this trend was previously confined to Somali waters, but in the context of kidnap and ransom off Aceh, it seems that a political element was involved with the Free Aceh Movement being held responsible for these activities by the Indonesian Government.[106] Given the existence of such a political element, it seems that kidnap and ransom to finance secessionist activities could very well fall into the next category of violent activity at sea: terrorism.

Terrorism

States have argued for decades about the legal meaning of terrorism and the need for a comprehensive instrument to deal with the issue.[107] As yet, however, there is no international legal instrument which provides a comprehensive definition of terrorism. There are a number of instruments which clearly deal with the phenomenon or aspects of it, but they singularly fail to define it.[108] The United Nations General Assembly has, however, indicated what it believes the nature of terrorism to be in a number of resolutions. In General Assembly Resolution 51/210 which is entitled *Measures to Eliminate International Terrorism* it stated that it:

1. Strongly condemns all acts, methods, and practices of terrorism as criminal and unjustifiable, wherever and by whomsoever committed;
2. Reiterates that criminal acts intended or calculated to provoke a state of terror in the general public, a group of persons or particular persons for political purposes are in any circumstance unjustifiable, whatever the considerations of a political, philosophical, ideological, racial, ethnic, religious or other nature that may be invoked to justify them.[109]

In short, it might be said that terrorism, in a colloquial sense, is politically motivated violence which is perpetrated against both military and civilian targets by non-state actors. Whatever the motivation for terrorism, it is clear that the use of violence will constitute a crime under the criminal law of all states.

While maritime terrorism remains relatively insignificant in comparison to piracy and armed robbery against ships in the Asia Pacific region, analysts agree that it is a phenomenon which is likely to become increasingly common as terrorist groups realize the potential for exerting pressure on target states which this form of

---

[105] Ibid 17.
[106] Ibid.
[107] Laqueur states that between 1936 and 1981 no less than 109 different definitions of terrorism were advanced in a variety of forums. See Walter Laqueur, 'Reflections on Terrorism' (1986) 65 *Foreign Affairs* 86. See also the chapter by Alex Conte in this volume.
[108] See the conventions discussed in the chapter by Alex Conte at footnotes 58-69 and accompanying text.
[109] GA Res 51/210 (1996).

terrorism will afford them.[110] The Sri Lankan Tamil Tigers and Filipino Abu Sayyef secessionists have undertaken a number of maritime terrorist attacks and have engaged in piratical activity to fund their operations.[111] The Al Quaeda network also signalled its terrorist intentions with an attack upon the *USS Cole* in Yemen in 2000.[112] The chaos which maritime terrorism could create should not be underestimated. Not only could it cause a significant loss of life, but it could also threaten important SLOC and cause massive environmental damage, particularly in the multiplicity of narrow straits in the South East Asia region or the sensitive ecosystems of the South Pacific.[113] If a very large oil tanker of 250,000 tonnes or greater were sunk in the Malacca Straits, for example, the major oil route to the Far East would be blocked and significant global economic and security consequences would ensue. The Free Aceh Movement (GAM), which is seeking autonomy from Indonesia, has indicated in the past that it would be prepared to disrupt shipping in the Malacca Straits in order to further its cause.[114]

It was, in fact, an earlier terrorist incident which gave rise to the drafting and adoption in 1988 of possibly the most important legal instrument designed to fight criminal activity at sea, regardless of location. Following the hijacking of the *Achille Lauro* in 1985 the IMO sponsored Convention for the Suppression of Unlawful Acts Against the Safety of Maritime Navigation and its associated Protocol for the Suppression of Unlawful Acts Against the Safety of Fixed Platforms Located on the Continental Shelf was adopted.[115] The main purpose of this Convention is to deal with the jurisdictional issues arising from criminal offences perpetrated on vessels and their personnel and to facilitate the prosecution or extradition of offenders involved in such offences.

Although SUA was adopted under the auspices of the IMO largely to deal with the threat of terrorism against ships, the convention has considerably wider scope than this and covers a range of criminal activity, including armed robbery and piracy, directed at ships and fixed continental shelf platforms. Under article 3

---

[110] For a recent response to this assumption see the Council for Security Cooperation in the Asia-Pacific Maritime Cooperation Working Group, *Statement Against Maritime Terrorism* (19 February 2002, Seoul, Republic of Korea).

[111] William Joseph Ackerman, 'Transnational Crime and Terrorism and its Effects on the Maritime Industry' (2003) 13 *Port Technology International* 223; Rohan Gunaratna, 'Trends in Maritime Terrorism – The Sri Lankan case', *Lanka OutLook*, Autumn 1998, Spotlight on Sri Lanka <http://www.is.lk/is/spot/sp0316/clip8.html> at 10 March 2005.

[112] For an account of the facts and US responses see Raphaeil Perle and Ronald O'Rourke, *CRS Report to Congress: Terrorist Attack on USS Cole*, 30 January 2001, Findlaw <http://news.findlaw.com/cnn/docs/crs/coleterrattck13001.pdf> at 10 March 2005.

[113] See Stanley B Weeks, 'Sea Lines of Communication (SLOC) Security and Access' (Policy Paper 33, University of California Institute on Global Conflict and Cooperation, 1998).

[114] 'Gam says it controls ship lanes', *Nation*, 4 September 2001. On 25 August 2001, the coal transporter *Ocean Silver* was hijacked by members of GAM who were armed with guns and grenade launchers. The hijackers released six crew members, but held another six hostage and demanded a ransom for their release. *IMB Report 2001*, above n 103, 36.

[115] For documents detailing the *Achille Lauro* incident see (1985) 24 *International Legal Materials* 1509. See also Freestone and Halberstam, above n 97.

SUA specifies as offences a number of acts against shipping, including the seizure or destruction of ships and the endangering of safe navigation by the use of violence against any person on a ship or by damaging a ship, its cargo or equipment, including its navigational facilities. States are required to make the offences identified by the convention punishable under their laws[116] and establish jurisdiction over offences committed on or against their ships or in their territory or by their nationals.[117] States may also assert jurisdiction over offences committed by stateless persons habitually resident within their territory, offences where their nationals are victims and offences aimed at compelling a state to do or abstain from doing some act.[118] The offences identified in the Convention are deemed to be included as extraditable offences in extradition treaties between states parties,[119] and a state party in whose territory an alleged offender is found is either obliged to extradite him to a requesting state party or to prosecute him.[120] In order to ensure that this latter is possible, states parties are required to ensure that the appropriate jurisdictional arrangements are in place to allow prosecution to take place.[121]

One of the noticeable features of SUA is its territorial application. By article 4 the convention applies to ships which are navigating, scheduled to navigate into, through or from waters beyond the outer limit of the territorial sea of a single state or the lateral limits of its territorial sea with adjacent states. This means that an offence committed in contemplation of a vessel making an international voyage, or in the course of making an international voyage beyond the territorial sea of the state will be subject to the jurisdiction of any of the convention states into whose hands the perpetrator of an offence might fall. A problem with which SUA does not grapple, however, is that of whether an individual might still claim the political offence exception in cases of politically motivated terrorism. The convention is silent on this matter, so it must be assumed that this remains a distinct possibility and could be used to undermine the effectiveness of the instrument.[122]

While it is recognized that there is a broad array of practical issues affecting the control of violence at sea, none the less, the existence of a soundly based and

---

[116] Art 5 SUA.
[117] Art 6(1) SUA.
[118] Art 6(2) SUA.
[119] Art 11 SUA.
[120] Art 10 SUA.
[121] Art 6(4) SUA.
[122] A diplomatic conference is to be held under the auspices of the IMO in 2005 to adopt changes made to SUA and *Protocol for the Suppression of Unlawful Acts Against the Safety of Fixed Platforms Located on the Continental Shelf*, opened for signature 10 March 1988, 1678 UNTS 304 (entered into force 1 March 1992) ('SUAPROT') to make them more responsive in dealing with maritime terrorism. A range of new offences is likely to be added to art 3 and art 8 will provide for the boarding of vessels suspected of being involved in terrorist activities. See the *Report of the Legal Committee (LEG)*, 89th session, 25–29 October 2004, IMO <http://www.imo.org/Newsroom/mainframe.asp?topic_id=280&doc_id=3662> at 22 November 2004.

predictable legal framework for combating such violence is a prerequisite for effective action. A sound legal basis for taking measures against armed robbers, pirates and terrorists might also be seen as a confidence building measure since it must be underpinned by strong levels of cooperation. Indeed, cooperation is central to the provisions of UNCLOS on piracy where all states are duty bound to cooperate in the suppression of piracy,[123] and in SUA where cooperation is identified as a primary means of preventing violence against ships and their personnel. Article 12 of SUA states that states parties must afford each other the greatest measure of assistance in connection with criminal proceedings brought in respect of the convention offences in article 3. Article 13 of SUA further provides:

1. States Parties shall cooperate in the prevention of the offences set forth in Article 3, particularly by:
(a) taking all practicable measures to prevent preparations in their respective territories for the commission of those offences within or outside their territories;
(b) exchanging information in accordance with their national law, and co-ordinating administrative and other measures taken as appropriate to prevent the commission of offences set forth in Article 3.

While SUA is potentially one of the most potent weapons in the legal armoury of states, it has not attracted a significant number of ratifications from states in the Asia Pacific region, despite calls upon these states to do so from the UN and the shipping industry.[124] As the UN Secretary-General has noted in his 1998 Report on Oceans and the Law of the Sea, SUA 'provides another more useful vehicle for prosecution than the nineteenth century piracy statutes'.[125] More recently, the UN General Assembly has urged states to ratify SUA to help combat violence at sea. In Resolution 56/12 entitled *Oceans and Law of the Sea*[126] the General Assembly urged states to become parties to SUA and SUAPROT and to ensure its effective implementation through the adoption of legislation aimed at ensuring that there is a proper framework for responses to incidents of armed robbery at sea.

At the industry level, the Safe Navigation and Environment Committee (SNEC) of the Asian Shipowners Forum at its meeting in November 2001 observed:

---

[123] Art 100 UNCLOS.
[124] IMO, *Summary of Status of Conventions as at 30 October 2004* <http://www.imo.org/HOME.html> at 22 November 2004. For details of ratifications see IMO, *Status of Complete Listings of Conventions* <http://www.imo.org/includes/blastDataOnly.asp/data_id%3D10614/status.xls> at 22 November 2004. The Convention entered into force 1 March 1992. States in the Asia Pacific region which are parties to SUA and SUAPROT are Australia, China, India, Japan, Marshall Islands, New Zealand, Russian Federation, Samoa, Tonga, USA, Vietnam and Vanuatu.
[125] UN Doc A/53/456 (1998) [151].
[126] UN Doc A/RES/56/12 (2001).

Following the recent terrorists attacks on the United States, the SNEC expressed concerns that cargo ships could become easy targets of pirates or hijackers who may be linked to terrorist groups. In this respect, the SNEC was of the view that governments should be encouraged to ratify the 1988 Convention for the Suppression of Unlawful Acts Against the Safety of Maritime Navigation (Rome Convention as it is commonly called) and to implement its provisions in their national legislation as soon as possible. The Convention should provide a very useful tool for governments to combat acts of piracy and armed robbery against ships.[127]

In the light of these calls to ratify SUA, it would seem that a concerted effort to secure ratification and implementation of SUA in Asia Pacific would be a significant step forward in combating violence at sea in the region.

IMO recommendations

In June 1999 the Maritime Safety Committee of the IMO issued a circular entitled *Recommendations to Governments for preventing and suppressing piracy and armed robbery against ships*,[128] in which the IMO suggested that states should develop action plans for dealing with piracy, as well as establishing the necessary infrastructure and operational arrangements for the purposes of preventing and suppressing piracy and armed robbery against ships.[129] On the question of jurisdiction, the IMO recommended that states take such measures as may be necessary to establish their jurisdiction over the offences of piracy and armed robbery at sea, including adjustment of their legislation to enable them to apprehend and prosecute persons committing such offences.[130] While the IMO did not recommend ratification of SUA, none the less, this would go a long way to meeting the issues raised in its *Recommendations*. As a further adjunct to the assumption of state jurisdiction over the offences of piracy and armed robbery against ships, however, the IMO stated that a person apprehended outside the territorial sea of any state for committing these crimes should be prosecuted under the laws of the investigating state by mutual agreement with other substantially interested states, including the flag state or states within whose jurisdiction an offence occurs.[131] While the potential expansion of the jurisdictional bases which

---

[127] Press Release, 2 November 2001.
[128] MSC/Circ.622/Rev.1 (1999).
[129] Ibid [4]. At an international conference involving fifteen regional States which took place in Tokyo in March 2000 the IMO and a number of ship-owners and their associations issued the *Tokyo Declaration* and a *Model Action Plan* which closely follows the IMO *Recommendations*. These relate primarily to reporting structures and the development of effective communications between the various law enforcement agencies of regional States. The conference *communiqué* noted, however, that anti-piracy activities 'including potential cooperation can only be done subject to relevant international treaties, each Participating Administration's domestic legislation as well as its availability of adequate resources to sustain these activities'.
[130] Above n 128, [17].
[131] Ibid [16].

the IMO has recommended is welcome, the history of the ratification of SUA does not suggest that rapid implementation is likely to occur.

A further initiative suggested by IMO is the adoption of a *Regional Agreement on Cooperation in Preventing and Suppressing Acts of Piracy and Armed Robbery against Ships*.[132] The agreement, which remains in draft form, stresses the need for international cooperation in suppressing piracy and armed robbery at sea. While it reiterates the right and obligation of states to take measures to suppress piracy and armed robbery in its own waters, it none the less also recognizes that jurisdictional boundaries inhibit effective action against fugitive offenders. The draft regional agreement therefore sets out a process for cooperation which would allow the vessels of one state to pursue offenders into the national waters of another state. Such pursuit would only be permitted where a law enforcement liaison officer is embarked on the law enforcement vessel of the other state and gives his or her permission for pursuit into national waters.[133] This form of devolved state authorization which would allow a foreign state to engage in law enforcement activities appears to be some way from becoming a reality, but it does not preclude other forms of bilateral cooperation in the interim.

The Proliferation Security Initiative

In the post 9/11 period one of the policies that has been developed which is likely to have a significant impact on freedom of navigation is the Proliferation Security Initiative (PSI). This policy, which was announced by US President George W Bush in Poland on 31 May 2003 represents an attempt to stop trafficking in weapons of mass destruction (WMD). The policy permits national authorities of reciprocating states to stop and search ships and aircraft carrying suspect cargo and to seize illegal weapons or missile technologies. In essence, the fifteen states[134] who are now participants in the PSI commit themselves to board suspicious vessels flying their own flags; to consent to the boarding and search of their vessels by other states who are members of the PSI; to stop and search suspicious vessels in their territorial seas and their contiguous zones; to require suspicious aircraft in their airspace to land for inspection; to carry out rigorous inspections at their ports and airfields and not to transport WMD to or from states of concern. The PSI is not a legal instrument, but rather an understanding among the fifteen participating states that by acting in this reciprocal way they are simply applying existing rules of international law. As Byers says, '... much of the PSI involves nothing more than the consistent and rigorous application of existing rights under national and international law'.[135] Despite this observation, however, it should be noted that the

---

[132] Ibid, Appendix 5.
[133] Ibid, art 5.
[134] Australia, Canada, France, Germany, Italy, Japan, the Netherlands, Norway, Poland, Portugal, Russia, Singapore, Spain, the UK and the US.
[135] Michael Byers, 'Policing the High Seas: The Proliferation Security Initiative' (2004) 98 *American Journal of International Law* 526, 528.

US has signed a bilateral agreement with Liberia in which both states grant each other reciprocal rights to board suspect vessels flying their respective flags on the high seas. Because this agreement applies to all areas of high seas, its potential sphere of application is considerable. Liberia is second only to Panama in terms of tonnage under its flag, so this brings a considerable amount of shipping within the purview of the agreement. If the US were to reach similar agreements with other flag of convenience states, it would have search rights to nearly ninety five per cent of world shipping. While in terms of most of the PSI members this would be underpinned by a degree of reciprocity, in terms of Liberia and Panama, which do not have navies, the right of stop and search on the high seas is likely to consist of one-way traffic.

Conclusion

The nature of the maritime environment and the geopolitical realities of Asia Pacific make it a crucible for the development of the law of the sea. The pressures created by the lack of precision in the drafting of UNCLOS are more likely to be tested to their limit in this region than in any other part of the world. In addition to this the regional incidence maritime violence (piracy, armed robbery at sea and terrorism) and the respective counter-measures designed to deal with it add a new dimension to limitations on freedom of navigation and the security of maritime trade. While attempts have been and continue to be made to resolve some of the more pressing issues through a variety of mechanisms, it is apparent that the tensions between the perceived need of certain coastal states to extend their jurisdictional competences ever further seaward and the resistance by the maritime powers to the extension of coastal state power create a climate of uncertainty and insecurity. Although it can be argued that the claim and counter-claim of coastal states and maritime powers by way of testing the acceptability or otherwise of their demands is simply part of the usual international intercourse which results in the organic development of the law, none the less it would be short-sighted to fail to recognize that not taking action to resolve these issues in a more structured way could result in conflict. As the tenth anniversary of the entry into force of UNCLOS looms, it becomes even more apparent that the Convention was not an end in itself, but only a beginning. There is still much work to be done if the law of the sea is to be a suitable vehicle not only for maintaining freedom of navigation but for building security and confidence in the maritime areas of the Asia Pacific region.

Chapter 5

Climate Change in Oceania: Responses to the Kyoto Protocol

Geoff Leane

Introduction

Climate change issues are of great importance in the Pacific region given the particular vulnerability of its small island developing states. They are in an invidious position having not experienced the development cycle of industrialized states that is the motivating force behind greenhouse gas emissions, yet are among the most vulnerable likely victims of global warming due to their particular geographies and fragile economies. They are juxtaposed with two industrialized states – Australia and New Zealand – whose responses to the challenge of climate change might generously be described as ambiguous. The region is really a microcosm of the international order in this at least, and the Kyoto Protocol assumes great symbolic as well as practical importance as its aspirations and limitations are magnified by the peculiarities of the region and its disparate actors.

This chapter will first give a broad outline of the structure, status and limitations of the Kyoto Protocol to the United Nations Framework Convention on Climate Change (UNFCCC).[1] The discussion will then move to a review of policy responses in the region, concentrating on Pacific Forum states of the South Pacific and in particular Australia and New Zealand, the two industrialized states in the region.

The Kyoto Protocol

Background

An international response to climate change concerns began with the establishment of an Intergovernmental Panel on Climate Change (IPCC) in 1988 as a joint initiative of the World Meteorological Organization and the United Nations

---

[1] *United Nations Framework Convention on Climate Change*, opened for signature 9 May 1992, 1771 UNTS 107 (entered into force 21 March 1994) ('UNFCCC'); *Kyoto Protocol to the United Nations Framework Convention on Climate Change*, opened for signature 11 December 1997, (1998) 37 ILM 22 (entered into force 16 February 2005) ('Kyoto Protocol').

Environment Program. It warned of possible threats and the need for an institutional response, which in 1992 took the form of the UNFCCC at the Rio 'Earth Summit'.[2] The Convention was signed by 155 states, and was the first international environmental agreement to be negotiated by almost all of the international community. The ambition of the Convention (article 2) was to stabilize so-called greenhouse gases (GHGs) 'at a level that would prevent dangerous anthropogenic interference with the climate system'. This objective was further articulated in five principles (article 3), including those of intergenerational equity, the precautionary principle and the need to take account of the special circumstances of developing countries through an emerging principle of 'common but differentiated responsibility' in international environmental law. States made commitments to mitigate climate change (article 4) but the means of implementation were left substantially to states' discretion, though they might include not only abatement of emissions but also enhancement of greenhouse 'sinks' (human-induced land-use change and forestry activities) and possible trading in emission reduction units.

The Kyoto Protocol to the UNFCCC allows parties to choose their preferred mix of regulation through 'command and control' measures and economic instruments which lean toward market-based responses. The former tend to be more democratic, transparent and enabling of accountability, though often expensive and inefficient. They may also be less encouraging of innovation compared to economic instruments, which tend to foster technological development as emitters try to reduce compliance costs. Economic instruments may in theory at least be more flexible, and although public participation is limited in the formative stages it may come into play later as consumers exercise product choices. In New Zealand, for example, economic instruments include carbon charges and the creation of a market in tradable emission permits. It should be noted, however, that the so-called economic instruments are still, at least in their formative stages, regulatory creations of government and may continue to require a regulatory and administrative support framework. Whilst economic instruments may be more cost effective it is not always possible to demonstrate this.[3]

In light of the relative resources available to different states and their incommensurate contributions to present elevated levels of GHGs, parties were assigned different levels of commitments in pursuit of the goals of the Convention 'in accordance with their common but differentiated responsibilities and respective

---

[2] For a more comprehensive history see Daniel Bodansky, 'The History of the Global Climate Change Regime' in Urs Luterbacher and Detlef Sprinz (eds), *International Relations and Global Climate Change* (2001) 23, 40. The threats included an increase in global mean surface temperatures of 1.4-5.8 degrees Centigrade, rising sea levels (9-88 cm by 2100), flooding of low-lying coastal areas, changing rainfall patterns resulting in floods and droughts, and a more variable climate generally with increased threats of extreme weather events: UNFCCC, *A Guide to the Climate Change Convention and its Kyoto Protocol* (2002) 5.

[3] See, e.g. Klaus Bosselmann, Jenny Fuller and Jim Salinger, *Climate Change in New Zealand: Scientific and Legal Assessments* (2002) 79: a 1994 OECD survey indicated that in 90 per cent of cases validating data on the incentive impacts of economic instruments was inconclusive or unavailable.

capabilities' (article 3(1) of the UNFCCC). In particular, developed (OECD) states and those with economies 'in transition' (EITs) – for example, Hungary, Bulgaria, Belarus, the Czech Republic and the Russian Federation – were grouped in Annex I to the Convention. Those states were originally required to reduce their GHG emissions[4] to 1990 levels by the year 2000, though in fact over the 1990s the OECD states from Annex I actually increased emissions by 6.6 per cent whilst emissions from the EITs declined by more than 40 per cent.[5] OECD states from Annex I are also listed in Annex II, and thereby assigned responsibility for providing financial resources (via the UN Global Environment Facility) to assist developing states and for providing environmentally friendly technologies to both developing states and EITs.

The original framework was to be developed in annual Conferences of the Parties (COPs), the supreme decision-making body of the Convention, beginning in 1995. COP-1 produced the 'Berlin Mandate' to pursue more ambitious commitments via some new legal instrument, eventually realized in the Kyoto Protocol at COP-3 in December 1997. Although the scientific evidence for global warming is still controversial, the context for an institutional response includes the IPCC findings in 2001 that confirm 'an increasing body of observations giv[ing] a collective picture of a warming world' with 'new and stronger evidence that most of the warming observed over the last 50 years is attributable to human activities'.[6]

Not only did the Kyoto Protocol demand stronger measures on GHG emissions but it also established some innovative mechanisms by which goals might be realized. With respect to emissions, most developed states must reduce their emissions, in varying degrees below 1990 levels, over a five year average in the 'first commitment period' 2008–2012. The collective commitment of the developed states is to a reduction of at least five percent below 1990 levels, although much greater reductions are expected to be necessary in the future. As to mechanisms for achieving their targets, states have a range of policy instruments available to them. Conventional methods might include, for example, carbon taxes, energy efficiency measures and modified agricultural practices. More innovative and largely market-oriented measures were included at the behest of the so-called 'umbrella group' of countries,[7] namely the so-called 'JUSCANZ' group comprising Japan, the United States, Canada, Australia and New Zealand plus Russia and Norway. Among such measures were the inclusion of GHGs other than carbon dioxide, reductions achieved through clean technology investment in developing countries, establishment of an emissions trading market for the purchase of 'credits' from states which have reduced emissions by more than their stipulated target, and carbon credits for contributions to carbon 'sinks', usually by growing

---

[4] For six stipulated gases: carbon dioxide, methane, nitrous oxide, hydrofluorocarbons, perfluoroarbons, sulphur hexafluoride.
[5] UNFCCC, *Guide to the Climate Change Convention*, above n 2, 11.
[6] *Third Assessment Report of the IPCC*, quoted in UNFCCC, Guide to the Climate Change Convention, above n 2, 5.
[7] See, e.g. Frank Loy, 'On a collision course? Two potential environmental conflicts between the U.S. and Canada' (2002) 28 Canada-United States Law Journal 11.

trees. Carbon sinks are based on the theory that the process of photosynthesis sequesters atmospheric carbon and stores it in living tissue. The importance of these carbon sinks is attested to by the claim that global deforestation between 1850 and 1990 accounts for one third or more of carbon dioxide emissions – reforestation can substantially redress that loss.[8] Ironically, having successfully lobbied for the inclusion of these mechanisms two of the most GHG-intensive states, the United States (which originally agreed to a 7 per cent reduction on 1990 levels) and Australia (one of the few states which negotiated an actual increase – of 8 per cent – on 1990 levels), declined to ratify the Protocol (see discussion below).

Joint Implementation (JI) is another market-oriented policy option whereby a government or private entity in an Annex I state invests in an emission-reducing project in another Annex I state, claiming credit for the resulting 'emission reduction units' against its own target. Its most obvious application would be in EIT states where there is more likely to be scope for low cost abatement projects. With respect to developed states implementing such projects in less-developed states provision is made for a 'Clean Development Mechanism' (CDM) which again allows the Annex I state to use the 'certified emission reductions' to help meet its own targets. It was agreed at COP-6 in Bonn that CDMs may include afforestation and reforestation projects, though an Annex I country may only claim an amount equal to one percent of its base year emissions. In effect the implementing country is utilizing comparative advantage *vis a vis* the host country as in trade generally. However, as an aspect of the more general discord on North-South issues, including climate change but also relating to many other issues such as poverty, debt and trade, CDMs too become controversial and sensitive. They may, for example, be seen as exploitation of vulnerable developing states or as a breach of equitable principles in relation to the historical responsibility of developed states for global warming generally. On the other hand the CDM program, commenced in 2000, is expected to generate investment in developing countries.

The Kyoto Protocol was itself incomplete and further Conferences of the Parties continued, notably at COP-7 in 2001 with the package known as the Marrakesh Accords which finalized implementation rules for the Protocol. There are broadly five elements to the program. First are the commitments to legally binding emission targets in relation to 1990 baseline emissions; states so committed are listed in Annex B to the Protocol. For example, Canada and Japan must reduce by 6 per cent, Russia and New Zealand must maintain 1990 levels, the European Union must collectively reduce by 8 per cent but can re-distribute its quota between member states.

Secondly, parties may pursue these binding commitments by a variety of means. They have a wide range of domestic policy options at their disposal to

---

[8] J Ford-Robertson, J Maclaren and S Wakelin, 'The Role of Carbon Sequestration as a Response Strategy to Global Warming, with a Particular Focus on New Zealand' in Alexander Gillespie and William Burns (eds) *Climate Change in the South Pacific: Impacts and Responses in Australia, New Zealand, and Small Island States* (2000) 189, 189.

reduce emissions – for example, through enhanced energy efficiency, carbon taxes, sustainable agriculture – but also to absorb emissions in so-called 'carbon sinks', for example by planting trees. Their inclusion in the subsequent COP-6 2001 Bonn Accord resulted from intense pressure from the Umbrella Group of countries. The European Union unsuccessfully resisted, and the practice has been criticized for including 'business as usual' reforestation, for justifying the dubious practice of substituting new, fast-growing, managed forests for old-growth native forest, and for providing states with the opportunity to actually increase emissions.[9] Other policy options already mentioned include JI, CDMs and emissions trading.

Thirdly, the Protocol seeks to minimize impacts on developing countries. Those impacts may be manifest in different ways, including flooding of small island states as a result of rising sea levels, droughts, floods and so on due to more extreme and variable weather events, and constraints on urgent development needs in least developed states. Annex I parties are committed to minimizing such impacts, including the creation of an 'adaptation fund' to be administered by the Global Environment Facility, which is the financial agent of the Convention and Protocol.

Fourthly, information needs – clearly vital to the integrity of the Protocol – are to be met by various accounting, reporting and review procedures such as a national registry for GHG transactions, submission of an annual inventory and review by expert review teams. That information provides the basis for the final element – compliance. This regime is comprised of a Compliance Committee which is in turn constituted by 'facilitative' and 'enforcement' branches. The former provides advice and assistance toward compliance, and makes decisions on the basis of a three-quarters majority. The latter is empowered to impose consequences on errant parties, and its decisions require not only a three-quarters majority but also a majority of both Annex I and non-Annex I parties. Annex I Parties are given one hundred days to remedy any shortfall in compliance, failing which they must carry it into the next commitment period along with a 30 percent penalty.

Although global warming is usually characterized as an 'environmental' problem given its material impacts on our physical environment its genesis is of course in 'development' issues: population growth, land use, materialism, patterns of energy consumption, technological innovations and so on. They are outcomes of growing affluence in developed economies but also of growth aspirations in developing states. Ambitions to regulate – or more crudely to manipulate – development in light of global warming issues, indeed of environmental issues generally, must address the quandary of how to deal with developed versus less developed states given their wildly disparate historic contributions to the problems and their respective resource constraints in attempting to address them. For example, the developed states have contributed ten times more than the developing

---

[9] For a more detailed critique of the practice see, e.g. Dayna Scott, 'Looking for Loopholes' (Fall, 2001) 27 *Alternatives Journal* 22. Thus (at 24) it was estimated that concessions to the Umbrella Group would mean that emissions from industrialized nations could be allowed to increase by 7 per cent above 1990 levels rather than the overall 5 per cent reduction by 2010 mandated by the Kyoto Protocol.

states in the recent buildup of greenhouse gases, including 84 per cent of emissions since 1800.[10] Thus there is an inevitable mix of elements of both retributive justice (in assigning responsibility to those who cause the problem, though manipulable empirical data make this difficult) and distributive justice (in shifting costs and benefits between interdependent parties).[11] As well as these essentially intra-generational issues there are further ethical issues of inter-generational equity. We visit these problems (and solutions) on future generations, or alternatively we are asking present generations to pay the price for the indulgences of past generations in order to benefit future generations.

In any event it is likely that the impacts of climate change will fall disproportionately on developing states with marginal agricultural sectors reflecting small scale and low technology. They lack both capital resources and redundancies in their production systems that would support adaptive responses to relatively sudden changes.[12] Developed industrial states will in all probability prove more resilient. Thus, say some, why should less developed states be expected to do anything, and in any event what can they possibly do? In the South Pacific these issues echo loudly with the wealthy industrialized states of Australia and New Zealand being responsible both for disproportionate contributions to the problem and for measures to mitigate it. The small island states in turn are likely to be disproportionately and perhaps even catastrophically affected and lack the resources and potential adaptive strategies to mitigate. The ethical question is arguably fairly straightforward and most acutely observed in the stance taken by the United States as the only major developed state to repudiate the Kyoto Protocol. The question is this: that even if the United States considers that the dangers of global warming pose an acceptable level of risk, does it then have the right to impose dangerous threats on the most vulnerable states given that effective global action on what other states have judged to be dangerous threats is all but impossible without US co-operation?[13] Of course the US is free to make that judgement in respect of its own nationals, but what if any right does it have to effectively impose it on the overwhelming majority of dissenting states who must endure the United States' disproportionate contribution to the threat? Unsurprisingly the US decision not to ratify the Protocol drew sharp criticism from other states,[14] though some observers are more sympathetic to the US position and sceptical of the motives and policy positions of Kyoto states, especially the

---

[10] D Brown, 'The U.S. Performance in Achieving Its 1992 Earth Summit Global Warming Commitments' (2002) *Environmental Law Reporter* 10741, 10762.

[11] See, e.g. M Paterson, 'Principles of Justice the Context of Global Climate Change' in Luterbacher and Sprinz, above n 2, 121.

[12] See, e.g. Urs Luterbacher and Detlef Sprinz, 'Global Climate Change in the Context of Interactions Between Society and Environment' in Luterbacher and Sprinz, above n 2, 1, 6.

[13] See, e.g. Brown, above n 10, 10757.

[14] See, e.g. Steven Freeland, 'The Kyoto Protocol: An Agreement Without A Future?' (2001) 24 *University of New South Wales Law Journal* 532, 538, citing (at note 21) condemnation by the European Parliament ('appalling and provocative'), Japanese lawmakers ('shocking'), China ('irresponsible') and the U.N. Secretary General ('unfortunate').

member states of the European 'bubble'.[15] These questions become more acute in the South Pacific where the asymmetry between contribution to the problem, likelihood of serious local consequences and leverage in global policy is most pronounced.

Status of the Protocol

In order to enter into force article 25(1) stipulated that at least 55 states must ratify the Protocol (in whatever form), a requirement that has now been met.[16] As well, however, those ratifying states must include sufficient Annex I parties to account for at least 55 per cent of 1990 carbon dioxide emissions from the Annex I group. That requirement was finally satisfied in 2004 with ratification by Russia. The Protocol will now enter into force on 16 February 2005.

By November 2004, 129 states had given notice of ratification. They represent some 61.6 per cent of total Annex I party emissions.[17] Given the withdrawal of the United States in March 2001, representing some 36 per cent of Annex I party emissions of carbon dioxide in 1990, the next best hope – indeed the only hope – for the Protocol coming into force was the accession of the Russian Federation, accounting for some 17 per cent of the relevant emissions.[18] That was by no means certain; after initially signalling its intent to ratify Russia appeared to reverse its position. Suggested reasons for the Russian delay are varied. One argument runs that the post-1990 Russian economy has shrunk so significantly that it will be in a position to sell substantial carbon credits under the Protocol, but that with the withdrawal of the United States (which would likely have been the major buyer) those credits will have considerably less value than was first thought. A contrary argument runs that the Russian economy needs to recover to (or better) Soviet-era levels and that the Protocol will inhibit that ambition. The argument is qualified by the observation that Russia can utilize presently unrealized production efficiencies. Its emissions per unit of Gross Domestic Product (GDP) are double those of the U.S. and at least four times those of Western European countries, so that it could theoretically double its GDP without increasing emissions by realizing comparable efficiencies.[19] Ironically Russia's assent to the Protocol will probably have a negative effect on the environment, at least in the short term. The substantial carbon credits which Russia will bring to the international carbon trading market will tend to lower the price of these 'permits to emit' and discourage the implementation of higher cost abatement measures by those who

---

[15] For example, Bruce Yandle and Stuart Buck, 'Bootleggers, Baptists, and the Global Warming Battle' (2002) 26 *Harvard Environmental Law Review* 177.
[16] In May 2002 with the accession of Iceland.
[17] UNFCCC, *Kyoto Protocol: Status of Ratification* (2004) <http://unfcc.int/essential_background/kyoto_protocol/statuts_of_ratification/items/2613.php> at 2 December 2004.
[18] UNFCCC, *Guide to the Climate Change Convention*, above n 2, 39.
[19] Michael Grubb, 'Jumping to Conclusions on Kyoto', *The Moscow Times* (Moscow), 9 January 2004, 8 <http://www.themoscowtimes.com/stories/2004/01/09/006.html> at 20 February 2004.

purchase them.[20] Yet another argument holds that Russia has been indulging in 'brinksmanship' in search of either concessions or of a *quid pro quo* in the form of, for example, European support for its entry into the World Trade Organization (which was in fact announced at the same time).[21]

Meanwhile the United States position has been to rely on voluntary and market forces rather than government regulation.[22] Rather than seeking to achieve an actual reduction in emissions the goalposts have been moved to reducing 'greenhouse gas intensity', that is to say, the ratio of emissions to Gross National Product. Some estimates are that this would allow an actual increase in carbon dioxide emissions of as high as 43 percent above 1990 levels even if targets and voluntary reductions were realized.[23] In any event this emissions intensity focus in reality amounts to 'business as usual' since its successes derive from efficiency gains which were already taking place.[24] It is in effect a plan to do nothing.[25] For this among other reasons the US has been said to be in violation of its commitments under the UNFCCC[26] and the Kyoto Protocol, to both of which it is a signatory. On the other hand the Bush administration has taken the unusual step of formally opposing the Protocol.[27]

The Russian and United States positions raise interesting questions under the Vienna Convention on the Law of Treaties. Had Russia not acceded to the Protocol and thus brought it into force then signatories would have been placed in a difficult position. From a legal perspective obligations prior to coming into force are covered under article 18 of the Vienna Convention on the Law of Treaties, namely the obligation not to defeat the object and purpose of a treaty prior to its entry into force. States which have indicated consent to be bound are obliged to 'refrain from acts which would defeat the object and purpose' pending entry into force 'provided that such entry into force is not unduly delayed'.[28] The meaning of the provision is unclear – for example, the extent of the obligation – and there is a dearth of

---

[20] See, e.g. Bjart Holstmark and Knut Alfsen 'Implementation of the Kyoto Protocol without Russian Participation' (Discussion Paper No. 376, April 2004, Statistics Norway, Research Department, copy on file with author).

[21] Peter Baker, 'Russia Backs Kyoto to Get on Path to Join WTO', *The Washington Post* (Washington), 22 May 2004, A15 <http://www.washingtonpost.com/wp-dyn/articles/A46416-2004May21.html> at 15 December 2004.

[22] See, e.g. Christopher Joyner, 'Burning International Bridges, Fuelling Global Discontent: The United States and Rejection of the Kyoto Protocol' (2002) 33 Victoria University of Wellington Law Review 27, 46.

[23] Ibid 69.

[24] Brown, above n 10, 10758.

[25] Loy, above n 7, 15.

[26] Brown, above n 10, 10757.

[27] Jutta Brunnee, 'The United States and International Environmental Law: Living with an Elephant' (2004) 15 *European Journal of International Law* 617, 645 (citing The White House, 'Text of a Letter from the President to Senators Hagel, Helms, Craig and Roberts', 13 March 2001).

[28] *Vienna Convention on the Law of Treaties*, opened for signature 23 May 1969, 1155 UNTS 331 (entered into force 27 January 1980), art 18(b).

practice on its application but it is likely to mean that not all acts which would be prohibited after coming into force must be avoided. Rather a state must refrain from acts which actually invalidate the purpose of the treaty, for example, destroying objects whose return is the subject of the treaty.[29]

With regard to the Protocol the implication is that a ratifying state could legally do almost anything (or nothing) in respect of its omissions so long as it did not make compliance impossible in the first commitment period. That is similarly the case with those states which still have not ratified, particularly the United States and Australia. They are parties to the UNFCCC and signatories to the Protocol though they have not ratified it. Thus whilst not legally bound to meet the emission targets of the Protocol they are nonetheless required under international law to refrain from actions which would make the discharge of Kyoto obligations impossible.[30] In practice that permits considerable latitude – what level of greenhouse gas emissions would be sufficient to render impossible adherence to treaty obligations given, for example, uncertainty with respect to future technological innovations, economic cycles, policy alternatives, and so on? In any event the United States has expressly disavowed the Kyoto Protocol and so is presumably not restricted even by the article 18 language. Both countries claim to have adopted voluntary programs (discussed below). As well state and local authorities have in many cases adopted climate change initiatives that in practice may come to have a cumulative impact notwithstanding inaction by central governments in both countries.

But now that entry into force of the Protocol is finally assured it means that thirty industrialized countries will be legally bound to meet their respective quantitative emission targets. Important climate change institutions will now take their place in the regime – the international carbon trading market for buying and selling emission credits, the Clean Development Mechanism for encouraging investment in developing-country projects, and the Adaptation Fund for assistance to developing countries in dealing with impacts of climate change. At the time of writing only four industrialized countries have not yet ratified the Protocol – the United States and Australia, together accounting for more than a third of industrialized state emissions, and Liechtenstein and Monaco.

Limitations of the Protocol

The efficacy of the Protocol is compromised in a variety of ways. There is no pretence that it will 'solve' the climate change problem. Even with implementation some 75 per cent of global emissions are not covered; it will probably only reduce global emissions by around 1 per cent by the end of the first commitment period, whilst the best available science suggests that global emissions need to be reduced by some 60 per cent by the end of the century merely to stabilize them at 1990 levels, though those levels are themselves some 25 per cent higher that pre-

---

[29] See, e.g. Anthony Aust, *Modern Treaty Law and Practice* (2000) 93-5.
[30] Ibid.

industrial levels.[31] Similarly, even full implementation of the Protocol is projected to reduce warming by only one twentieth of one degree centigrade, and to have only a minimal effect on sea levels.[32] Thus, many of the predicted impacts of climate change are most likely to occur regardless of present international policy responses. With some justification one veteran of the climate change regime describes its history as a 'sort of elegantly choreographed evasion'.[33]

The underlying reasons for the limited ambitions of the Protocol are of course many and complex but might be crudely summarized by the observation that greenhouse gas emissions go to the very core of modern economic activity. Curtailing them presents real but unknowable challenges both to the affluent, materialist cultures of developed states and to the growth ambitions of developing states. Both the sources and impacts are truly global. They are not amenable to the more straightforward amelioration of, for example, substances that deplete the ozone layer – the subject of the Montreal Protocol on the Protection of the Ozone Layer. In that case the sources of the ozone depleting substances were limited in number and readily identifiable, and substitute products were available.

The ongoing refusal of the United States to ratify the Protocol presents an insurmountable barrier to even the modest aspirations of the first commitment period. As noted above, the United States contributed some 36 per cent of Annex I party emissions of carbon dioxide in 1990, more than double the next largest emitter (the Russian Federation) and half as much again as fifteen European Union states combined.[34] It initially agreed to reduce those 1990 levels by 7 per cent, but over the 1990s its GHG emissions increased by some 13 per cent and continue to grow.[35] It would now have to reduce emissions by close to one third to meet its Kyoto target. It has taken some steps in regard to its ratification of the UNFCCC – for example, its reporting responsibilities, its research commitments and (arguably) its minimum obligations to provide finance to developing nations, but has failed to comply with its emission reduction responsibilities under the UNFCCC[36] or to ratify the Kyoto Protocol. Its reasons for not ratifying seemingly boil down to some combination of the lack of binding commitments for the developing world, scientific uncertainty as to the quantum and timing of climate change and (unsubstantiated) fears of the economic cost of policy responses. The first and last of these issues motivated the 1997 U.S. Senate vote (95-0) to resist any Kyoto agreement that did not include targets for developing countries or which threatened significant damage to the U.S. economy. Domestic political resistance flows from

---

[31] IPCC, *First Assessment Report* (1990), Overview <http://www.ipcc.ch/pub/reports.htm> at 15 December 2004.

[32] See William Burns, 'The Impact of Climate Change on Pacific Island Developing Countries in the 21st Century' in Gillespie and Burns, above n 8, 233, 249.

[33] Hon. Simon Upton (then New Zealand Minister for the Environment), 'Risks Surrounding the Kyoto Protocol' in The New Zealand Institute of International Affairs, *Seminar Papers: Climate Change: Implementing the Kyoto Protocol* (1999) 1, 13.

[34] Joyner, above n 22, 39.

[35] Brown, above n 10, 10751.

[36] Ibid 10768.

both the Democratic Party (fearing a threat to its labour base) and the Republican Party (fearing a threat to its corporate base).[37] Present prospects for U.S. ratification of the Kyoto Protocol appear bleak.[38]

The absence of binding commitments on developing countries, at least for the time being, is obviously a serious constraint on the efficacy of measures to address climate change. Under the Kyoto Protocol they effectively face no limits on their greenhouse gas emissions, notwithstanding that many are significant contributors (in absolute terms though not per capita) – for example, in terms of quantum of emissions China ranked second in 1998, India sixth, South Korea eighth, South Africa eleventh and Mexico twelfth.[39] By way of illustration, in 1999 the industrialized countries contributed some 51 per cent of total world carbon emissions, which share is expected to drop to around 41 per cent by 2020 if emissions are not controlled.[40]

Finally, the present Kyoto regime does not incorporate greenhouse gas emissions from international flights and shipping, though there is pressure from Europe to reduce these emissions in the second commitment period from 2012. It is expected that they will be debated at COP-10 at Buenos Aires in December 2004. They have been conservatively estimated at 3.5 per cent and 1.8 per cent respectively of global emissions of greenhouse gases, though environmental groups claim that these numbers may actually double if indirect effects are included.[41] Of concern is the expected growth in world transport demand – perhaps as much as 55 per cent over the period 1995–2020.[42]

So the Kyoto Protocol is at best a hesitant first step, and any significant efforts to address climate change must be deferred until at least the second commitment period. Developing states will have to be included in binding commitments and the United States must be persuaded to participate, though present indications are that its emissions are likely to be so high as to make any meaningful reduction unlikely in the near term. But the symbolism of the present ambitions of the Protocol is nonetheless signficant, most particularly in the willingness of the developed states to set at least a modest example and to acknowledge at least in principle the notion of common but differentiated responsibility. Policy responses in the Pacific region ought to be considered in that context, though as we shall see they offer no more cause for optimism than does the wider international response.

---

[37] Ibid 10749.
[38] For a more sympathetic reading of the U.S. response to Kyoto see, e.g. Yandle and Buck, above n 15.
[39] Senator The Hon. Nick Minchin 'Responding to Climate Change: Providing a Policy Framework for a Competitive Australia' (2001) 24 *University of New South Wales Law Journal* 550, 553.
[40] Yandle and Buck, above n 15, 183.
[41] Maarten Messiaen, 'New Take-Off Proposed for Kyoto' *Inter Press Service News Agency*, 29 November 2004 <http://www.ipsnews.net/africa/interna.asp?idnews=26458> at 15 December 2004.
[42] Ibid.

Regional responses

That wider global order is reflected immediately in the disparate array of states which constitute the South Pacific region. They vary radically in degrees of industrialization, geography, climate, natural resources, patterns of energy use, sources of GHGs, and so on. The most obvious demarcation is between the various small, developing island states and the larger developed states of Australia and New Zealand. Australia might reasonably be characterized as the major regional power, with New Zealand in closer geographical and cultural proximity to the small island states, of which Fiji would be the largest in demographic and economic terms. In the context of climate change Australia and New Zealand are, in per capita terms, major contributors to greenhouse gas emissions whilst the small island states contribute only negligible emissions but are extremely vulnerable to climate change impacts. One might then simplistically characterize the former as perpetrators of climate change and the latter as victims. Certainly remedial measures would be expected from the high-polluting, resource-rich developed states and assistance with mitigation measures might be expected for the developing states. The parallels between the region and the wider international order are again obvious and the notion of common but differentiated responsibility apposite.

In looking to the policy responses of regional states the most striking contradiction is the presence of Australia as one of only two regional states (along with Tonga) not to ratify the Protocol, again seeming to mirror the wider context in its mimicry of the United States. It has implemented a 'voluntary' program aimed at realizing its Kyoto target of an 8 per cent increase of emissions over 1990 levels. New Zealand has ratified and is implementing policies which will maintain emissions at 1990 levels, though it expects to make a small economic gain as a result. The small island developing states are not required to meet any emission targets – their concerns are with mitigating the impacts of climate change.

Australia

Background

Australia accepts the IPCC's conclusions on climate science 'as the most authoritative available'[43] and accepts 'the reality that climate change is occurring'.[44]

---

[43] Hon. Dr. David Kemp MP (Australian Federal Minister for the Environment and Heritage), 'Australia's Approach to Climate Change' (Opening Address at the Beyond Kyoto: Economic Impacts and Alternative Mitigation Strategies Conference, Institute of Public Affairs, Melbourne, 28 February 2003), Department of the Environment and Heritage <http://www.deh.gov.au/minister/env/2003/sp28feb03.html> at 15 December 2004.
[44] Ibid.

From an ecological perspective the impacts of global warming on Australia are difficult to predict[45] but are expected to include impacts on vulnerable ecosystems in the arid and semi-arid areas of the south-west and inland, alpine systems and coral reefs. Climate variation is expected to include increases in the intensity of heavy rains and tropical cyclones with associated risks to human life, property and infrastructures. Water supply and agricultural production will be vulnerable, particularly in the south-west and inland regions.

Australia contributes just over 1 per cent of total greenhouse emissions but its per capita emissions are among the world's highest[46] and notwithstanding its relatively small population it is one of the top twelve emitters.[47] Under a 'business as usual' scenario Australia's emissions would be expected to grow by around 26 per cent over 1990–2010, with energy sector emissions expected to grow by 40 per cent.[48]

From an economic perspective Australia claims to be peculiarly vulnerable to greenhouse gas reduction measures in having an energy-intensive economy and in having an international competitive advantage in low cost energy from huge reserves of coal and gas.[49] For example, by offering cheap electricity from low cost coal Australian governments were able to induce energy-intensive users like the aluminium industry to locate in Australia in the early 1980s. Australia lacks extensive hydro resources and has followed a policy of not developing nuclear power, though it does have great potential for renewable energy sources such as solar and wind power.

The policy implications of a coal-dependent economy are significant for Australia. The production and use of coal accounts directly for some 38 per cent of Australia's total greenhouse gas emissions – compared to 31 per cent from all other energy sources and 31 per cent from other activities such as agriculture.[50] In terms of carbon dioxide emitted per unit of energy provided, coal is almost twice as intensive as natural gas and one and a half times as intensive as petroleum products.[51] As well, coal extraction releases large amounts of methane, which is considerably more potent a greenhouse gas than is carbon dioxide. Not surprisingly, in light of this dependence on coal, critics say that the coal industry has exerted an

---

[45] See, e.g. Australian Government, *Living with climate change: An overview of potential climate change impacts on Australia* (2002), Australian Greenhouse Office <www.greenhouse.gov.au/science/impacts/overview/index.html> at 3 February 2004.
[46] Australian Government, *National Greenhouse Strategy*, Executive Summary, vii <www.greenhouse.gov.au/pubs/ngs/ngs.html> at 15 December 2004. See also Clive Hamilton, 'Climate Change Policies in Australia' in Gillespie and Burns, above n 8, 51, 63.
[47] Hon. Dr. David Kemp MP (Australian Federal Minister for the Environment and Heritage), 'Australia's Domestic Climate Change Approach' (Speech to COP-9, Milan, 9 December 2003) <http://www.deh.gov.au/minister/env/2003/sp09dec03.html> at 15 December 2004.
[48] Australian Government, *National Greenhouse Strategy*, above n 46, vii.
[49] Kemp, 'Australia's Approach to Climate Change', above n 43. These policy positions have been strongly criticized elsewhere – see, e.g. Hamilton, above n 46 and W. Hare, *Australia and Kyoto: In or Out?* (2001) 24 University of New South Wales Law Journal 556.
[50] Hugh Saddler, 'Australia and Greenhouse Gas Emissions' (2002–2003) 51 *Dissent* 51.
[51] Ibid.

extraordinary influence on policy responses to Kyoto – for example, in pressuring the government in 1995 to abandon a carbon tax in return for voluntary agreements under the Greenhouse Challenge program, and even then only requiring 'no regrets' actions which would be at least cost-neutral.[52] Similarly in 2000 the government was effectively dissuaded from a domestic emissions trading scheme which would have placed a cost on excessive greenhouse gas emissions,[53] and work on an international emissions trading scheme was abandoned in 2004.

In addition to its reliance on low-cost fossil fuels, other specific factors influencing Australia's ability to reduce greenhouse gas emissions include a relatively high economic growth rate, a wide range of climatic zones, relatively high population growth, very long distances between urban centres and land use patterns which are still undergoing significant change.[54] However, the economic model used to justify Australia's claim to a peculiar vulnerability in pursuing emission reductions came under widespread criticism for *inter alia* its bias toward business interests.[55]

A further complication for Australia arises from its constitutional arrangements. As a federal state it is governed under a division of powers framework between the central federal government and the various state and territorial governments (as are, for example, the United States and Canada but not, for example, New Zealand or the United Kingdom). In the Australian case certain specified powers are assigned to the Commonwealth Parliament with legislative powers over the remainder left to the legislative authority of the states. Various areas in which governments would need to regulate in respect of climate change policy lie with the states; examples include energy and land clearing.[56] Under the National Greenhouse Strategy (see below) the policy adopted has been one of cooperation between the Commonwealth, State, Territory and Local governments. Representatives of each level of government are responsible for managing the program's principles, guidelines, goals and measures, and are in turn responsible to the Council of Australian Governments.[57] The Agreement does not, however, create legally binding obligations and there is no guarantee of its effective implementation by the states – only political pressure can be applied. Should it choose to the Commonwealth could introduce its own legislation to implement its obligations under the UNFCCC and (if it ratifies) the Kyoto Protocol. Such legislation would likely be a valid exercise of the Commonwealth external affairs power (s 51 (xxix) of the *Australian Constitution 1900*). That power has been interpreted to include federal legislative competence in matters that are of

---

[52] Ibid 51-2.
[53] Ibid 53.
[54] Australian Government, *Tracking to the Kyoto Target* (2004) 3 <http://www.greenhouse.gov.au/projections/tracking/pubs/tracking2004.pdf> at 16 December 2004.
[55] Hare, above n 49, 558.
[56] Laura Horn, 'The Kyoto Protocol: Australia's Commitment and Compliance' (2001) 24 *University of New South Wales Law Journal* 583, 584-5.
[57] Ibid.

inherently international concern as well as legislation pursuant to an international treaty or convention.[58] Either, and certainly a combination of both would seem sufficient to ground the authority of the federal government to legislate in respect of the Kyoto Protocol should it choose to ratify. However, actions by the various state governments are also important, and New South Wales in particular has been pro-active in adopting more forceful regulatory strategies than has the federal Howard government.[59] But as with environmental law generally, the policy choice has been to favour a model of cooperative federalism.[60]

Australia ratified the UNFCCC in 1992 and signed the Kyoto Protocol in 1998, but has declined to ratify the Protocol. Its stated reason is the Protocol's lack of application of binding targets to developing countries with the associated threat of loss of jobs and investment to developed countries. The claim is that Australia will become less competitive and the resulting 'carbon leakage' (as GHG industry moves to developing states) would undermine the Protocol itself.[61] Generally with respect to climate change negotiations Australia has been characterized as being 'at best, a reluctant partner and, at worst, a country whose engagement is little more than a naked defence of its coal and aluminium industries'.[62] With respect to developing countries and the dangers of their pursuing the emissions intensive growth path of developed countries, Australia (like the United States) has adopted a hard line in demanding, if not targets and binding commitments then possibly some kind of incentive structures.[63] It has, however, undertaken to meet its Kyoto target.[64] Its commitment under the Protocol was to limit greenhouse emissions to 108 per cent of 1990 levels over the period 2008–2012. The only other states allowed to actually increase emissions were Norway (by 1 per cent) and Iceland (by 10 per cent).

Policy responses

A sectoral analysis of greenhouse gas emissions (1996 data) showed the (non-transport) Energy sector to be the largest contributor at 55 per cent, followed by Agricultural production (excluding land clearing) at 20 per cent, the Transport sector at 17 per cent, Waste at 4 per cent and Industrial Processes at 2 per cent.[65]

The recent policy discourse within which Australia has responded to climate change issues has been characterized as 'ecological modernisation', that is to say

---

[58] James Crawford 'The Constitution and the Environment' (1991) 13 *Sydney Law Review* 11.
[59] R Taplin and X Yu, 'Climate Change Policy Formulation in Australia: 1995–1998' in Gillespie and Burns, above n 8, 95, 105-107.
[60] Robert Hughes, Geoffrey Leane and Andrew Clarke, *Australian Legal Institutions: Principles, Structures and Organisation* (2nd ed, 2003) 112.
[61] Kemp, 'Australia's Approach to Climate Change', above n 43.
[62] Hare, above n 49.
[63] Kemp, 'Australia's Approach to Climate Change', above n 43.
[64] Ibid.
[65] Australian Government, *National Greenhouse Strategy*, above n 46, ix.

the assumption that environmental issues can be accommodated within, or internalized in, existing political, economic and social institutions.[66] That 'shallow ecology' approach goes back to the Brundtland Report assumption that there is no necessary contradiction between economic growth and environmental imperatives – indeed that the former is necessary to finance the latter. Environmental policy more generally has historically been caught up in the tensions of Australia's federalist system of government; control of the environment was traditionally a responsibility of the states but became controversial in the 1980s as the federal government asserted its foreign affairs power in certain environmental conflicts. Nonetheless the requirement for harmonization of federal and state legislation presents itself in respect of Kyoto measures as in other areas; for example, in legislation to give legal recognition to carbon sequestration rights in pursuit of an emissions trading scheme.[67] A number of 'carbon trades' have already been contracted, for example, between Japanese interests and Australian forestry interests.[68]

At the same time the federal government was attempting to articulate a national strategy on Ecologically Sustainable Development.[69] During the early 1990s the federal government sponsored working groups whose aim was to suggest appropriate policy responses on Ecologically Sustainable Development generally and on the Greenhouse issue. A variety of (but not all) stakeholders participated and reached a surprising degree of consensus within the 'ecological modernisation' paradigm, that is to say by utilizing existing institutional and social structures.[70] One of the outputs was the National Greenhouse Response Strategy (NGRS), though it apparently did not ultimately reflect the original consensus of the working group participants and was in fact disowned by them.[71] This preliminary work motivated Australia to confidently sign the UNFCCC in December 1992 – indeed it was the eighth state to do so.

The NGRS was criticized for lacking new measures, lacking firm commitments and for relying on ad hoc government processes and commercial decisions – in other words for simply maintaining the status quo.[72] The imposition of a carbon tax was considered but rejected after strong opposition from industry. A program of voluntary emission reductions was adopted, but with an explicit commitment to 'the business objectives of development and growth' and with no penalty for withdrawal.[73] By 1995 the program was arguably an 'abject failure' and

---

[66] Harriet Bulkeley, 'The Formation of Australian Climate Change Policy: 1985–1995' in Gillespie and Burns, above n 8, 33, 35.

[67] For more detail see, e.g. David Jones, 'The Kyoto Protocol, Carbon Sinks and Integrated Environmental Regulation: an Australian Perspective' (2002) 19(2) *Environment and Planning Law Journal* 109, 122-9.

[68] Ibid 125.

[69] Bulkeley, above n 66, 35.

[70] Ibid 40-42.

[71] Ibid.

[72] Ibid 45.

[73] Ibid 47. For a summary critique of the NGRS see also Taplin and Yu, above n 59, 96-7.

offered little prospect of reconciling economic and environmental values.[74] The NGRS was further developed in 1995 with the addition of Greenhouse 21C, a program which sought to bring together all relevant actors in responding to the Berlin COP in 1995.

One outcome of Greenhouse 21C was the establishment of the Greenhouse Challenge program which was to facilitate cooperative partnerships between government and industry. The program was voluntary, and only required the pursuit of 'no regrets' actions. It survived a change in government in 1996. The results have included active participation by the aluminium industry (which consumes 19 per cent of all electricity sold in Australia) and the electricity generation industry, but not the coal industry.[75] There have, however, been some recent signs of coal industry cooperation, for example in the establishment of the COAL21 action plan with the federal government (with a particular emphasis on carbon sequestration, which involves capturing carbon dioxide and burying it underground).

It was in this context that Australia approached the Kyoto Protocol with less confidence than the 1992 UNFCCC. The Australian government's approach leading up to the 1997 Kyoto Conference was to argue for 'differentiation', that is to say an approach that states should suffer equally in pursuing greenhouse gas emission reductions and that therefore they should be subject to different targets depending on relative economic costs. Thus it was argued that Australia was heavily dependent on fossil fuels for domestic energy and for export revenue – therein lay its international competitive advantage – and was therefore deserving of more lenient targets. That position was strongly criticized by many Australian economists, who suggested that the government's economic models on impacts, costs and benefits were misleading and further that the model chosen was substantially financed by the fossil fuel industry.[76]

There appeared to be a number of glaring contradictions in the government's 'differentiation' policy response to Kyoto.[77] The model it presented in international forums assumed that there were no 'no regrets' reductions (that is, costless energy savings measures) available whereas its domestic strategy depended largely on the existence of just such options.[78] For example, the Greenhouse Challenge program requires only that 'no regrets' actions be pursued; if these are in fact available then the model Australia presented internationally must exaggerate the cost of emission reduction programs. If they are not available then the domestic program must be a

---

[74] Bulkeley, above n 66, 49.
[75] Saddler, above n 50, 52.
[76] Hamilton, above n 46, 54-8. These accusations received some support in a report by the Commonwealth Ombudsman (at 58). See also Mark Diesendorf, 'A Critique of the Australian Government's Greenhouse Policies' in Gillespie and Burns, above n 8, 79.
[77] These arguments are largely drawn from Hamilton, above n 46, 63-6.
[78] Hamilton, above n 46, 57.

farce.[79] In fact there is compelling evidence that Australia is a relatively energy-inefficient user and therefore has potential for significant efficiency gains.[80]

The policy ran contrary to long-established 'polluter pays' principles – as perhaps the highest per-capita polluter in the world Australia was demanding permission to actually continue to increase emissions to a degree second only to Iceland. That would make it even more difficult for Australia to conform to what will presumably be a much stricter post-Kyoto regime. Because it anticipated relatively high population growth as a consequence of its immigration policies – a policy choice presumably driven by economic benefits – Australia argued for per capita targets, notwithstanding the implications that such a policy would have for the emissions of those developing countries (with high population growth) that Australia wanted included in the Kyoto targets.

In the event Australia 'won' concessions at Kyoto which went considerably further than merely easing its allegedly unfair reduction burden; rather it would in all likelihood actually result in surplus emission savings which under the projected Kyoto emissions trading system it could sell to other signatory states, thus effecting a wealth transfer from other developed countries to the country with perhaps the highest per capita emissions in the world![81] One critic summarizes this outcome as 'the outstanding anomaly from Kyoto', achieved by threats to withdraw if it was not granted.[82]

As well as being permitted to actually increase its emissions by 8 per cent it was also permitted to include emissions from land clearing in its total, thus inflating the 1990 base level. The so-called 'Australia' clause allowed countries with net positive land-use emissions, that is to say where there was actually a net loss of forest 'sinks' with their associated capacity to absorb greenhouse gases, to include those positive emissions in the 1990 base year calculation. The effect is to increase the base year number and, for a country like Australia which was one of only three allowed to actually increase emissions, to allow a larger increase in 2008–2012. Australia was the only country to qualify for this concession as all other industrialized countries were experiencing a net growth in forests and therefore negative land-use emissions. It has been estimated that Australia thereby effectively obtained an increase of something like 19 per cent in its 1990 emissions – which in turn it can grow by another 8 per cent in the first adjustment period – worth some $10 billion.[83] As these emissions appear to be declining without intervention it may be that the target of 8 per cent increase can be achieved without policies to reduce emissions in the energy sector.[84] Indeed it has been estimated that the 'Australia' clause will allow it to increase fossil fuel and related emissions

---

[79] Saddler, above n 75.
[80] Hamilton, above n 46, 70.
[81] Ibid 72-4.
[82] Ibid 76; also Hare, above n 49, 560.
[83] D Victor, *The Collapse of the Kyoto Protocol and the Struggle to Slow Global Warming* (2001) 63.
[84] Diesendorf, above n 76, 79.

by some 22-33 per cent during the first commitment period.[85] For example, between 1990 and 2002 Australia's total net emissions were said to have grown by 1.3 per cent,[86] but this number includes a fall of more than 75 per cent in the Land Use category. Without that category total net emissions would have shown an increase of more than 23 per cent.[87] Put another way, the reduction in Land Use emissions from 1990 accounted for some 31 per cent of the overall decline in emissions per dollar of Gross Domestic Product[88] – such is the impact of the 'Australia' clause. The irony of Australia still refusing to ratify the Protocol becomes still sharper.

As to further policy initiatives, the conservative Howard Government, elected in 1996, had implemented a number of new greenhouse initiatives in 1996–1997. One was the Activities Implemented Jointly (AIJ) program, which sought to implement the UNFCCC option of joint emission reduction projects between developed and developing states, though no government funding was provided and little activity has ensued.[89] The Prime Minister's Greenhouse Package was introduced in the lead up to Kyoto in 1997, including such measures as a Renewable Energy Innovations Investment Fund, fuel efficiency goals, energy efficiency codes and labelling requirements, and a program to establish carbon 'sinks'. The package was, however, seen as disappointing by many commentators.[90] Although there are indications of significant interest by industry in reducing emissions – for example, by signing on to the Greenhouse Challenge program – such undertakings are only voluntary and only some 17 per cent of projected reductions were direct consequences of the program, the balance being likely to have occurred in any event.[91] In 1998 the government established the Australian Greenhouse Office (AGO) under the environment portfolio to co-ordinate greenhouse policy, issue discussion papers and deliver federal government programs. It was the first such institution of its kind in the world.

The National Greenhouse Strategy (NGS), which superseded the NGRS and included the above initiatives, is meant to provide a strategic framework within which to realize Australia's Kyoto ambitions. In terms of emission reduction programs a major initiative has been the Mandatory Renewable Energy Targets (MRET) scheme, aimed at utilizing Australia's solar, wind, water and biomass resources. Its original target was a 2 per cent uptake of renewable energy by 2010 (versus a goal of 15 per cent by 2010 proposed by the European Union), although this was later converted to an absolute target.[92] Since 2001 large wholesale

---

[85] Jones, above n 67, 116.
[86] Australian Government, 'Analysis of Recent Trends and Greenhouse Indicators 1990 to 2002' (2004) Australian Greenhouse Office, National Greenhouse Gas Inventory <www.greenhouse.gov.au/inventory2002/trends/index.html> at 11 May 2004.
[87] Ibid.
[88] Ibid.
[89] Taplin and Yu, above n 59, 101.
[90] Ibid 104.
[91] Ibid 107-108.
[92] Of 9500 GigaWatt/hour, which of course is a static target which would represent a proportionately smaller achievement in the event of energy demand increasing: see Sarojini

purchasers of electricity have been required to obtain legislated amounts of their electricity from such renewable sources as wind farms and hydro-electric power; the prescribed levels increase gradually over a ten year period with penalties for non-compliance.[93] An innovatory aspect is the legislative creation of a renewable energy market in tradeable certificates, that is to say, the commercialization of renewable energy technologies. There are also grants-related programs to encourage the development of commercial renewable energy and alternative fuels.

Further programs include the Greenhouse Gas Abatement Program, which targets large-scale, cost-effective projects in various sectors, and a joint government-industry International Greenhouse Partnerships Office to facilitate Joint Implementation and Clean Development Mechanism projects in other countries. Other programs seek, for example, improved fuel efficiency in motor vehicles (a non-binding target of 15 per cent improvement by 2010), enhanced greenhouse sinks (a trebling of the plantation estate by 2020), and greenhouse best practice in waste and industrial processes. As in New Zealand, however, there seems to be a conspicuous absence of ambitious strategies for the agricultural sector. Local government participation is facilitated through a Cities for Climate Change Protection Program under the International Council for Local Environmental Initiatives. Monitoring strategies include an enhanced National Greenhouse Gas Inventory and National Carbon Accounting System, along with ongoing investment in climate science (for example, the role of Antarctica and the Southern Ocean in the climate system). Trade in emission permits has been estimated to be worth up to A$12 billion per annum, although the present government is unwilling to implement a domestic emissions trading system until it ratifies the Kyoto Protocol, the Protocol has entered into force (which it now has) and an international trading regime is in place.[94]

Finally, the Australian government has entered into a number of bilateral partnerships or collaborations on climate change – partners include the United States, the European Union, Japan, China and New Zealand. Projects typically relate to climate change science, including accounting and monitoring strategies, energy innovations and, in the case of China, capacity building. The New Zealand partnership includes common interest areas such as agriculture (particularly methane emissions from livestock) and the particular challenges faced by Pacific Island neighbours.

Conclusions

Given Australia's reliance on cheap fossil fuels for its industrial and export base it will be necessary to develop technologies for cleaning up fossil fuel emissions; promising possibilities are thought to lie with coal gasification and sequestration of

---

Krishnapillai, 'Bad Neighbour Policy – Australia, Kyoto, and the Pacific' (August–September 2002) *Arena* 14, 14.
[93] Jones, above n 67, 122.
[94] Ibid 119, 121.

carbon dioxide in underground strata and aquifers. In the longer term there is the prospect of a hydrogen economy whereby improved technology may offer the prospect of extracting molecular hydrogen from various common elements (such as water) to power a future energy system rather than relying on fossil fuels. Nonetheless Australia's ability to meet its 108 per cent target in the first commitment period is almost entirely dependent on a dramatic decrease in emissions due to land-use changes, that is to say mostly from a decrease in the removal of forest cover and to a lesser extent from reforestation.[95] It will be recalled that the net positive emissions from land-use change were the subject of the so-called 'Australia' clause which enable that country, and only that country, to inflate its 1990 emissions and thereby benefit from a less demanding target in the first commitment period since it was permitted to increase that high level to 108 per cent. So those land-use changes not only served to provide a more amenable target but also serve as the means to achieve it; that is to say, the very generous emissions target was effectively a consequence of undesirable land-use practices, whilst the reversal of those practices will allow Australia to meet its target using sink credits rather than actually reducing emissions! Its past poor practices effectively allow it to evade the pain of authentic emission reductions.

In general, Australia's climate change strategy eschews tax and regulation strategies in favour of voluntary, co-operative schemes with industry using 'cost-effective technology' that does not threaten economic growth. This last imperative, together with international competitiveness, appears to be the primary motivation behind its greenhouse strategy. But for reasons discussed above both its international and domestic policy responses to the Kyoto Protocol appear to be incoherent.[96]

The pattern of emissions since 1990 is not particularly encouraging. By 1995 net greenhouse gas emissions (including the Land Use sector) had risen 6 per cent over 1990 levels, including an 8 per cent rise for the Energy sector (which accounted for more than half of all emissions), and a separate government study suggested even higher increases in the energy sector of 11 per cent in 1995–1996 with possible increases of 40 per cent by 2010.[97] In 2000 greenhouse gas emissions stood at 105 per cent of 1990 levels and, based on existing policies, were projected to reach 111 per cent by 2010[98] according to the government's own data. That emissions might yet exceed the already generous 108 per cent target, notwithstanding the artificial inflation of the base year emissions resulting from the 'Australia' clause, must give rise to a certain cynicism. Business-as-usual emissions, that is to say without Kyoto policy measures, were projected to be 123

---

[95] Australian Government, *Tracking to the Kyoto Target*, above n 54, 4-5.
[96] See, e.g. Saddler, above n 50, Bulkeley, above n 66, Hamilton, above n 46, Diesendorf, above n 76, Taplin and Yu, above n 59.
[97] Taplin and Yu, above n 59.
[98] Kemp, 'Australia's Approach to Climate Change', above n 43. This figure was revised in 2004 with new data suggesting that the Kyoto target of 108 per cent was achievable (see Australian Government, *Tracking to the Kyoto Target*, above, n 54) though it is probably still too soon to tell.

per cent of 1990 levels over the first commitment period.[99] Emissions for 2020 are projected to be 126 per cent over 1990 levels, mainly due to growth in the energy sector.[100]

The latest available greenhouse gas inventory data submitted for the period 1990–2002 demonstrates the pattern of emissions – they declined to their lowest post-1990 levels in 1992, rose over the intervening years to their highest point in 1998, then declined for the next few years to 2001 and finally increased again by 1.5 per cent in 2002.[101] Again the sectoral data are more revealing; for example, over 1990–2002 Energy sector emissions (the largest contributor) rose by 30 per cent and Agriculture by 11 per cent, but growth in all sectors was outweighed by a 76 per cent fall in the Land Use, Land Use Change and Forestry sector due to a significant reduction in the area of forest conversion. In terms of emissions intensity over 1990–2002 there was a 12.5 per cent reduction in emissions per capita and a 31 per cent reduction in emissions per dollar of Gross Domestic Product. The latter was due to a variety of factors, including higher growth in the services sector as compared to manufacturing, and the substantial reduction in the Land Use, Land Use Change and Forestry sector. Over the period to 2020 emissions per real dollar of Gross Domestic Product are expected to fall to 52 per cent of 1990 levels.[102] But of course 'per unit' measures of emissions are misleading as the critical measure in terms of climate change is the absolute level of emissions, and that level continues to grow in Australia.

Australia's Kyoto policies have not gone unnoticed by the vulnerable island states of the South Pacific: they were described as 'self-serving' by the Cook Islands Prime Minister, and were impliedly criticized by a call for greater emission reductions by the South Pacific Forum meeting of leaders in 1997.[103]

The post-Kyoto image from Australia then is of one of the world's wealthiest nations, producing one of the highest per capita levels of greenhouse emissions in the world, with an excellent environmental 'history' backed by first rate science, extracting extraordinary self-serving concessions at Kyoto and then refusing to ratify the Protocol. It had ironically been viewed as a repository of world-class climate change science since the early 1970s,[104] and had been 'an exemplary international environmental citizen', a position from which the greenhouse policy response represents a 'radical departure'.[105] Of the four developed states still

---

[99] Australian Government, *Tracking to the Kyoto Target*, above n 54, 2.

[100] Hon. Dr. David Kemp MP (Australian Federal Minister for the Environment and Heritage), 'Australia Moves Closer to Kyoto Target' (Press Release, 18 September 2003) Department of Environment and Heritage <http://www.deh.gov.au/minister/env/2003/mr18sep03.html> 16 December 2004.

[101] Australian Government, 'Analysis of Recent Trends and Greenhouse Indicators 1990 to 2002', above n 86.

[102] Australian Government, *Tracking to the Kyoto Target*, above n 54.

[103] Taplin and Yu, above n 59, 113.

[104] Reid Basher, 'The Impacts of Climate Change on New Zealand' in Gillespie and Burns, above n 8, 121, 137.

[105] X Yu and R Taplin, 'The Australian Position at the Kyoto Conference' in Gillespie and Burns, above n 8, 113.

declining to ratify the Protocol – at the time of writing the United States, Australia, Liechtenstein and Monaco – two of them number among the worst polluters, are among the few richest countries in the world, were successful in extracting major concessions from other negotiating parties, and yet still refuse to enter into binding commitments. Those who see the United States as something of a rogue state in the climate change regime might see Australia similarly mirrored in the South Pacific. Only its relatively small size prevents it from seriously eroding the practical effect of the Kyoto Protocol, though it doubtless undermines the Protocol's symbolic importance both internationally and regionally.

New Zealand

Background

New Zealand contributes only 0.2 per cent of total Annex I state emissions, although on the basis of 'all greenhouse gas' emissions it is the fourth highest per-capita emitter.[106] It occupies an interesting space, geographically and politically, between on the one hand a large, regionally dominant Australia with high greenhouse emissions and an ongoing resistance to compulsory Kyoto reductions, and on the other hand the highly vulnerable small island states of the South Pacific.[107] As the other industrialized 'European' society in the region, and with a high degree of economic interdependence with Australia, it tends to co-ordinate policy with Australia including with respect to climate change. On the other hand it strongly identifies with the Pacific island states, and as well has constitutional responsibility for the islands of Tokelau.

Unusually for a first-world country, the New Zealand economy is significantly dependent on primary production, wherein lies its comparative advantage in the world community. It therefore relies on an equable and stable climate to maintain this advantage and the prosperity it brings. The corollary is that New Zealand's agricultural sector produces an unusually large (for a developed nation) proportion of its greenhouse gas emissions – a little over 49 per cent in 2002.[108] In terms of climate change impacts New Zealand, a mid-latitude country, is likely less vulnerable than either the hot and dry expanses of Australia or the low lying atolls of the Pacific. It is likely to experience reduced snowpack and a shorter snow season, together with shrinkage of glaciers but generally (as compared to Australia) its '... cooler, wetter, mid-latitude location may lead to some benefit

---

[106] Alexander Gillespie, 'Defending the Irresponsible: A Reply to Chapman and Gray' (1998) 2 *New Zealand Journal of Environmental Law* 233, 247.
[107] Basher, above n 104, 136.
[108] New Zealand Government, *Report on revised projections for the Kyoto Protocol – first commitment period 30 April 2004* (2004) New Zealand Climate Change Office <http://www.climatechange.govt.nz/resources/reports/revised-projections-kyoto-/index.html> at 19 October 2004.

through the ready availability of suitable crops and likely increases in agricultural production'.[109] This optimistic view is not, however, shared by all.[110]

New Zealand is one of the few developed countries which expects to make a small net economic gain from the first Kyoto commitment period, mainly due to the carbon sink credits it will receive from reforestation.[111] As compared to 'business as usual', a small decline in Gross Domestic Product (0.08-0.26 per cent) is predicted to be offset by a gain in income from international sales of sink credits for an overall increase in Gross National Product of 0.05-0.52 per cent.[112]

New Zealand's obligation under the Kyoto Protocol is to maintain emissions at 1990 levels over the first commitment period, notwithstanding that it is the fourth highest per capita emitter on an 'all greenhouse gas' basis.[113] That was a very successful outcome, at least for New Zealand, after negotiations conducted as 'self-interested hard-ball from beginning to end'.[114] A peculiarity of New Zealand emissions is the concentration of methane, a particularly potent heat-trapping gas. This concentration is a consequence of the relatively small population of humans as compared to ruminants (such as cattle and sheep). At the time of the Kyoto meeting methane accounted for some 45 per cent of New Zealand's total greenhouse gas emissions, and represented some ten times the average global per capita rate for methane emissions.[115] Fortuitously for New Zealand, its emissions of non-carbon dioxide greenhouse gases (particularly methane and nitrous oxide) actually fell over the period 1990–1996 due to extraneous variables such as lower prices for beef and sheep meat, although the trend was partially reversed in the mid-1990s.[116] Another problematic policy issue for New Zealand has been the transport sector (accounting for some 40-45 per cent of carbon dioxide emissions) which is characterized by a high and growing level of car ownership (second only

---

[109] IPCC Working Group II, *Summary for Policymakers: The Regional Impacts of Climate Change: An Assessment of Vulnerability* (November 1997) [6.4] (reproduced in Gillespie and Burns, above n 8, Appendix IV).

[110] See, e.g. Ken Piddington, 'A commentary on the Minister's Chatham House Speech of 14 June' in New Zealand Institute of International Affairs, above n 33, 1-2.

[111] New Zealand Government, *National Interest Analysis: Kyoto Protocol to the UN Framework Convention on Climate Change* (13 February 2002) 5, New Zealand Climate Change Office <http://www.climatechange.govt.nz/resources/consultation/round1/national-interest-analysis.pdf> at 17 December 2004.

[112] New Zealand Climate Change Program, Climate Change Working Paper: Assessment of Economic Modelling (November 2001) New Zealand Climate Change Office <www.climatechange.govt.nz/resources/economic/index.html> at 20 October 2004.

[113] Alexander Gillespie, 'New Zealand and the Climate Change Debate: 1995–1998' in Gillespie and Burns, above n 8, 165.

[114] The Hon. Simon Upton (Kyoto negotiator and then Minister for the Environment), quoted in Gillespie, 'Defending the Irresponsible', above n 106, 248.

[115] Gillespie, 'New Zealand and the Climate Change Debate', above n 113, 179.

[116] Gillespie, 'Defending the Irresponsible', above n 106, 242-4.

to the United States at 69 vehicles per 100 population),[117] an aging car fleet and the absence of emission controls on vehicles.[118]

Policy Responses

The New Zealand Climate Change Program was initiated in 1988 by a Labour government to consider what national response might be required of New Zealand. In 1990 the Labour government, and then successive National governments, adopted climate change policies and greenhouse gas reduction targets. This pre-Kyoto program initially envisaged a 20 per cent reduction in GHGs by 2005 by the soon-to-be defeated Labour government and similarly by the Opposition National Party (though with a target date five years earlier, that is by 2000).[119] By 1992, with a forecast growth in emissions between 1990–2000, the aim of 20 per cent reduction was abandoned by the governing National Party, and in 1993 its policy was changed to one of stabilization of net carbon dioxide emissions at 1990 levels by 2000,[120] still a decade earlier than the later first commitment period from Kyoto. The recent history of New Zealand energy efficiency was particularly poor: between 1973 and 1987 its intensity of energy use (energy used per unit of Gross Domestic Product) grew by more than 30 per cent in contrast to a 20 per cent overall reduction for OECD states.[121] There was therefore arguably scope for significant emission reductions on the demand side through efficiency measures as well as supply side options such as wind power. More recently, carbon dioxide emissions actually grew by one third over the period 1990–2002.[122]

As a general context for policy responses to the Kyoto Protocol it should be noted that in the mid-1980s New Zealand undertook a major re-structuring of its economy, characterized principally by a down-sizing of government and an embrace of market mechanisms as opposed to a regulatory state. It was a self-imposed regime of neo-liberal economics reflecting the so-called Washington consensus. Initially introduced by a Labour government and followed by all subsequent governments, these economic reforms have exerted a powerful gravitational pull on government policy and are reflected in an ongoing move away from a regulatory state and toward a more market-driven economy. There is an aversion to either increasing the cost of emission-producing processes and uses to

---

[117] Ibid 245.
[118] Gillespie, 'New Zealand and the Climate Change Debate', above n 113, 183.
[119] For a detailed (and critical) review of New Zealand climate change policy in the early 1990s see Kirsty Hamilton, 'New Zealand Climate Change Policy Between 1990 and 1996: A Greenpeace Perspective' in Gillespie and Burns, above n 8, 143.
[120] Ibid 153-5.
[121] Ibid 148.
[122] New Zealand Climate Change Office *New Zealand's Greenhouse Gas Inventory 1990–2002: Executive Summary* (April 2004) New Zealand Climate Change Office <www.climatechange.govt.nz/resources/reports/nir-apr04/html> at 27 July 2004.

reflect environmental and 'Kyoto' externalities through, for example, taxation policies, or to subsidizing alternative processes and uses.

The relationship between Kyoto measures (in the framework of international legal obligations) and the domestic regime for regulating the environment requires an understanding of the New Zealand *Resource Management Act 1991* (RMA). The RMA was a consolidating statute, replacing or amending over 50 statutes, and was heavily influenced by the 1987 Brundtland Report and its emphasis on sustainable development and integrated resource management.[123] It adopted a principled and comprehensive approach to sustainable development which was considered innovative at the time and which earned it a reputation as one of the more advanced environmental statutes in the world. Control of greenhouse gas emissions falls within the ambit of the Act (under s.15(1)(c) and s.2), particularly in the sense that both pursue the priority of sustainability. Climate change policies might arguably have been more completely incorporated into the existing mechanisms of the RMA, primarily through the use of resource consents for emitters and the development of appropriate plans by regional authorities, but also including carbon tax and carbon trading mechanisms. However, that has not been the policy choice of governments to date.[124] One of the virtues of a regulatory framework – an enhanced degree of public participation – is thereby lost in the embrace of economic instruments, although contrary arguments might be made for economic instruments in terms of least-cost responses, flexibility, technological innovation and lower transaction costs.[125] In the event the Domestic Policy Option Statement (DPOS) supported the use of stand-alone economic instruments with the RMA consigned to a complementary role. In 2004 the RMA was amended to remove the ability of regional councils to directly control greenhouse gas emissions through resource consents and regional plans, the government's desire being to address emissions through national policies.

But in terms of policy in the mid-1990s two principles came to drive the climate change response in New Zealand.[126] The first was one of minimal interference with markets: for example, a market-oriented approach to research by various non-government agencies was introduced in 1992 by the (conservative) National government,[127] with few resources available for government agencies. As an aside, an interesting feature of the New Zealand climate change regime is said to be the voluntary networking of scientists from various specialty areas – climate scientists, agricultural scientists, hydrologists, coastal specialists, environmental managers, industry experts and social and medical researchers. This rather ad hoc

---

[123] For a more detailed account of Kyoto policies in the context of the RMA see Bosselmann, Fuller and Salinger, above n 3, 83-102.

[124] Ibid 88-98. The authors are critical of that choice (at 102-109), and argue that risks such as inconsistency between regional plans could be overcome by issuing a National Policy Statement.

[125] See, e.g. ibid 98-102.

[126] Gillespie, 'New Zealand and the Climate Change Debate', above n 113, 169-179.

[127] For example, Hamilton, above n 119, 149-152.

model is said to be both efficient and effective in the absence of substantial state funding.[128]

The second principle required 'least economic cost' policies, which in practice translated as an emphasis on carbon sequestration in forests rather than lower emissions at source. This latter policy is known as a 'net approach' (as opposed to the 'gross approach' of emission reductions), and in 1994 it was proposed that such sequestration constitute 80 per cent (lowered to 60 per cent in 1997) of the proposed climate change response.[129]

New Zealand's negotiating stance at Kyoto was, like that of Australia, controversial in demanding the inclusion of carbon sinks in emission accounting and in seeking commitments from developing countries.[130] As was the case with Australia and other sink supporters,[131] this promotion of carbon sinks as a policy option resulted in criticism from other Kyoto states – not only on grounds of narrow self-interest but also because there were still many scientific uncertainties surrounding their operation, because of methodological problems in accounting for them and because the carbon would eventually be released. In fact New Zealand may be well placed to allow large increases in greenhouse gas emissions on the basis of credits it will receive for carbon sinks, much of which will flow from 'business as usual' forestry.[132] In terms of reductions in carbon dioxide emissions through sinks the average for Annex I countries (according to 1997 estimates) was 8 per cent but for New Zealand was 81 per cent, the highest of any Annex I country.[133] It was in that context that one commentator characterized New Zealand's approach as 'parochial self-interest, combined with sleight of hand'.[134]

The post-Kyoto policy response of the ruling National Government took the form of the DPOS, the primary objective of which was to pursue 'least cost' measures, which in turn were judged to be the use of economic instruments which would reach to all rather than merely large emitters via pricing mechanisms. The relevant instruments were taken to be environmental taxes and a domestic emissions trading system. The domestic trading system would interface with the international system, requiring emitters to hold certificates sufficient to cover their greenhouse gas emissions; they could sell any surplus or purchase more in the event of falling short.[135] Other policy objectives within the DPOS included maintaining international credibility, equity with respect to impacts, practicality and durability over time, and flexibility.

---

[128] Basher, above n 104, 139 (though no evidence is offered).
[129] Ibid.
[130] Hamilton, above n 119, 143.
[131] For example, Canada, Norway, Iceland, the United States and the Russian Federation.
[132] Bosselmann, Fuller and Salinger, above n 3, 121.
[133] Gillespie, 'Defending the Irresponsible', above n 106, 235.
[134] 'Kyoto' (1997) 3 *ECO Newsletter* 2 (quoted in Gillespie, 'Defending the Irresponsible', above n 106, 234).
[135] For a more detailed analysis of the emissions market see, e.g. Paul Radich, 'Kyoto and the Emissions Trading Market' (2001) *New Zealand Law Journal* 463; Paul Radich, 'The Emissions Market' (2002) *New Zealand Law Journal* 14.

A Labour government was elected in 1999 and proceeded with a consultation process and a Preferred Policy Package in 2002. Its stated 'overall climate change goal is that New Zealand should have made significant greenhouse gas reductions on business-as-usual and be set towards a permanent downward path for gross emissions by 2012'.[136] The policy response was again dominated by non-regulatory, market-based options, mostly aimed at modest emission reductions which would be swamped in importance by the sink credits which New Zealand had aggressively (and controversially) promoted as a member of the JUSCANZ group. An overview of projections[137] for the first commitment period (2008–2012) illustrates the point.

Total GHG base year (1990) emissions were 61.64 million tonnes of carbon dioxide-equivalent (Mt CO2-equivalent), so the commitment for 2008–2012 is for an aggregate 308 Mt CO2-equivalent for the five years. Best estimates for 'business-as-usual', that is to say in the absence of Kyoto policies, are for 399 Mt CO2-equivalent, an increase of 30 per cent. By 2002 total emissions had already grown by 21.6 per cent, including large increases for methane from dairy cows (up 65 per cent), transport (up 61 per cent) and electricity generation (up 58 per cent, with growth in electricity production coming from thermal rather than hydro generation).[138] Existing Kyoto policies are estimated to reduce that business-as-usual total to 360 Mt CO2-equivalent, still an increase of 17 per cent over the base year. But sink credits for the same period are projected at 95 CO2-equivalent, thus generating an emissions 'credit'. In other words, emissions will actually increase significantly over 1990 levels, but will be more than compensated for by reforestation – hence New Zealand's aggressive advocacy of carbon sinks and a 'net' emissions approach.

On a sectoral basis, Agriculture is the largest source of greenhouse gas emissions with 49 per cent of total emissions, and on a business-as-usual basis was expected to grow by 26 per cent above 1990 in the first commitment period.[139] There was a growth of 15.5 per cent to 2002. Agriculture is at present largely exempt from Kyoto measures though emissions in this sector are expected to ease somewhat due to land use changes such as forestry, tenure reviews, conversion to lifestyle blocks and intensive horticulture. The Energy (including transportation) sector contributed 43 per cent of total emissions, with a projected business-as-usual growth of 43 per cent above 1990 levels by the first commitment period.[140] There was a 35 per cent increase in emissions from this sector to 2002. Note that the domestic transport sector accounted for some 45 per cent of carbon dioxide

---

[136] New Zealand Climate Change Office, Q&A on GHG Inventory and New Zealand's net position <www.climatechange.govt.nz/resources/info-sheets/qa-inventory-net-position.html> at 27 July 2004.

[137] New Zealand Government, *Report on revised projections for the Kyoto Protocol*, above n 108.

[138] New Zealand Climate Change Office, Q&A, above n 136.

[139] New Zealand Government, *Report on revised projections for the Kyoto Protocol*, above n 108.

[140] Ibid.

emissions but has not been subject to any explicit policy response other than a general expression of concern for its environmental impacts.[141]

The Industrial Processes sector contributes only 5 per cent of total emissions, with business-as-usual estimates of 29 per cent growth above 1990 levels in the first commitment period.[142] Emissions in this sector increased by 20.5 per cent over 1990–2002. The Waste sector contributed some 3 per cent of total emissions in 2002 through landfill disposal and waste water.[143] Business-as-usual projections for the first commitment period are not currently available, but emissions had actually fallen by 17.7 per cent in 2002.

There are a range of programs through which actual reductions in emissions, as compared to 'business as usual', are expected to be achieved.[144] That is to say, these are reductions which would not have occurred but for the various government policies either presently in place or planned. Firstly, the National Energy Efficiency and Conservation Strategy (NEECS) seeks to improve energy efficiency by some 20 per cent and to increase energy supplies from renewable energy sources. The expected impact over the first commitment period is 5 Mt CO2-equivalent. Secondly, the New Zealand Waste Strategy aspires to 'moving towards zero waste by 2010' through reductions in waste together with re-use, recycling and recovery economic incentives for a total abatement of 6 Mt CO2-equivalent. Thirdly, a Project to Reduce Emissions program provides incentives for projects which will reduce emissions below 'business as usual' during the first commitment period. Incentives take the form of emission units which are awarded to projects which would not otherwise be economically viable. The units will be internationally tradable when the Protocol comes into force. The value of the units will be determined by the future international market, leaving current tenderers to make their own value estimates, though some assistance is available from the emerging European Union Emissions Trading Scheme. Estimates are for savings of some 8-12 Mt CO2-equivalent. Some four million emission units have been awarded to date, with another six million to be available from late 2004. Fourth, Local Government Initiatives will take the form of a three year program, beginning in 2004, called 'Communities for Climate Protection'. It is based on the 'Cities for Climate Protection' program that has proven successful internationally in reducing emissions both from local councils and their constituent communities through energy efficiency, waste reduction, sustainable transportation and other locally oriented initiatives. It is expected to realize some 0.6 Mt CO2-equivalent. Fifth, there is a Small to Medium Enterprises and Business Opportunities policy aimed at encouraging smaller businesses to reduce emissions and their exposure to emissions charges. They are expected to generate some 3 Mt CO2-equivalent in emissions abatement. Finally, the government plans to introduce price based measures, including an emissions charge on fossil fuels and industrial process

---

[141] Bosselmann, Fuller and Salinger, above n 3, 74.
[142] Ibid.
[143] Ibid.
[144] See generally New Zealand Government, *Report on revised projections for the Kyoto Protocol*, above n 108.

emissions from 2007. The charge will approximate the international emissions price with a cap of NZ$25 per tonne of CO2-equivalent – at NZ$15 per tonne the charges are expected to generate some 11 Mt CO2-equivalent. Enterprises whose viability is then particularly at risk may voluntarily pursue international best practice in return for carbon charge exemptions under a program of Negotiated Greenhouse Agreements (NGAs). Note that agriculture is not subject to the charge, but in return is required to enter into a Memorandum of Understanding to implement an agricultural research strategy to reduce methane and nitrous oxide gases.

Other policy strategies relate to transport, waste, climate change research and public awareness. The various policies are to be differentially applied to four economic groups: those whose competitiveness is most at risk, general energy users including businesses, institutions and households, on-farm agriculture and 'others' for whom policy responses are difficult (for example, due to lack of abatement options and/or measurement difficulties).

As required by the Kyoto Protocol the government formulated a National Energy Efficiency and Conservation Strategy (NEECS) and passed the Energy Efficiency and Conservation Act 2000 to promote energy efficiency, conservation and renewable energy sources, though without a specific regulatory framework. The NEECS aims to achieve a 20 per cent improvement in energy efficiency by 2012 together with a substantial increase in renewable energy sources.

Thus Kyoto policies in New Zealand have as yet barely targeted the energy sector (just a commitment to efficiency), the transport sector (environmental impacts merely noted) and the agriculture sector (a commitment to more research).[145] The reluctance to implement meaningful policy measures in the agricultural sector is perhaps the most significant policy anomaly, as government (that is to say taxpayers) are to bear the Kyoto costs of the sector's non-carbon dioxide emissions. The obvious reasons are the difficulty of reducing these emissions and the importance of the sector to the New Zealand economy, though in the long term some practical measures must be implemented. There is now a Pastoral Greenhouse Gas Research Strategy which seeks to develop abatement technologies which will lower ruminant methane and nitrous oxide emissions by at least 20 per cent at the end of the first commitment period.[146]

In any event, overwhelming the policies for actual emission reductions are the anticipated sink credits from Landuse Change and Forestry. The best estimate of carbon sequestration from sinks is 95 Mt CO2-equivalent, largely due to high levels of planting in the mid-1990s – over the period 1992–2002 planted forests were taking over farmed land at an average rate of 40 000 ha per year, but planting rates declined to some 15 000 ha per year in 2003.[147] The government's forecast

---

[145] Ibid.

[146] Mark Leslie and Peter O'Hara, 'A Pastoral Greenhouse Gas Research Strategy' (October 2003) New Zealand Ministry of Agriculture and Forestry <http://www.maf.govt.nz/mafnet/rural-nz/sustainable-resource-use/climate/pastoral-greenhouse-gas-strategy/index.htm> at 22 October 2004.

[147] New Zealand Government, *Report on revised projections for the Kyoto Protocol*, above n 108.

planting rates are for 30 000 ha per annum. As the plantings from the 1990s mature in the mid-2020s a future government will in fact face net liabilities from Kyoto forests, at least for a period of 2 to 5 years. Carbon sequestration from these forest sinks increased by 17.7 per cent over the period 1990–2002.

The government has proposed a Forest Industry Framework Agreement to promote and co-ordinate climate change policy for the sector, and has set aside funding for new initiatives contingent on the signing of a Memorandum of Understanding. As well, and in light of the importance of forestry to New Zealand's ability to meet its Kyoto commitments, the government has felt it necessary to issue a 'clarification' to the industry on the management of the benefits and liabilities which will accrue under Kyoto rules for sink credits.[148] In short, the government has decided to retain all sink credits and to assume any associated liabilities, at least for the first commitment period. Those liabilities arise because credits claimed for 'Kyoto' forests (those planted since 1990) create contingent liabilities in the future when the same forests are harvested or otherwise degraded. Replacement emission units will have to be purchased on the international market and may be more expensive if and when the price of carbon credits increases over time. Should these liabilities be devolved to private individuals and companies they would not only face these possible capital losses but other ongoing obligations, such as insurance of some kind to ensure their ability to discharge the liabilities and the costs of monitoring and verification of carbon data. However, there is a Permanent Forest Sink Initiative which aims to enable landowners, particularly those with largely marginal land, to establish permanent forests which cannot be harvested until after 35 years have elapsed and then on a 'continuous canopy basis'.[149] Rights (in the form of tradable Kyoto emission units) and obligations (regarding costs and replacement of units in the event of forest loss) will be the subject of contracts between landowners and the Crown, and will include an insurance requirement to guarantee landowner liabilities in the event of accidental or deliberate loss of forest.

New Zealand has also entered into Climate Change Partnerships with Australia and the United States. The NZ-US partnership began in July 2003 and, at the time of writing, included 32 projects in such priority areas as climate change science, greenhouse gas accounting in forestry and agriculture, climate change research in Antarctica and cooperation with developing countries.[150] The Australia-New Zealand Bilateral Climate Change Partnership announced a number of projects in December 2003, including climate monitoring and prediction in the

---

[148] New Zealand Government, *Clarification on sink credits* (2004) New Zealand Climate Change Office <www.climatechange.govt.nz/sectors/forestry/sink-credits.html> at 27 July 2004.

[149] New Zealand Government, *Questions and answers on the Permanent Forest Sink Initiative* (2004) New Zealand Climate Change Office <www.climatechange.govt.nz/resources/info-sheets/qa-forest-sink-intiative.html> at 27 August 2004.

[150] Hon. Pete Hodgson, 'NZ-U.S. consolidate partnership on climate change' (Press Release, 16 July 2004) New Zealand Government <http://www.beehive.govt.nz/PrintDocument.cfm?DocumentID=20342> at 27 July 2004.

South-West Pacific Region, facilitation of local government engagement on climate change issues, common energy efficiency regulatory requirements and further research into climate variability and predictability. There is a fairly high degree of collaboration between New Zealand and Australia, for example within the scientific establishment but also within economic, environmental and foreign policies although clearly their respective policy responses to climate change differ. For example, in November 2004 seven new partnership projects under the Bilateral Climate Change Partnership were announced in such areas as methane emissions from livestock and nitrous oxide from agriculture, adaptation strategies with developed countries, extension of a joint end-use energy efficiency scheme to Fiji and improved climate observations for Pacific Island Countries.[151]

Conclusions

In summary, New Zealand's policy response to the Kyoto Protocol might reasonably be described as disappointing. It is one of only four states (excluding two Economies in Transition) to have negotiated for itself a no-reduction position from 1990 base levels of GHGs. It was a vigorous promoter of self-serving JUSCANZ initiatives on carbon sinks and the various 'flexible' policy options which allows it to avoid any significant pain of actual emission reductions by utilizing forest sinks. Indeed it is likely to make an economic gain from its Kyoto measures. In that sense it could not be said to have exercised leadership in the difficult task of persuading the international community to make the hard decisions which will surely be necessary to make any substantial impact on global warming.

Small Island States

The Alliance of Small Island States[152] (AOSIS) emerged as an independent grouping at the fourth round of negotiations leading to the UNFCCC. The Pacific Island Countries (PICs) fall within a general category of Small Island Developing States (SIDS). Many of the South Pacific states belong to a regional grouping known as the Pacific Forum – the fourteen members are Australia, the Cook Islands, the Federated States of Micronesia, Fiji, Kiribati, Nauru, New Zealand, Niue, Palau, Papua New Guinea, Republic of the Marshall Islands, Samoa, Solomon Islands, Tonga, Tuvalu and Vanuatu. Among the Forum's objectives is the 'sustainable management of its resources', along with other objectives such as

---

[151] Hon. Pete Hodgson, 'Joint Australia, New Zealand action on climate change' (Press Release, 4 November 2004) New Zealand Government <http://www.beehive.govt.nz/PrintDocument.cfm?DocumentID=21393> at 20 December 2004.

[152] Defined by the UN as being of less than 10 000 square km in land area and with less than 500 000 inhabitants. The group includes states from the Atlantic, Indian and Pacific Oceans, the Caribbean, the Mediterranean (Cyprus, Malta) and the South China Sea (Singapore).

economic prosperity and good governance.[153] But generally their vulnerability to climate change is the most pressing environmental issue they presently face, particularly with respect to rising sea levels and their impacts on coastal environments, bleaching of coral reefs and unpredictable changes in productivity in marine ecosystems.[154] Coastal populations are under particular threat: in Fiji, for example, half of the population live within sixty kilometres of the coast and 90 percent of villages are located on the coast.[155] Their economies are similarly threatened as the major sectors – fishing, tourism and agriculture – will all be affected by climate change.[156] Further implications follow with respect to destabilizing effects on the social and political orders of what are already in many cases only marginally viable states.

Generally, they lack the resource and infrastructures for a significant scientific establishment, with monitoring often supported by Australia and New Zealand. They are generally characterized by small, weak and dependent economies and will be largely dependent on other states to manage climate change impacts. Given that any solutions will depend on negotiations between major states, through the Kyoto Protocol or otherwise, then climate change will remain an external issue for Pacific Island states notwithstanding that they are likely to be its first victims.[157] The reluctance of their most important neighbour, Australia, to ratify the Protocol suggests the weak degree of influence these states exert even in their own region. Indeed all of the so-called JUSCANZ 'Kyoto-hostile' states – Japan, the United States, Canada, Australia and New Zealand – are Pacific Rim states and seemingly impervious to the likely plight of the small and largely fragmented Pacific Island states.

They are indeed particularly vulnerable to climate change impacts.[158] It has been predicted that over the period 2000–2100 the global mean sea level will rise 0.09–0.88m.[159] The particular threat to SIDS has been recognized by the international community – for example, in the discussions of the UNFCCC and the UN Global Conference for the Sustainable Development of Small Island

---

[153] See, e.g. Pacific Islands Forum, *Special Leaders' Retreat: The Auckland Declaration* (2004) <www.forumsec.org.fj> at 6 April 2004.

[154] Laurence Cordonnery, 'Environmental Law Issues in the South Pacific and the Quest for Sustainable Development and Good Governance' in Anita Jowitt and Tess Newton (eds), *Passage of Change: Law, Society and Governance in the Pacific* (2003) 233, 234.

[155] Ashleigh Lezard et al, *Climate Change in the Pacific* (2003) 3 World Wildlife Federation <http://www.wwfpacific.org.fj/climate_change/CC%20Booklet%20(lite).pdf> at 20 December 2004.

[156] Ibid.

[157] Cordonnery, above n 154.

[158] For a more complete assessment see, e.g. Burns, above n 32, 233.

[159] J T Houghton et al (eds), *IPCC, Climate Change 2001: The Scientific Basis* (2001) 16, cited in Alexander Gillespie, 'Small Island States in the face of climatic change: the end of the line in international environmental responsibility' (2004) 22 UCLA *Journal of Environmental Law and Policy* 107, 110. Other estimates vary – for example, an IPCC projection of 0.15-0.95m, with a best estimate of 0.49m by 2100 (quoted in Burns, above n 32, 235).

Developing States.¹⁶⁰ In many cases SIDS rise only a few metres above sea level and are therefore at risk for significant land loss – examples include the Marshall Islands, Tuvalu, Kiribati, Tonga and Vanuatu.¹⁶¹ Kiribati, for example, could lose 12.5 per cent of its land mass from a one metre rise in sea levels, and in fact has already seen two of its uninhabited islands disappear under rising sea levels.¹⁶² Other impacts such as coastal erosion, dislocation of population and costs of adaptation will be common to other affected countries though usually with less severity.¹⁶³ Those impacts would be further exacerbated by any increase in violent weather events. Amelioration measures are likely beyond the economic capabilities of these states – for example, effective sea walls in the Marshall Islands are estimated to cost US$100 million in a country with a gross domestic product of only US$80 million.¹⁶⁴

Notwithstanding the uncertainty surrounding likely impacts of global warming, vulnerability assessments for the Pacific Island states suggest that they are highly vulnerable to climate change and sea levels, that they have considerable natural resilience which is impaired by human pressures, that they themselves make only insignificant contributions to global environmental changes, and that they have a low capacity to respond to change.¹⁶⁵ This vulnerability is acknowledged in the preamble to the UNFCCC, 'recognizing ... that low-lying and other small island countries ... are particularly vulnerable to the adverse effects of climate change', in Principle 2 that '... those that are particularly vulnerable to the adverse effects of climate change ... should be given full consideration', in (article 4) Commitment Four that 'the developed country Parties ... shall ... assist the developing country Parties that are particularly vulnerable to the adverse effects of climate change in meeting costs of adaptation to those adverse effects' and in (article 4) Commitment Eight that 'the Parties shall give full consideration to ... [necessary] actions ... including [those] ... related to funding, insurance and the transfer of technology ... especially on ... (a) small island states; (b) countries with low-lying coastal areas'. The South Pacific SIDS have, through the Pacific Forum, similarly called for 'urgent action to reduce greenhouse emissions and for further commitments in the future by all major emitters'.¹⁶⁶

All of the Pacific Forum states except Australia and Tonga have ratified (or acceded to) the Kyoto Protocol, and three of them – the Cook Islands, Niue and Nauru – have added a Declaration that article 3 of the Protocol (stipulating an overall 5 per cent reduction of 1990 emissions by Annex I countries over the first commitment period) is 'inadequate to prevent dangerous anthropocentric

---

¹⁶⁰ Gillespie, above n 159, 112-13.
¹⁶¹ Ibid.
¹⁶² Burns, above n 32, 235.
¹⁶³ For a more complete treatment of likely effects on SIDS, see Gillespie, above n 159.
¹⁶⁴ Burns, above n 32, 236.
¹⁶⁵ John Hay, 'Climate Change in the Pacific: Science-based Information and Understanding' in Gillespie and Burns, above n 8, 269, 285.
¹⁶⁶ *Forum Communiqué*, Thirty Third Pacific Islands Forum, Fiji, August 2002, [24]-[25] (quoted in Gillespie, above n 159, 120).

interference with the climate system'.[167] As developing (or in some cases least developed) countries they are not required to meet any specific emission reduction targets under the Kyoto Protocol.

An interesting problem for the future may be that of environmental refugees from states such as Tuvalu. Its total land size is only 26 square km, its highest point is only 4-5m above sea level and its population only 11 000.[168] It has already requested that Australia and New Zealand take some of its people as the islands become less habitable; New Zealand has agreed to plan a thirty year immigration program but Australia has declined. As well Tuvalu is threatening to file a lawsuit with the International Court of Justice against the United States and Australia over the refusal of those countries, respectively the largest emitter of greenhouse gases and the biggest per capita emitter of greenhouse gases, to ratify the Kyoto Protocol.[169] In that context the response of New Zealand and particularly Australia must be a considerable disappointment to the Pacific Forum states.[170] More generally, there is also a question as to whether there might be a claim in state responsibility for the impacts of climate change on vulnerable states.[171]

Regional cooperation has, however, offset some of the disadvantages of under-developed island states. They coordinate climate change policy through the Alliance of Small Island States (AOSIS), whose priorities are understandably in tension with industrialized states including Australia and New Zealand, neither of whom were required to actually reduce emissions below 1990 levels. Actual climate change efforts are financed by the Global Environment Facility (a joint program of the World Bank and UN Development Programme) under the Pacific Island Climate Change Assistance Program (PICCAP), to which Australia is a significant contributor.[172] More generally there is a South Pacific Regional Environment Programme (SPREP), supported by Australia and New Zealand, that monitors regional environmental issues such as marine pollution and biodiversity as well as climate change.[173] In addition there are government agencies – for

---

[167] UNFCCC, *Kyoto Protocol: Status of Ratification*, above n 17.

[168] 'Tiny country struggles to keep its head above water' (November 2003) 15 *Global Environmental Change* 5.

[169] Kalinga Seneviratne, *Tuvalu Steps Up Threat to Sue Australia*, U.S. (2002) Pacific Islands Report <www.tuvaluislands.com/news/archives/2002/2002-09-10.htm> at 18 August 2004.

[170] This was most clearly demonstrated at the 1997 South Pacific Forum, where this disappointment drew an aggressive response from Australian Prime Minister Howard: see Basher, above n 104, 138. See also ibid.

[171] See, e.g. Phillip Barton, 'State Responsibility and Climate Change: Could Canada be Liable to Small Island States?' (2002) 11 *Dalhousie Journal of Legal Studies* 65.

[172] In 2003 Australia substantially increased its contribution to the GEF to $68 million for the third replenishment period, some 40 per cent of which was targeted at climate change projects including the PICCAP. See Kemp, 'Australia's Approach to Climate Change', above n 43.

[173] Note a more sceptical view of such programs as being tainted by 'ecocolonialism' and 'scientific neocolonialism'; see, e.g. Michael Edwards 'Parochialism and Empowerment:

example, in New Zealand the Climate Change Office and the National Institute of Water and Atmospheric Research – which participate in various climate change initiatives in the Pacific, including the Global Climate Observing System which monitors climate on a global scale.

Under the Kytoto Protocol's Clean Development Mechanisms program for Annex I states to facilitate emission reductions in non-Annex I states there would seem to be opportunity for Australia and New Zealand to offset their relatively high domestic costs of emission reduction with low-cost projects in the neighbouring South Pacific, for example in energy and land use. Australia has undertaken a number of emission reduction projects in the South Pacific and Indonesia,[174] but New Zealand has not yet taken any formal initiatives.

Summary and Conclusions

The Kyoto Protocol is a significantly limited instrument for addressing the threat of climate change. It will come into force in 2005 with Russia's ratification, and may reasonably be expected to meet its modest ambition of a 5 per cent reduction in greenhouse gas emissions in the first commitment period. Its major limitations are three-fold: the absence of the United States as the most prolific emitter, the lack of binding commitments for developing states such as China, and the modesty of its ambitions given the necessary reduction in emissions to even stabilize greenhouse gas concentrations. Each is a reflection of the realpolitik of the international order, wherein the trade-off between economic growth and the unknown net impacts of emission reduction measures lead to an unenthusiastic response from many states. Nowhere was this clearer than largely market-oriented concessions granted to the JUSCANZ group, of whom two states (the United States and Australia) still refused to ratify the Protocol. One thing seems likely though: if the developed states (including the United States) fail to meet even the modest aspirations of the first commitment period then it seems unlikely that developing states will embrace any future regime which requires legally binding commitments to reduce their own emissions.

The limitations of the Protocol have particular significance for Pacific Island states. They are especially vulnerable both in terms of geography and of economics. They will most likely be disproportionately affected by climate change notwithstanding that their contribution to the problem is negligible. Similarly they lack (individually at least) any political influence sufficient to sway powerful states, and are unable to exert significant influence even in their own Pacific region in respect of Australia in particular.

It must be particularly galling to the Pacific Island states that one of the Pacific Forum members – Australia – is one of the highest per capita emitters of

---

Responding to Ecocolonialism and Globalisation in the SouthWest Pacific' in Gillespie and Burns, above n 8, 251.

[174] See, e.g. Peter Alsop, 'Joint Implementation: A Survey of Principles and Practical Issues' in Gillespie and Burns, above n 8, 209, 226-8.

greenhouse gases and was able to plead a 'special case' and negotiate one of the most favourable state regimes for emission targets and abatement practices, yet still refuses to ratify. As a party to the original Framework Convention on Climate Change it has undertaken voluntary measures but in spite of its being permitted an 8 per cent increase in emissions (the most favourable of any major developed state) it appears unlikely to meet even that target.

Similarly New Zealand, the other significant regional power and major per capita emitter, was a member of the reluctant group of JUSCANZ states and was successful in negotiating a 'no-reduction' emissions position. Although it is unusually dependent on agriculture and must deal with the difficult issue of methane emissions from livestock, it is one of the few states which may actually realize an economic gain from the first commitment period. Its reluctance to accept a reduction on 1990 emission levels, its reliance on carbon sinks rather than actual emissions, its reluctance to make hard choices (for example, in agriculture) and its promotion of developing country commitments all point to its being one of the 'Kyoto-reluctant' states. New Zealand may compare favourably to Australia and the United States but that is damning with faint praise.

Neither Australia nor New Zealand appear willing to exercise leadership in the region, at least in this, and the small island states are unable to bring meaningful pressure to bear. In that sense the region might be seen as a microcosm of the broader international order both in terms of power relations and in the efficacy of the Protocol. Notwithstanding that the Kyoto Protocol is finally coming into force, it may well be defined not by its achievements but by its limitations. Its first and most vulnerable victims may well be the small Pacific island states, whilst at least one of their affluent neighbours might be characterized as one of the 'villains' of what may prove to be a fatally compromised regime.

Chapter 6

What Bioprospecting Means for Antarctica and the Southern Ocean

Michelle Rogan-Finnemore

Introduction

Setting the scene

This chapter explores the issue of bioprospecting in the Antarctic. First, it presents the component parts of the Antarctic Treaty System including, importantly, those articles of the Antarctic Treaty itself which require the closest examination in the context of commercial activities, like bioprospecting, in the Antarctic region. Consideration is then given to the definition of Antarctica, the Southern Ocean and bioprospecting itself. The chapter then moves on to discuss the implications of the specific obligations contained within the Antarctic Treaty focusing on the obligation for free availability of information and results and the use of Antarctica for peaceful purposes only. The contentious nature of the Antarctic territorial claims is then considered along with what unresolved sovereignty means for the region in the context of any resource utilization. The chapter concludes with consideration of the future of Antarctic bioprospecting.

Some readers may wonder why a chapter on Antarctica and the Southern Ocean is included in a book about International Law and the South Pacific region. Whilst the small island nations have little direct interest in the Antarctic region, New Zealand and Australia have a direct and substantial interest. They are two of the twelve original signatories to the Antarctic Treaty and are Antarctic territorial claimant states which maintain an active role within the Antarctic Treaty System. The Antarctic and especially the Southern Ocean region are geographically proximate to both and they have historic and present-day connections to the region. For example, the New Zealand Ministry of Foreign Affairs and Trade includes an Antarctic Policy Unit which is responsible for New Zealand representation within the Antarctic Treaty arena and New Zealand often plays a key role in negotiating Antarctic law and policy.

The Antarctic region is often defined by a series of extreme descriptors. These include 'highest', 'driest', 'coldest' and 'windiest'. While it is true that on average, across the entire Antarctic continental region, these terms are accurate this generalization hides the fact that the Antarctic region is a large, diverse area of the earth which supports a range of environments covering both terrestrial and marine ecosystems. These environments are often referred to as 'extreme', carrying with it an implication that living and surviving there, especially from an anthropogenic standpoint, is difficult. Yet, it is these extreme conditions to which many living organisms have indeed adapted that make the Antarctic region a target of bioprospectors.

Antarctica has no permanent human population and no legally recognized sovereign. Seven states claim territory in Antarctica and two other states reserve the right to make a future claim,[1] but none of these claims are formally recognized by the international community. Therefore there is no 'Antarctic government' as such. Instead the region is governed by an international system known as the Antarctic Treaty System which currently has 47 participating states. This system has functioned effectively for the past 43 years, but that is not to say that it has not had to weather both internal and external challenges. These challenges have even led some to argue that the system be replaced by an international institution, such as the United Nations.

New challenges to the system regularly emerge. Bioprospecting is the latest challenge to the Antarctic Treaty System. Global bioprospecting is a lucrative industry. Bioprospecting efforts involve the search for novel biodiversity that can be utilized in a product or process which may then be commercialized. Scientists' recent appreciation of Antarctica's potential as a source of novel biodiversity has aroused growing interest in the continent and its surrounding marine environment. This growing interest has reawakened Antarctic challenges similar to those presented in the early days of sealing and whaling, in the negotiation of a fisheries conservation and management agreement, in the management of the Antarctic tourism industry and in the negotiations of a mineral extraction regime.

Not since the late 1970s debate on Antarctic mineral resource extraction have the potential commercial stakes been so high. Even Southern Ocean fishing and the Antarctic tourism industry may pale in comparison to the commercial and therefore economic potential of a bioprospecting industry developing from Antarctic-derived biodiversity.

The real legal challenge to the system stems from the obligations as stated in the Antarctic Treaty 1959,[2] the lack of a recognized sovereign for the region and the current global debates surrounding benefit-sharing from and access to the world's natural resources. The issue is further complicated because of the conflicting uses for Antarctica and multiple threats to this unique environment. These include the value of the region for scientific research; the increasing value of the region in economic terms; and the value of Antarctica, including its intrinsic value and wilderness value,[3] as recognized in the Protocol for

---

[1] The seven claimant states are Argentina, Chile, Australia, France, New Zealand, Norway, and the United Kingdom; the United States and Russia each reserve the right to make a future claim.

[2] *The Antarctic Treaty*, opened for signature 1 December 1959, 402 UNTS 71 (entered into force 23 June 1961) ('Antarctic Treaty').

[3] See, generally, David Leary (Presentation at the Bioprospecting in the High Seas Conference, Dunedin, 28–29 November 2003).

Environmental Protection to the Antarctic Treaty 1991.[4] This presents the Antarctic Treaty parties with a complicated situation for a region with conflicting uses and multiple threats.

Bioprospecting activities in the Antarctic are the single most urgent issue that has challenged the effective operation of the Antarctic Treaty System since the adoption (and subsequent abandonment) of the Convention on the Regulation of Antarctic Mineral Resources 1988[5] in the late 1980s. Understanding the legal implications of allowing this activity to continue in the region is of critical importance to the Antarctic Treaty System.

The Antarctic Treaty System

The Antarctic Treaty System (ATS) refers to 'the whole complex of international legal instruments and arrangements made for the purpose of coordinating relations among states with respect to Antarctica'.[6] The phrase is legally defined in the most recent ATS instrument, the Protocol on Environmental Protection to the Antarctic Treaty 1991[7] (Protocol), which provides in its article 1(e) that 'Antarctic Treaty System' means 'the Antarctic Treaty, the measures in effect under that Treaty, its associated separate international instruments in force and the measures in effect under those instruments'. The Handbook of the Antarctic Treaty System,[8] although not a legal document as such, also includes within the System 'the results of Meetings of Experts, the decisions of Special Consultative Meetings and, at a non-governmental level, reflects the work of the Scientific Committee on Antarctic Research (SCAR)'.[9]

While the component parts of the Antarctic Treaty System cover a range of Antarctic and Southern Ocean issues, its 'three pillars'[10] are often said to be:

1. Safeguarding peace;
2. Ensuring freedom of scientific research; and
3. Protection of the Antarctic environment.

The first two pillars were proposed at the genesis of the Antarctic Treaty System in 1959, while the third pillar is reflected in subsequent legal instruments beginning in 1964.

---

[4] *Protocol on Environmental Protection to the Antarctic Treaty*, opened for signature 4 October 1991, 30 ILM 1991 (entered into force 14 January 1998) ('Protocol').
[5] *Convention on the Regulation of Antarctic Mineral Resources*, opened for signature 25 November 1988, 27 ILM (1988) (not yet in force) ('CRAMRA').
[6] Harlan Cohen (ed), *Handbook of the Antarctic Treaty System* (9th ed, 2002) 1.
[7] Above n 4.
[8] Cohen, above n 6.
[9] Ibid.
[10] Kees Bastmeijer, *The Antarctic environmental protocol and its domestic legal implementation* (2003) 12.

Central to the ATS is the Antarctic Treaty which was negotiated in less than two years and signed at the Washington Conference.[11] It is the core legal instrument which provides the foundation for the development and evolution of the system. The Antarctic Treaty has been called 'unique',[12] referring partially to its relative simplicity. Fourteen articles and a preamble have managed to effectively control a geographic region which occupies one tenth of the Earth's surface. The Treaty's two key objectives are stated initially in the preamble as: first, the use of Antarctica exclusively for peaceful purposes; and second, support for international cooperation in scientific investigation in Antarctica. The original parties to the Antarctic Treaty agreed in the preamble statements that these objectives were 'in the interest of all mankind'. These objectives are directly supported in the Antarctic Treaty in articles I, II, and III. They are indirectly supported primarily by articles IV, V, VII, and VIII. All of these articles are discussed in more detail below in the context of bioprospecting.

The Antarctic Treaty is by virtue of its article XIII(1) open for accession by any Member State of the United Nations, or by any other state which may be invited to accede. Forty-five states have ratified the Antarctic Treaty (Figure 6.1). As a multilateral accord, the Treaty is given credit for its success, especially in maintaining non-militarization and denuclearization of the Antarctic region, as well as promoting scientific cooperation.[13] The Antarctic Treaty consists only of obligations; it also contains little more than moral sanctions to ensure compliance and observance of its principles. In addition, it also lacks effective arbitration procedures and any provisions referring to economic exploitation of the region.[14]

Sovereignty defined

Sovereignty has been described as the term for 'the plenary competence of a state, or as the totality of the rights and duties of a state which are recognised by international law ... which connotes the exclusive right of a state to perform state functions within its own territories'.[15] Therefore, central to the notion of sovereignty is the territory within which the state exercises its exclusive sovereign rights. Huber J, in the *Island of Palmas*[16] case said that 'much depends upon which state possesses territorial sovereignty over a given area ... if there is no sovereignty over an area, that area inevitably comes under an international regime of some sort'.[17] Since territory is central to the notion of sovereignty, a sovereign must have

---

[11] Conference on Antarctica (Washington, DC, 15 October–1 December 1959).

[12] Gerald S Schatz and the Antarctican Society, 'Transnational Science and Technology in the absence of Defined Sovereignty: Development in the Polar Regions and in Legally Similar Situations' in Gerald S Schatz (ed), *Science Technology and Sovereignty in the Polar Regions* (1974).

[13] See Christopher Joyner, *Governing the Frozen Commons: the Antarctic regime and environmental protection* (1998) 21.

[14] See generally, F M Auburn, *The Ross Dependency* (1972) 33.

[15] Gillian Triggs, *International law and Australian sovereignty in Antarctica* (1986) 150.

[16] *Island of Palmas* (1928) 2 RIAA 829.

[17] Ibid.

acquired territory. This may be achieved in a number of ways including discovery of territory that is terra nullius, the primary mode of acquisition of Antarctic territory to date. However, simply discovering a territory is not enough and today, the most problematic of issues surrounding territorial claims to Antarctica is whether these claims have actually been perfected. Discovery of territory only provides an inchoate title to the territory at best; effective occupation of the territory is then required[18] to perfect that title. There has been much debate surrounding the concept of effective occupation[19] and what that phrase actually means. The debate has implications especially in the context of the vast, remote and harsh environment such as Antarctica.

The US, a non-claimant signatory state and an active player in the Antarctic Treaty arena, developed a stance of non-recognition of the Antarctic claims on the basis that effective occupation was a necessary requirement and had not been achieved. This has constantly been its position[20] even though the US itself reserves the right to make a claim in the future grounded on acts similar to those made by the Antarctic territorial claimants.

It is not the intention of this chapter to debate the legitimacy of the territorial claims to Antarctica.[21] The next section is limited to a discussion of the territorial claims situation that we are currently presented with, that is, the territorial claims situation frozen as at 1961 by the Antarctic Treaty, and within which we must resolve any legal issues related to the Antarctic region, including those in relation to bioprospecting. The chapter then goes on to investigate the article IV obligation to compromise on sovereignty and the impact of this obligation on Antarctic resource use.

The territorial claims to Antarctica

Antarctica was the last continent to be discovered. While no one disputes that Antarctica was terra nullius before its discovery, there is some debate on who actually was the first to discover continental Antarctica. The US, Russia and the UK all claim the honour based on discovery expeditions of Palmer, Bellinghausen and Cook, respectively.

By 1955, seven states had laid territorial claims to sectors of Antarctica, principally based on discovery. In 1908, the UK was the first to announce its claim to the entire Antarctic peninsula. In the 1940s both Chile and Argentina claimed

---

[18] *Clipperton Island* (1931) 2 RIAA 1105.
[19] See, e.g. *The Legal Status of Eastern Greenland* [1933 PCIJ (ser A/B) No 53.
[20] The position of the US was first expressed by US Secretary of State Hughes: 'It is the considered opinion of this department that the discovery of lands unknown to civilization, even when coupled with the formal taking of possession, does not support a valid claim of sovereignty, unless the discovery is followed by an actual settlement of the discovered territory'.
[21] See generally, Triggs, *International law and Australian sovereignty in Antarctica*, above n 15 for a full discussion of the legitimacy of the Antarctic territorial claims.

areas in the peninsula region, so that these three sectors overlap[22] and are mutually contested. The other four claims, those of New Zealand, Australia, France and Norway, were declared beginning in 1923. The claims of New Zealand and Australia stem from the UK claim and are based on the voyages of James Clark Ross who circumnavigated the Antarctic continent. All of the seven claims, except one, converge at the south geographic pole and have a northern boundary at the 60° South Latitude line.[23] All but one employ the sector principle[24] to define their territory. A large portion of Antarctica remains unclaimed (Figure 6.2). In addition to the seven claimant states, the US and Russia reject all seven of the territorial claims, whilst themselves maintaining that they each have a legal basis to claim Antarctic territory should they ever wish to do so.[25] To date, none of the claims or basis of claims is recognized internationally, except in some cases by other 'neighbouring' Antarctic claimant states.[26]

Today, the Antarctic territorial claims issue remains unresolved. The question as to whether the claims to territorial sovereignty in Antarctica are valid has never been decided upon by international arbitration or adjudication.[27] This is the situation we are presented with and which forms the background for any discussion involving the control and use of Antarctic natural resources.

Legal status of Antarctic marine areas

The Southern Ocean is a highly biodiverse zone and therefore a likely target of Antarctic bioprospectors. As the status of marine offshore zones depends on the legal status of the land adjacent to it, for the Antarctic the unresolved situation regarding territorial claims creates a complicated jurisdictional situation for the Southern Ocean marine environment. In the absence of sovereignty ashore in continental Antarctica, a recognized coastal state or states is absent. As a consequence, some argue that the

---

[22] The overlapping claims are those of the United Kingdom, Argentina, and Chile.

[23] Norway does not employ the sector principle to define its claim in Antarctica, preferring to leave the northern and southern extent of their claim undefined. This may effectively create a zone of unclaimed territory at the south geographic pole. Chile does not designate a northern boundary for its Antarctic land, claiming contiguity with the Chilean landmass.

[24] See Triggs, *International law and Australian sovereignty in Antarctica*, above n 15 for a full discussion of the sector principle. While not a basis of claim to Antarctic territory, states appear to employ the principle as a convenient way to define their boundaries in the south polar region.

[25] The United States and Russia (as recognized successor from the USSR) each maintain a basis for claim.

[26] Australia, New Zealand, France, Norway and the United Kingdom reciprocally recognize the validity of each other's claims.

[27] The UK in 1947 and again in 1955 made an application to the International Court regarding the sovereignty dispute arising from the overlapping claims of the UK, Argentina and Chile. Both Argentina and Chile refused to submit to the jurisdiction of the International Court on this point therefore the situation was not considered.

high seas extend to the coastline of Antarctica, although most claimant states[28] assert some form of jurisdiction over coastal waters adding a further dimension to any discussions related to off-shore areas and marine living resources.

As all of the Antarctic territorial claims involve sectors which include a coastal area of the Southern Ocean, each of these territorial claims, if perfected, generate as a right marine off-shore zones.[29] The United Nations Convention on the Law of the Sea (UNCLOS)[30] established that a coastal state has sovereignty over an adjacent territorial sea to a limit of twelve nautical miles.[31] There is also a contiguous zone that extends for another twelve nautical miles, in which states may exercise limited control.[32] Part V of UNCLOS establishes that the Exclusive Economic Zone (EEZ) extends for up to 200 nm from the baseline of the territorial sea.[33] Within the EEZ the sovereign coastal state has the rights:

> for the purpose of exploring and exploiting, conserving and managing the natural resources, whether living or non-living, of the waters super-adjacent to the sea-bed and of the sea-bed and its subsoil, and with regard to other activities for the economic exploitation and exploration of that zone ...[34]

The sovereignty of the Sub-Antarctic Islands is generally not contested, so that for these islands there exist undisputed maritime zones with their respective recognized sovereigns. The unclaimed sector of Antarctica clearly does not generate maritime zones and therefore the marine off-shore area of the unclaimed sector is considered high seas.

At the time of the negotiation of the Antarctic Treaty in the late 1950s, international law recognized the existence of territorial seas of between three and 12 nautical miles. By the 1980s, the world had also come to recognize the existence of at least 200 nautical miles of fishing zones and Exclusive Economic Zones. The rights of a coastal state over the continental shelf were first advanced in the US Truman Proclamation of 1945 and were affirmed in 1958 as not depending

---

[28] See, e.g. New Zealand's position as described in an email from Trevor Hughes to Michelle Rogan-Finnemore, 28 December 2003, which notes that as regards New Zealand's position on the legal status of the Ross Sea in the Ross Dependency Region: 'This is a complex issue. Essentially we regard the seas around Antarctica as the high seas, ie international waters. With the other States Parties to CCAMLR we have agreed to conserve and manage the living resources south of the Antarctic Convergence (minus whales which come under IWC) through the Convention. We regard ourselves as having the right, however, under the 1923 Order in Council "providing for the government of the Ross Dependency" and the 1977 Territorial Sea and EEZ Act, to declare an EEZ in the Ross Dependency.'

[29] Note that there is further complication with determining baselines in Antarctica due to the ice that occupies coastal regions of Antarctica and annual sea ice formation that effectively doubles the size of the Antarctic continent in winter.

[30] *UN Convention on the Law of the Sea*, opened for signature 10 December 1982, 1833 UNTS 3 (entered into force 16 November 1994) ('UNCLOS').

[31] UNCLOS art 2-4.

[32] UNCLOS art 23.

[33] UNCLOS art 57.

[34] UNCLOS art 56(1)(a).

on occupation, effective or notional or any express declaration of a coastal state.[35] The International Court of Justice endorsed this view in 1969, stating 'the rights of the coastal state in respect of the continental shelf ... exist ipso facto and ab initio by virtue of its sovereignty over the land'.[36] There is, therefore no need for a formal declaration over the continental shelf.

This meant that states claiming sovereignty in Antarctica argued that a fishing zone or an EEZ was a non-severable attribute of Antarctic sovereignty.[37] All Antarctic territorial claimants were therefore able to regard their slice of the Antarctic pie as including control over resources on the seabed and subsoil in at least that area covering up to 200 nm. Australia in particular took the view that to assert a fishing zone[38] would not be an extension of an existing Antarctic claim nor for that matter a new claim by them, but merely the exercise of a function necessarily appurtenant to an existing claim.[39] Non-claimants states have a different view, concluding that the non-acceptance of Antarctic territorial claims means that offshore areas are designated as high seas.[40]

Any Southern Ocean bioprospecting activities would therefore also involve discussion of Antarctic territorial claims and the sovereignty dispute. Some argue that regulation of bioprospecting activities in the Southern Ocean, regardless of the lack of agreement on sovereignty, is already possible within the context of the Convention on the Conservation of Antarctic Marine Living Resources (CCAMLR)[41] which purports to regulate 'all marine living organisms'. There has also been a suggestion that the International Seabed Authority (ISA) may have a role to play in regulating Antarctic marine bioprospecting activities.[42] While Antarctica is a unique area in international law, Burke argues that the Southern Ocean shares many of the problems of high seas around the globe.[43] Therefore lessons learned from the negotiations of the UNCLOS may well be of value in the

---

[35] *Convention on the Continental Shelf*, opened for signature 29 April 1958, 450 UNTS 311 (entered into force 10 June 1964) art 2(3).

[36] *North Sea Continental Shelf (Federal Republic of Germany/Denmark; Federal Republic of Germany/Netherlands)* [1969] ICJ Rep 1969, 3, [69].

[37] Keith Brennan, 'Recent International Developments regarding Antarctica' in Richard A Herr, Robert Hall and Bruce W Davis (eds), *Issues in Australia's Marine and Antarctic Policies* (1982) 93. See also Triggs, *International law and Australian sovereignty in Antarctica*, above n 15, 225-26.

[38] Australia does exert an Australian Fishing Zone (AFZ) around its external territories including Antarctica.

[39] Also see *Note No 35/2004 of the Permanent Mission of Australia to the United Nations to the Division for Ocean Affairs and the Law of the Sea*, 12 May 2004, regarding Australia's intention to make a submission to the Commission on the Limits of the Continental Shelf for the coast of Australia and its external territories.

[40] Michael J Peterson, *Managing the Frozen South: The Creation and Evolution of the Antarctic Treaty System* (1988) 69.

[41] *Convention on the Conservation of Antarctic Marine Living Resources*, opened for signature 20 May 1980, [1982] ATS 9 (entered into force 7 April 1982) ('CCAMLR') art 1(1).

[42] Julia Jabour-Green, 'Bioprospecting in the High Seas' (Report from the Bioprospecting in the High Seas Conference, Dunedin, 28–29 November 2003), 7.

[43] Dillon Burke, *Exploiting the Last Ocean* (PhD Thesis, University of Canterbury, 2001) 82.

context of Southern Ocean marine bioprospecting whether the parties agree to allow involvement of the ISA or not. Antarctic Treaty Consultative State parties have not taken the opportunity to discuss these points.

Defining Antarctica and the Southern Ocean

There appears to be no universally accepted definition of 'Antarctica' or 'Antarctic';[44] even at the Washington Conference there was no agreement as to the definition of these two terms.[45]

For the purposes of this discussion 'Antarctic' and the 'Antarctic region' are defined utilizing the article VI Antarctic Treaty limits. Article VI states that the Antarctic is 'the area south of 60° South Latitude, including all ice shelves ...'. The term 'Antarctica', however, is usually used when referring to the continent itself.[46] For the purposes of this chapter, 'Antarctica' means the Antarctic continent, off-lying islands and the ice shelves.

The Scientific Committee of Antarctic Research (SCAR) defines 'Antarctic' simply as the area bounded by the Antarctic Convergence.[47] The Convergence is a biological boundary which is constantly shifting. This makes it an impractical legal boundary. However, CCAMLR establishes as its territorial scope the area south of coordinates which roughly approximate to the Antarctic Convergence.[48]

For the purposes of this chapter, the area referred to as the 'Southern Ocean' will be defined as the marine area south of the Antarctic Convergence and/or the coordinates, as listed in CCAMLR which roughly approximate that convergence. It therefore consists of a conglomeration of large parts of the South Pacific, South Atlantic, and South Indian Oceans each with its own distinct attributes.[49]

Also for the purposes of the present discussion, all areas including the islands of the Sub-Antarctic region which are not the subject of disputed sovereignty are excluded from these discussions unless specifically referred to otherwise.

Bioprospecting

Defining 'bioprospecting'

Internationally there is no universally agreed definition of 'bioprospecting'. While the activity builds on traditional techniques employed by humans since civilization

---

[44] William M Bush, *Antarctica and International Law* (1982) vol 1.
[45] See, e.g. comments by the UK in document UK0511955B and Argentina in document AR30071940, in Bush, above n 44.
[46] This also includes ice shelves and the islands lying within the Antarctic Circle.
[47] SCAR, *Constitution, Procedures and Structure of the Scientific Committee on Antarctic Research* (1958) s 1.
[48] CCAMLR art I(4).
[49] 'Southern Ocean' in Mary Trewby (ed), *Antarctica: An Encyclopedia from Abbott Ice Shelf to Zooplankton* (2002) 176.

began, advancements in technology have raised the activity to a new level over a relatively short period of time. Presently, there are no international legal agreements which specifically define or use the term 'bioprospecting'. Even the United Nations Convention on Biological Diversity 1992[50] (CBD) and The Bonn Guidelines on Access to Genetic Resources[51] (Bonn Guidelines), recently created legal instruments whose objectives involve the protection of biological diversity and regulation of access to and benefits derived from living resources, do not utilize the term. A comprehensive definition of bioprospecting has eluded Antarctic Treaty parties.

A clear definition of the activity is important to Antarctic Treaty parties for a number of reasons. First, without an adequate definition there is difficulty understanding the breadth and extent of the activity currently being carried out in the Antarctic. This makes adequate regulation of the activity and development of robust policy impossible. Second, any definition of the activity should clarify questions surrounding whether the activity can primarily be viewed as falling within the category of scientific research or within the context of commercialization. This distinction is critical within the Antarctic Treaty System, as the system prioritizes activities for the benefit of scientific cooperation in the Antarctic region and not for the promotion or advancement of commercial opportunities. While commercialization is generally defined as 'to exploit for profit',[52] in the Antarctic, commercialization is also equated with non-governmental activities. Such activities within the Antarctic Treaty System are generally deemed inferior to those associated with scientific research carried out as part of national Antarctic programmes.

Bioprospecting versus biodiscovery

Recently, bioprospecting is being viewed as 'a broad concept embracing a number of phases to investigate a region's biodiversity and to collect samples of biological organisms'.[53] While there is no agreed universal definition for the term 'bioprospecting', some have suggested that since the activity can be broken down into a number of phases, the definition and nomenclature should also be broken down into component parts. The suggestion has been made that the activity be characterized by two distinct terms: 'biodiscovery' and 'bioprospecting'.[54]

Biodiscovery would encompass phase one, which is the phase of scientific research into a region's biodiversity including sample collection, where generally the initial size of any collected sample from nature is small and therefore the

---

[50] *Convention on Biological Diversity*, opened for signature 5 June 1992, 1760 UNTS 79 (entered into force 29 December 1993) ('CBD').

[51] *Bonn Guidelines on Access to Genetic Resources and Fair and Equitable Sharing of the Benefits Arising out of their Utilization*, COP VI Decision VI/24 ('Bonn Guidelines').

[52] *Collins Concise English Dictionary* (1995).

[53] Julia Jabour-Green, above n 42, 7.

[54] See, e.g. Julia Jabour-Green and Dianne Nicols, 'Bioprospecting in Areas outside of National Jurisdiction: Antarctica and the Southern Ocean' (2003) 4 *Melbourne Journal of International Law* 76, 78.

environmental impact is minimal. In some cases, this phase may utilize ex-situ samples that were collected from a region for another purpose and are no longer needed for that purpose, or have been described and archived. This type of ex-situ utilization therefore would only include the initial collection in Antarctica or the Southern Ocean (for the initial purpose). It poses no new threat from environmental impact as there is no return trip to the Antarctic for sample collection, unless any isolated natural chemical cannot be synthesized in a laboratory.

Bioprospecting would cover the second and subsequent phases, including the recollection if required, of the biological resource for the purpose of further investigation. Jabour-Green and Nicols[55] describe the second and subsequent phases as:

1. Isolation, Characterisation and Culture;
2. Screening for Pharmaceutical Activity; and
3. [Commercialisation including] Development of Product, Patenting, Trials, Sales and Marketing.

Bioprospecting projects require many years lead time prior to any commercialization. The initial phase of the activity (phase one) is simply the start of any process that may realize a commercial outcome.[56] The distinction into the two categories of phases implies that each phase has different objectives, different outcomes, and different requirements attached to them.[57]

For convenience and because there are legal implications associated with all phases of the activity, the term bioprospecting is used throughout this chapter to include all stages in the process unless specifically stated otherwise.

Relationship with biodiversity

The target of bioprospecting is the biodiversity of a region, including plants and animals (including micro-organisms), in a range of environments. The likelihood of isolating a novel or useful biochemical increases with biodiversity. That is, the greater the biodiversity that is studied, the more likely it is for a 'hit'.[58]

Therefore bioprospecting efforts are often linked with efforts to understand the biodiversity of an area.[59] While Antarctica's known biodiversity is low, it is predicted that at least the waters of the Southern Ocean contain a biodiverse range

---

[55] Ibid 85-7. Jabour-Green and Nicols defines four phases in the process: 1 Sample Collection; 2 Isolation, Characterisation and Culture; 3 Screening for Pharmaceutical Activity; 4 Development of Product, Patenting, Trials, Sales and Marketing.
[56] Roberta Farrell and Shona Duncan, 'Uniqueness of Antarctica and Potential for Commercial Success' (Paper presented at the Bioprospecting in Antarctica Workshop, Christchurch, 7–8 April 2003) 8.
[57] Jabour-Green, above n 42, 7.
[58] Murray Munro, 'Biodiversity and Bioprospecting in Antarctica' (Presentation delivered at the Graduate Certificate in Antarctic Studies Programme, Christchurch, 9 December 2003).
[59] See, generally, Farrell and Duncan, above n 56. See also ibid.

of micro-organisms. Also hot spots around volcanic areas such as Mount Erebus are likely to be biodiverse regions. Of particular importance to bioprospectors are organisms that survive in extreme environments. The organisms that thrive in the frozen ground and brackish internal waters of Antarctica and in the surrounding marine environment of the Southern Ocean, do so because they have developed 'unique biological coping strategies'.[60] Often it is these unique coping strategies that can be isolated and developed to address a specific target or purpose.

Biodiversity then is important for bioprospecting. 'Biological diversity' (or biodiversity) for the purposes of the CBD is defined as meaning:

> ... the variability among living organisms from all sources including, inter alia, terrestrial, marine and other aquatic ecosystems and the ecological complexes of which they are part; this includes diversity within species, between species and of ecosystems.[61]

Researchers have yet to fully investigate this uniqueness in the Antarctic region. Because it is poorly known, the biota and especially the micro-biota (including microscopic bacteria, plants and animals) of Antarctica and the Southern Ocean hold an interest to biodiversity researchers and also interest the biotechnology industry.[62] Biotechnology is also defined in the CBD as meaning 'any technological application that uses biological systems, living organisms, or derivatives thereof, to make or modify products or processes for specific use'.[63]

For biotechnology companies the probability of a 'hit', that is, the probability that a natural product sample contains a compound that can be commercially developed into a useful product, is wholly dependent on the number of samples obtained and, most importantly, the biodiversity of the samples. The more novel the biodiversity investigated, the more likely it is that something useful will be found.

The Antarctic Treaty

For the purposes of any discussions regarding resource exploitation in the Antarctic and specifically to provide background to any discussion surrounding bioprospecting activities in the region, attention is drawn to a few key articles of the Antarctic Treaty.

---

[60] Ian Sample, 'Cold rush threatens pristine Antarctic', *The Guardian* (UK), 2 February 2004, The Week, 1.
[61] CBD art 2.
[62] See John Bowman, 'Antarctica a Global "Hot Spot": Biodiversity and Biotechnology' (Paper presented at Looking South-Managing Technology, Opportunities and the Global Environment, The Australian Academy of Technological Sciences and Engineering Symposium, Australia, November 2001).
[63] CBD art 2.

Article I

Article I is obvious in its initial statement that 'Antarctica shall be used for peaceful purposes only'. While no definition of 'peaceful purposes' is given, the article lists prohibitions as examples in support of the peaceful purposes objective. These include prohibition of any measures of a military nature such as the establishment of military bases and fortifications, prohibition of the carrying out of military manoeuvres and of the testing of any type of weapons in Antarctica. Article V indirectly supports the article I objective, specifically prohibiting nuclear explosions in the Antarctic Treaty area, an activity of primary concern to the two superpowers at the time and clearly an activity that would breach the peaceful purposes objective.

Articles II and III

Articles II and III are here considered together, as while article II succinctly states the second objective of the Antarctic Treaty, it is article III that directly supports this objective by defining ways in which the objective can be effectively promoted. At the time of the negotiation of the Antarctic Treaty, articles II and III were viewed as being the minimum the parties could 'get away with and still end up with a credible Treaty'.[64]

Article II states that 'Freedom of scientific investigation in Antarctica and cooperation toward that end, as applied in the International Geophysical Year, shall continue …'. The reference to applications in the International Geophysical Year (IGY) are important for at least two reasons. First, the IGY allowed for the valid participation of the Soviet Union in Antarctic for the first time in the legitimate name of science.[65] Inclusion on this basis was critical and it was an affirmation of the apolitical nature of IGY activities. Second, there were obvious mutual benefits of closing the Antarctic to a Soviet military presence,[66] even while continuing to provide shared access to research for all participants.

The success of the IGY presented a possibility that political disputes could be removed from the region by devoting the area exclusively to peaceful purposes. It also presented at least a temporary solution to the Antarctic sovereignty dilemma in that promotion of scientific investigation and research in the region could be used to underline the international value and significance of the region. In the US government's opinion this would 'diminish the status of national territorial pretensions and also illustrate the limited nature of the contribution any one nation could make towards the solution of most Antarctic problems'.[67]

Freedom of scientific investigation therefore was, and continues to be, a principal object of the Antarctic Treaty which is also evidenced by other articles of the Antarctic Treaty and its preamble. The scientific community seized a unique

---

[64] J A Heap, 'Cooperation in the Antarctic: a quarter of a century's experience' in Francisco Vicuna (ed.) *Antarctic Resources Policy: Scientific, legal and political issues* (1983) 103, 105.
[65] Robert A Swan, *Australia in the Antarctic* (1961) 275.
[66] See Susan Buck, *The Global Commons: an introduction* (1998) 57.
[67] Swan, above n 65.

opportunity when the political community recognized the advantages of scientific cooperation in the region in order to avoid political conflicts and perhaps violence.[68]

Article III directly supports the article II objective by providing examples of how this objective could be promoted, stating:

1. In order to promote international cooperation in scientific investigation in Antarctica, as provided for in Article II of the present Treaty, the Contracting Parties agree that, to the greatest extent feasible and practicable:
(a) information regarding plans for scientific programs in Antarctica shall be exchanged to permit maximum economy of and efficiency of operations;
(b) scientific personnel shall be exchanged in Antarctica between expeditions and stations;
(c) scientific observations and results from Antarctica shall be exchanged and made freely available.

The success of the IGY meant that parties envisioned that these requirements would be easy to maintain. However, it was not envisioned that the proviso for the free availability and exchange of scientific observations and results requirement would prove problematic in any commercial era if it ever were to develop. In fact, little attention was directed towards the prospect of commercial operations in the region. It is paragraph 1(c) that requires the greatest level of consideration in the context of the legal implications of bioprospecting in the Antarctic, as some believe that the commercial nature of that activity prevents observations and results from being exchanged and made freely available as required. Any limits placed on this fundamental objective of freedom of scientific investigation in the Antarctic will require careful analysis. Further consideration is given to this issue below.

Article IV

While the two key objectives of the Antarctic Treaty are often cited as critical to the success of the Antarctic Treaty, it is article IV, which deals with unresolved sovereignty and the territorial claims to Antarctica, that was undoubtedly 'the political key'[69] which was critical to the signing of the Antarctic Treaty in the first place. Article IV was necessary to appease all signatory state parties regarding their territorial claims. Therefore while it only indirectly supports the two key objectives of the Treaty, the absence of this article would arguably have resulted in no treaty for the region at all. Article IV is therefore the critical element in the Antarctic Treaty, often called the 'cornerstone'[70] of the Treaty as it addresses disputed territorial sovereignty in Antarctica. Article IV was initially, and presently remains, critical to the success of the Antarctic Treaty and therefore the Antarctic Treaty System. Joyner calls it the legal 'flexi-glue that allows the Treaty to work

---

[68] See Buck, above n 66, 56-8.
[69] Christopher Beeby, *The Antarctic Treaty* (1972) 10.
[70] F M Auburn, *Antarctic law and politics* (1982) 104.

for governments who hold diametrically opposed positions on the contentious question of territorial sovereignty over the continent'.[71]

Article IV has two paragraphs. Article IV (1) reads:

1. Nothing contained in the present Treaty shall be interpreted as:
(a) a renunciation by any Contracting Party of previously asserted rights of or claims to territorial sovereignty in Antarctica;
(b) a renunciation or diminution by any Contracting Party of any basis of claim to territorial sovereignty in Antarctica which it may have whether as a result of its activities or those of its nationals in Antarctica, or otherwise;
(c) prejudicing the position of any Contracting Party as regards its recognition or non-recognition of any other State's rights of or claim or basis of claim to territorial sovereignty in Antarctica.

This complex provision is at times criticized as a 'purgatory of ambiguity',[72] but this criticism, according to Joyner, ignores the chief purpose of article IV, namely to provide a politically workable arrangement for all states involved.[73]

The complexity arises from the need to provide protection for varying views and positions on sovereignty in Antarctica. For those seven states which asserted a territorial claim before 1959 the article's subparagraph 1(a), protects their respective claims and does not require them to abandon their claim. Subparagraph 1(b) protects the basis of any claim (without comment as to legitimacy or otherwise) thus protecting not only the position of the basis for the territorial claimants but also those states who have stated that they too have a basis of claim and reserve the right to make a future claim. While providing additional protection for the position of the seven claimant states, this provision was inserted primarily for the protection of the US and then USSR. Finally paragraph 1, section (c), allows states that do not recognize any or all of the claims or basis for claims to become a party to the Treaty without jeopardizing their position as regards sovereignty in Antarctica. This applied not only to non-claimant states but also to those states with overlapping territorial claims.

Article IV was also important to those states that participated in the Washington negotiations but who, at the time of the signing of the Antarctic Treaty, had neither territorial claim nor basis of claim to any portion of Antarctica. Originally there were three such states, clearly in the minority amongst the twelve original signatories.[74] Today, the seven claimant states represent the minority amongst the 45 states that are now party to the Antarctic Treaty. For every decision

---

[71] Joyner, above n 13, 58.
[72] Triggs, *International law and Australian sovereignty in Antarctica*, above n 15, 137.
[73] See generally, Joyner, above n 13, 56-8.
[74] The original signatories were the seven claimant states (Argentine, Chile, UK, France, Australia, New Zealand and Norway); In addition the US and USSR maintained they had a basis of claim but did not make a claim to territory; the three additional original signatories were Japan, South Africa and Belgium, all of whom had participated in the IGY by carrying out scientific research in Antarctica.

made in the Antarctic Treaty forum, an accommodation must be made to appease the varying views of this diverse group of states.

Article IV, paragraph 2 then goes on to establish rules for the future (that is, beyond the situation as it existed in 1959) by stating that:

> 2. No acts or activities taking place while the present Treaty is in force shall constitute a basis for asserting, supporting or denying a claim to territorial sovereignty in Antarctica or create any rights of sovereignty in Antarctica. No new claim, or enlargement of an existing claim, to territorial sovereignty in Antarctica shall be asserted while the present Treaty is in force.

This makes it clear that the positions of those Treaty signatory states with an interest in territory in Antarctica can neither be made worse nor improved by any acts or activities in Antarctica undertaken during the currency of the Antarctic Treaty, nor may any new assertions to territory be made by signatories.

This leaves little doubt that the territorial claims to Antarctica continue to persist today. While the issue as to sovereignty remains unresolved, the legal operation of the territorial claims are held in abeyance by article IV and the position as it existed in 1959 has not been legally challenged. The question as to whether the claims to territorial sovereignty in Antarctica are valid has never been decided upon by international arbitration or adjudication. It is within this context that any discussion regarding living or non-living resource use in the Antarctic must be addressed. This creates complicated issues surrounding access to and ownership of resources which are discussed below.

Article VIII

Because of the unresolved nature of Antarctic territorial claims, issues surrounding jurisdiction are complex, the problem being the allocation of jurisdictional powers among the Antarctic Treaty states. Only article VIII of the Antarctic Treaty makes mention of jurisdiction in Antarctica, stating:

> without prejudice to the respective positions of Contracting Parties relating to jurisdiction over all other persons in Antarctica, observers designated under paragraph 1 of Article VII and scientific personnel exchanged ... and members of staff accompanying any such persons, shall be subject only to the jurisdiction of the Contracting Party of which they are nationals in respect of all acts or omissions occurring while they are in Antarctica ...

This provision fails to address jurisdictional issues related to persons who are not part of a national Antarctic programme, so that individuals who are part of private expeditions to Antarctica are not covered by this provision. While initially this was not a problem, as all expeditions to Antarctica were state-led expeditions, the increase in private expeditions is one reason that states have implemented domestic legislation closing the jurisdiction gap and covering these individuals while in

Antarctica.[75] Any application of the general principle of jurisdiction, that is, giving claimant states jurisdiction over all persons in their Antarctic claimed territory, could well 'give rise immediately and directly to disputes about sovereignty'.[76] Further consideration is given to Antarctic sovereignty below.

Article IX

The Antarctic Treaty contained little in the way of institutional provisions when it was negotiated and signed. For example, it deliberately avoided the creation of a treaty secretariat. The Antarctic Treaty's Article IX is the sole provision of an institutional nature, providing for the holding of periodic meetings but not being prescriptive as to when and, except initially, where they should occur. Article IX(1) simply states that representatives of the 'Contracting Parties ... shall meet at the City of Canberra within 2 months after the date of entry into force of the Treaty, and thereafter at suitable intervals and places ...'. Until 1994 the parties met every second year, rotating amongst contracting state venues. However, since 1994 the parties have met annually, the increase in frequency of meetings reflecting the increase in the number of issues of substance that are now discussed in the Antarctic Treaty forum.

Article IX(1) stipulates three purposes for the meetings. These are (1) exchanging information; (2) consulting together; (3) formulating and considering, and recommending to their Governments, measures in furtherance of the principles and objectives of the Treaty. It is the second purpose that has served as the basis for the accepted title for the (now annual) Antarctic Treaty Consultative Meetings (ATCMs). Final reports from each ATCM become the documents that support the evolution of the Antarctic Treaty and thus add to the system.[77] Membership and participation at ATCMs represent 'supranational tribunals as a way to accommodate differences but acknowledge and reinforce common values'.[78]

Paragraph 2 of article IX goes on to establish each contracting party's level of participation at these meetings by designating states as either a 'Consultative State' or a 'Non-Consultative State'. For those states with a genuine interest in Antarctica, Consultative State status is important, as only Consultative States have voting rights and full participation rights at ATCMs.

In order to obtain Consultative State status, an Antarctic Treaty signatory state must meet certain activity criteria. Specifically the state must 'demonstrate its interest in Antarctica by conducting substantial scientific research activity there ...'.[79] No definition of 'substantial scientific research activity' is provided, however the paragraph lists two illustrative examples: firstly, establishment of an Antarctic scientific station or secondly, dispatch of a scientific expedition in

---

[75] See, e.g. for New Zealand, *Antarctica Act 1960*.
[76] Beeby, above n 69, 11.
[77] See the web site of the Antarctic Treaty Secretariat at <http://www.ats.org.ar/> for electronic copies of most recent ATCM Reports.
[78] Anne-Marie Slaughter, 'The real new world order' (1997) 76 *Foreign Affairs* 183, 187.
[79] Antarctic Treaty art IX (2).

Antarctica. This requirement for substantial activity only applies to acceding states, the original twelve Antarctic Treaty signatories automatically acquiring and unqualifiedly retaining Consultative State status.

In addition to the Antarctic Treaty requirements for obtaining Consultative State status, a further qualification has now been established by the Protocol on Environmental Protection to the Antarctic Treaty 1991,[80] (Protocol) whereby in order for a state to obtain Consultative State status, a signatory state must meet the criteria as laid down in the Antarctic Treaty *and* must also have ratified, accepted and approved the Protocol.[81]

All other states which have acceded to the Antarctic Treaty initially have Non-Consultative State status. They have observer status at all ATCMs, have the ability to prepare and present Information Papers, but do not have voting privileges. Should a Non-Consultative State wish to acquire Consultative State status they must ratify the Protocol, meet the requirements of article IX of the Antarctic Treaty and apply for Consultative State status at an ATCM. It is only then, by consensus of all Antarctic Treaty Consultative States, that their higher status may be approved.

Discussion

Articles II and III implications in the context of bioprospecting

The few discussions to date surrounding the legal implications of bioprospecting in the Antarctic have focused on the article II and III obligations of the Antarctic Treaty. Exactly what the extent of these obligations are for Antarctic Treaty state parties is unclear. Doubt is raised over whether bioprospecting is an activity that can legally be carried out in the Antarctic while continuing to allow state parties to meet this obligation.

The second fundamental obligation of the Treaty, freedom of scientific investigation, is first mentioned in the preamble. As noted above, the Treaty then states the obligation in a general way in its article II (saying that 'Freedom of scientific investigation in Antarctica and cooperation toward that end, as applied in the International Geophysical Year, shall continue') and, in support of this, article III goes on to give specific indications of what was envisioned by the Treaty Parties in article II. Recall that article III states:

1. In order to promote international cooperation in scientific investigation in Antarctica, as provided for in Article II of the present Treaty, the Contracting Parties agree that, to the greatest extent feasible and practicable:
(a) information regarding plans for scientific programs in Antarctica shall be exchanged to permit maximum economy of and efficiency of operations;

---

[80] Above n 4.
[81] Protocol art 22(4).

(b) scientific personnel shall be exchanged in Antarctica between expeditions and stations;
(c) scientific observations and results from Antarctica shall be exchanged and made freely available.

Bush argues that articles II and III simply 'crystallize[d] pre-existing state practice'. He also noted that the phrase 'freedom of scientific investigation' implied a 'freedom of movement in and around Antarctica by surface and air, at least for the purposes of scientific investigation'.[82] While this seems like a trivial practice, it is the first glimpse at the compromise on sovereignty that the Treaty parties would have to agree to, as usually movement within a territory is under the control of the sovereign. Generally, it gave Antarctic Treaty state parties the right to freely move about the Antarctic continent, regardless of any State's position as to territorial claims.

The provisions were codified by Recommendation VIII-6 (1975)[83] which states the standard format for exchange of information. This standard format includes providing details to other Antarctic Treaty Consultative State parties such as advance notification of research plans and logistics and supply arrangements. Today, the exchange and free availability obligation has come to be more widely interpreted. Many states cite the phrase to imply that all information related to scientific investigation on the continent should be shared and be made available for free or without reservation to anyone who requests the information. Some believe the obligation is for the information to be placed into the 'public domain' and they agree that this was not necessarily synonymous with ease of access to data.[84]

Whatever the current extent of the obligation, in practice it appears that the 'freedom of scientific investigation' obligation has historically been met by all Antarctic Treaty State parties primarily through the cooperative arrangement of the Antarctic Treaty Consultative Meeting system and related organizations such as the Council of Managers of National Antarctic Programmes (COMNAP), all National Antarctic Science Program information is prepared and presented to all Treaty parties at the annual meetings. Many of the programmes operate cooperative arrangements when providing air, marine and surface support, so that generally there is no restriction on freedom of scientific investigation in a practical sense. It is the more specific obligation laid down in article III that may prove to be the most difficult to interpret and apply in the context of bioprospecting activities in the Antarctic, specifically regarding patenting of an Antarctic derived product or process and confidentiality agreements.

---

[82] William Bush, 'The Next 40 Years: The Challenge of Economic Globalisation and 21st Century Security Threats' in Julia Jabour-Green and Marcus Haward (eds), *The Antarctic: Past, Present and Future* (2002) 126, 153.
[83] *ATCM Recommendation VIII-6*, ATCM VIII (1975).
[84] See Legal Workgroup Report from the Bioprospecting in Antarctica Workshop, Christchurch, 2003.

Article III: further consideration

Bush notes that the Antarctic Treaty parties realized as early as 1973 that it was article III, with its obligation to make 'freely available' scientific results and observations from Antarctica, which would have implications for the exploitation of economic resources of the region.[85] This is because activities related to the exploration of economic resources have the potential to place limits on free availability of observations and results. The question is: if this potential is realized, are these limits inappropriate within the article III obligations of the Antarctic Treaty?[86]

While there has been little problem to date with article III, subparagraphs (1)(a) or (1)(b), in any discussions involving bioprospecting in the Antarctic, problems do appear to arise as regards the extent of the obligation in subparagraph (1)(c). An Antarctic Treaty document of 1972[87] describes article III(1)(c) as making 'possible the exchange of scientific information freely and directly between scientific organisations'. However, the precise nature of the disclosure and exchange requirements imposed by article III(1)(c) is uncertain.[88] To date, little debate on the issue has been required as scientific investigation has primarily been a result of government funded and supported expeditions which carries with it obligations to disclose and publish results. Scientists also clearly recognize the value of publishing their data, observations and results in peer reviewed journals. Publishing results has at least a two-fold benefit for these scientists: one, publication often meets their obligations prescribed by National Antarctic Programmes for logistical support for their field research component; and two, publishing often attracts new or continuing funding for their research.

With the emergence of privately funded commercial research activities, publication is not always an obligation prescribed by the funding organization. This may lead to unpublished Antarctic observations and results and may also involve protection of information associated with intellectual property and 'trade secrets'. In the case of bioprospecting there may already exist exclusive collaborative arrangements between Antarctic researchers and commercial companies which have funded the research which call for confidentiality and exclusive rights to any discoveries.

However, this is not the first instance of the Antarctic Treaty System dealing with limited availability of observations and results from Antarctica. The issue has

---

[85] See Bush, above n 44, 55; *Report of a Meeting of Experts organized by the Fridtjof Nansen Foundation on existing law relevant to the authorization or prohibition of mineral exploration for commercial purposes in the Antarctic Treaty area*, Antarctic Treaty Document AT30051973, s 23.

[86] See Jabour-Green and Nicols, above n 54; Jabour-Green and Nicols prefer to utilize the phrase 'commercialisation of science' instead of 'exploration of economic resources' when asking this question.

[87] See Bush, above n 44; *Report and recommendations of the VIIth Antarctic Treaty Consultative Meeting*, Antarctic Treaty Document AT30101972.01, [11].

[88] See Jabour-Green and Nicols, above n 54, 104.

been discussed in the context of an Antarctic mineral regime. When CRAMRA was finalized it included article 16 dealing with the availability and confidentiality of data and information. The article is a partial reiteration of the article III(1)(c) obligation with a two-part proviso and one potentially significant difference. It reads:

> Data and information obtained from Antarctic mineral resource activities shall, to the greatest extent practical and feasible, be made freely available, provided that:
> (a) as regards data and information of commercial value deriving from prospecting, they may be retained by the Operator in accordance with Article 37;[89]
> (b) as regards data and information deriving from exploration or development, the Commission shall adopt measures relating, as appropriate, to their release and to ensure the confidentiality of data and information of commercial value.

The inclusion of this article within CRAMRA implies that the parties were flexible as to the extent of the obligation to make data and information freely available, even going so far as to 'ensure the confidentiality of data and information of commercial value'. The article does not make 'results' part of the exchange agreement. Whether this was a deliberate omission or simply an oversight is unclear. It was one of the CRAMRA Commission's functions to facilitate and promote the exchange of information and specifically 'to adopt measures relating to the availability and confidentiality of data and information, including measures pursuant to Article 16'.[90] Inclusion of these provisions in CRAMRA was a signal that the Antarctic Treaty Consultative parties would not limit nor prohibit an activity from taking place in the Antarctic region if that activity generated data of a confidential or commercial character. So that while CRAMRA was never ratified, the implication of inclusion of such a provision may imply that *any* activity that generates confidential data or data of commercial value will not prima facie mean that the confidential nature of the data will be in breach of the article III(1)(c) 'freely available' obligation and therefore the activity may proceed.

Intellectual property rights, patents and the Article III obligation

Intellectual property (IP) is a generic term that refers to a range of private property rights[91] accorded to 'creations of the mind'.[92] Since the US Supreme Court case of *Diamond v Chakrabarty*[93] these creations of the mind may include IP rights associated with micro-organisms, and micro-organisms are emerging as an

---

[89] CRAMRA art 37 deals with obligations surrounding 'prospecting'.
[90] CRAMRA art 21(1)(h).
[91] *Agreement on Trade-Related Aspects of Intellectual Property Rights*, opened for signature on 15 April 1994, 1869 UNTS 229 (entered into force 1 January 1995) ('TRIPS Agreement') preamble, [4].
[92] Kim Connelly-Stone, 'Patents, Property Rights and Benefit-sharing Issues in Relation to Bioprospecting' in Alan Hemmings and Michelle Rogan-Finnemore (eds), *Antarctic Bioprospecting* (2005) (In press).
[93] *Diamond v Chakrabarty* (1980) 447 US 303.

important element of Antarctic biodiversity. Micro-organisms are also an important target of bioprospectors.

IP rights vary globally and there are many different types of IP rights in use today. Generally, however, there are three major categories of IP: patents, trademarks and copyright. Of these three, patents are of most import to any study concerning bioprospecting and genetic resources.[94] Patents are the primary means of granting exclusive use of a novel product or process to the inventor for a limited time period. Patents are granted on a national basis and therefore domestic laws dictate the treatment, protection and enforcement of patenting rights. In New Zealand for example, patenting rights are provided for under the Patents Act 1953.[95] A patent is an intellectual property right granted by a state authority that excludes others from the use or benefit of a patented invention for a limited time. In New Zealand, a patent lasts for 20 years. They are however also subject in some cases to international agreements and constraints.

There presently appears to be nothing specific in the domestic law of states which prevents an individual or organization from protecting the IP associated with an Antarctic-derived novel product or bioproduct, as long as that product fulfils the essential patent criteria under the domestic legislation. The criteria do not allow for patenting the discovery itself, that is, the inventor must add an inventive step which results in a novel product or process. There is no evidence that patenting offices give consideration to the fact that the product or process may have been derived from the Antarctic region. In fact, many patents already exist in relation to Antarctic-derived products and processes.[96] All of the Antarctic-related patents applied for to date have been from within an Antarctic Treaty Party state.

Allowing patenting of products and processes associated with Antarctic bioprospecting raises two issues. The first issue is of a general nature, that is, that allowing patenting would lead to greater involvement of commercial interests in the Antarctic; this has generally been seen as against the spirit of the Antarctic Treaty. This was the same argument that was delivered with the negotiation of CRAMRA, that is, that setting up a regulatory framework which provided certainty of access and property rights regarding mineral resources would only encourage commercial involvement and would act as incentive to mine. With the abandonment of CRAMRA and the continued moratorium on mining it is impossible at this stage to know whether this would have proved correct.

Secondly and more specifically, it is in the context of the Antarctic Treaty and its article III(1)(c) obligation that the lawfulness of patenting must be considered. The mandate for the free exchange of information has led to fears that commercially focused research, and in particular, patenting would be in breach of article III and therefore would be contrary to the Antarctic Treaty.

---

[94] Nicholas Mason, *Forging a New Global Commons: Introducing common property into the global genetic resource debate* (MA Thesis, University of Canterbury, 2004) 18.
[95] *The Patents Act 1953* (NZ).
[96] See Sample, above n 60. Already some 92 patents referring to Antarctic organisms or molecules extracted from them have been filed in the US and a further 62 patents have been filed in Europe.

While Bush argues that commercial activities may not breach the article I peaceful purposes obligation, he takes an extreme position on the article III obligation, stating that *all* research of a commercial nature (whether it leads to IP protection or not) is in danger of breaching the article III requirements. Bush noted that '[a] growth in the demand for research of economic relevance is likely to run counter to the Antarctic Treaty requirement that "scientific observations and results from Antarctica shall be exchanged and made freely available"'.[97] Counter arguments exist, based on the notion that the patent system is in fact a device which allows scientific information and new discoveries to enter the public domain, while protecting the inventor's rights for a limited time period.

Generally, a patent applicant has to meet four requirements in order to be successful. Three of these four requirements refer specifically to the invention itself (novelty, non-obviousness and usefulness). The fourth requirement is that the product or process be described with adequate specification and disclosure. In the United States for example, the US Constitution clearly states that the patent system was established in order to 'promote the Progress of Science and the useful Arts by securing for limited times to Authors and Inventors the exclusive right to their respective Writings and Discoveries'.[98] Thus, the United States patent law finds its rationale for allowing patenting in its instrumental power to promote scientific progress, not in a basic right to one's own intellectual property. The patent encourages disclosure of information that otherwise might not be open to scrutiny by others while protecting the exclusive right of use of the inventor.

In New Zealand that sentiment was supported in the *Pharmaceutical Management Agency Ltd*[99] case, when Gault J. recently put it thus: 'The patent system rests on the policy that a limited term monopoly will be granted as an incentive to innovation but subject to the invention and the best method of carrying it out being disclosed and made available ...'.[100]

The patent holder may only control the exploitation of the information, the information itself cannot be locked up.[101] Whether this really satisfies the article III(1)(c) obligation is at the heart of any debate. While patents promote knowledge sharing by requiring the details of the patented invention to be placed in the public domain,[102] and while this disclosure and sharing of information clearly supports the spirit of article III, it is not clear whether patenting breaches the legal letter of the Article III(1)(c) obligation. While the legal letter of the law is usually of fundamental importance the spirit of cooperation that has existed amongst Antarctic Treaty parties has arguably supported the robustness and effectiveness of the Antarctic Treaty System to date and may be of at least equal importance.

---

[97] Bush, above n 82, 138.
[98] *United States Constitution*, art 1 s 8.
[99] *Pharmaecutical Management Agency Ltd. v Commissioner of Patents* (2000) 2 NZLR 529.
[100] Ibid 533.
[101] Andrew Allen, 'Biotechnology, Research and IP Law' (2002) 8 *Canterbury Law Review* 237, 239.
[102] Australian Law Reform Commission, *Genes and ingenuity: gene patenting and human health report* (2004) 58.

The clause 'to the greatest extent feasible and practicable' allows Antarctic Treaty parties some discretion,[103] and some even argue that this qualification may reduce the level of obligation or in fact eliminate the obligation during times when it is not feasible or practical to meet it.[104] The onus is left to the goodwill and efficiency of the state.[105] Attention has also been drawn to the use of the word 'shall' in the phrase and not the more obligatory word 'will'. However, in practice the parties have had the expectation that the obligation will be met. It also should be noted that the acquisition of intellectual property rights is only one phase of any bioprospecting project. The first stage, the discovery or collection of biological resources or material, does not itself constitute or create intellectual property – a discovery does not equate to an invention.[106] Therefore any consideration of the legality of bioprospecting in the context of the article III obligation should discuss the legality of the individual phases of the activity. In the majority of cases, the act of bioprospecting does not lead to a patent or to commercialization of a discovery; it is the development of a product or process that may lead to restrictions on free availability of information and results.

Care must also be taken when considering the position of the developing nations that are parties to the Treaty. There is a widespread belief amongst developing nations that the IP right systems are mainly designed by the developed nations for the specific purpose of exploiting the natural resources of developing nations[107] and are not necessarily a device established to promote the progress of science. Third world governments see no evidence that patents encourage research, saying this is a benefit often cited by industrialized countries.[108] This belief must be examined carefully in a system that has often been referred to as a 'rich man's club'[109] but which now consists of developed and developing nations.

For this reason, any regulation within the Antarctic Treaty System on the use of Antarctic living resources, which includes patenting rights may see opposition from the developing nations that are Consultative State parties to the Antarctic Treaty.[110] Consensus may thus be difficult to achieve on any bioprospecting regulation which allows for protection of IP rights.

Antarctic sovereignty

Watts put it succinctly when he said '[i]t is impossible to discuss any legal issue in the Antarctic context without sooner or later, and usually it is sooner, having to refer to the differences over sovereignty'.[111] An essential requirement for the

---

[103] Jabour-Green and Nicols, above n 54, 100.
[104] See Legal Workgroup Report, Bioprospecting in Antarctica Workshop, Christchurch, 2003.
[105] Peter Beck, *The International Politics of Antarctica* (1986) 104.
[106] Connelly-Stone, above n 92.
[107] Krishna R Dronamraju, *Biological and social issues in biotechnology sharing* (1998) 1.
[108] Fowler, *Biotechnology, Patents and the Third World*, 219.
[109] Beck, above n 105, 184.
[110] Keith Suter, *Antarctica: private property or public heritage?* (1991) 23, calling inclusion of India in ATS a 'shrewd move'.
[111] Sir Arthur Watts, *International Law and the Antarctic Treaty System* (1992) 111.

functioning of the Antarctic Treaty System has always been balancing sovereignty considerations.[112] This is reflected initially in article IV of the Antarctic Treaty and subsequently in the conventions and numerous recommendations which restate and reaffirm the article IV agreement.

The unresolved nature of Antarctic sovereignty is a source of contention amongst the Antarctic Treaty parties themselves, which while abated due to article IV of the Antarctic Treaty has the potential to reignite in the future. Commercial opportunities involving Antarctic resource use and management may well be the source of such ignition. The unresolved nature of Antarctic sovereignty is also a source of contention between the Antarctic Treaty parties and third party states many of which believe the resources of the Antarctic region should be utilized for the benefit of all mankind.

Similar issues were faced during the negotiation of CRAMRA and accommodations were created to address these internal and external conflicts. The internal conflicts included: the varying views on sovereignty between claimant and non-claimant states; differences between developed nations and those that were least developed or developing states; and between those states that were likely to directly engage in the activity and those who would not or who would indirectly participate through the activities of other parties.[113] The external conflicts are much broader and include the international community's reluctance to accept that the regulation of Antarctic resources should only be conducted among the Antarctic Treaty Consultative State parties, exclusively for the benefit of those states.

Hanessian hoped article IV would 'ultimately permit the claims issue to die a natural death'.[114] But Triggs notes 'the issue of sovereignty has re-emerged [as it did in the minerals debate] with the need for effective regulation for the conservation and exploitation of ... living resources'.[115] Exploitation, ownership and distribution of any benefits derived from natural resources from Antarctica challenge the 'frozen' sovereignty situation, arguably with implications for peace and international scientific cooperation in the region under the Antarctic Treaty System.

In the interests of all mankind

While lessons can be learned from CRAMRA, consideration must also be directed to emerging norms for utilizing resources in areas beyond national jurisdiction and those global resources which many believe should either be utilized for the benefit of all mankind or alternatively, should not be utilized at all. This involves consideration of global commons and the principle of common heritage of mankind.

---

[112] See Davor Vidas, *Implementing the Environmental Protection Regime for the Antarctic* (2000) 266.
[113] See Rudiger Wolfrum, *The Convention on the Regulation of Antarctic Mineral Resource Activity* (1991) 13; see also Gillian Triggs, 'Negotiations of a Minerals Regime' in Gillian Triggs (ed) *The Antarctic Treaty Regime: Law, Environment and Resources* (1987) 182, 187.
[114] J Hanessian, *The Antarctic Treaty (1959)* (1960) 9 *International and Comparative Law Quarterly* 436, 468.
[115] Triggs, *International law and Australian sovereignty in Antarctica*, above n 15, 150.

Common property or common pool resources are said to be located in resource domains known simply as commons. Antarctica has been described as an international commons,[116] a disputed commons,[117] and Joyner states that 'the natural and legal situation of the Antarctic plainly intimate that the region qualifies as a global commons area'.[118] The unresolved nature of the territorial claims is the sticking point for declaring that the region is a true global commons.

Often because of the unresolved nature of the territorial claims, Antarctic resources are referred to as the common heritage of mankind.[119] Birnie and Boyle note that although the term common heritage is used loosely to refer either to all resources of nature, living and non-living, or to the global environment as an ecological entity, for legal purposes the term is only narrowly defined by the meaning given to it in two conventions,[120] namely the 1979 Moon Treaty[121] and the 1982 UNCLOS.[122] As utilized in both these conventions, the concept of common heritage of mankind implies that the non-living resources of these areas, areas that are beyond national jurisdiction, 'cannot be appropriated to the exclusive sovereignty of states but must be conserved and exploited for the benefit of all, without discrimination'.[123] Importantly, the concept differs from common property, in that it allows for all states to share in the benefits even if unable to participate in the process of extraction and exploitation.

While a case may be made that the resources of the Antarctic region should be made the common heritage of mankind, such a view remains controversial and 'does not take full account of the complex legal and political arrangements for the region'.[124] Any definite statement regarding Antarctic living resources as common heritage would require that benefits derived from operations such as bioprospecting should be for the benefit of all mankind, not simply for the Antarctic Treaty states, Antarctic Treaty Consultative states or for only those states which claim territory in Antarctica.

Many developing countries view all genetic resources as part of the common heritage of mankind.[125] What all this may mean for areas beyond national jurisdiction or simply for the Antarctic region which maintains its unresolved sovereignty status is unclear and requires investigation. It is likely that any new attempt to declare Antarctic resources as common heritage would see Antarctic Treaty Consultative State parties claim to be the exclusive custodians of the

---

[116] See, e.g. Buck, above n 66.
[117] Harlan Cleveland, *The Global Commons* (1990).
[118] Joyner, above n 13, 44.
[119] See, e.g. Buck, above n 66, 64-6; Joyner, above 13, 32-3.
[120] Patricia Birnie and Alan Boyle, *International Law and the Environment* (2nd ed, 2002) 143.
[121] *Agreement Governing the Activities of States on the Moon and Other Celestial Bodies*, opened for signature 5 December 1979, 1363 UNTS 3 (entered into force 11 July 1984).
[122] UNCLOS arts 136, 137.
[123] Birnie and Boyle, above n 120, 143.
[124] Ibid 144.
[125] Vandana Shiva, 'Biotechnological Development and the Conservation of Biodiversity' in Vandana Shiva and Ingunn Moser (eds), *Biopolitics: A feminist and ecological reader on biotechnology* (1995) 193, 209.

resources with ultimate responsibility for governance in the Antarctic. This approach was reflected in, for example, Recommendation VIII-8 on 'Activities of States that are not Consultative Parties'. While the recommendation reaffirms the Antarctic Treaty preamble sentiments that it is 'in the interests of all mankind' to govern the Antarctic, it also recognizes and places a special responsibility on Antarctic Treaty Consultative parties, a view reaffirmed in both CRAMRA and the Protocol.

Before the negotiations of CRAMRA began, it was said that the Consultative Parties were signalling greater flexibility. Referring to this increase in flexibility, Wolfrum said, in answer to the question: 'Who is going to profit from the utilization of Antarctic mineral resources ... that it would be the claimant states, the non-claimant states and the world community'.[126] The same question will undoubtedly be asked in the context of bioprospecting.

Conclusions

Antarctic-related bioprospecting activities are currently under way and have been for some time within the framework of National Antarctic research programmes. That is, bioprospecting activities have been approved and carried out in the Antarctic in the same way that any other scientific project or programme is carried out. If the activity continues to be carried out in this manner and if there is no serious environmental impact associated with such activities it is arguably likely that Antarctic bioprospecting can and will continue and not much will change. To date, little formal discussion concerning the legal implications of continuing to allow the activity to take place in the Antarctic has been undertaken.

Any formal discussions must broadly address two matters. First, consideration must be given to the legal obligations within the Antarctic Treaty and the Antarctic Treaty System. This involves matters regarding the idea of 'peaceful use' of the Antarctic, includes consideration of the obligation for the free availability of information and results and will once again involve examination of the complicated Antarctic sovereignty situation. Secondly, any discussions regarding Antarctic resources will certainly involve consideration of a moratorium on the use of Antarctic living resources or discussions of appropriate property models, access to Antarctic living resources and benefit-sharing criteria.

The Antarctic Treaty parties may, this time, have a genuine opportunity to act in the interests of all mankind. A declaration that Antarctic biodiversity should be protected and valued simply because of its intrinsic value and that it should therefore not be used as part of any commercial exercise would send a clear signal to the international community that the Antarctic Treaty Consultative states genuinely are considering the interests of all mankind. However any statement to this effect is, at best, a long way off or could never be made. It remains to be seen if and when the bioprospecting issue will be fully and formally discussed within the Antarctic Treaty System and what the outcome of any such discussion might be.

---

[126] Rudiger Wolfrum, 'The Use of Antarctic Non-Living Resources: The Search for a Trustee?' in Rudiger Wolfrum (ed), *Antarctic Challenge* (1983) 143, 163.

Figure 6.1 Parties to the Antarctic Treaty System's Component Instruments as at December 2004

Party		ATS Instrument			
		Antarctic Treaty	CCAS	CCAMLR	Env. Protocol
1.	Argentina	✓	✓	✓	✓
2.	Australia	✓	✓	✓	✓
3.	Austria	C	-	-	C
4.	Belgium	✓	✓	✓	✓
5.	Brazil	✓	✓	✓	✓
6.	Bulgaria	✓	-	C	✓
7.	Canada	C	✓	C	✓
8.	Chile	✓	✓	✓	✓
9.	China	✓	-	-	✓
10.	Colombia	C	-	-	C
11.	Cuba	C	-	-	-
12.	Czech Republic	C	-	-	✓
13.	Denmark	C	-	-	C
14.	Ecuador	✓	-	-	✓
15.	Estonia	C	-	-	-
16.	European Community	-	-	✓	-
17.	Finland	✓	-	C	✓
18.	France	✓	✓	✓	✓
19.	Germany	✓	✓	✓	✓
20.	Greece	C	-	C	✓
21.	Guatemala	C	-	-	-
22.	Hungary	C	-	-	C
23.	India	✓	-	✓	✓
24.	Italy	✓	✓	✓	✓
25.	Japan	✓	✓	✓	✓
26.	Korea, Republic	✓	-	✓	✓
27.	Korea, DPR	C	-	-	C
28.	Namibia	-	-	✓	-
29.	Netherlands	✓	-	C	✓
30.	New Zealand	✓	C	✓	✓
31.	Norway	✓	✓	✓	✓
32.	Papua New Guinea	C	-	-	-
33.	Peru	✓	-	C	✓
34.	Poland	✓	✓	✓	✓
35.	Romania	C	-	-	✓
36.	Russian Federation	✓	✓	✓	✓

37.	Slovak Republic	C	-	-	C
38.	South Africa	✓	✓	✓	✓
39.	Spain	✓	-	✓	✓
40.	Sweden	✓	-	✓	✓
41.	Switzerland	C	-	-	C
42.	Turkey	C	-	-	-
43.	Ukraine	✓	-	✓	✓
44.	United Kingdom	✓	✓	✓	✓
45.	United States	✓	✓	✓	✓
46.	Uruguay	✓	-	✓	✓
47.	Vanuatu	-	-	C	-
48.	Venezuela	C	-	-	-

Key:
✓   'First-level' Party which has Ratified, Accepted or Approved that instrument. For the Antarctic Treaty such a Party is termed a 'Consultative Party', and for CCAMLR a 'Member of the Commission'
C   'Second-level' Contracting Party to that instrument
-   Not a Party to that instrument

Chart created and data compiled by Alan D. Hemmings, originally for the Proceedings of the Bioprospecting in Antarctica Workshop: Antarctic Bioprospecting, 2005 (In press). Used with permission.

Sources:
Antarctic Treaty and *Protocol on Environmental Protection to the Antarctic Treaty*: United States. 2004. 'Report of the Depository Government of the Antarctic Treaty and its Protocol in accordance with Recommendation XIII-2'. XXVII ATCM IP 36.
Cohen, H.K. (ed.). 2002. *Handbook of the Antarctic Treaty System*. Ninth Edition. Department of State. Washington, DC.
Convention for the Conservation of Antarctic Seals: United Kingdom. 2004. 'Report submitted to Antarctic Treaty Consultative Meeting XXVII by the Depository Government for the Convention for the Conservation of Antarctic Seals in accordance with Recommendation XII-2, paragraph 2(d)'. XXVII ATCM IP 1.
Convention on the Conservation of Antarctic Marine Living Resources: Australia. 2004. 'Report by the head of the Australian delegation in his capacity as representative of the Depository Government for the Convention on the Conservation of Antarctic Marine Living Resources to the Twenty-Seventh Antarctic Treaty Consultative Meeting'. XXVII ATCM IP 65.
Commission for the Conservation of Antarctic Marine Living Resources. 2003. *Report of the Twenty-Second Meeting of the Commission*. CCAMLR Secretariat, Hobart.

Map of the Antarctic Region

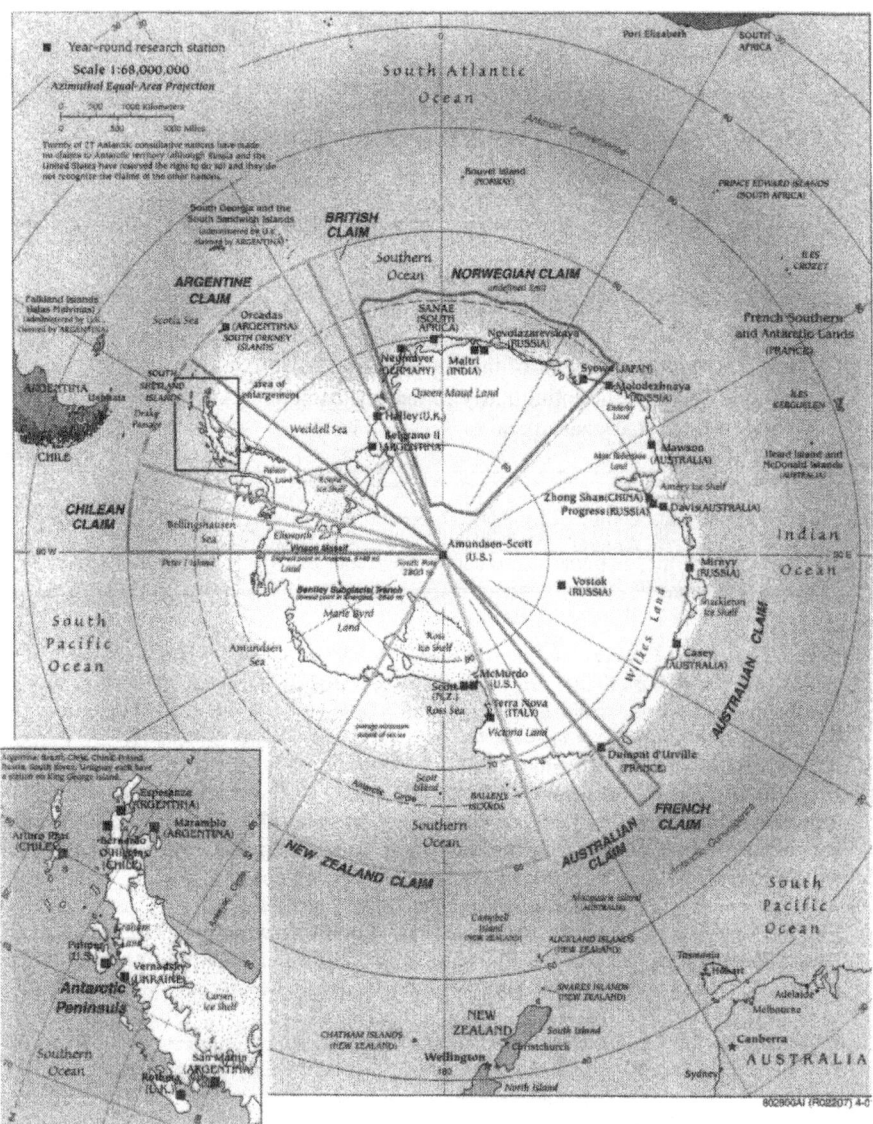

Figure 6.2 Map of the Antarctic Region showing the boundaries of the seven territorial claims

Chapter 7

Development and the International Trade Regime: Challenges for South Pacific Island States

Barbara von Tigerstrom[*]

Introduction

The South Pacific region is home to a diverse group of island states with unique characteristics. By global standards, all of these island states are relatively small in terms of both population and land area. Most of them are former colonies – some are still in dependent relationships of various types with neighbouring or faraway states – and they have close economic ties with each other and with the present or past dominant powers, including preferential trade arrangements and, in some cases, common currency and other forms of cooperation. As small island developing states (SIDS), the Pacific island countries face particular challenges in economic development. They also suffer from a degree of inherent disadvantage in international trade, which is increasingly emphasized as a driver of development.

The idea behind free trade is that each country will find and exploit its areas of comparative advantage in an environment of open competition. This is expected to increase efficiency overall and encourage countries to make the best possible use of the resources available to them. It assumes that each country is in a position to make an economically rational and efficient choice and that if it does so, it can compete in a global market. However, there is increasing appreciation of the difficulties that this presents in practice and of the need for more attention to the particular characteristics of different countries. Pacific island countries illustrate the challenges faced by small island developing states in this context:

> In the Pacific islands, where the consequence of nature's legacy is seen in most stark relief, one already finds several micro-states that have virtually no exports of either goods or services (Tuvalu, Niue, Nauru, Kiribati, Marshall Islands to name but a few), but survive from remittances and aid flows. In the larger states of the region (Fiji,

---

[*] Research assistance by Alison Heath (LLB (Hons) student, University of Canterbury) and helpful discussions with Dr Caroline Foster (Lecturer, University of Auckland Faculty of Law) are gratefully acknowledged.

Solomon Islands, Vanuatu, Samoa) trade has been based on either preferences or sovereignty and small transient market niches which create quasi-rents of similar commercial effect on investors to that of trade preferences.[1]

The physical, geographical, economic and demographic characteristics of these states make it difficult for them to diversify their economies and to be competitive in a free trade environment. Their experience calls into question some of the assumptions that underlie the rules of the international trading system, and their representatives as well as informed observers have begun to suggest that those rules should be modified to take into account their special needs. This raises broader questions about the extent to which the international regime can and should differentiate between countries in imposing legal obligations and applying legal rules. The principle of special and differential treatment for developing and least-developed countries is well-established in the World Trade Organization (WTO). However, its adequacy and effectiveness are deeply contested. Demands for further special treatment by groups of developing states present an important test for the multilateral system because they challenge it to provide a legal framework that addresses the diverse needs of some of its most vulnerable members. Regional trade agreements present some of the same challenges on a smaller scale.

This chapter surveys these issues from the perspective of the small island countries of the Pacific. It begins by briefly outlining the development challenges of the region and of small island developing states. It will then examine the extent to which the World Trade Organization (WTO) has accommodated the special needs of developing countries and small economies. Although many of the region's countries are not presently members of the WTO, the WTO regime affects non-members indirectly as well as current and prospective members. The third section will focus on regional trade agreements in the South Pacific, again considering attempts to address the development needs of small island countries in the region. By putting these together, we more fully appreciate the position of Pacific island countries in the world trading system, and work toward a preliminary assessment of the ways in which the legal framework does or does not respond to their needs.

The challenges of economic development in Forum Island Countries

Development status of the Forum Island Countries

All of the Forum Island Countries (FICs)[2] are considered to be developing countries, and five of them – Kiribati, Samoa, Solomon Islands, Tuvalu and

---

[1] Roman Grynberg, 'Towards Doha-lite' (2004) 3 *World Trade Review* 427, 428.
[2] This category includes all of the members of the Pacific Forum except Australia and New Zealand: Cook Islands, Federated States of Micronesia (FSM), Fiji, Kiribati, Nauru, Niue, Palau, Papua New Guinea (PNG), Republic of the Marshall Islands (RMI), Samoa, Solomon Islands, Tonga, Tuvalu and Vanuatu. They are sometimes also referred to as 'Pacific Island Countries' (PICs).

Vanuatu – are least developed countries (LDCs) according to the United Nations (UN) list, which is based on income, 'human assets' and economic vulnerability.³ States can 'graduate' from this list, and Samoa is eligible to be considered for graduation in 2006.⁴ Kiribati and Tuvalu met some of the criteria for graduation in 2003 but were not recommended for graduation, partly because they were the most economically vulnerable countries in the list.⁵ Vanuatu is not expected to graduate until at least 2009, since it still meets the human assets and vulnerability criteria.⁶ It has been suggested that 'if more sophisticated modalities were employed for graduation and reclassification of countries arguably most of the fourteen FICs would be classified as LDCs'.⁷

The Asian Development Bank (of which all FICs except Niue are developing member countries) has divided these countries into three groups: high natural resource, high poverty countries (Papua New Guinea, Solomon Islands and Vanuatu); moderate resource, good social development countries (Cook Islands, Fiji, Federated States of Micronesia, Samoa and Tonga); and low resource, small and vulnerable countries (Kiribati, Republic of the Marshall Islands, Nauru and Tuvalu).⁸ This typology highlights the considerable diversity within this group of countries, although they also face some common challenges.⁹ Some of them have experienced 'solid' economic growth in recent years, while the others have seen weak or negative growth and recent downturns.¹⁰ Variations in population, land and sea area, and resources are reflected in their economies. However, there are some broad similarities. Tourism, agriculture and fisheries are important to most economies of the region; manufactured goods are significant exports only in a few cases. Most of the FICs are highly dependent on outside sources of income, including official development assistance (ODA), remittances and trust funds.¹¹ They are highly 'open' economies, with high ratios of trade to gross domestic

---

³ UN Committee for Development Policy, Report on the sixth session (29 March 2004–2 April 2004), UN Doc E/2004/33, 15.
⁴ UN Committee for Development Policy, Report on the fifth session (7–11 April 2003), UN Doc E/2003/33, [22], [35].
⁵ Ibid [23].
⁶ Ministry of Foreign Affairs and Trade (New Zealand), 'Economic Update – Vanuatu – July 2004' <http://www.mfat.govt.nz/foreign/regions/pacific/econupdate/2004/july04/vanuatu.html> at 20 November 2004.
⁷ Roman Grynberg, 'The Pacific Island States and the WTO: Towards a post-Seattle Agenda for the Small Vulnerable States' (Paper presented at the Global Conference on the Development Agenda for Small States, London, February 2000) World Bank <http://wbln0018.worldbank.org/html/smallstates.nsf/(attachmentweb)/ThePacificIslandStates/$FILE/ThePacificIslandStates.pdf> at 15 December 2004.
⁸ Asian Development Bank, *Responding to the Priorities of the Poor: A Pacific Strategy for the Asian Development Bank 2005–2009* (2004) 19.
⁹ See ibid 2 and the introduction to this volume for a further discussion of diversity within the region.
¹⁰ Ibid 2.
¹¹ Ibid 3.

product (GDP) and heavy reliance on imports and exports, and almost all have a negative balance of trade (meaning that they import more than they export).[12]

By some measures, the development status of these countries tends to be relatively high compared to other developing and least developed countries.[13] However, the sense of security that this might give may be somewhat deceptive. The UN has recently raised concerns about the lack of progress on key development indicators in the Pacific Islands,[14] and the Asian Development Bank characterizes the region as 'underperforming' in terms of its 'disappointing' economic growth.[15] Poverty is a growing problem, with the numbers of people living in poverty increasing and traditional safety-nets breaking down.[16] In addition, relatively high average indicators for the region conceal 'wide disparities' in human development and poverty indicators.[17]

The development challenges facing these countries include economic, political, social and environmental factors. Political instability and conflict have been significant problems for some FICs, and governance issues are common challenges throughout the region.[18] The islands must deal with a range of environmental threats – some, like climate change, largely beyond their control,[19] others, like depletion of marine and forest resources or waste management, potentially mitigated by local strategies.[20] A recurring theme in assessments is concern about the high degree of vulnerability that these countries have to external influences, be they environmental, economic or geopolitical. For example, because they tend to be dependent on external assistance, the changing aid environment has a disproportionate impact on Pacific island states. With the end of the Cold War and hence the islands' declining strategic value, the 'passing of ... opportunities to attract extra aid led to the comment at a Pacific regional meeting in 1990 that the Cold War had ended, and the Pacific islands had lost'.[21] Although there is some evidence of recent revitalisation of aid in the region (which may be related in part to 'new' security concerns such as terrorism and transnational crime[22]), these countries are experiencing increased pressure to become economically self-

---

[12] Ibid 3, 50; A V Hughes, *A Different Kind of Voyage: Development and Dependence in the Pacific Islands* (Asian Development Bank, Pacific Studies Series, 1998) 66.

[13] For example, those FICs that are included in the Human Development Index (HDI) tables for 2004 are classified as 'Middle human development'; all except PNG have HDI values above the average for developing countries or LDCs, respectively: United Nations Development Programme, *Human Development Report 2004: Cultural Liberty in Today's Diverse World* (2004) 140-41.

[14] United Nations, 'Mauritius Conference on Small Islands Aims to Boost Pacific Islands' Lagging Performance' (Press Release ENV/DEV/798, 24 November 2004).

[15] Asian Development Bank, above n 8, 3.

[16] Ibid 7.

[17] Ibid 9.

[18] Ibid 11-14.

[19] See the chapter by Geoffrey Leane in this volume.

[20] Asian Development Bank, above n 8, 10; Hughes, above n 12, 113-14.

[21] Hughes, above n 12, 27.

[22] See the chapters by Neil Boister and Alex Conte in this volume.

sufficient, in particular through trade. There are important examples of economic 'success stories' in the region, where opportunities have been recognized and exploited with impressive creativity.[23] However, some of these have faced significant barriers,[24] others have been relatively short-lived, and some carry with them social and political costs.[25]

Special challenges for small island developing states

While some of the development challenges facing the FICs are particular to specific countries, some of them are inherent in the characteristics of small island developing states. The difficult position of these states is increasingly being recognized by the international community. All of the FICs are SIDS as defined by the UN,[26] a group that is recognized to be facing particular challenges in development. Being simultaneously small states, island states and developing states, one might say that they are disadvantaged three times over. The special vulnerability that this status carries with it has been the subject of recent attention in the UN, the WTO and the World Bank, among others. In 1994, a UN Global Conference on the Sustainable Development of Small Island Developing States was held in Barbados. A Declaration and Programme of Action on Small Island Developing States were adopted at the Conference, setting out actions to be taken by SIDS and the international community in fourteen priority areas.[27] Progress on the implementation of the Programme of Action will be assessed at a meeting in Mauritius in January 2005. Both the UN Millennium Declaration and the Monterrey Consensus on Financing for Development take note of the difficulties faced by these states and call upon UN member states to implement the Barbados Programme of Action.[28] The World Bank has recently given attention to this issue,

---

[23] See, for example, ibid 61-2; Asian Development Bank, above n 8, 5; Ron Crocombe, *The South Pacific* (2001) 326-7.

[24] For example, the export of kava (a root with relaxing properties, with a long history of traditional use in Polynesia) for herbal products in Western countries seemed promising at first, but suffered serious setbacks following reports of possible liver toxicity which led to bans in many countries.

[25] See for example, the discussion of 'sovereignty for sale and rent' – the exploitation of niches such as offshore banking, 'flags of convenience', waste dumping, gambling and passport sales – in Crocombe, above n 23, 362-78.

[26] Office of the High Representative for the Least Developed Countries, Landlocked Developing Countries and Small Island Developing States, 'List of SIDS' <http://www.un.org/special-rep/ohrlls/sid/list.htm> at 13 October 2004.

[27] *Programme of Action for the Sustainable Development of Small Island Developing States*, [4]-[11] UN Doc A/CONF.167/9 (1994); *Declaration of Barbados* [III]-[IV] UN Doc A/CONF.167/9 (1994).

[28] *United Nations Millennium Declaration*, GA Res 55/2, [17] UN Doc A/RES/55/2 (2000); *Report of the International Conference on Financing for Development*, [19] UN Doc A/CONF.198/11 (2002). See also *Declaration and state of progress and initiatives for the future implementation of the Programme of Action for the Sustainable Development of Small Island Developing States*, GA Res S-22/2, Annex, UN Doc A/RES/S-22/2 (2000).

and has formed a joint task force on small states with the Commonwealth Secretariat.[29] As will be discussed below, the WTO has established a work programme on small economies (including SIDS) as part of the current round of negotiations.

There is no single accepted definition of a 'small' state or economy; an appropriate definition will depend on the context and the particular issues being examined.[30] In the context of trade and development, a population of 1.5 million is often suggested as a threshold for defining this group, but higher thresholds may also be used, and some states with somewhat larger populations (such as Papua New Guinea, with approximately 5 million) may be included on the ground that they share the relevant characteristics.[31] Size is of course relative: although in the global context all of the FICs are considered small, within this group, some are members of a subgroup variously designated as 'small' or 'smaller' island states (SIS).[32] According to some classification schemes, these (and some other FICs) would be considered members of the subcategory of 'micro' states, and other FICs 'very small' states.[33] There is evidence to suggest that these distinctions even among small states are significant in economic and trade terms.[34]

There is considerable diversity within the group of small states. However, they tend to share certain common characteristics and challenges.[35] A large proportion of the world's small states are also islands (or multi-island states),[36] which compounds some of the difficulties they face. Many small states and especially small island states are physically remote and isolated. Remoteness entails dependence on transport providers and high transport costs, which are exacerbated by small volumes. This raises the price of imports and exports. In multi-island states, high costs and difficulties with market access exist even within

---

[29] See Commonwealth Secretariat and World Bank, *Small States Meeting Challenges in the Global Economy (Report of the Commonwealth Secretariat/World Bank Joint Task Force on Small States)* (2000).

[30] Mario A Gutiérrez, 'Is Small "Beautiful" for Economic Integration?' (1996) 30 *Journal of World Trade* 173, 173. To make matters more difficult, there are numerous different terms and categories used in different contexts, e.g. small states, small economies, small vulnerable states/economies, 'small and poor' states. This chapter will focus on small states/economies and the subcategory of small island developing states.

[31] Commonwealth Secretariat and World Bank, above n 29, 3.

[32] These are Cook Islands, Kiribati, Nauru, Niue, Republic of the Marshall Islands and Tuvalu. This subgroup holds annual leaders' summits to discuss relevant issues, and as will be seen below, is subject to some special provisions in regional trade agreements.

[33] See L Alan Winters and Pedro M G Martins, 'When comparative advantage is not enough: business costs in small remote economies' (2004) 3 *World Trade Review* 347, 349, 360.

[34] Ibid 376.

[35] For useful summaries of these characteristics, see Commonwealth Secretariat and World Bank, above n 29, 6-19; *Programme of Action for the Sustainable Development of Small Island Developing States*, [4]-[11] UN Doc A/CONF.167/9 (1994); *Declaration of Barbados* [III]-[IV] UN Doc A/CONF.167/9 (1994). The discussion here draws from these sources.

[36] Of the 45 small developing states identified by the Commonwealth Secretariat/World Bank Task Force, 34 are islands: above n 29, 5.

a single state; in addition, effective public administration is difficult and expensive. There will often be limited competition in the domestic market because remoteness discourages foreign producers and service providers, and the domestic market may be too small to support more than one producer.

The limited land area of small states means that there will often be pressure on natural resources. Fresh water will often be scarce and its supply easily threatened. The resource base of small states is typically narrow and this is reflected in the production of a narrow range of goods and services. As a result, there are limited opportunities for diversification, leaving producers and the national economy vulnerable to depletion of key resources, global fluctuations in prices and other factors largely beyond their control. The narrow resource base and small area mean that small states are extremely vulnerable to natural disasters and environmental change, because these have the potential to wipe out the supply of key resources for the whole country. This is compounded by the fact that small island states are particularly susceptible to natural disasters such as hurricanes. In the longer term, a rise in sea level may threaten the very existence of some small island states, and in the short term, disasters and environmental degradation often affect the entire population and physical environment, with potentially devastating consequences.

A small population often means limited institutional capacity in the public and private sectors. Government departments and private firms are relatively small, affecting their capacity and competitiveness, respectively. Economies of scale cannot be achieved in production by small firms or in the provision of public services. These services are thus relatively costly to provide, and as noted above this may be exacerbated by high transport costs. At the same time, sources of revenue are limited, many small states relying heavily on tariffs for a substantial proportion of public revenue. The domestic market is small with limited competition and diversification. The economies of small states tend to be relatively 'open' to trade and investment, and rely heavily on these. However, access to external capital is limited and many small states are dependent on ODA.

From this brief summary it will be appreciated that small states, and especially small island states, face significant challenges in a number of related areas. Although small states tend to do relatively well on some development indicators (such as education and health),[37] they often have more poverty than their per capita income would suggest.[38] Overall, the picture that emerges is one of states that are highly vulnerable. Vulnerability in this context means 'exposure to exogenous shocks over which the affected country has little or no control, and relatively low resilience to withstand and recover from these shocks'.[39] Key determinants are lack of diversification, export dependence and the impact of natural disasters. Almost all of the states classified as 'most vulnerable' are small

---

[37] Commonwealth Secretariat and World Bank, above n 29, 16. Note, however, that the exceptions to this are said to include low income countries in the Pacific.

[38] Ibid. This is thought to be due to uneven distribution of income, especially in multi-island states.

[39] Ibid 19.

states, and about two thirds of these are islands.[40] This vulnerability means that in global or regional regimes the stakes for small island developing states are high. Shifts in trade and development policy – such as declining levels of ODA and increasing emphasis on free trade as a strategy for promoting economic development – are likely to have a disproportionate impact on these countries. The following sections examine the ways in which these shifts are reflected in multilateral and regional trade agreements and the extent to which the current approach adequately meets the needs of this vulnerable group of countries.

Small island developing states of the Pacific and the WTO

Only three of the FICs (Fiji, Papua New Guinea and Solomon Islands) are currently Members of the WTO, and have been members since 1996. Three others (Samoa, Tonga and Vanuatu) are observers and are in various stages of negotiating their accession.[41] WTO Members are all parties to the Uruguay Round package of agreements, including the current version of the earlier General Agreement on Tariffs and Trade (GATT), the General Agreement on Trade in Services (GATS), the Agreement on Trade-Related Aspects of Intellectual Property Rights (TRIPS) and the Understanding on Rules and Procedures Governing the Settlement of Disputes (DSU), as well as agreements on subsidies and countervailing measures, agriculture, sanitary and phytosanitary measures, technical barriers to trade and anti-dumping.[42] These agreements constitute an ambitious programme of trade liberalization, building on the earlier GATT commitments. The basic obligations under the GATT are still the cornerstones of the WTO regime: the most-favoured nation (MFN) treatment obligation, which requires equally favourable treatment of imports from all WTO members; the national treatment obligation, which requires equally favourable treatment of imports as compared to domestic products; progressive reduction of tariffs; and the elimination of quantitative restrictions on trade (such as quotas). The aim of these rules is to move toward free trade through the reduction of various forms of trade barriers on a multilateral basis.

---

[40] Ibid 20. Fiji, Kiribati, Samoa, Solomon Islands, Tonga and Vanuatu are all listed in this category: ibid 22.

[41] The process of accession to the WTO is further discussed below at notes 139-145 and accompanying text. Vanuatu's Final Accession Package was completed in 2001 but has yet to be adopted. At the date of writing, consultations were still under way regarding the accession of Samoa and Tonga. New Zealand completed a bilateral accession agreement with Tonga in early 2004, which sets out the terms for New Zealand exports to Tonga upon that country's accession to the WTO: Jim Sutton, 'NZ signs WTO accession agreement with Tonga' (Press Release, 8 March 2004).

[42] *General Agreement on Tariffs and Trade*, opened for signature 30 October 1947, 58 UNTS 187 ('GATT'); Annexes 1 through 3 to the *Marrakesh Agreement Establishing the World Trade Organization*, opened for signature 15 April 1994, 1867 UNTS 3 (entered into force 1 January 1995) ('WTO Agreement').

A substantial proportion – approximately two thirds – of WTO Members are developing countries, and currently 32 are LDCs.[43] The category of developing countries is not defined and Member states may self-identify as developing countries (subject to challenges by other Members disputing this status). In the case of LDCs, however, the WTO adopts their designation by the UN.[44] The promotion of economic development is among the objectives of the multilateral trade regime. However, the extent to which the WTO agreements adequately fulfil this objective and respond to the challenges faced by developing countries has been one of the most pressing and contentious issues in the WTO. It is an issue of great importance to current and potential FIC members of the WTO, which as SIDS face significant challenges in international trade.

Developing countries and the WTO

In establishing the WTO, the parties recognized the 'need for positive efforts designed to ensure that developing countries, and especially the least developed among them, secure a share in the growth in international trade commensurate with the needs of their economic development'.[45] Views on the Organization's effectiveness in pursuing this goal are decidedly mixed, with many developing country representatives arguing that not only are these countries not deriving sufficient benefit from trade liberalization, but the implementation of their own WTO obligations is creating additional hardships rather than benefits. Tensions between developed and developing countries have been a perennial feature of WTO negotiations.

Developing countries and LDCs are provided with various forms of special and differential treatment (SDT) under the WTO agreements.[46] First, there are provisions allowing greater flexibility to developing countries in implementing their obligations under the WTO agreements. These may take the form of exemptions, lesser or more flexible commitments, or longer transitional time periods for compliance. There are also provisions for technical assistance to be provided to developing countries in the implementation of their obligations, participation in dispute settlement, and preparation of trade policy review reports. A third category of provisions requires developed country Members to take account of the interests of developing countries in implementing the WTO agreements and application of trade policies. Finally, there are provisions designed

---

[43] World Trade Organization, *Understanding the WTO* (2004) World Trade Organization <http://www.wto.org/english/thewto_e/whatis_e/tif_e/tif_e.htm> at 24 November 2004. Solomon Islands is one of the LDC Members.
[44] See above n 3 and accompanying text.
[45] WTO Agreement, preamble.
[46] The WTO Secretariat has identified 145 SDT provisions in the WTO agreements, falling into six categories: provisions aimed at increasing developing countries' trade opportunities, provisions requiring Members to safeguard the interests of developing countries, flexibility of commitments and action, transitional time periods, technical assistance, and provisions relating to LDCs. *Implementation of Special and Differential Treatment Provisions in WTO Agreements and Decisions*, WTO Doc WT/COMTD/W/77 (2000) 3 (Note by Secretariat).

to increase market access by developing countries. This involves reducing trade barriers for products from developing countries, including tariffs and other barriers, so that these countries will have greater trading opportunities. Developed countries agreed that in reducing their tariffs and other barriers for developing country products, they will not expect developing countries to reciprocate with equivalent reductions – a departure from the usual expectation of reciprocity in trade concessions.[47]

Preferential tariffs and other differential and more favourable treatment of developing countries that would otherwise violate the MFN treatment principle have been permitted, first by a temporary waiver,[48] and since 1979 by a permanent decision known as the 'Enabling Clause',[49] now incorporated as part of the GATT.[50] The Enabling Clause provides that notwithstanding the MFN obligation in article I of the GATT, 'contracting parties may accord differential and more favourable treatment to developing countries, without according such treatment to other contracting parties'.[51] This applies to preferential tariffs granted by developed countries to developing countries under the Generalized System of Preferences (GSP) as well as mutual reduction of tariffs and non-tariff barriers among developing countries.[52] Differential and more favourable treatment authorized by this decision should be designed 'to facilitate and promote the trade of developing countries' and 'to respond positively to the development, financial and trade needs of developing countries'.[53]

These various forms of SDT are intended to address the difficulties or challenges that developing countries face in the international trading system and to ensure that developing countries benefit from increased trade liberalization. They also reflect different theories of the relationship between trade and development, and as the SDT provisions have been established over the years, they have mirrored the predominance of one or another of these theories in various historical periods. A brief review of this evolution will enable a better understanding of current debates and proposals for reform. In turn, this provides the context for appreciating the particular difficulties of SIDS in the multilateral trade regime.

---

[47] GATT art XXXVI(8).
[48] *Waiver Decision on the Generalized System of Preferences*, GATT BISD 18th Supp, 24, GATT Doc L/3545 (1971).
[49] *Decision on Differential and More Favourable Treatment, Reciprocity and Fuller Participation of Developing Countries*, GATT BISD 26th Supp, 203, GATT Doc L/4903 (1979) ('Enabling Clause').
[50] *General Agreement on Tariffs and Trade 1994*, Annex 1A to the *Marrakesh Agreement Establishing the World Trade Organization*, opened for signature 15 April 1994, 1867 UNTS 3 (entered into force 1 January 1995) ('GATT 1994'). This subparagraph stipulates that decisions of the GATT contracting parties form part of the Agreement.
[51] Enabling Clause, above n 49, [1].
[52] Ibid [2]. The GSP is a scheme of voluntary, non-reciprocal tariff preferences granted by developed countries on products of interest to developing countries. Developing countries grant mutual preferential treatment to each other under the Generalized System of Trade Preferences (GSTP).
[53] Ibid [3].

The original GATT contained no special provisions explicitly addressing the needs of developing countries.[54] Although a substantial proportion of the original contracting parties were developing countries, there was no formal recognition of their status, and the general approach was one of uniform rights and obligations for all parties.[55] The GATT provisions as revised in the mid-1950s made it possible for developing countries to use quantitative restrictions for balance of payments reasons and to assist and protect their 'infant industries'.[56] Allowing developing countries to maintain protectionist policies reflected the prevailing development strategy of import substitution, which involved protection of domestic industries and maintenance of trade barriers to encourage the substitution of locally-manufactured products for imports.[57] Increasing interest in export-led growth as another development strategy was reflected in changes made over the next few decades, including Part IV of the GATT and the Enabling Clause, which focused on nonreciprocal concessions to increase market access for developing country products, with the aim of ensuring that developing countries could increase their export earnings and benefit from the growth in international trade.[58] These provisions established non-reciprocity as a fundamental principle:[59] developed countries, when they make commitments to lower trade barriers, do not expect developing countries to reciprocate, and in particular do not expect and will not seek concessions or contributions by the developing countries 'which are inconsistent with their individual development, financial and trade needs'.[60]

The protectionist and export-led strategies co-existed for a time, despite some tension between them: at the same time that production for export was supposed to be increasing and developing countries were supposed to be exploiting their areas of comparative advantage, protectionist policies were thought to be working against this by allowing inefficiency in their domestic production.[61] More recently, the prevailing approach has tended to favour full liberalization of both developed and developing country policies – the former to improve market access and the latter to encourage efficiency in developing countries' production – which would resolve this contradiction.[62] In the 1980s, the disappointing development

---

[54] To a limited extent some provisions achieved this indirectly, for example, an exception to the MFN principle for trade preferences between colonies and colonial powers: GATT art I:2(b). This 'would have covered a substantial part of trade between developed and developing countries at the time the GATT was created': Michael J Trebilcock and Robert Howse, *The Regulation of International Trade* (2nd ed, 1999) 369.
[55] Constantine Michalopoulos, 'The Role of Special and Differential Treatment for Developing Countries in GATT and the World Trade Organisation' (Working Paper No 2388, World Bank, 2000) 2.
[56] GATT arts XII, XVIII.
[57] Michalopoulos, above n 55, 3; Trebilcock and Howse, above n 54, 381; Peter Gallagher, *Guide to the WTO and Developing Countries* (2000) 1.
[58] GATT art XXXVI:2, 3.
[59] GATT art XXXVI:8; Enabling Clause, above n 49, [5].
[60] Enabling Clause, above n 49, [5].
[61] Trebilcock and Howse, above n 54, 371.
[62] Ibid 383.

performance of many countries, especially compared with the experience of East Asian countries which had unilaterally adopted liberal trade policies and focused on exports, led many to question the value of protectionist policies for development, and the pendulum began to swing toward liberalization. In the 1990s the 'Washington Consensus' emerged, outlining a development strategy based on, *inter alia*, liberalization of trade and investment, privatization and deregulation.[63] Though it has not gone unquestioned, the neoliberal approach to development has come to represent the received wisdom, in particular of the international financial institutions and subsequently of the WTO. Essentially, this view holds that free trade benefits developing countries by providing opportunities for export-led growth and by increasing efficiency and competitiveness in their own economies and industries. Commitments under the WTO agreements are, from this point of view, helpful to developing countries because they encourage reform of those countries' policies in ways that will ultimately help, not hinder, their economic development.[64]

The aim under this approach, then, is to integrate developing countries into the global trading system, not provide them with exceptions or exclusions that would insulate them; commentators caution that there is no real benefit in being granted 'immunity from rules that make sense'.[65] However, it is recognized that, at least initially, integration may be difficult for developing countries. Special treatment of developing countries is therefore justified to the extent that it helps them to adjust to liberalization and participate in the global trade regime. This is reflected in the SDT provisions dating from the Uruguay Round negotiations, which emphasize technical assistance and longer implementation periods. This has been referred to as an 'adjustment model' of SDT:[66] it assumes that developing countries can be – and should be – fully integrated on equal terms following an initial, assisted period of adjustment.

The Uruguay Round has been described as representing a significant shift from the fundamental principle of non-reciprocity to 'limited non-reciprocity'[67] or 'flexibility in the context of reciprocity'.[68] Under this approach, commitments are 'agreed on a reciprocal basis, and flexibility applies to the differential application of such commitments'.[69] Though it is now firmly entrenched in the WTO regime,

---

[63] Although the Washington Consensus as originally proposed (in 1989) contained 10 policy reforms recommended for Latin America, the term has since come to be more loosely used to refer generally to a neoliberal theory or strategy for development. See John Williamson, 'What Should the World Bank Think about the Washington Consensus?' (2000) 15(2) *World Bank Research Observer* 251.

[64] See, e.g. J Michael Finger and L Alan Winters, 'What Can the WTO Do for Developing Countries?' in Anne O Krueger (ed), *The WTO as an International Organization* (1998) 365; Gallagher, above n 57, 14.

[65] Ibid 388.

[66] Frank J Garcia, 'Beyond Special and Differential Treatment' (2004) 27 *Boston College International and Comparative Law Review* 291, 299.

[67] Ibid 305.

[68] Michalopoulos, above n 55, 20.

[69] Ibid.

this new model has been criticized as unrealistic and unfair by some commentators and developing country representatives. SDT was always intended to be temporary in the sense that states would 'graduate' from developing country status and hence cease to be eligible, but the adjustment model assumes that developing countries will be able to comply fully with their obligations even while they retain that status. The transitional time periods provided are said to be inadequate, with periods expiring before sufficient progress on implementation and capacity building can be made.[70] The technical assistance arrangements have not been viewed as particularly successful, and developing countries still face significant barriers to participation in the WTO.[71] More fundamentally, this approach, which emphasizes 'extra time or extra help to "catch" up to a level playing field',[72] obscures the fact that the playing field is unlikely to be level, and even if it were, the unequal economic and political power of the players is likely to prevent identical treatment from amounting to equal treatment.

However, the older approaches to SDT are not unproblematic, either. The existing preference arrangements have several weaknesses, with the result that they are not particularly effective in achieving their objective of increasing export opportunities for developing countries. One issue is the product coverage of these arrangements, which in some cases has excluded the products of most export interest to the beneficiary countries.[73] In addition, the arrangements have historically been subject to various forms of conditionality which may exclude some countries.[74] Rules of origin may present a further barrier and in some cases the costs of meeting the rules of origin requirements may even exceed the value of the preferences.[75] Furthermore, it is widely recognized that even when preferences are utilized, their value is being steadily eroded as the level of tariffs decreases through successive rounds of negotiations and tariff bindings.[76] Tariff preferences only provide an export advantage to developing or least developed countries where

---

[70] Garcia, above n 66, 305-306; Michalopoulos, above n 55, 22.

[71] Garcia, above n 66, 309; Michalopoulos, above n 55, 27-8.

[72] Garcia, above n 66, 299.

[73] Stefano Inama, 'Market Access for LDCs: Issues to be Addressed' (2002) 36(1) *Journal of World Trade* 85, 93. For example, the exclusion of textiles and clothing by the United States and Canada, and of agricultural products by Japan and (until recently) the EU, has limited the value of trade preferences for LDCs. See also Garcia, above n 66, 303, regarding developing countries generally.

[74] Inama, above n 73, 94; Garcia, above n 66, 304. States' ability to impose non-trade related conditions can be expected to be more limited following a recent decision of the WTO Appellate Body: see below at n 107.

[75] Inama, above n 73, 93; Alexander Keck and Patrick Low, 'Special and Differential Treatment in the WTO: Why, When and How?' (Staff Working Paper No ERSD-2004-03, WTO, 2004) 9-10. Rules of origin determine when a product is considered to originate from a particular country for customs and tariff purposes; typically they demand that a given proportion of content and/or of value added to a manufactured product originate in that country. They may also require that the last process of manufacture have occurred in that country.

[76] Keck and Low, above n 75, 10-11; Garcia, above n 66, 304; Michalopoulos, above n 55, 24.

those countries' products enjoy a significant margin of preference over products coming from other countries. When the overall level of tariffs decreases, this margin and the value of preferences is eroded. Although the reduction of tariffs is generally considered to be positive, the unintended side-effect of tariff preference erosion undermines the primary existing method of increasing trade opportunities for developing countries.

Tariff preferences also exemplify a wider problem with SDT in the WTO regime: many of the SDT provisions are non-binding, unenforceable statements of principle or exhortations. The provisions regarding special and more favourable treatment are permissive rather than mandatory. For tariff preferences, this means that the arrangements that exist are generally unilateral initiatives that could be withdrawn or changed without any possibility of recourse by affected developing countries.[77] The instability of tariff preferences has the effect that developing countries hoping to take advantage of them have little security, and this limits their ability to make long-term plans or attract relevant investment.[78] All of these weaknesses have led many to suggest that reciprocal, bound tariff concessions on an MFN basis will be more beneficial to developing countries in the long run.[79]

The fact that developing countries cannot rely on or enforce the provisions that purport to accommodate their needs and interests creates uncertainty for them, working against the stated purpose of facilitating their full participation in the trade regime. This concern is linked to the perception that developing countries made a 'bad bargain' in the Uruguay Round and that developed countries have not lived up to their end of the bargain.[80] The shift from non-reciprocity to 'flexible reciprocity' entailed the expectation that as developing countries liberalized their trade policies and moved toward full integration with the multilateral trade regime, they would benefit from further liberalization on the part of developed countries as well. Developing countries looking forward to the reduction of trade barriers, particularly in areas of export interest such as agriculture and textiles, have largely been disappointed. Not surprisingly, then, the non-binding status of SDT provisions and the lack of adequate progress on market access are among the current issues under discussion in the WTO.

Developing countries' growing insistence that progress be made on these issues has led to greater attention to them in recent years. The current round of negotiations, launched in 2001 at the Fourth Ministerial Conference in Doha, has been dubbed the 'Development Round' and negotiations are taking place within the framework of the 'Doha Development Agenda' (DDA). The Ministerial Declaration adopted at Doha (Doha Declaration) states that 'trade can play a major

---

[77] There are some exceptions to this: some preferences are set out in treaty arrangements (the SPARTECA agreement discussed below being one example), and developing countries that are excluded from an arrangement can challenge it as being inconsistent with the permissive provisions (see below at n 107). Unilateral discretion and instability remain the general rule, however.

[78] Inama, above n 73, 92-3; Keck and Low, above n 75, 10-11.

[79] See, e.g. Keck and Low, above n 75, 11-12.

[80] See, e.g. Garcia, above n 66, 297-8.

role in the promotion of economic development and the alleviation of poverty' and recognizes 'the need for all our peoples to benefit from the increased opportunities and welfare gains that the multilateral trading system generates'. It expresses an intention to place the needs and interests of developing countries 'at the heart of the Work Programme adopted in this Declaration' and to 'make positive efforts designed to ensure that developing countries, and especially the least-developed among them, secure a share in the growth of world trade commensurate with the needs of their economic development'.[81]

The DDA covers a wide range of complex issues which are being negotiated in various bodies within the WTO.[82] The Doha Declaration and a decision on 'Implementation-Related Issues and Concerns'[83] (Implementation Decision) establish a framework for reviewing SDT and addressing the difficulties encountered by developing countries in implementing their obligations. This work is to include consideration of ways to make SDT more effective and the potential for making some of the provisions mandatory rather than non-binding.[84] Sceptics still insist that 'the agenda of the Work Programme has been totally set by major developed countries guided by their own economic interests. The priority of the development of the developing countries is not reflected in it'.[85] There is undoubtedly some truth to this view, and it can only be disproved by substantial progress on issues of interest to developing countries in the negotiations. One thing is clear, however: the review of SDT and the emphasis on development issues has meant renewed focus on, and debate about, these issues. As a result, there is an opportunity to examine and revisit the rationales, forms and effectiveness of SDT. Part of this debate, of particular interest to the FICs, involves discussion of the distinctions between different types of developing countries and the treatment of small developing states in the multilateral trade regime.

Differentiation between developing countries in the WTO

Although developing countries have many interests in common, it is trite to say that the group of developing countries is very diverse in terms of size, level of development, natural and human resources, and other factors.[86] This diversity means that developing countries do not necessarily have shared interests on every issue or speak with one voice. It also complicates discussions of optimal trade rules

---

[81] *Ministerial Declaration*, WTO Doc WT/MIN(01)/DEC/1 (2001) ('Doha Declaration') [2].
[82] For an overview, see WTO, *How the negotiations are organized* <http://www.wto.org/english/tratop_e/dda_e/work_organi_e.htm> at 1 December 2004. A discussion of the full range of these issues would be far beyond the scope of this chapter. Some of the key issues include agriculture (including special consideration of cotton), non-agricultural market access, services, trade facilitation, and intellectual property.
[83] *Implementation-Related Issues and Concerns*, WTO Doc WT/MIN(01)/17 (2001) (Decision of 14 November 2001).
[84] Ibid [12]; Doha Declaration, above n 81, [44].
[85] Bhagirath Lal Das, *WTO: The Doha Agenda: The New Negotiations on World Trade* (2003) 4-5.
[86] Trebilcock and Howse, above n 54, 367.

for developing countries, given that the rules that are appropriate for some likely will not be so for all. Despite the widespread recognition of vast differences in developing country needs and capacity, with few exceptions the same rules apply to them all: 'Singapore and Korea are supposed to be treated the same way as Ghana and Saint Lucia; Argentina and Brazil the same as the Maldives and Senegal'.[87] If SDT for developing countries is supposed to be a response to the particular challenges faced by those countries, can it do so adequately while ignoring such important distinctions? The extent to which SDT responds appropriately to the actual difficulties of various developing countries will be an important measure of its legitimacy, which is increasingly under challenge.

There are a number of different ways in which we may classify developing countries into subgroups: by income level, by primary exports, by import and export ratios, by their geographical characteristics (in particular landlocked countries and island countries), or by their membership in negotiating groups or groups of beneficiaries under preference regimes (for example the Africa, Caribbean and Pacific or 'ACP' Group).[88] The only subcategory of developing countries that is given official recognition and special treatment in the WTO agreements is the LDCs. The Enabling Clause formally recognized LDCs as a subcategory of developing countries, providing for 'special treatment' of LDCs in the context of preferences and urging developed countries to 'exercise the utmost restraint in seeking any concessions or contributions' by LDCs and not to expect any 'concessions or contributions that are inconsistent with the recognition of their particular situation and problems'.[89] Developed country Members have put in place various additional preferences for LDCs under the authority of the Enabling Clause. For example, the European Union adopted an amendment to its GSP scheme that provides duty-free access to most products from LDCs.[90] In 1999, a decision was taken to waive MFN obligations of developing countries to the extent required to allow them to provide tariff preferences to LDCs.[91]

---

[87] Michalopoulos, above 55, 25.

[88] For a review of various classifications, see Richard R Barichello, Alex McCalla and Alberto Valdes, 'Developing countries and the world trade organization negotiations' (2003) 85 *American Journal of Agricultural Economics* 674.

[89] Enabling Clause, above n 49, [2(d)], [6]. See also [8], which provides that '[p]articular account will be taken of the serious difficulty of the least-developed countries in making concessions and contributions in view of their special economic situation and their development, financial and trade needs'.

[90] *Commission Regulation (EC) No 416/2001 of 26 February 2001 Amending the GSP so as to extend duty and quota free access to least-developed countries* [2001] OJ L 60/43. This is known as the 'Everything But Arms' (EBA) amendment because the preferential access is to apply to all LDC products except arms, although the particularly 'sensitive' products – bananas, rice and sugar – will be included only after a transitional period. For other examples, see Inama, above n 73.

[91] *Preferential Tariff Treatment for Least-Developed Countries*, WTO Doc WT/L/304 (1999) (Decision on Waiver). This is an example of the encouragement of 'South-South' trade as a means of promoting development.

In respect of many of the SDT provisions, LDCs are provided with additional protections, flexibility or assistance as compared to other developing countries. Under the Agreement on Agriculture, for example, whereas developing countries are given ten years to implement reduction commitments, LDCs are not required to make any reduction commitments at all.[92] Another type of provision is seen in the TRIPS Agreement, which allows a transitional period of 10 years for LDCs (as opposed to four years for other developing countries) for the implementation of most of its provisions.[93] The needs of LDC Members are to be given priority in technical assistance under the Agreement on Technical Barriers to Trade.[94] There is also a separate Decision on Measures in Favour of Least-Developed Countries[95] which contains a range of provisions regarding implementation, preferences, technical assistance and ongoing review. Its first paragraph reiterates the general principle that LDCs, 'for so long as they remain in that category, while complying with the general rules set out in the [Uruguay Round] instruments, will only be required to undertake commitments and concessions to the extent consistent with their individual development, financial and trade needs, or their administrative and institutional capabilities'.

Apart from LDCs, distinctions between developing countries are formally recognized in only a small handful of instances in the WTO. The Agreement on Subsidies and Countervailing Measures (SCM Agreement) provides an exemption from the prohibition on export subsidies for developing countries with a per capita income of less than $1000 as well as LDCs.[96] Other developing countries must phase out their export subsidies during an eight-year transitional period.[97] These provisions in the SCM Agreement represent an important – though limited – precedent for formal differentiation between developing countries.[98] A ministerial decision regarding the implementation of the Uruguay Round Agreement on

---

[92] *Agreement on Agriculture*, Annex 1A to the *Marrakesh Agreement Establishing the World Trade Organization*, opened for signature 15 April 1994, 1867 UNTS 3 (entered into force 1 January 1995), art 15.2.

[93] *Agreement on Trade-Related Aspects of Intellectual Property Rights*, Annex 1C to the *Marrakesh Agreement Establishing the World Trade Organization*, opened for signature 15 April 1994, 1867 UNTS 3 (entered into force 1 January 1995), arts 65, 66.

[94] *Agreement on Technical Barriers to Trade*, Annex 1A to the *Marrakesh Agreement Establishing the World Trade Organization*, opened for signature 15 April 1994, 1867 UNTS 3 (entered into force 1 January 1995) ('TBT Agreement'), art 11.8.

[95] *Decision on Measures in Favour of Least-Developed Countries*, WTO Doc LT/UR/D-1/3 (1994).

[96] *Agreement on Subsidies and Countervailing Measures*, Annex 1A to the *Marrakesh Agreement Establishing the World Trade Organization*, opened for signature 15 April 1994, 1867 UNTS 3 (entered into force 1 January 1995) ('SCM Agreement'), art 27.2(a), Annex VII.

[97] Ibid art 27.2(b). Export subsidies which are 'inconsistent with its development needs' must be eliminated more quickly: art 27.4.

[98] Michalopoulos, above n 55, 26. This is despite the fact that the particular provision has little value in development terms: ibid.

Agriculture also refers to 'net food-importing developing countries' along with LDCs as the group to be given special consideration.[99]

Another way in which differentiation can occur is for developing countries to cease to be eligible for specific forms of SDT where certain criteria are met. In the SCM Agreement, when a developing country reaches 'export competitiveness', its exemption will end (for low-income developing countries and LDCs) or its transitional period will be shortened (for 'other' developing countries).[100] This is a specific example of the more general principle of 'graduation', which holds that developing countries will increase their contributions, concessions and participation in the trade regime as 'the progressive development of their economies and improvement in their trade situation' permit.[101] Though this principle is generally accepted, there is a lack of clear mechanisms to draw such distinctions and tailor countries' eligibility for SDT accordingly.

These examples show that differentiation among developing countries for specific purposes, though rare, is not unheard of or impossible in the WTO. Indicators such as per capita income or share of world trade could be used to differentiate between developing countries for some purposes.[102] The World Bank, for example, distinguishes between developing countries based on income levels, and it has been suggested that these distinctions could be recognized in the WTO.[103] It has also been suggested that developing countries classified as 'heavily indebted' by the World Bank and the International Monetary Fund be treated the same as LDCs, given that they likely have an equal need for additional benefits.[104] To date, no such proposals have been accepted.

One possibility for differentiation is the allocation of tariff preferences on a targeted basis to certain developing countries.[105] This involves developed countries unilaterally differentiating by giving additional preferences to subcategories of developing countries. An initial question is whether they are able to do this without violating their obligations under the WTO agreements. As we saw above, the Enabling Clause (a decision of the GATT contracting parties which has been incorporated into the agreement) allows for preferential treatment of developing countries notwithstanding the MFN obligation in the GATT. This decision

---

[99] *Decision on Measures Concerning the Possible Negative Effects of the Reform Programme on Least-Developed and Net Food-Importing Developing Countries*, WTO Doc LT/UR/D-1/2 (1994).

[100] SCM Agreement art 27.5. For low-income developing countries and LDCs, an eight-year transitional period will begin as for other developing countries; for other developing countries the transitional period will be shortened to two years. Low-income developing countries and LDCs must only reach export competitiveness in 'one or more products' to lose their exemption; for other developing countries the shortened transitional period applies only to subsidies for the given product in which export competitiveness has been reached. Export competitiveness is defined in art 27.6.

[101] Enabling Clause, above n 49, [7].

[102] Michalopoulos, above n 55, 35.

[103] Ibid.

[104] Michalopoulos, above n 55, 26.

[105] Keck and Low, above n 75.

explicitly allows '[s]pecial treatment of the least developed among the developing countries' in the context of differential and more favourable treatment.[106] However, the extent to which preferences and special treatment can be given selectively to *other* subcategories of developing countries was the subject of a recent dispute in the WTO. The dispute involved the tariff preferences granted by the European Communities (EC), which included, in addition to general arrangements available to all developing countries and special arrangements for LDCs, other special arrangements applied selectively to developing countries complying with certain environmental or labour standards or combating drug production and trafficking.

Under the drug arrangements, eligible countries listed in an annex to the relevant EC regulation were granted duty free access for certain products, whereas other developing countries were subject to either reduced or normal tariff rates.[107] India (supported by other developing countries which had been excluded from the scheme) challenged the preferences under the drug arrangements, arguing that preferential tariffs should be available equally to all developing countries.[108] The Panel agreed, deciding that the Enabling Clause required identical preferences to be granted to all developing countries without differentiation (except with regard to LDCs, which were permitted special treatment).[109] Upon appeal, however, the Appellate Body reversed this decision, though it ultimately agreed with the Panel that the EC's drug arrangements as they stood could not be justified under the Enabling Clause.[110] The Appellate Body was of the opinion that similarly situated developing countries could not be treated differently, but this did not mean that preferences need be identical for all developing countries.[111] Developing countries may have different needs according to their levels of development and particular circumstances, and preferential treatment responding to these differences is permissible – in fact it could even be said to be encouraged, given that paragraph 3(c) of the Enabling Clause requires preferential treatment to be 'designed and, if necessary, modified, to respond positively to the development, financial and trade needs of developing countries'.[112] The particular needs of various groups of developing countries must have some objective basis, there must be a sufficient nexus between the measures and these special needs, and the preferences must be

---

[106] Enabling Clause, above n 49, [2(d)].
[107] *European Communities – Conditions for the Granting of Tariff Preferences to Developing Countries*, WTO Doc WT/DS246/AB/R, AB-2004-1 (2004) [5] (Report of the Appellate Body).
[108] India originally challenged the environment and labour rights arrangements as well but subsequently decided to limit its complaint to the drug arrangements. Ibid [4].
[109] *European Communities – Conditions for the Granting of Tariff Preferences to Developing Countries*, WTO Doc WT/DS246/R (2003) (Report of the Panel).
[110] *European Communities – Conditions for the Granting of Tariff Preferences to Developing Countries*, WTO Doc WT/DS246/AB/R, AB-2004-1 (2004) (Report of the Appellate Body).
[111] Ibid [153], [156].
[112] Ibid [161], [162].

available to all developing countries sharing those needs.[113] The case for such measures is strengthened to the extent that these special needs are recognized in international instruments and the measures are designed as rational responses to those needs.[114]

It is questionable whether unilaterally granted additional preferences are the best way of ensuring fair and effective differentiation. Even with the limits set by the recent Appellate Body decision, leaving the definition of subcategories and appropriate measures up to unilateral decisions of individual developed countries is not ideal.[115] Also, as explained above, it is well-recognized that the effectiveness of tariff preferences is limited and declining, which affects the potential for this mechanism to achieve meaningful differentiation among developing countries. Differentiation could also occur with respect to exemptions or reduced commitments, extended transition periods or entitlements to additional assistance, for example. The decision was based on the particular wording of the Enabling Clause regarding the GSP, and did not directly address other forms of SDT or differentiation. However, it does have broader significance to the extent that it outlines the distinction between discrimination and legitimate differentiation. Special treatment for subcategories of developing countries must be based on objective criteria relevant to development needs – rather than, for example, political aims or securing market access for developed country products – and they must be available to all similarly situated countries.[116] In the case of SIDS, their particular challenges and development needs have been identified and recognized by the international community.[117] This would strengthen the case for differentiated treatment. In principle, if appropriate forms of additional SDT could be identified and applied to all countries sharing the relevant characteristics, this would enhance rather than detract from the fairness of the multilateral regime.

'Small economies' and the WTO

The issue of differentiation between developing countries has been taken up as part of the re-examination of SDT in the Doha Round negotiations. Of particular relevance to the small island states in the South Pacific region, this recent discussion has included consideration of the particular challenges faced by 'small economies'. The three FIC Members of the WTO are part of an informal grouping of small economies; the others whose accessions are in progress participate in this

---

[113] Ibid [163]-[165]. The EC drug arrangement preferences did not meet these conditions because they were not based on objective criteria and were not available to all similarly situated countries. Ibid [180], [182]-[183].

[114] *European Communities – Conditions for the Granting of Tariff Preferences to Developing Countries*, WTO Doc WT/DS246/AB/R, AB-2004-1 (2004) [163]-[164] (Report of the Appellate Body).

[115] Michalopoulos, above n 55, 25-6.

[116] For discussion on this point see Robert Howse, 'Appellate Body Ruling Saves the GSP, at Least for Now' (2004) 8(4) *Bridges Monthly Review* 5.

[117] See, e.g. *Declaration of Barbados*, above n 27; *United Nations Millennium Declaration*, above n 28.

group to a more limited extent in their capacity as WTO observers. The group is seeking recognition of the difficulties faced by SIDS and other small, vulnerable economies in the world trading system. These issues have been raised by individual Members and in group proposals at each Ministerial Conference of the WTO since its establishment and were formally acknowledged on several occasions, but no concrete measures have yet been taken.[118]

The Doha Ministerial Declaration, which sets out the mandate for the current Doha Round of negotiations, includes the following paragraph:[119]

> 35. We agree to a work programme, under the auspices of the General Council, to examine issues relating to the trade of small economies. The objective of this work is to frame responses to the trade-related issues identified for the fuller integration of small, vulnerable economies into the multilateral trading system, and not to create a sub-category of WTO Members. The General Council shall review the work programme and make recommendations for action to the Fifth Session of the Ministerial Conference.

This work programme has been progressing in dedicated sessions of the WTO Council on Trade and Development (CTD).[120] As of November 2004, eight dedicated sessions had been completed. Several proposals have been discussed, and under the Doha Declaration mandate, recommendations were to be prepared for the Fifth Ministerial Conference, due to take place in December 2005 in Hong Kong. At this point it seems somewhat unlikely that agreement will be reached on substantive recommendations by that date, however the work programme will be included in General Council's report to the Ministerial Conference.[121] Despite the relative lack of attention that this work programme has received amidst the mass of complex negotiations ongoing in the Doha Round, its importance to the members of the small economies group cannot be underestimated. The representative of Fiji stated at one of the dedicated session meetings that its government 'would judge the success of the Doha Development Agenda largely by the extent to which it provided solutions to particular economic and administrative problems of the small developing countries which were among the most vulnerable of all WTO Members'.[122]

---

[118] See *Dominica: Statement by The Honourable Norris Charles, Minister for Trade and Marketing*, WTO Doc WT/MIN(96)/ST/127 (1996); *Saint Lucia: Statement by H.E. Mr. Edwin Laurent, Ambassador, Permanent Representative to the WTO*, WTO Doc WT/MIN(96)/ST/98; *Ministerial Declaration*, WTO Doc WTO/MIN(98)/DEC/1 (1998) [6]; *Preparations for the 1999 Ministerial Conference: Proposals for Addressing Concerns on Marginalization of Certain Small Economies*, WTO Doc WT/GC/W/361 (1999); *Preparations for the Fourth Session of the Ministerial Conference*, WTO Doc WT/GC/W/441 (2001); *Fiji: Statement by the Honourable Kaliopate Tavola on Behalf of Small Vulnerable Economies*, WTO Doc WT/MIN(03)/ST/87.
[119] *Ministerial Declaration*, WTO Doc WT/MIN(01)/DEC/1 (2001).
[120] *Work Programme on Small Economies: Framework and Procedures*, WTO Doc WT/L/447 (2002).
[121] 'CTD: Focus on S&D, Small Economies' (2004) 8(10) *Bridges Monthly Review* 8.
[122] *Note on the Meeting of 17 July 2003*, WTO Doc WT/COMTD/SE/M/5 (2003) [26].

Submissions and discussions in these dedicated sessions have raised a range of issues regarding the difficulties faced by small, vulnerable economies in the global trade regime.[123] Many of these echo the characteristics of small states described above. Of particular relevance in the context of the WTO are the following typical characteristics of small states:

- A high degree of trade openness and dependence on trade (both imports and exports);
- Reliance on a narrow range of sources of income, often including a large proportion of income from tariff revenues;
- Concentration of exports in one or a few products and a small number of markets;
- Limited opportunities for diversification because of limited resource bases and limited human resources, and disincentive to diversify because of diseconomies of scale;
- Vulnerability and lack of resilience of domestic economies to natural disasters and fluctuations in world prices of key exports;
- Relative inefficiency of domestic firms for structural reasons, such as the small size of domestic markets, inability to take advantage of economies of scale, and high transport and other costs;
- Difficulty attracting investment;
- Very small share of global trade; and
- Limited human and other resources to participate effectively in the WTO institutions and procedures.

It has been argued that some of the WTO rules have 'threatened the viability of the economic base of [small] countries and their political and social stability', and that the rules 'do not respond to the specific development and trade needs of countries with small developing economies'.[124] The precise nature of the problems identified becomes clearer upon examination of the proposals made for reform.

An initial proposal made in 2002[125] raised a number of issues and proposed solutions; some of these were later elaborated and clarified in subsequent

---

[123] See especially *Work Programme on Small Economies: Issues relating to the Trade of Small Economies (Revision)*, WTO Doc WT/COMTD/SE/W/1/Rev.1 (2002) (Communication from Barbados, Belize, Bolivia, Cuba, Dominican Republic, El Salvador, Fiji, Guatemala, Haiti, Honduras, Jamaica, Mauritius, Nicaragua, Papua New Guinea, Paraguay, Solomon Islands, Sri Lanka, Trinidad and Tobago).
[124] Ibid [8].
[125] *Work Programme on Small Economies: Concrete proposals to address certain specific concerns and problems affecting the Trade of Small Economies*, WTO Doc WT/COMTD/SE/W/3 (2002) (Communication from Barbados, Belize, Bolivia, Cuba, Dominican Republic, Guatemala, Honduras, Mauritius and Sri Lanka). Fiji and Papua New Guinea were later noted as co-sponsors of this proposal: *Report of the Committee on Trade and Development in Dedicated Session to the General Council*, WTO Doc WT/COMTD/SE/1 (2003) [7], [10].

documents.[126] The proposals can be grouped under several headings. The first is preferences and market access. As noted above, the gradual liberalization of trade and reduction of tariffs results in the erosion of tariff preferences for developing countries. The proposals emphasize that this preference erosion is a particular concern for small economies because trade preferences have been of vital importance to them. This is due to a number of factors just mentioned, such as heavy reliance on a small number of export products and export markets, and lack of competitiveness because of structural constraints. The erosion of preferences along with challenges to existing preferences in the WTO have 'compounded the vulnerability of the small economies'.[127] It is also noted that given the small economies' insignificant share of world trade, preferences for these countries' products would result in minimal distortion. The 2002 proposal suggests an agreement that 'the liberalization process shall preserve the existing margins of preference for products exported by small economies'.[128] The difficulty of achieving this is apparent, given that preference erosion may be an inevitable by-product of progressive tariff reductions, and the WTO membership is unlikely to abandon this key strategy for trade liberalization. A later proposal seems to accept this, suggesting that in view of this erosion, 'adequate alternative arrangements' should be created which would 'offset the inherent structural disadvantages of these economies', including grant and concessionary financing.[129] It also suggests that existing preferences for products of 'trade preference dependent small economies' should be 'grandfathered', which would address the issue of challenges to existing preferences.[130] In a similar vein, it is also suggested that the GATT rules regarding free trade agreements be modified to allow regional trade agreements in which small economies would receive preferential treatment on a non-reciprocal basis.[131]

---

[126] *Questions from the United States and Initial Responses in Regard to Proposals Contained in WTO Document WT/COMTD/SE/W/3*, WTO Doc WT/COMTD/SE/W/7 (2002); *World Programme on Small Economies (Further elaboration of key proposals outlined in WT/COMTD/SE/W/3)*, WTO Doc WTO/COMTD/SE/W/11 (2004) (Communication from Barbados, Fiji, Mauritius, Papua New Guinea, Solomon Islands and Trinidad and Tobago).

[127] *World Programme on Small Economies (Further elaboration of key proposals outlined in WT/COMTD/SE/W/3)*, WTO Doc WTO/COMTD/SE/W/11 (2004) [2] (Communication from Barbados, Fiji, Mauritius, Papua New Guinea, Solomon Islands and Trinidad and Tobago).

[128] *Work Programme on Small Economies: Concrete proposals to address certain specific concerns and problems affecting the Trade of Small Economies*, WTO Doc WT/COMTD/SE/W/3 (2002) [1] (Communication from Barbados, Belize, Bolivia, Cuba, Dominican Republic, Guatemala, Honduras, Mauritius and Sri Lanka).

[129] *World Programme on Small Economies (Further elaboration of key proposals outlined in WT/COMTD/SE/W/3)*, WTO Doc WTO/COMTD/SE/W/11 (2004) [5] (Communication from Barbados, Fiji, Mauritius, Papua New Guinea, Solomon Islands and Trinidad and Tobago).

[130] Ibid. 'Grandfathering' means that existing arrangements are allowed to continue notwithstanding rules with which they might be inconsistent.

[131] *Work Programme on Small Economies: Concrete proposals to address certain specific concerns and problems affecting the Trade of Small Economies*, WTO Doc WT/COMTD/SE/W/3 (2002) [2] (Communication from Barbados, Belize, Bolivia, Cuba, Dominican Republic, Guatemala, Honduras, Mauritius and Sri Lanka).

The next main issue that is raised relates to subsidies and in particular export subsidies. In general, export subsidies are prohibited under the SCM Agreement. As noted above, developing countries are provided with a transition period within which to phase out these subsidies, and low-income developing countries (with per capita GNP of less than $1000) and LDCs are exempt from the prohibition together.[132] Those small economies which are not LDCs or low-income developing countries have therefore been required to gradually eliminate export subsidies.[133] The proposals argue that these rules do not give enough flexibility to small economies, which may need to continue providing export subsidies to compensate for 'inherent cost disadvantages and resource constraints' faced by their producers.[134] It is therefore proposed that small economies receive the same exemption from the export subsidy prohibition as LDCs and low-income developing countries.

A number of specific issues and proposals relate to the constraints faced by small states in terms of administrative, human and financial capacity, and relatively high costs of implementation for those states.[135] These concerns cut across many different areas, including anti-dumping measures, subsidies and safeguards; sanitary and phytosanitary standards and technical barriers to trade; and participation in dispute settlement and negotiations. Proposals to address these concerns range from general calls for greater flexibility, longer transitional periods, and increased technical assistance and capacity building, to specific reforms. Specific requests in respect of dispute settlement include the right to compensation in the event that a small economy successfully challenges another Member's measures, regardless of the 'losing' party's subsequent compliance with its obligations,[136] and compulsory mediation in disputes involving small economies.[137]

---

[132] See above n 96 and accompanying text.

[133] Although the eight-year transition period has since passed, it is possible to apply for extensions and many developing countries have done so. SCM Agreement art 27.4.

[134] *World Programme on Small Economies (Further elaboration of key proposals outlined in WT/COMTD/SE/W/3)*, WTO Doc WTO/COMTD/SE/W/11 (2004) [8] (Communication from Barbados, Fiji, Mauritius, Papua New Guinea, Solomon Islands and Trinidad and Tobago). See also *Work Programme on Small Economies: Concrete proposals to address certain specific concerns and problems affecting the Trade of Small Economies*, WTO Doc WT/COMTD/SE/W/3 (2002) [3] (Communication from Barbados, Belize, Bolivia, Cuba, Dominican Republic, Guatemala, Honduras, Mauritius and Sri Lanka).

[135] *Work Programme on Small Economies: Concrete proposals to address certain specific concerns and problems affecting the Trade of Small Economies*, WTO Doc WT/COMTD/SE/W/3 (2002) [4] (Communication from Barbados, Belize, Bolivia, Cuba, Dominican Republic, Guatemala, Honduras, Mauritius and Sri Lanka).

[136] Under the *Understanding on Rules and Procedures Governing the Settlement of Disputes*, Annex 2 to the *Marrakesh Agreement Establishing the World Trade Organization*, opened for signature 15 April 1994, 1867 UNTS 3 (entered into force 1 January 1995) ('DSU'), compensation (in the form of the grant of trade concessions) is voluntary, to be agreed by negotiation between the parties and is only available where the 'losing' party fails to comply with the recommendations of the dispute settlement report: art 22.

[137] Under the DSU, mediation and other forms of alternative dispute settlement may be undertaken voluntarily if both parties agree: art 5.

It is also proposed that small economies with insufficient domestic capacity be permitted to designate a regional authority to carry out certain functions that are required under the WTO agreements to be performed by a competent national authority.[138]

Finally, the issue of accessions has been raised as an area of difficulty for small economies. Accession to the WTO is a complex process which must be undergone by any state wishing to become a WTO Member after its establishment. The terms of accession must be agreed between the acceding state and the existing members of the WTO. This may involve years of negotiations, and can result in acceding states having to make commitments beyond those that are strictly required by the WTO agreements themselves ('WTO-plus' commitments) or those accepted by other Members. It also means that developing countries and LDCs do not necessarily receive the benefit of SDT that founding WTO Members are entitled to; as part of the terms of accession they may be, and often are, required to waive some of these special provisions such as transitional periods or exemptions. Although the WTO is said to be a 'rules-based' system, the terms of accession largely depend on negotiating power, with existing Members having the upper hand since their disagreement can block another state's accession. Concerns have been raised about LDCs and small economies, in particular, being disadvantaged in the accession process, in terms of both the strains that the process places on their limited institutional capacities and the obligations which they accept as a condition of accession.[139] The experience of Vanuatu, whose accession has been on hold since 2001, is cited as an example of the difficulties faced by SIDS and LDCs in this context.[140] Like other acceding LDCs, Vanuatu (and more recently Samoa) faced demands for WTO-plus commitments that were beyond those made by other similarly-situated Members and arguably inappropriate to their development needs.[141]

The difficulties of acceding LDCs have received some attention, although attempts to address them appear not to have much practical effect.[142] The small economies proposal points out that similar challenges are faced by these states, and these are yet to be addressed. It notes that small economies are unable to participate effectively in accession negotiations and suggests that acceding small economies 'should not be required to accept more obligations than small

---

[138] For example, making determinations in anti-dumping or countervailing measures investigations, or the implementation of provisions under the TBT Agreement, above n 94.

[139] Roman Grynberg and Roy Mickey Joy, 'The Accession of Vanuatu to the WTO: Lessons for the Multilateral Trading System' (2000) 34(6) *Journal of World Trade* 159; Ratnakar Adhikari and Navin Dahal, 'LDC Accession to the WTO – Learning from Nepal, Cambodia and Vanuatu' (2004) 8(3) *Bridges Monthly Review* 3; Jane Kelsey, 'Acceding Countries as Pawns in a Power Play: a case study of the Pacific Islands' (Paper presented at the WTO Public Symposium 'Multilateralism at a Crossroads', Geneva, 27 May 2004), available online at Action, Research and Education Network of Aotearoa <http://www.arena.org.nz/pacwto.htm> at 15 December 2004.

[140] Ibid. Vanuatu is both a SIDS and an LDC.

[141] Ibid.

[142] Adhikari and Dahal, above n 139, 4.

economies that are founder Members of WTO, nor obligations that founder Members have not themselves undertaken'.[143] This would bring the treatment of small economies into line with that recommended for LDCs in WTO General Council Guidelines, which exhort Members to 'exercise restraint in seeking concessions and commitments' from LDCs, provide that SDT 'shall be applicable to all acceding LDCs' and require transitional periods and assistance to be given to acceding LDCs for the implementation of their obligations.[144] However, acceding LDCs have been unable to insist on compliance with these guidelines in accession negotiations and they appear not to have been followed.[145]

Responses to the above proposals by developed countries and other developing countries have been mixed. As might be expected, specific requests for assistance and administrative changes have tended to be more favourably received than requests for exemptions or other forms of special treatment.[146] A recurring theme in the discussions is the tension between providing for appropriate responses to the difficulties of small economies, on the one hand, and avoiding the creation of a sub-category of developing states, on the other. The work programme mandate in the Doha Ministerial Declaration explicitly states that the objective of the work programme is *not* to create a sub-category of WTO Members. At a most recent meeting of the dedicated session, the Chair remarked on the apparent conflict in this mandate which 'forbids the creation of a new sub-category while calling for action on the needs of small economies'.[147] Others have suggested that a 'characteristic-specific' approach which links particular needs and responses may be an alternative to a 'sub-category' approach.[148]

This is reinforced by the fact that as discussions progress, the boundaries have become blurred between small economies and other vulnerable states, and between the dedicated sessions of the small economies work programme and other parts of the Doha Round negotiations. For example, landlocked developing countries – of whom many, but not all, are also small economies – have claimed that they are subject to some of the same disadvantages as small economies, and therefore should be included within the scope of the work programme.[149] Other

---

[143] *Work Programme on Small Economies: Concrete proposals to address certain specific concerns and problems affecting the Trade of Small Economies*, WTO Doc WT/COMTD/SE/W/3 (2002) [7] (Communication from Barbados, Belize, Bolivia, Cuba, Dominican Republic, Guatemala, Honduras, Mauritius and Sri Lanka).

[144] *Accession of Least-Developed Countries*, WTO Doc WT/L/508 (2003) (General Council, Decision of 10 December 2002).

[145] Adhikari and Dahal, above n 139, 4.

[146] See, e.g. *Questions from the United States and Initial Responses in Regard to Proposals Contained in WTO Document WT/COMTD/SE/W/3*, WTO Doc WT/COMTD/SE/W/7 (2002).

[147] 'CTD: Focus on S&D, Small Economies', above n 121, 8.

[148] Ibid.

[149] See, e.g. *Note on the Meeting of 25 April 2002*, WTO Doc WT/COMTD/SE/M/1 (2002) [8]; *Communique of the Fifth Annual Ministerial Meeting of Landlocked Developing Countries (LLDCs)*, WTO Doc WT/COMTD/SE/2 (2004). The affinities between LDCs, SIDS and landlocked developing countries have been recognized, for example by the United Nations which maintains a single High Representative for these three sub-groups.

Members which do not fit into either of these categories have argued that they face some of the same specific difficulties such as high transport costs,[150] and it has been suggested that some issues are common to many developing countries.[151] A 'characteristic-specific' rather than a 'sub-category' approach thus has some appeal, but the complexity of this approach is daunting.

At the same time, it is increasingly clear that there is substantial overlap between the discussion of some topics in the dedicated sessions of the work programme and other ongoing DDA negotiations. Members are apparently split over whether it is better to deal with a full range of issues in the dedicated sessions or to limit this discussion only to issues that are not part of negotiations elsewhere. There is a trade-off between the focused attention to the particular needs of small economies that is possible in the dedicated sessions and the need to integrate or 'mainstream' the issues raised there into the negotiations on relevant topics. Small economies themselves have raised issues particular to their circumstances outside the dedicated sessions, for example in relation to services, agriculture and fisheries.[152] Clearly the concerns of small developing states are not limited to those discussed in the dedicated sessions proposals, but reach into many different aspects of the WTO regime.

This suggests that although small states are disproportionately affected by various aspects of the WTO regime, some of the difficulties that they face are the result of systemic features of the regime that may not be adequately addressed by piecemeal reforms to address special needs. For example, the difficulties with accessions, which have great significance for the many FICs and other SIDS that are not yet Members, can arguably only be addressed by fundamental changes to the accessions process, not by any amount of pleading for 'restraint' in certain cases.[153] Another example is the effectiveness of dispute settlement for small WTO members, which cannot credibly threaten significant retaliation against a larger

---

[150] See, e.g. *Note on the Meeting of 17 October 2003*, WTO Doc WT/COMTD/SE/M/6 (2003) [25] (statement by the representative of Chile).

[151] See, e.g. *Note on the Meeting of 25 April 2002*, WTO Doc WT/COMTD/SE/M/1 (2002) [14].

[152] *WTO Negotiations on Agriculture: Proposals by Small Island Developing States (SIDS)*, WTO Doc G/AG/NG/W/97 (2000) (Communication from Dominica, Jamaica, Mauritius, St Kitts and Nevis, St Lucia, St Vincent and the Grenadines, and Trinidad and Tobago); *The GATS and the Annex on Financial Services: International Regulations and Financial Services (Revision)*, WTO Doc S/FIN/W/29/Rev.1 (2003) (Communication from Antigua and Barbuda, Belize, Fiji Islands, Guyana, Papua New Guinea, the Maldives, Solomon Islands and St Kitts and Nevis); *Fisheries Subsidies*, WTO Doc TN/RL/W/136 (2003) (Communication from Antigua and Barbuda, Belize, Fiji, Guyana, the Maldives, Papua New Guinea, Solomon Islands, St Kitts and Nevis).

[153] This is the main thesis of Grynberg and Joy, above n 139. They argue (at 172) that the accession process is 'inherently flawed' by the imbalance of power between existing and acceding Members that results from the way the process is designed, 'rather than simply by the size disparity between LDCs and small vulnerable States like Vanuatu on the one hand and large WTO members such as the United States, the EU and Japan on the other'.

economy to pressure it into compliance with a panel or Appellate Body decision.[154] The prospects for systemic reforms are not encouraging,[155] but they are sufficiently important that further efforts may be worthwhile.

In other respects, the difficulties faced by SIDS and other small economies might be addressed by targeted provisions such as longer transition periods, partial exemptions, preferences and technical assistance. There are strong arguments in favour of such special treatment. They would result in only minimal distortion of global markets and minimal impacts on other members, given small economies' tiny share of world trade.[156] It is undisputed that small (especially small island) economies face serious challenges in international trade due to their inherent characteristics, to the extent that some believe their producers can never be competitive in a free trade environment.[157] The argument for special accommodation is therefore compelling.

The question remains, though: what kinds of special treatment are likely to be beneficial? As we have seen, preferences have been important to some countries but have not been very effective overall, and their value is steadily declining. Exemptions from or reductions in liberalization commitments are another possibility, but they are widely believed to be counterproductive for developing countries. Exemptions from other kinds of commitments might be more promising, for example in the areas of intellectual property protection or customs valuation which are costly and of questionable benefit to the countries themselves.[158] Financial and technical assistance are also likely to be useful and important.[159] Unfortunately, some commentators note that the willingness of developed country Members to agree to proposals for SDT tend to depend more on the political acceptability of the proposed measures than their merit in development terms. As a result, it has been suggested that the most desirable outcomes for small developing countries are the least feasible, and the least desirable are the most feasible.[160]

---

[154] This issue has been highlighted in the recent dispute between Antigua and Barbuda and the United States over US restrictions on internet gambling: *United States – Measures Affecting the Cross-border Supply of Gambling and Betting Services*, WTO Doc WT/DS285/R (2004) (Report of the Panel). Although Antigua and Barbuda won a favourable decision at the panel stage, there is very little it can do to pressure the United States to comply with the ruling (assuming it is upheld on appeal). See 'US-Antigua Gambling Dispute Raises Systemic Issues' (2004) 8(40) *Bridges Weekly Trade News Digest*.

[155] Grynberg and Joy, above n 139, 173.

[156] According to one analysis, a list of 62 small, low-income countries collectively amount to only about 1.1 per cent of total world trade: Aaditya Mattoo and Arvind Subramanian, 'The WTO and the poorest countries: the stark reality' (2004) 3 *World Trade Review* 385.

[157] Winters and Martins, above n 33. The severity of their disadvantages and the extent to which they can be overcome is more contentious: see, e.g. Satish Chand, 'Trade gains for small island economies' (2004) 3 *World Trade Review* 409; Christopher Findlay, 'Policy reform in small "remote economies"' (2004) 3 *World Trade Review* 422.

[158] Mattoo and Subramanian, above n 156, 403.

[159] Ibid 404-405.

[160] Ibid 405. See also Michalopoulos, above n 55, 26.

Assuming that agreement could be reached on useful forms of differentiated SDT for small economies, there is also the added complication that at least some of the measures might also suit the needs of other developing countries with particular characteristics. The principle enunciated by the Appellate Body in the *EC – Tariff Preferences* decision that favourable treatment should be available to all similarly situated developing countries seems reasonable. This suggests that a subcategory approach may need to be abandoned in favour of a more nuanced system where specific forms of SDT are available to developing countries sharing relevant characteristics.[161] The major obstacle here is the added complexity of the provisions that might be required for such a tailored response – with their associated costs and potential for political conflicts – in an already complex system. Perhaps, though, these difficulties are not insurmountable and it would be preferable to accept and share the cost of added complexity rather than leave the burden resting on states least able to bear it. The proposals by small economies have helped to draw attention to the flexibility that might be required if we are to take seriously the objective of tailoring trade rules to diverse states' circumstances and development needs.

Regional trade agreements in the Pacific

Despite the central importance of the WTO, regional trade agreements (RTAs)[162] have continued to flourish, their proliferation increasing rather than declining since the establishment of the WTO.[163] RTAs continue to be popular for a number of reasons. Bilateral or regional trade agreements have an important role in solidifying political relationships with nearby states. Given the slow and difficult nature of multilateral negotiations, RTAs often provide faster and easier routes to trade liberalization with one's major trading partners. The pace of RTA negotiations worldwide has accelerated recently, in part due to frustrations with WTO negotiations. RTAs thus are an increasingly important part in many states' trade relationships. RTAs are also said to be important for developing countries, because they may promise deeper and more secure trade preferences.[164] However, far from being an alternative to the WTO, they coexist alongside this multilateral regime, and are affected by it. The GATT and GATS set out criteria that must be met by RTAs in order that these agreements not be considered breaches of

---

[161] Compare the proposal of Keck and Low for an 'implicit threshold approach' to SDT in which access to SDT on a provision-specific basis would be based on measurable criteria: above n 75, 22ff. See also Bernard Hoekman, Constantine Michalopoulos and L Alan Winters, 'More Favourable and Differential Treatment of Developing Countries: Towards a New Approach in the WTO' (Working Paper 3107, World Bank, 2003) 18-20.
[162] The WTO uses the term 'regional trade agreement' to refer to any trade agreement between two or more states, regardless of whether they are located in the same geographical region. These agreements are also referred to by other names such as free trade agreements, preferential trade agreements or economic partnership agreements.
[163] World Trade Organization, 'Regional Trade Agreements: Facts and Figures', <http://www.wto.org/english/tratop_e/region_e/regfac_e.htm> at 15 December 2004.
[164] Michalopoulos, above n 55, 24.

Members' most-favoured nation treatment obligations. As long as at least one of the parties to an RTA is a WTO Member, these criteria will affect the shape of the agreement. This means that even the position of non-WTO Members will be indirectly, but quite significantly, affected by WTO obligations. This section looks at the RTAs to which the FICs are or might become parties, within this broader context. It examines the extent to which the emerging framework of regional integration might address the development needs of SIDS in this part of the world.

Overview of relevant agreements

As in other regions of the world, the countries of the South Pacific are part of a growing network of RTAs. The region is home to one of the oldest and most comprehensive bilateral trade agreements, the Australia/New Zealand Closer Economic Relations Trade Agreement (CER Agreement).[165] This agreement and its associated protocols and other instruments establish free trade in goods and most services between Australia and New Zealand, mutual recognition for most goods and other forms of harmonization and cooperation. The stated aim of the two countries is to work toward a single economic market.[166] Each of them has also entered into bilateral agreements with other countries, including Singapore and Thailand, and in 2005 they will begin negotiating a free trade agreement with the ASEAN Free Trade Area.[167] As members of Asia-Pacific Economic Cooperation (APEC), Australia and New Zealand (along with Papua New Guinea, the only FIC member of APEC[168]) have also committed to the 'Bogor Goals', which include the establishment of a free trade area in the Asia-Pacific region by 2010 for developed members and 2020 including developing economies.[169]

A free trade area has existed between Australia and Papua New Guinea since 1977.[170] A preferential trade agreement is also in place among the four states of the

---

[165] *Australia New Zealand Closer Economic Relations Trade Agreement*, opened for signature 28 March 1983, [1983] ATS 2 (entered into force 1 January 1983).
[166] 'Australia and New Zealand Closer Economic Relations (CER) Ministerial Communique' (Joint Communique, 11 December 2004).
[167] 'Joint Declaration of the Leaders at the ASEAN-Australia and New Zealand Commemorative Summit' (30 November 2004). ASEAN (the Association of Southeast Asian Nations) includes Brunei Darussalam, Cambodia, Indonesia, Laos, Malaysia, Myanmar, Philippines, Singapore, Thailand and Vietnam.
[168] The Pacific Islands Forum Secretariat has observer status in APEC.
[169] 'APEC Economic Leaders' Declaration of Common Resolve' (Leaders' Declaration, 15 November 1994). The APEC Leaders restated their commitment to these goals in the most recent declaration from November 2004: '12th APEC Economic Leaders' Meeting Santiago Declaration: One Community, Our Future' (Leaders' Declaration, 20–21 November 2004).
[170] *Agreement on Trade and Commercial Relations between the Government of Australia and the Government of Papua New Guinea*, opened for signature 6 November 1976, [1977] ATS 7 (entered into force 1 February 1977) ('PACTRA'); *Agreement on Trade and Commercial Relations between the Government of Australia and the Government of Papua New Guinea*, opened for signature 21 February 1991, [1991] ATS 37 (entered into force 20 September 1991) ('PACTRA II').

'Melanesian Spearhead Group' (MSG): Papua New Guinea, Solomon Islands, Vanuatu and Fiji. The MSG was formed in the late 1980s primarily as a political group, but more recently evolved into the 'Pacific islands' first serious experiment in freeing-up trade and investment among themselves'.[171] The agreement provides for duty-free trade in a range of goods between the MSG member states. Although this does not account for a significant proportion of members' trade and some consider the agreement to be a failure,[172] it represents an important experiment in trade liberalization for the region.[173]

The FICs have enjoyed preferential market access in Australia, New Zealand and other trading partners under several trade agreements. The South Pacific Regional Trade and Economic Cooperation Agreement (SPARTECA),[174] in force since 1981, provides for non-reciprocal duty free access to New Zealand and Australian markets for products from FICs. Under this agreement, almost all exports from these countries enter New Zealand and Australia duty free and without quantitative restrictions.[175] As members of the African, Caribbean and Pacific (ACP) group, many of the FICs have been eligible for preferential market access in the EU under the Lomé Conventions,[176] now succeeded by the Cotonou Agreement[177] (to be discussed below). Under the Compacts of Free Association with the United States, most products from the Marshall Islands, the Federated States of Micronesia and Palau may be imported duty free into the United States.[178] As developing and least-developed countries, FICs have also been beneficiaries of the Generalized System of Preferences and preference arrangements of various countries.

---

[171] Hughes, above n 12, 30. Fiji was not an original member but joined in 1996 following the establishment of the trade agreement: Crocombe, above n 23, 597.

[172] Jane Kelsey, *Big Brothers Behaving Badly: The Implications for the Pacific Islands of the Pacific Agreement on Closer Economic Relations (PACER)* (Interim Report, 2004) Action, Research and Education Network of Aotearoa <http://www.arena.org.nz/bigbully.pdf> at 15 December 2004, 12. See also World Bank, *Embarking on a Global Voyage: Trade Liberalization and Complementary Reforms in the Pacific*, Report No. 24417-EAP (2002), 12-13.

[173] Hughes, above n 12, 30.

[174] *South Pacific Regional Trade and Economic Cooperation Agreement*, opened for signature 14 July 1980, [1982] ATS 31 (entered into force 1 January 1981) ('SPARTECA'), as amended. As between Papua New Guinea and Australia, PACTRA rather than SPARTECA applies: *Exchange of Notes constituting an Agreement on the continued application of the Agreement on Trade and Commercial Relations between Australia and Papua New Guinea of 6 November 1976*, signed 17 February 1982 and 17 March 1982, [1982] ATS 6 (entered into force 17 March 1982).

[175] World Bank, above n 172, 28.

[176] Most recently *Fourth ACP-EEC Convention of Lomé*, opened for signature 15 December 1989 (1990) 29 ILM 783.

[177] *Partnership Agreement Between the Members of the African, Caribbean and Pacific Group of States of the one part, and the European Community and its Member States, of the other part*, signed 23 June 2000 [2000] OJ L 317/3 (entered into force 1 April 2003) ('Cotonou Agreement').

[178] *Compact of Free Association*, 48 USC §§ 1901, 1931 (2003).

These non-reciprocal arrangements – both unilateral preferences and more stable agreements providing for preferential treatment – are illustrative of the pre-Uruguay Round approach to trade and development. As described above, this approach, reflected in the Enabling Clause and Part IV of the GATT, focused on non-reciprocal trade preferences for developing countries as a means of encouraging export-led growth. The subsequent shift toward reciprocal commitments and the full integration of developing countries into the world trading regime has more recently begun to make itself felt in the region. At the same time, tariff preferences have diminished in value and importance as their margins are eroded by liberalization. In addition, recent developments reflect renewed concern about compliance with WTO disciplines on RTAs. Rules governing RTAs have been contained in the GATT since its inception, but have taken on greater importance as the number and significance of RTAs increases and more effective dispute settlement (post-Uruguay Round) makes them more vulnerable to challenge by third countries.

Preferential treatment among parties to an RTA would, in principle, violate the obligation of MFN treatment in the GATT, which requires equally favourable treatment to be given to the like products of all parties. However, in recognition of the potential benefits of RTAs, article XXIV of the GATT allows them to coexist with the multilateral regime provided they meet certain conditions. The first main condition is that upon the formation of a customs union or free trade area, the barriers to trade for third countries (i.e. those that are not part of the customs union or free trade area) must not be higher than before its formation.[179] This is known as the 'external trade' requirement. The second main condition, known as the 'internal trade' requirement, is that duties and other restrictions on 'substantially all trade' among the parties to the RTA must be eliminated.[180] The meaning of 'substantially all trade' has not been precisely defined, but coverage of a comprehensive range of sectors and a substantial proportion of trade is likely required. In summary, then, in order for an RTA's parties to be protected from allegations of MFN violations under the GATT, the RTA must comprehensively eliminate trade barriers among its parties and not result in higher barriers for third parties.

---

[179] GATT art XXIV:5. In the case of a customs union, the rule is that duties and other regulations must not 'on the whole' be higher than their 'general incidence' prior to its formation: art XXIV:5(a). For free trade areas, the rule is stated in more absolute terms: art XXIV:5(b). Greater flexibility is afforded to customs unions because a customs union will have common external tariffs and other restrictions (as well as liberalising trade within the union, as in a free trade area), and achieving this consistency means that some members of the union may have higher external barriers following the formation of the union. This is permitted provided that the overall level of barriers for the customs union as a whole will not be greater.

[180] GATT art XXIV:8. A similar but somewhat more relaxed internal trade requirement is found in the GATS, which allows liberalization of trade in services among parties to an RTA if the agreement has 'substantial sectoral coverage' and provides for 'the absence or elimination of substantially all discrimination ... between or among the parties' in the covered sectors: GATS art V:1. A footnote to this article states that 'substantial sectoral coverage' is 'understood in terms of number of sectors, volume of trade affected and modes of supply' and that 'agreements should not provide for the *a priori* exclusion of any mode of supply'.

All RTAs are to be notified to the WTO. The Committee on Regional Trade Agreements is responsible for supervising their consistency with GATT article XXIV. In practice, the supervision process has not had much effect, but there is also the possibility of RTAs being challenged in dispute settlement proceedings. This has been important in the context of the EU's arrangements with the ACP countries, under the Lomé and now Cotonou agreements. These agreements do not fit the GATT definition of an RTA because they do not provide for elimination of restrictions on substantially all trade; rather they (like SPARTECA within the Pacific region) provide for preferential access to EU markets, but not reciprocal or necessarily comprehensive liberalization. They were also supplemented by protocols to provide market access for certain key commodities, like bananas and sugar. Regional trade agreements among developing country parties are covered by the Enabling Clause[181] and therefore need not comply with the GATT article XXIV requirements. For example, the MSG trade agreement was notified to the WTO under the Enabling Clause, not GATT article XXIV.[182] However, this does not apply in the case of an RTA that includes both developed and developing country parties. Historically these have been granted waivers by the GATT contracting parties and, more recently, by the WTO members. However, the most recent waiver for the Cotonou Agreement, granted in 2001, will only last until 31 December 2007.[183] Moreover, these waivers have not protected certain aspects of the scheme from challenges by other WTO members who are excluded from their benefits. A long and complex dispute over the EU scheme for bananas pitted the EU and the ACP countries receiving preferential market access, on the one hand, against other developing countries excluded from preferences, backed by the United States (whose multinationals have substantial interests in non-ACP banana production), on the other. Following a series of decisions finding that the EU was in violation of its WTO obligations, the EU was forced to modify its bananas regime and to seek a further waiver for a transitional period.[184] Although these developments directly affected the African and Caribbean ACP countries, it also had wider implications. More recently, the EU's sugar regime, one part of which involves preferential arrangements for ACP sugar, has been successfully challenged in the WTO, with important implications for ACP countries and in particular Fiji, as a major Pacific island producer of sugar.[185] As we saw above, the

---

[181] Above n 49, [2(c)].

[182] *Melanesian Spearhead Group Trade Agreement*, WTO Doc WT/COMTD/N/9 (1999) (Notification from Papua New Guinea).

[183] *European Communities – The ACP-EU Partnership Agreement*, WTO Doc WT/MIN(01)/15 (2001) (Decision of 14 November 2001).

[184] *European Communities – Transitional Regime for the EC Autonomous Tariff Rate Quotas on Imports of Bananas*, WTO Doc WT/MIN(01)/16 (2001) (Decision of 14 November 2001).

[185] *European Communities – Export Subsidies on Sugar*, WTO Doc WT/DS265/R (2004) (Report of the Panel). The complaint was brought by Australia, Brazil and Thailand. Fiji and other ACP countries were third parties. The EC has announced that it will appeal this decision.

EU's scheme of unilateral GSP preferences was also challenged in respect of its differentiation between subcategories of developing countries.[186]

These disputes have showed that WTO members are willing to challenge preferential arrangements from which they are excluded, and the more effective procedures for dispute resolution put in place in the Uruguay Round mean that these challenges have more 'teeth' than previously. The Bananas dispute had resulted in $200 million worth of trade sanctions by the US against the EU,[187] providing a sharp incentive to the EU to ensure the WTO-compatibility of its preferential trade arrangements for ACP countries. This environment, combined with the shift in thinking about trade and development, away from non-reciprocal preferences toward full integration of developing countries on a reciprocal basis, has led to major changes in trade arrangements involving developing countries. The South Pacific is no exception to this trend.

A new generation of agreements has recently been concluded that have the potential to significantly change the trading environment for FICs. The EU-ACP relationship is now governed by the Cotonou Agreement, which replaces the Lomé Conventions and is intended to establish new WTO-compliant arrangements. Existing preferences under the Lomé regime will remain in place during a transitional period, ending in 2007.[188] During this period, new 'Economic Partnership Agreements' (EPAs) will be negotiated between the EU and regional groupings of ACP countries. Unlike previous arrangements, these will be reciprocal free trade agreements to liberalize trade in both directions. The Pacific ACP group includes all of the FICs, even those that were not previously party to the Lomé Conventions.[189]

Within the region, the Pacific Island Countries Trade Agreement (PICTA),[190] concluded in 2001, provides for the gradual establishment of a free trade area among the FICs. It is open only to FICs, not to Australia or New Zealand. The Cook Islands, Fiji, Kiribati, Nauru, Niue, Papua New Guinea, Samoa, Solomon Islands and Tonga are presently parties to PICTA,[191] and the agreement came into force in April 2003. This agreement is often referred to as a 'stepping stone'

---

[186] *European Communities – Conditions for the Granting of Tariff Preferences to Developing Countries*, WTO Doc WT/DS246/AB/R, AB-2004-1 (2004) (Report of the Appellate Body).

[187] 'Dispute Settlement Update: Bananas; US-EC Steel' (2001) 43(5) *Bridges Weekly Trade News Digest*, <http://www.ictsd.org/weekly/01-12-20/story2.htm> at 29 December 2004.

[188] The WTO waiver, above n 184, is designed to cover this transitional period.

[189] Note that this doesn't necessarily mean all of these countries need be party to the eventual EPA. As in other regions, there are questions about the extent to which all members of the regional group will share the same interests in the EPA negotiations. Members that are LDCs will continue to benefit from unilateral preferences under the EBA scheme (see above n 90) and may consider that they have little more to gain from an EPA.

[190] *Pacific Islands Countries Trade Agreement*, opened for signature 18 August 2001 (entered into force 13 April 2003) ('PICTA').

[191] Vanuatu has passed ratification legislation for PICTA but this legislation was not yet commenced at the time of writing: *Pacific Island Countries Trade Agreement (PICTA) Act* (Vanuatu) No. 6 of 2003.

toward the liberalization and integration of FICs. A separate agreement including Australia and New Zealand was negotiated alongside PICTA. The Pacific Agreement on Closer Economic Relations (PACER)[192] is a framework agreement providing for trade negotiations in the region. The current parties to PICTA, along with Australia and New Zealand, are also parties to PACER.[193] The latter agreement has been in force since October 2002. It does not itself establish a free trade area but sets out obligations to negotiate in certain circumstances: the parties will enter into negotiations for reciprocal free trade arrangements within eight years of the agreement coming into force or earlier as agreed,[194] and if any of the FIC parties, or the parties to PICTA jointly, enter into negotiations for a free trade agreement with a non-Forum country, they will undertake consultations with Australia and New Zealand 'with a view to the commencement of free trade arrangements'.[195] The most likely trigger for this obligation to consult with Australia and New Zealand is the negotiations with the EU under Cotonou. Therefore, although an eventual Cotonou EPA itself may not have a large impact on FICs, given the relatively low volume of their imports from Europe,[196] the EPA negotiations will have important implications. For the Compact countries (Federated States of Micronesia, Republic of the Marshall Islands and Palau), a similar obligation to provide equally favourable treatment to the United States is triggered when any of them agrees to lower its barriers to another developed country.[197] The FICs are now in a position of interlocking obligations, such that once the first free trade agreement including a developed country party is negotiated, obligations to other developed country trading partners will be triggered.

The conclusion of PACER and PICTA and the evolution of the FICs' relationship with the EU under the Cotonou Agreement represent significant changes for the region. The next section will take a closer look at these changes within the global context and at the extent to which they respond to the needs and concerns of SIDS as articulated in the multilateral context.

Special and differential treatment in regional trade agreements

As noted above, participation in RTAs is attractive from the point of view of developing countries because these may offer more stable and secure preferences than the unilateral preference arrangements of developed countries. They also promise deeper integration among a smaller group of trading partners who might

---

[192] *Pacific Agreement on Closer Economic Relations*, opened for signature 18 August 2001, [2004] ATS 10 (entered into force 3 October 2002) ('PACER').
[193] Again, Vanuatu has passed ratification legislation but this legislation was not yet commenced at the time of writing: *Pacific Agreement on Closer Economic Relations (PACER) Act* (Vanuatu) No. 5 of 2003.
[194] PACER art 5.
[195] Ibid art 6 (3), 6(4).
[196] Wadan Narsey, 'PICTA, PACER and EPAs: Where are We Going? Tales of Fags, Booze and Rugby' (Working Paper No. 6/2004, Pacific Institute of Advanced Studies in Development and Governance, Employment and Labour Market Studies Program, 2004) 16.
[197] See World Bank, above n 172, 23.

be expected to be more understanding of one another's particular needs. If one accepts the prevailing wisdom that liberalization by developing countries is beneficial for their development but requires a period of adjustment, RTAs represent an important opportunity to move toward liberalization in a gradual way – a view that is reflected in the 'stepping stone' approach to PACER and PICTA. For SIDS, in particular, RTAs may provide ways of overcoming some of their inherent disadvantages. The formation of a larger market by establishing a free trade area among a number of small states potentially allows greater economies of scale, competition and attractiveness to investors. Regional integration may also make it easier for small states to be heard on the international scene, pooling their resources and political influence in negotiations with other trading partners. In theory, at least, regional integration sounds like a promising strategy for SIDS, particularly if the multilateral regime seems unresponsive to their needs. The present reality is somewhat more complex, however.

A primary concern is the extent to which regional arrangements allow for SDT and for differentiation among developing country members in order to provide treatment appropriate to each party's needs. PACER and the Cotonou Agreement both include a commitment to SDT in the eventual RTAs to be negotiated under these agreements. Any trade agreement negotiated under PACER is to 'recognise the differences in development status of the Parties by the inclusion of appropriate measures providing for special and differential treatment of developing countries'.[198] The Cotonou Agreement in several places reaffirms the parties' commitment to SDT[199] and provides that negotiations for the EPAs 'shall take account of the level of development and the socio-economic impact of trade measures on ACP countries'.[200]

Special and differential treatment in RTAs can manifest itself in different ways. First, the division of the Forum members' trade agreements into PICTA and PACER, rather than moving directly to a single free trade area including all Forum members, in effect provides differentiated treatment to the FICs as a group. The FICs that are parties to PICTA will liberalize trade among themselves first before including Australia and New Zealand. Most imports into FICs are from Australia and New Zealand, and the amount of trade among the FICs is relatively small.[201] This means that the impact on FICs will be modest at first, increasing gradually as trade barriers are reduced among them and then more rapidly when Australia and New Zealand join the group. A built-in transition period is thus provided for, during which FICs can adjust to the loss of tariff revenue and increased competition with their domestic products. The next step is a free trade area including Australia and New Zealand, which will have a larger impact. Then, once free trade within the whole region is established, the stated goal is to move toward

---

[198] PACER art 7(c).
[199] Cotonou Agreement arts 34(4), 35(3).
[200] Ibid art 37(7).
[201] World Bank, above n 172, 8 (trade among the PICTA countries amounts to only 4 per cent of their total trade).

full integration with the global trading regime.[202] Similarly, the Cotonou Agreement between the ACP countries and the EU contemplates that groups of ACP countries will move toward regional integration as a first step, then that these will enter into agreements with the EU, and finally that they will achieve full integration with the global economy.[203] This 'stepping stone' approach could be described as analogous to the adjustment model of SDT in the WTO, allowing longer transitional periods to developing countries for the adjustment that will be necessary to cope with trade liberalization. Full integration into the global economy is the eventual goal, but is to take place gradually for these states in recognition of their more limited capacity for adjustment.

PACER, the Cotonou Agreement and the Compacts of Free Association also provide for assistance to be granted by the developed country parties. Article 11 of PACER provides that a programme of work for financial and technical assistance, including trade facilitation and promotion, capacity building and structural adjustment, will be developed. It states that the parties recognize the need for 'significant additional resources' for this programme of work and that it 'shall be supported by an adequate level of funding' by Australia and New Zealand and other interested donors. A programme of trade facilitation is also provided for (in article 9 and Annex I). These provisions are reminiscent of technical assistance SDT in the WTO agreements, and similarly reflect an obligation of parties who are in a position to offer assistance to help developing country parties implement their obligations and obtain greater benefit from trade liberalization. In addition, the Cotonou Agreement and Compacts of Free Association contain more general provisions on development and financial assistance. In these agreements, trade liberalization is one part of a larger framework for economic cooperation. Although PACER has similar goals – to promote sustainable development and eliminate poverty in the region – it deals only with trade as a presumed driver of development, leaving other forms of development assistance to separate ad hoc arrangements.

The regional agreements therefore contemplate SDT for FICs as a group by setting out a framework for gradual integration, establishing the principle of SDT for the trade agreements to be negotiated, and providing for various types and amounts of assistance by developed country trading partners. The existing agreements also contain another layer of differentiation in the form of special provisions for LDC and SIS parties. The SIS (Small Island States), it will be recalled, are the smallest of this group of small states, and include the Cook Islands, Kiribati, Nauru, Niue, Republic of the Marshall Islands and Tuvalu. Two of these, Kiribati and Tuvalu, are also LDCs, as are Samoa, Solomon Islands and Vanuatu. This means that of the nine FICs that are parties to PACER and PICTA, six are

---

[202] PACER art 3(2).
[203] Cotonou Agreement arts 1, 34(1). These state that the objective of the agreement and its economic and trade cooperation framework is the 'gradual integration of ACP [countries] into the world economy'. The APEC Bogor Goals also reflect a two-stage strategy, in this instance providing for liberalization among developed countries first, followed by developing countries.

either SIS or LDC parties (or both); of the fourteen FICs that are parties to the Cotonou Agreement and part of the Pacific Group of ACP states, nine belong to the SIS and/or LDC categories. As noted above, there is evidence to suggest that the very smallest states (which would include the Pacific SIS) face particularly intense, and to some extent insurmountable, challenges in international trade.[204] In principle, then, special treatment for these countries is justified.

All three of these agreements contain provisions allowing special treatment for LDC and SIS parties. PICTA provides that in the establishment of the free trade area, 'Least Developed Countries and Small Island States may be integrated in accordance with different structures and by different time frames than other Parties'.[205] They have a different schedule of reduced import duties which allows higher rates.[206] The LDC and SIS parties must be represented and their particular constraints considered in the context of rules of origin,[207] and they are permitted to maintain higher tariffs to protect developing industries for a longer period.[208] PACER also provides, in language identical to PICTA, that LDC and SIS parties may be integrated by different structures and time frames.[209] Article 7(d) explicitly allows SDT for LDC and SIS parties as an exception to the requirement that any new trade arrangement between FICs and Australia and New Zealand must not discriminate between FIC parties. Trade facilitation is to be designed to take account of the 'special needs and resource and capacity constraints of Least Developed Countries and Small Island States'.[210] The Cotonou Agreement provides for special treatment for least-developed, landlocked and island ACP states.[211] Differentiation is among the fundamental principles of the agreement and the 'vulnerability of landlocked and island countries shall be taken into account'.[212] Article 35(3) specifically states that this vulnerability is to be taken into account in economic and trade cooperation.

Differentiation between developing countries is therefore established as a guiding principle of these framework agreements, in addition to SDT for developing country parties generally. The full extent of special treatment to be provided will only be apparent in the RTAs that are to be negotiated within the framework: an eventual Forum-wide free trade agreement under PACER and the EPA between the EU and Pacific ACP states. However, both agreements explicitly contemplate differentiation and PACER specifically provides for SDT for LDC and SIS parties to a free trade agreement. This is in contrast to the multilateral regime, which, as we have seen, has resisted recognizing any subcategories of developing countries other than LDCs.

---

[204] See, e.g. Winters and Martins, above n 33, 376.
[205] PICTA art 3(1).
[206] Narsey, above n 196, 3.
[207] PICTA arts 5(3), 5(6)(m).
[208] Ibid art 14(3).
[209] PACER art 3(6).
[210] Ibid art 9(4).
[211] Cotonou Agreement arts 85-90.
[212] Ibid art 2.

Two main questions arise from this. First, is the differentiated treatment contemplated by these agreements in compliance with the WTO rules on RTAs? PACER and the Cotonou Agreement are not themselves RTAs, but they provide for the negotiation of RTAs that are intended, by the terms of both agreements, to be WTO-compliant.[213] Second, assuming that the current approach with its two layers of differentiation is permissible, is it likely to be beneficial for FICs, including for the smallest among them?

As explained above, the GATT provisions require an RTA to eliminate restrictions on substantially all trade among the parties. This has been thought to mean that agreements that only partially liberalize trade – in particular that provide for non-reciprocal liberalization – may not meet this condition. Arrangements like the Lomé Conventions between developed and developing country parties, where the developing country parties did not eliminate their trade barriers, were vulnerable to challenge for this reason. It would seem that differentiation among developing countries, such that some of them – here SIS parties – might have lesser obligations, might run into the same difficulties.[214] The lack of clarity on this point and the implications for RTAs involving developing countries have placed this question on the agenda for WTO negotiations. The Doha Ministerial Declaration contains an agreement to negotiate to clarify and improve the disciplines applying to RTAs, and these negotiations are to 'take into account the developmental aspects of regional trade agreements'.[215] The particular issue of SDT and differentiated obligations in RTAs has been raised as part of these negotiations. The ACP group has submitted a paper drawing attention to the fact that the existing rules on RTAs do not provide for SDT in 'North-South RTAs', despite the fact that SDT is 'a key principle and integral part of the legal architecture of WTO', and proposing that 'appropriate flexibility shall be provided for developing countries in meeting the "substantially all trade" requirement in respect of trade and product coverage' and to allow certain protective non-tariff measures for developing countries.[216] This could provide the necessary flexibility for RTAs not only to provide SDT for developing countries generally, but also to differentiate between subcategories of developing countries as may be appropriate in each particular region. The present rules would only constrain certain kinds of SDT and differentiation, since asymmetrical obligations of technical assistance, for example, would not run afoul of the GATT rules. The potential constraint is nevertheless important. This is therefore another aspect of the current WTO negotiations that will be significant for SIDS. If differentiation and SDT are not

---

[213] PACER art 2(2)(e); Cotonou Agreement arts 34(4), 36(1), 37(7).
[214] Note, however, that this probably only applies to Cotonou EPAs and an RTA negotiated under PACER, but not to PICTA, since PICTA is an RTA among developing countries only and therefore covered by the Enabling Clause rather than GATT art XXIV.
[215] Doha Declaration, above n 81, [29].
[216] *Developmental Aspects of Regional Trade Agreements and Special and Differential Treatment in WTO Rules: GATT 1994 Article XXIV and the Enabling Clause*, WTO Doc TN/RL/W/155 (2004) [7], [11] (Communication by the Mission of Botswana on Behalf of the ACP Group of States).

permitted in RTAs, this will work to undermine whatever progress may be made on these issues in the multilateral regime.

The next question, then, involves the extent to which the emerging framework of RTAs involving FICs has the potential to adequately address their particular needs. Views on this point are mixed, although there appear to be some common concerns. Some of the differences of opinion reflect uncertainty about the likely impact of changes in trade policy on Pacific island populations and economies. They also reflect different judgements about what counts as a benefit. For example, the effect of RTAs in 'locking in' domestic trade and economic policy reforms is seen by some as a benefit, by others as a harm. Similarly, trade creation following the creation of a regional free trade area – that is, displacement of local production by imports from another producer from within the free trade area – can be seen as either a harm or a benefit, depending on one's perspective. It has a negative impact on the local producers who lose their market share, but a positive impact on the other producers and on overall efficiency.

Given these differences in perspective and the inherent uncertainty involved in predicting outcomes in a complex system, we are unlikely to reach any definitive conclusions on the likely impact of the current framework. Divergent views have led commentators to offer directly conflicting advice as to the best course of action for FICs.[217] However, it is significant that some common points seem to emerge from the debate. Numerous commentators have questioned the benefits of the 'stepping stone' approach to economic integration of small developing countries like the FICs. In theory, a gradual, step-by-step process of integration seems like a good idea for these countries: it allows them to adjust more slowly to the policy changes that are required and their impacts. This seems consistent with the rationale supporting longer transitional periods as a form of SDT for developing countries in the multilateral system. However, moving toward full integration through a series of progressively larger RTAs presents some specific problems.

First, it is suggested that a trade agreement among only the FICs would result in more trade diversion than trade creation. That is, it is more likely that imports from outside the free trade area will be displaced by imports from within the area (trade diversion), rather than domestic production being displaced by imports from within the area (trade creation). Although in either scenario there are winners and losers, trade diversion is seen as negative overall: it results in the importing country losing tariff revenue (because tariff-attracting imports from outside the free trade area are displaced by tariff-free imports from within the area) and a higher cost, less efficient product gaining market share (because the tariff-free import can be higher priced and still compete with external tariff-attracting imports which would otherwise have an advantage). The government loses and a less efficient outcome results.

---

[217] For example, Kelsey, above n 172, 34-6, sets out various alternative 'escape routes' from PACER (primarily ways to avoid triggering the obligation to negotiation an RTA under PACER), while Narsey, above n 196, 18-19, suggests that it may be preferable for PICs to pro-actively trigger PACER and negotiate an RTA with Australia and New Zealand simultaneously with the EU-Pacific ACP EPA.

Compounding this problem is the fact that those industries within the region that successfully grow and capture market shares within the free trade area will not necessarily succeed when the next steps toward integration are eventually taken. A producer that is able to be competitive within the region while it is still protected from external imports often will not remain competitive on a larger or global stage once external barriers are lowered. Therefore, the effort and resources that are invested in these producers during the first phase of limited integration may ultimately be wasted and even greater adjustment required in the long run.[218] In the case of RTAs among small developing countries particularly, it is thought unlikely that integration will be sufficient to overcome the disadvantages of small economic size and make industries competitive. Finally, where a free trade area is established among developing countries, there is a tendency for this to increase income disparities between those countries, with the richest members becoming richer and those least well-off being further disadvantaged. Clearly this could damage rather than promote regional cooperation and solidarity.

There seems to be a degree of consensus supporting these concerns, which are based on experiences with the MSG trade agreement and other regional agreements among developing countries as well as economic modelling.[219] If correct, they predict that the gradual approach to integration, although it appears to be a logical response to the particular circumstances and needs of FICs, will not in fact be beneficial for them. The proposed remedy then depends on whether commentators view the ultimate goal of integration as desirable for these states or not: either they should attempt to halt the 'stepping-stone' process before it goes any further,[220] or move more quickly toward integration with developed country trading partners and/or broader liberalization on an MFN basis in the multilateral system.[221] However, both of these courses of action seem unlikely, and it appears that pursuing the stepping stone approach may be another example of the broader tendency for less desirable forms of differential treatment to be favoured because they are politically more feasible.[222]

As for differentiated treatment of SIS within RTAs, the extent to which this is likely to be beneficial depends on the specific forms of SDT that are adopted. PICTA and PACER provide for 'different structures and time frames' for integration of LDC and SIS parties. Longer transition periods for these countries may well be appropriate given their dependence on a limited range of revenue

---

[218] Another concern is that this will increase resistance to further liberalization because the producers that are successful within the region have a vested interest in ensuring they are not exposed to global competition. See, e.g. World Bank, above n 172, 12.

[219] See World Bank, above n 172, 7-14, 22; Nathan Associates Inc., 'Regional Approaches to Integrating Small Economies into the World Trade System' (Research Paper, Submitted to USAID, 2002), 7-10; Gutiérrez, above n 30, 211-13; Kelsey, above n 172, 25; Narsey, above n 196, 7-9.

[220] Kelsey, above n 172, 41, advising FICs to avoid negotiating with the EU or otherwise triggering PACER, freeze accessions to the WTO and consider withdrawing from PICTA and PACER.

[221] See, e.g. Narsey, above n 196, 18; World Bank, above n 172, 30.

[222] See above n 160.

sources and more limited capacity. Under PICTA they are allowed to maintain higher import tariffs (in general and for the protection of developing industries) and this may be contemplated under PACER and Cotonou as well. Reducing developing countries' liberalization commitments to allow them to maintain protectionist policies has fallen out of fashion as a general rule; however, the appropriateness of this strategy in the particular case of very small developing countries may need to be reassessed. There is evidence that very small island countries will find it difficult or impossible to compete in a free trade environment,[223] so the usual prescription of liberalization for developing countries may not apply. Certainly technical assistance and other means of dealing with the limited capacity of these countries on a long term or even permanent basis would seem to be appropriate forms of SDT.

Conclusion

The difficulties facing small states like the FICs in international trade are finally beginning to receive some sustained attention in the WTO with the Doha Declaration work programme on small economies. However, at the same time, changes in the trade regime seem to be exacerbating some of these difficulties: tariff reductions are eroding margins of preference for developing countries that helped them to compete in foreign markets, pressures toward reciprocal liberalization mean sharp declines in tariff revenues upon which many small developing states rely for income, and many countries are increasingly unsympathetic to the use of protective measures to help domestic industries compete in home or export markets. These changes are affecting WTO Members and non-Members alike, directly and indirectly, so there is no way of opting out of the changing global regime and small states are extremely limited in their capacity to influence the regime to reflect their interests.

Requests for special treatment for SIDS and other small, vulnerable economies challenge the prevailing wisdom in trade and development that expects developing countries to be able to diversify their economies, exploit areas of comparative advantage and work toward competitiveness in free regional and global trade. Although differences of opinion remain, there is widespread agreement that for small states and especially SIDS, it is difficult – perhaps even impossible – to be competitive in a free trade environment: 'there may be some very small economies that face such great absolute disadvantages that exporting at world prices is either impossible or generates factor incomes that are too low to subsist. In the limit free trade could mean no trade for these countries'.[224] Although these countries are urged to diversify their economies to decrease their vulnerability and dependence, diversification further exacerbates the lack of economies of scale, so there may be a trade-off between diversification, on the one hand, and efficiency and competitiveness, on the other. There are also obstacles to

---

[223] See, e.g. Winters and Martins, above n 33.
[224] Winters and Martins, above n 33, 348.

developing new industries. For example, it has been suggested that SIDS take advantage of new communications technologies that make remoteness less of a disadvantage by exploiting niches in internet-based service industries, and some have begun to do so.[225] However, they have faced opposition by other states[226] and difficulties with regulatory capacity which are also typical of small states.

Although the situation is by no means hopeless, it seems clear that the challenges facing SIDS must be taken seriously and that they do, in fact, reflect inherent disadvantages that are not likely to disappear if their governments would only 'try harder'. Of course the 'right policies' will mitigate some disadvantages and increase opportunities (if we could only agree on what the right policies are). Many analysts believe, however, that long-term, even permanent, assistance and support will be required – unpopular as this view may be. In particular, assistance with supply capacity and regulatory capacity will be required to enable small states to take advantage of trade opportunities.[227] In addition, countries dependent on tariff revenue will need both immediate and long-term support to deal with the fiscal impact of the loss of revenue from liberalization.[228] Since tariff reductions will result in savings for developed country trading partners, this could be seen as merely reversing the flow of revenue from developing to developed countries.

In addition, a good case has been made for some forms of special treatment in trade rules, for example exemptions from some commitments that are costly and of little or no benefit to the implementing country itself,[229] extended transition periods and assistance with compliance. More controversial are exemptions or reduced commitments that allow SIDS to subsidize or protect their producers – although these are attractive to many countries they are considered ultimately to be counterproductive, because they will impair the competitiveness of those producers even further in the long run.[230] There is also urgent need for attention to systemic issues that impose particular burdens on small developing states, notably accessions to the WTO, limitations of dispute settlement in the WTO for small economies and costs of participation.

In respect of both assistance and deviations from trade rules, the cost to the rest of the world will be relatively very small. The tiny share of world trade represented by small developing states means that any distortion from SDT will be

---

[225] See, for example, Government of the Republic of Vanuatu, *Vanuatu's Internet Free Trade Zone* <http://www.vanuatugovernment.gov.vu/cyberspace.html> at 15 December 2004.

[226] For example the attempts by the United States to prohibit internet gambling that resulted in the dispute with Antigua and Barbuda: see above n 154.

[227] See, for example, Ransford Smith, 'Size matters' (2004) 3 *World Trade Review* 441, 445; Dominique Njinku, 'Uniform treatment for Africa in the DDA' (2004) 3 *World Trade Review* 433, 439.

[228] Although these revenue losses may be partly replaced by other sources such as sales taxes (World Bank, above n 172, 34ff), implementing these may be problematic (ibid 45ff; Kelsey, above n 172, 25).

[229] Mattoo and Subramanian, above n 156, 403. Examples they give include intellectual property protection under TRIPS and customs valuation requirements.

[230] Ibid, 403-404; Winters and Martins, above n 33, 376.

minimal, as is the relative cost of assistance.[231] It does not seem that it would be difficult for developed states to agree to many of the demands. However, as we saw above, several commentators have noted that responses to requests for special treatment do not necessarily reflect whether they would be effective and cost-efficient. There is a tendency, for various political reasons, to reject more desirable solutions in favour of less desirable ones. Recent negotiations have also shown a significant degree of resistance to the full range of proposals for accommodating the needs of SIDS.[232]

What does all of this mean for the FICs? We see all of these issues reflected in the experience of these countries in their global and regional contexts. Trade liberalization, through multilateral WTO commitments or gradually expanding regional arrangements, deprive FICs of an important form of revenue as they reduce their tariffs, and expose their producers to greater competition in domestic and export markets. Trade preferences that have been important for some of the island economies[233] are being eroded or subjected to legal challenges by other developing states. The WTO accessions process has been a significant barrier for Pacific island countries like Vanuatu and Samoa, which have faced what many perceive to be unreasonable demands from other WTO members. The regional environment has undergone a radical shift from nonreciprocal preferential arrangements (under SPARTECA and the Lomé Conventions) toward reciprocal trade liberalization as developed country trading partners seek to satisfy WTO disciplines on regional agreements. The new generation of regional agreements are significant in that they recognize the need for special treatment of the smallest developing countries as well as SDT for developing countries generally. This is an important example of differentiation, corresponding to a distinction drawn in economic studies between 'countries that will have the most extreme difficulty competing in the global market' and those that may stand a better chance at competing, with external assistance.[234] It was also seen that the 'stepping stone' approach to regional trade liberalization, however appealing in theory, may represent an example of countries accepting a less desirable solution to the challenges they face.

Many of the changes that would benefit the small island developing states of the Pacific must take place on the global stage where they have limited ability to influence events. However, they can participate in worldwide partnerships of SIDS and small economies which have been reasonably effective in raising the profile of these issues in the UN and the WTO. In addition, there are some strategies that

---

[231] See, e.g. Winters and Martins, above n 33, 378.

[232] See the draft document for the January 2005 UN meeting on SIDS, which shows that the EU has sought to delete or significantly amend virtually every point under the heading 'Trade: globalization and trade liberalization' and the United States has suggested deleting the whole section: *Draft strategy for the further implementation of the Programme of Action for the Sustainable Development of Small Island Developing States*, [65]-[67], UN Doc A/CONF.207/L.1 (2004).

[233] Hughes, above n 12, 72.

[234] Grynberg, 'Towards Doha-lite', above n 1, 428-9.

could be undertaken within the region itself which could help the FICs to deal with the daunting challenges of the international trading system. Although regional economic integration in the 'stepping stone' model is problematic, other forms of regional cooperation are more promising.[235] For example, proposals to share the burden of administrative requirements (such as trade remedies investigations) among groups of small states could be explored within the Forum or other regional frameworks. Efforts to increase supply capacity will likely be most effective with some external support, but important cooperative initiatives could be undertaken among the FICs. Australia and New Zealand arguably have an important responsibility to support the island countries in these efforts, not least because they will be the major beneficiaries of trade liberalization by FICs (through savings on tariffs by their exporters, who supply the largest proportion of goods to the islands). They also have an opportunity to show some leadership at the global level in responding to the concerns of SIDS.

---

[235] See Andrew S Downes, 'The trade environment and small countries' (2004) 3 *World Trade Review* 416, 420; Njinku, above n 227, 437-8.

Index

Abu Sayyef 132, 154
Aceh Liberation Front 132, 154
Achille Lauro 151, 154
ACP, *see* African, Caribbean and Pacific
Activities Implemented Jointly 179
Adaptation Fund 165, 169
African, Caribbean and Pacific 244, 128, 161, 162, 164, 165, 166, 167
AG, *see* Attorney General
AGO *see* Australian Greenhouse Office
AIJ, *see* Activities Implemented Jointly
Alliance of Small Island States 192, 195
al-Qaeda 104, 122
Antarctic Treaty 210-16
    Consultative Meetings 215, 127
    developing nations 222
    System 201-02
Antarctica
    commons, international 224
    jurisdiction 205, 214-15
    marine areas 204
    ownership of resources 214, 218, 220, 223
    sovereignty 202, 204-5, 213-14, 222-3
    territorial claims 203-4, 205, 206, 213
anti-terrorism treaties, *see* terrorism
AOSIS, *see* Alliance of Small Island States
APCs, *see* Asia Pacific Consultations
APEC, *see* Asian Pacific Economic Cooperation
APG-ML, *see* Asia Pacific Group on Money Laundering

archipelagic
    sea lanes passage 138, 139, 140
    states 137-9
    waters 138, 139
arms smuggling 42, 67
ASEAN, *see* Association of South East Asian States
Asia Pacific Consultations 73
Asia Pacific Group on Money Laundering 40, 62, 63
Asian Development Bank 231, 232
Asian Pacific Economic Cooperation 116-18, 125, 128, 258
    counter-terrorism cooperation 117, 125
    Shanghai Statement 117
Asian Shipowners Forum 156
asset forfeiture 38, 49, 62, 72
Association of South East Asian States 128, 258
asylum, *see* refugees
AT, *see* Antarctic Treaty
ATCM, *see* Antarctic Treaty Consultative Meeting
ATS, *see* Antarctic Treaty System
Attorney General 61, 62
Austrac, *see* Australian Transaction Report and Analysis Centre
Australia
    climate change
        'Australia Clause' 178, 179, 181
        context 172, 175
        contribution to 166, 173
        land use change 174, 181
        Kyoto policy responses 174, 175-80
        National Greenhouse Strategy 174, 179
        Partnerships 177, 180, 191

policy background 172
counter terrorism 96, 115, 117
historic bays 136
maritime surveillance 71
Police 77-8
refugee policy 24, 25, 26, 30
   'Pacific Solution' 30
   resettlement 29, 31

Australian Greenhouse Office 179
Australian Transaction Report and Analysis Centre 65

Banda Sea 139
baselines, *see* straight baselines
biodiscovery 208
biodiversity 208-10
bioprospecting
   definition 207-8
   intellectual property rights 219-22
   legal status in Antarctica 216
biotechnology 210
bioterrorism 104; *see also* terrorism
Black Sea bumping incident 141
boat people, *see* refugees
Brazil 145, 244
Bruntland Report 176, 186
burden sharing
   obligation 26-8
   practicality and feasibility 16
   promotion and implementation 27-8
Bush, George W 158

Cambodia 135, 136, 141
Canada 163, 164, 174, 193
Cape Verde 145
carbon charges 162
carbon sinks, *see* climate change
carbon trading market 167
Castle John 151
CBD, *see* Convention on Biological Diversity
CCAMLR, *see* Convention for the Conservation of Antarctic Marine Living Resources
CDM, *see* Clean Development Mechanism
China 135, 136, 141, 142, 145, 171, 180, 196
CHM, *see* Common Heritage of Mankind
Christmas Island 11, 12
CLAGS, *see* Combined Law Agency Groups
Clean Development Mechanism 164, 165
climate change
   carbon sinks 164, 187, 188
   commitments and targets 162-3
   developing countries 166, 171
   history 161-2
   impacts 166-7
      developing states 171-2
   policy instruments 163
   regional cooperation 195
Closer Economic Relations Australia New Zealand Trade Agreement 258, 263
Combined Law Agency Groups 60
common heritage of mankind 233-5
Commonwealth Secretariat 63, 234
COMNAP, *see* Council of Managers of National Antarctic Programmes
COMSEC, *see* Commonwealth Secretariat
Conferences of the Parties 163, 164
Convention for the Conservation of Antarctic Marine Living Resources 206, 207
Convention for the Regulation of Antarctic Mineral Resource Activity 219, 223, 225
Convention for the Suppression of Unlawful Acts Against the Safety of Navigation 151, 154, 157
Convention on Biological Diversity 208, 210
Convention on the Status of Refugees 12, 14, 15, 16, 17, 18, 20, 21, 26, 27, 32

Cook Islands 29, 40, 58, 60, 61, 64, 65, 68, 74, 115, 116, 118, 182, 192, 194, 231, 234, 262, 265
COPs, *see* Conference of the Parties
corruption 43-4, 55, 57, 74-5, 77, 82
Cotonou Agreement 82, 261-7
Council for Security Cooperation in the Asia Pacific 74, 128, 154
Council on Trade and Development 249
counter terrorism
   Counter-Terrorism Committee reporting obligations 115, 119-121
   impact on executive decision making 121-4
   international framework 102, 105-7, 115, 125
   New Zealand role 100, 104-5, 106, 115
Cour de Cassation 151
CRAMRA, *see* Convention for the Regulation of Antarctic Mineral Resource Activity
criminal justice 55, 67, 76, 77, 80
CSCAP, *see* Council for Security Cooperation in the Asia Pacific
CTD, *see* Council on Trade and Development
customary international law 14, 16, 56, 129, 139, 140, 141, 144

Danworth, John 105
DDA, *see* Doha Development Agenda
developed states
   environmental obligations 163-4, 170
   trade with developing states 272
   transnational crime, role in 36-7, 40, 76, 80, 81
developing states
   challenges to development 230, 232, 233
   differentiation in the WTO 237, 243-8

   impacts of climate change 170, 172
dispute settlement 237, 252, 260, 271
Doha Declaration, *see* World Trade Organization Doha Declaration
Doha Development Agenda 242, 243, 249, 254, 255, 267
Domestic Policy Option Statement 186, 187
DPOS, *see* Domestic Policy Option Statement
drug trafficking 39, 40-2, 48, 51, 57, 63, 68-9, 76, 80, 110
due regard 144, 145, 147

Earth Summit 162, 166
EC, *see* European Community
Ecologically Sustainable Development 176
Economic Partnership Agreement 262, 266
Economies in Transition 192, 163
EEZ, *see* Exclusive Economic Zone
EITs, *see* Economies in Transition
electronic crimes 39
endangered species 45, 70
environmental offences 51, 69
environmental refugees 195
EPA, *see* Economic Partnership Agreement
European Community 247, 248, 257
European Union 21, 82, 164, 165, 170, 179, 180, 189, 244
Exclusive Economic Zone 47, 71, 129, 133, 138, 140, 142-9, 205
EXCOM, *see* United Nations High Commissioner for Refugees Executive Committee
exports 231, 234, 240, 244, 250, 259
extradition 38, 50-51, 57, 66-8, 70, 102, 110, 112, 154

FADTC, *see* Foreign Affairs, Defence and Trade Committee

FATF, *see* Financial Action Task Force
Federated States of Micronesia 42, 44, 57, 70, 79, 116, 192, 231, 259, 263
FFA, *see* Pacific Islands Forum Fisheries Agency
FICs, *see* Pacific Islands Forum Island Countries
Fiji 41, 49, 51, 57, 59, 60, 63, 65, 67, 73, 105, 116, 172, 192, 231, 236, 249, 259, 261
Financial Action Task Force 40, 52, 62, 118-119, 125
Financial Intelligence Units 50, 65
first asylum, *see* refugees
FIU, *see* Financial Intelligence Units
FLNKS, *see* Kanak Socialist National Liberation Front
FON, *see* Freedom of Navigation
Foreign Affairs, Defence and Trade Committee 123
FORUM, *see* Pacific Islands Forum
Forumsec, *see* Pacific Islands Forum Secretariat
France 146, 147, 204
fraud 39, 45, 82 *see also* identity fraud
freedom of navigation 132, 142, 147, 148, 158
freedom of scientific investigation 211, 212, 216, 217
FRSC, *see* Pacific Islands Forum Regional Security Committee

GAM, *see* Aceh Liberation Front
GATS, *see* General Agreement on Trade in Services
GATT, *see* General Agreement on Tariffs and Trade
GDP, *see* Gross Domestic Product
General Agreement on Tariffs and Trade 236, 238, 239, 246, 251, 257, 260, 261, 267
General Agreement on Trade in Services 236, 257

Generalized System of Preferences 238, 244, 248, 259, 262
GHGs, *see* greenhouse gases
Global Environment Facility 163, 165, 195
globalization 45, 78, 79, 80, 104
Greenhouse Challenge Program 174, 177, 179
Greenhouse Gas Abatement Program 180
greenhouse gases 162, 163, 166, 172, 178, 185, 192, 195, 197
Greenpeace 103, 151; *see also* Rainbow Warrior
Gross Domestic Product 167, 182, 184, 185, 194, 232
Grotius, Hugo 127
GSP, *see* Generalized System of Preferences

hazardous materials 146, 148
hegemony 79-80
high seas 128, 132, 135, 138, 140, 142, 143, 145, 150, 151, 159, 205, 206; *see also* terrorism; maritime terrorism
historic bays
    claims in Asia Pacific region 136
Honiara Declaration 37-56, 60, 79
human trafficking 44, 45, 53, 57, 72, 73; *see also* people smuggling

IAEA, *see* International Atomic Energy Agency
ICJ, *see* International Court of Justice
identity fraud 39, 44, 54, 55, 74; *see also* fraud
IGY, *see* International Geophysical Year
IMB, *see* International Maritime Bureau
IMDG, *see* International Maritime Dangerous Goods
IMF, *see* International Monetary Fund

IMO, *see* International Maritime Organization
indigenous issues 53, 55, 72, 73, 81
INF, *see* irradiated nuclear fuel
innocent passage, right of 129, 135, 138, 139, 141-2
intellectual property rights 218, 219-222, 236, 256
Intergovernmental Panel on Climate Change 161
International Atomic Energy Agency 147, 148, 149
International Court of Justice 134, 136, 146, 195, 206
International Criminal Court 97, 102
International Geophysical Year 211, 212, 216
International Maritime Bureau 152, 153
International Maritime Dangerous Goods 148
International Maritime Organization 137, 147, 148, 149, 152, 154, 157-8
International Monetary Fund 63, 72, 246
international refugee law 11, 15, 16, 18, 33
International Seabed Authority 206, 207
IP, *see* intellectual property rights
IPCC, *see* Intergovernmental Panel on Climate Change
IPR, *see* intellectual property rights
Irian Jaya 43
irradiated nuclear fuel 148
ISA, *see* International Seabed Authority
Isatabu Freedom Movement 103

Jamia Islamia 132
Japan 72, 146, 147, 164
Japan, US, Canada, Australia and New Zealand Group 163, 188, 192, 193, 196, 197

Java Sea 139
JI, *see* Joint Implementation
Joint Implementation 164, 165, 180
JUSCANZ, *see* Japan, US, CANADA, Australia and New Zealand Group

Kanak Socialist National Liberation Front 103
Kiribati 115, 142, 192, 194, 230, 231, 262, 265
Kyoto Protocol; *see also* Australia; climate change; New Zealand
developing countries 165
first commitment period 163, 170, 191
goals 163
implementation 162, 164, 170, 174
limitations 169-71, 196
monitoring strategies 180, 191
regional responses 172
status 167-9

law enforcement cooperation 38, 48, 59, 70
Law Enforcement Cooperation Program 60
LDC, *see* Less Developed Country
LECP, *see* Law Enforcement Cooperation Program
Less Developed Country 164, 165, 166, 231, 237-43, 253
Liberia 159
Lombok Straits 131, 139
Lome Convention 259, 261, 262, 267, 272

Madrid bombings 102, 105
Malacca, Straits of, *see* Straits of Malacca
Malaita Eagles Force 103
Mandatory Renewable Energy Targets 179
maritime surveillance 52, 53, 70, 71
maritime terrorism, *see* terrorism

maritime zones 128-30, 133, 135, 137, 138, 205
Marshall Islands 40, 57, 62, 65, 68, 70, 115, 118, 119, 192, 194, 231, 259, 263
mass migrations 20
Melanesian Spearhead Group 259, 261, 269
MFN, *see* Most Favoured Nation
Micronesia, *see* Federated States of Micronesia
migration controls 32
military exercises 145
MLAT, *see* Mutual Legal Assistance Treaty
money laundering 39-40, 49-50, 58, 62-6, 82, 118, 119
Most Favoured Nation 236, 238, 242, 244, 246, 258, 260, 269
MRET, *see* Mandatory Renewable Energy Targets
MSG, *see* Melanesian Spearhead Group
mutual assistance 48-9, 61-2, 72
mutual legal assistance 38, 49, 62
MV Tampa 11, 12, 31

Nasonini Declaration 45, 54, 70, 75, 116, 118
National Energy Efficiency and Conservation Strategy 189-90
National Greenhouse Response Strategy 198, 90
national security 22, 34, 73, 102, 105, 125, 140
Nauru 11, 30, 40, 58, 61, 63, 64, 66, 68, 116, 119, 192, 231
navigational rights 128, 129, 132, 135, 138, 140, 142, 143, 144, 146
NEECS, *see* National Energy Efficiency and Conservation Strategy
Negotiated Greenhouse Agreement 190
New Zealand
 climate change

 context 183
 impacts 183
 Kyoto policy responses 185-92
 Partnerships 183
Green Party 143
parliamentary standing orders 123
Police 41, 60, 65, 120, 78
Resource Management Act 186
Security Intelligence Service 105, 106
NGA, *see* Negotiated Greenhouse Agreement
NGO, *see* Non-governmental Organisation
NGRS, *see* National Greenhouse Response Strategy
Niue 40, 52, 58, 62, 63, 64, 71, 115, 116, 118, 124, 192, 231, 234, 262
non-governmental organisation 9, 18, 128
non-refoulement 14, 15, 16, 17, 18-28
Norway 134, 158, 163, 168, 175, 204
NZP, *see* New Zealand Police
NZSIS, *see* New Zealand Security Intelligence Service

Oceania Customs Organisation 54, 59, 68, 72
OCO, *see* Oceania Customs Organisation
ODA, *see* Official Development Assistance
ODCCP, *see* Office for Drugs Control and Crime Prevention
OECD, *see* Organisation for Economic Cooperation and Development
OFC, *see* Offshore Financial Centre
Office for Drugs Control and Crime Prevention *see* United Nations Office for Drugs Control and Crime Prevention
Official Development Assistance 231, 235, 236

Offshore Financial Centre 39, 40, 77
Ombai-Wetar Straits 139
Organisation for Economic Co-operation and Development (OECD)
　Centre for Co-Operation with Non-Members 118
　Financial Action Task Force, *see* Financial Action Task Force
organized crime 39, 44-5, 49, 56, 57, 60, 120

PACER, *see* Pacific Agreement on Closer Economic Relations
Pacific Agreement on Closer Economic Relations 263, 264, 265, 266, 267, 269, 270
Pacific Immigration Directors Conference 54, 73
Pacific Island Climate Change Assistance Program 195
Pacific Island Countries Trade Agreement 195
Pacific Islands Forum
　environmental objectives 192
　Fisheries Agency 52, 71
　island countries 230-5, 259, 262, 263, 208
　Regional Security Committee 48, 53, 59, 71, 74, 76
　Secretariat 39, 47, 48, 54, 59, 61, 63, 66, 69, 72, 74, 75
Pacific Islands Law Officers' Meeting 37, 59, 66, 75
Pacific Pintail 146
Pacific Teal 146
Palau 40, 42, 58, 62, 65, 66, 115, 192, 259, 263
Panama 159
Papua New Guinea 42, 60, 61, 63, 66, 67, 68, 192, 259, 262
Particularly Sensitive Sea Areas 137
passports 13, 43
people smuggling 25, 29, 39, 44-5, 72, 73; *see also* human trafficking
Peru 131

Philip Straits 131
PICCAP *see* Pacific Island Climate Change Assistance Program
PICTA, *see* Pacific Island Countries Trade Agreement
PIDC, *see* Pacific Immigration Directors Conference
PILOM, *see* Pacific Islands Law Officers' Meeting
piracy 132, 149-53, 156
　IMO recommendations 157-8
PNG, *see* Papua New Guinea
preferential tariffs 238, 247
preferential treatment 246, 247, 251, 260
prison administration 53, 72
Proliferation Security Initiative 149, 158, 159
PSI, *see* Proliferation Security Initiative
PSSA *see* Particularly sensitive Sea Areas

radioactive waste, *see* hazardous materials
Rainbow Warrior 96, 103, 106
Reagan, Ronald 129
reefs 135, 136, 137, 138, 173, 193
refugees
　at sea 19, 13
　environmental, *see* environmental refugees
　human rights 10, 13, 14, 16, 17, 18, 22, 24
　mass flows 17, 18-25
　'Pacific solution' 11, 30, 31, 32
　policy 10, 23, 26
　protection 11, 12, 13, 21, 22, 27, 28, 32, 34
　relocations 16
　resettlement 17, 28, 29, 30, 34
　specific rights regime 21
　status of
　　determination procedures 10-13
　transfer of 11, 16, 30, 32
　UN contingency planning 27, 71

unconditional right to first asylum 24, 25, 26, 28, 30
regional security
   threats to South Pacific 131
regional trade agreements 257-263
   preferential treatment 260
   special and differential treatment 263-268
resettlement, *see* refugees
resettlement countries, *see* refugees
Resource Management Act, *see* New Zealand Resource Management Act
Rio 'Earth Summit', *see* Earth Summit
RMA, *see* New Zealand Resource Management Act
Royal Australian Navy 145
RTA, *see* regional trade agreements

Safety Navigation and Environment Committee 156-7
Safety of Life at Sea 148
Samoa 42, 58, 60, 61, 68, 70, 116, 192, 230, 231, 236, 253, 262, 272
Santa Maria 150, 151
SCAR, *see* Scientific Committee on Antarctic Research
Scientific Committee on Antarctic Research 201, 207, 235
scientific investigation, freedom of 211, 212, 216, 217
SCM, *see* Subsidies and Countervailing Measures
SDT, *see* Special and Differential Treatment
Sea Lines of Communication 131
sector principle 204
Security Council, *see* United Nations Security Council
Selden, John 128
September 11 100, 101, 111, 112, 116, 117, 124, 131
SIDS, *see* small island developing states
Singapore Straits 131, 139

SIS, *see* small island states
SLOC, *see* Sea Lines of Communication
small arms trafficking, *see* arms smuggling
small island developing states
   challenges 230, 233-6
   climate change
      environmental refugees 195
      impacts 165, 172, 183
   regional cooperation 195, 269, 273
SNEC, *see* Safety Navigation and Environment Committee
soft law 14, 17, 18, 19, 25, 27, 32, 34
SOLAS, *see* Safety of Life at Sea
Solomon Islands 33, 42, 58, 60, 68, 73, 103, 116, 192, 230, 236, 259, 262, 265
South China Sea 19, 131, 135, 139
South Korea 135, 141, 171
South Pacific
   Chief of Police Conference 59
   Regional Environmental Programme 69, 162, 195
   regional trade agreements, *see* regional trade agreements
   Regional Trade and Economic Cooperation Agreement 259, 261, 272
sovereignty 24, 32, 38, 52, 78, 83
   Antarctic, *see* Antarctic sovereignty
   coastal 129
   defined 202
   threats to 46
SPARTECA, *see* South Pacific Regional Trade Agreement
SPCPC *see* South Pacific Chief of Police Conference
special and differential treatment 230, 237, 240, 263, 272; *see also* regional trade agreements
Spratly Islands 131
SPREP, *see* South Pacific Regional Environmental Program

status determination procedures 13
straight baselines 129, 133, 134-7, 138, 142
Straits of Malacca 131, 139, 152, 154
Strasser, Rear Admiral Joseph 130
SUA, *see* Suppression of Unlawful Acts
Sub-Antarctic Islands 205
Subsidies and Countervailing Measures 236, 245, 246, 252
Sunda Straits 131, 139
Suppression of Unlawful Acts (Against the Safety of Navigation) 109, 151, 154, 157

Tamil Tigers 154
Tampa, *see* MV Tampa
tariff preferences 241, 242, 244, 246, 247, 248, 251, 257, 260, 262
taxation 53, 72, 186
technical barriers to trade, *see* trade
territorial asylum 13, 14, 16, 17, 23, 27, 32
territorial sea 128, 129, 133, 134, 135, 137, 138, 139, 140, 141-2, 155, 157, 205
territorial waters 11, 15, 25, 30, 32, 47, 71, 141
terrorism
  concept 100-102
  definition 98, 99, 103, 104, 153
  freedom fighters 99
  international conventions 57, 118, 158
  international cooperation 132, 149, 153, 154
  maritime 132, 149, 153, 154
  on the high seas, *see also* maritime terrorism
  United Nations action 111-115
toxic waste, *see* hazardous materials
tradable emission permits 162
trade
  liberalization 236, 251, 257, 259, 265, 272, 273
  technical barriers to 236, 245, 252
Trade-Related Aspects of Intellectual Property Rights 236, 245
transit passage 133, 140, 141
transnational criminal law 36, 37, 55, 57, 76, 78-9, 80
TRIPS, *see* Trade Related Aspects of Intellectual Property Rights
Tuvalu 68, 76, 115, 116, 137, 192, 194, 195, 229, 230, 231, 265

UDHR, *see* Universal Declaration of Human Rights
UN, *see* United Nations
UNESCAP, *see* United Nations Economic and Social Commission for Asia Pacific
UNGA, *see* United Nations General Assembly
UNHCR, *see* United Nations High Commissioner for Refugees
United Kingdom 146, 174
United Nations
  Economic and Social Commission for Asia and Pacific 128
  General Assembly
    Declaration on Measures to Eliminate International Terrorism 99, 111
    Resolution 51/210 (1996) 124, 153
  High Commissioner for Refugees
    Executive Committee 17, 25, 27, 28
  Office for Drugs Control and Crime Prevention, *see* Office for Drugs Control and Crime Prevention
  Security Council
    Resolution 1269 (1999) 100, 114
    Resolution 1368 (2001) 112, 114

Resolution 1373 (2001) 52, 70,
  97, 111, 112, 113, 114, 115,
  116, 117, 118, 119, 121,
  122, 123, 125
Resolution 1452 (2002) 115
Resolution 1455 (2003) 115,
  121, 122
Resolution 1456 (2003) 122,
  125
Terrorism Prevention Branch 96
United States of America 127, 136,
  140, 141, 145, 147
Universal Declaration of Human
  Rights 14
UNODC, see United Nations Office
  on Drugs and Crime
UNSC, see United Nations Security
  Council
Uruguay 145; see also World Trade
  Organization Uruguay Round
Urwin, Greg 47, 104
USS Cole 154
USS Dowdich 146

Vanuatu 40, 41, 42, 44, 58, 60, 62,
  63, 76, 231, 253, 259, 272

Vietnam 135, 141

Washington Consensus 185, 240
weapons of mass destruction 149,
  158
Western Naval Symposium 128
WMD, see weapons of mass
  destruction
World Bank 72, 195, 233, 246
World Trade Organization
  disputes 236, 252, 262; see also
    dispute resolution
  Doha Declaration 242, 243, 249,
    270
  small economies 251, 252, 255,
    263
  Uruguay Round 236, 240, 242,
    245, 260, 262
  Work Programme on Small
    Economies 234, 270
WTO, see World Trade Organization

Yugoslavia 21

Zaoui, Ahmed 22